ACTS:
The Expanding Church

ACTS:
The Expanding Church

By

EVERETT F. HARRISON

MOODY PRESS

CHICAGO

© 1975 by
THE MOODY BIBLE INSTITUTE
OF CHICAGO

Second Printing, 1978

Library of Congress Cataloging in Publication Data

Harrison, Everett Falconer, 1902-
  Acts: the expanding church.
  Bibliography: p. 414
  1. Bible. N.T. Acts—Commentaries. I. Bible.
N.T. Acts. II. Title.
BS2625.3.H37   226'.6'077   75-28445
ISBN 0-8024-0035-3

Printed in the United States of America

CONTENTS

FOREWORD

WITHOUT THE BOOK OF ACTS it would be hard to make sense out of the New Testament. The gospels end with the resurrection and ascension of Jesus Christ. The epistles, mostly by Paul, are largely doctrinal in nature, with only an occasional biographical or historical reference. So we ask all sorts of questions. What did the apostles do after the ascension? When was the Church founded? Who was Paul? How were the churches established to which the New Testament letters were written? These and other questions are answered by the book of Acts. Acts provides an account of the origin and early development of the Christian Church and serves as a historical bridge between the gospels and epistles.

But Acts does more than merely satisfy antiquarian interests; it provides practical instruction for Christians in a twentieth-century world. It shows that the wall of partition was broken down between Jews and Gentiles, and, by extension, between peoples of all races and tongues. It gives clear indications of the high spiritual standards that God has set for Christians. It provides examples of God's powerful working through His people and implies that this same power is available to believers today. It demonstrates that the Gospel had the power to defeat paganism and demonism in the first century and intimates that, for meeting twentieth-century paganism and Satanic forces, its power has not waned.

THE PUBLISHER

PREFACE

The aim in writing this commentary has been to deal adequately, though not exhaustively, with the book of Acts. Critical problems have not been overlooked, nor have practical applications been entirely avoided; but the main thrust has been to discern the meaning of the text.

As a rule, a summary, usually brief, is provided to introduce each passage of Scripture to be treated. This enables the reader to grasp the main content of each portion before its details are examined.

The biblical text is from the New American Standard Bible. Occasionally, in connection with the commentary, other renderings are given. Greek words are transliterated.

ABBREVIATIONS

BA	Biblical Archaeologist
BC	The Beginnings of Christianity
BS	Bibliotheca Sacra
ExpT	The Expository Times
HDB	Hastings' Dictionary of the Bible
IDB	Interpreter's Dictionary of the Bible
ISBE	International Standard Bible Encyclopaedia
JBL	Journal of Biblical Literature
JTS (NS)	Journal of Theological Studies (New Series)
KJV	King James Version
LXX	Septuagint (Old Testament in Greek)
NASB	New American Standard Bible
NEB	New English Bible
NovTest	Novum Testamentum
NTS	New Testament Studies
RSV	Revised Standard Version
TDNT	Theological Dictionary of the New Testament

INTRODUCTION

IT IS WIDELY RECOGNIZED that the titles of New Testament books were not provided by the writers but by the Church, in the course of the second century. This is demonstrated by the varying ways in which early writers refer to the same book. The manuscripts of Acts reflect considerable diversity: "'Acts," "Acts of Apostles," "Acts of the Apostles," "Acts of the Holy Apostles." There is no way of knowing what Luke's own choice would have been. The contents do not support completely the suggestion that only the deeds of apostles are to be recited, nor do they carry out the suggestion that the work of all the apostles is to be described.

Some moderns have proposed the title, "Acts of the Holy Spirit," as more accurately identifying the nature of this book. But however suitable this may be, it will not displace the familiar designations, "The Book of Acts," or "The Acts of the Apostles," and it fails to convey any suggestion of necessary human participation in the events that are to be recounted.

PLAN OF THE BOOK

The Great Commission of the risen Lord, as recorded in 1:8, is a key to the structure of the narrative, which reports the progress of evangelization in the same order as in that passage: Jerusalem, Judea, Samaria, the remotest part of the earth. This is true only in a representative sense, however, since there is an obvious selection of material. Omissions are evident, such as the witness in Galilee, Paul's sojourn in Arabia (Gal 1:17), and details of his labors in Syria and Cilicia (Gal 1:21). Jerusalem was the geographical focus for the outreach into Judea and Samaria, and it continues to have considerable influence through the remainder of the narrative. Antioch was the center from which evangelization of the Gentile world was undertaken.

Peter is the chief figure in the first half of the book, Paul in the second. Both men engaged in essentially the same kind of work: preaching, manifesting the mighty works wrought by the Spirit, and experiencing opposition to their witness, including bodily suffering and imprisonment. Sometimes these leading apostles are pictured as having associates; at other times they were alone. Certain other individuals gained prominence be-

11

cause of their witnessing activity: Stephen and Philip in the first half of the book; Barnabas, Silas, Aquila, Priscilla, and Apollos in the latter half. A notable feature of Paul's labors is the rigorous manner in which he clung to the plan of campaigning in the cities, leaving to his converts the task of bearing the message to surrounding areas.

In both halves of the book we find speeches or sermons, most of which are evangelistic in character. These are probably not intended to be verbatim reports of what was said on such occasions (they are too brief for that), nor are they imaginative creations by the writer of the book; they are, rather, digests of what was spoken.

A well-defined feature of Acts is the insertion of summaries from time to time, which serve the double purpose of generalizing the progress of the gospel on the basis of particular incidents cited (thereby suggesting that the material is only a fragment of what actually happened), and of providing a transition to new developments about to be recounted. The leading passages of this kind are 6:7; 9:31; 11:21; 12:24; 16:5; 19:20; and 28:30-31. However, there are others, such as 2:47; 5:14; 5:42; and 19:10, which seem to have something of this same summarizing character. Incidentally, there is no reason to conclude that the summaries were put into the text to cover up lack of information on the part of the writer. To give a complete account of early Christianity would require many books.

Quite naturally, the composition of Acts includes more than a mere recital of the progress of evangelism, for that story could not be fully told without mentioning the opposition that flared up in place after place. The reader receives the impression that this was the normal, expected thing. For the most part, persecution originated with the Jews, who were incensed at the proclamation of the resurrection of Jesus wrought by the power of God, since this exposed and condemned their own unbelieving attitude toward Jesus of Nazareth during His ministry, and their determined efforts to secure His death. The Sadducees took the lead in trying to restrain the apostolic testimony, but soon the torch passed into the hands of a passionate young Pharisee named Saul.

After his conversion a distinct lull in persecution is detectable in the area of Judea, only to be revived briefly by Herod Agrippa I in his action against James and Peter. Saul's conversion, especially after his prominence in opposing the Church, made many enemies for him among the Jews, so that wherever he went he found his own people prevailingly hostile to his person and his message. His very success in reaching Gentiles with the Gospel rankled with his countrymen, who seldom gave him much peace in his labors. Persecution occasionally came from other sources, as at Philippi and Ephesus, where in certain quarters the success of Paul brought an economic pinch that exploded into attempts to suppress his work.

The closing chapters of Acts revolve around Paul's seizure in Jerusalem, instigated by hostile Jews from the Ephesus area, followed by his protective detention by the Romans and a succession of hearings before Roman officials, concluding with his transfer to Rome after his appeal to Caesar.

Another element in the plan of the book is the portrayal of the life of the Church. We are enabled to see it growing in numbers, following up its evangelism with regular instruction of converts (2:42); laying great store by prayer (2:42; 4:31; 9:40; 10:9; 12:5; 13:3); providing for the physical needs of its members (2:45; 4:32-37; 6:1); developing simple organization as needed, including the appointment of the seven (6:1-6), the selection of James the Lord's brother as guiding head of the Jerusalem church when the apostles turned to evangelism beyond the city (12:17; 15:13), and the appointment of elders (11:30; 14:23; 15:2; 21:18). The apostles continued to function as Christ's authoritative appointees for the direction of the Church's life and work. In addition, prophets were raised up (11:27-30; 13:1) as well as teachers (13:1) for the guidance of the congregations.

Glimpses are afforded of believers partaking of fellowship meals (2:46) and also observing the Lord's Supper (2:42; 20:7). Faithfulness to their own gatherings did not rule out the continued use of the Temple and its services (3:1), and this very circumstance earned them the right to use the Temple courts for public preaching (5:25). Again and again we read of the remarkable unity of spirit and purpose that characterized the members of the Christian community (1:14; 2:44; 4:32), a unity born of the Holy Spirit (cf. Eph 4:3). That unity was marred briefly by the Ananias and Sapphira incident (5:1-11), but the affair only served to purify the company of believers who were shocked by this breach in their ranks.

The taking of the Gospel to the Samaritans does not seem to have disturbed the Church greatly, but the same cannot be said of the influx of Gentiles, especially after Paul and Barnabas had considerable success in reaching them on their first journey to Asia Minor. An element in the Jerusalem church demanded that Gentiles be subjected to circumcision. Paul, Barnabas, and others journeyed to Jerusalem to confer with the apostles and elders about this and to present the case for receiving Gentiles simply on the basis of their faith in Christ. This position was adopted by the Council, with the result that work among the Gentiles could then go forward with even greater freedom.

In summary, although the main thrust of the narrative in Acts is to accent the spread of the Gospel and to note in passing the opposition that was encountered, other factors, such as the spiritual life, organizational development, and internal problems of the Church, are not neglected.

AUTHORSHIP

Traces of the use of Acts by Christian writers of the late first and early second centuries have been claimed by some scholars, but no early testimonies to authorship are available. For this information it is necessary to go beyond the middle of the second century. The Canon of Muratori attributed the work to Luke. About this time Irenaeus did the same, emphasizing in his work *Against Heresies* the author's close relationship to Paul, calling him his follower. After this, many Fathers of the Church, including Clement of Alexandria, Tertullian, and Origen, continued the tradition.

The question remains whether the book of Acts itself substantiates this united testimony from the early centuries. The author did not identify himself by name, being content to note that he had written a former treatise to the man addressed in the opening words, a certain Theophilus. Yet the author's presence with Paul seems to be indicated at certain points in the narrative: the momentous venture into Europe from Asia (16:10-17), the journey from Macedonia to Jerusalem that led to Paul's arrest (20:5–21:18), and the journey to Rome (27:1–28:16). These passages are often referred to as "we" sections, because the narrative is couched in the first person plural. It is likely that 11:28 should be included also, where several Greek manuscripts of the so-called Western type, in describing the visit of Agabus to Antioch and his testimony to the church about a forthcoming famine, add the words, "when we were gathered together." This reading, if accepted, serves to make the author a probable resident of Antioch and a member of the church in that city.

A glance at the passages noted above reveals that this companion of Paul, whoever he was, made the sea trip to Rome with him. We are looking for a man, then, who not only traveled with Paul on some of his eastern campaigns but who presumably spent some time with him in Rome. By turning to the letters of Paul that in all probability were written from Rome (Ephesians, Colossians, Philemon, and Philippians) and noting the names of his associates during this period of detention, it should be possible to narrow the list of prospects and perhaps arrive at the identity of the one who wrote the "we" sections. By this process all individuals other than Luke may be set aside either because they are mentioned in the third person in Acts (in contrast to the author of the book) or because they did not make the journey to Rome with Paul. We have the apostle's statement that Luke was with him during his first imprisonment (Col 4:14) and also during his second (2 Ti 4:11). The aging apostle probably had need of the beloved physician's services as well as of his Christian companionship.

In the Colossians passage Luke is mentioned after Paul's helpers who belonged to the circumcision (Jewish believers). From this one may con-

14

clude that he was a Gentile. This judgment seems to be supported by an indication in his writings of a broad interest in the world of his time, as well as by his expert use of the Greek language. He did not identify with those who used the Jews' language (1:19).

But is the author of the "we" sections necessarily the author of the book as a whole? Some scholars have advanced the opinion that Luke's travel diary was taken over by another person who was responsible for the final form of Acts. But this is improbable for two reasons. If the man who was responsible for bringing together the materials of the book allowed the "we" form to remain unaltered, why did he not follow the same practice in his handling of other source material, such as is found in the early chapters, where participants presumably included themselves in the narrative? Also, it should be noted that the vocabulary and style of the "we" passages is thoroughly in accord with the vocabulary and style of the book as a whole. Unity of authorship is the best explanation of these phenomena.

Since Paul referred to Luke as a physician, the question may legitimately be raised as to whether Acts throws any light on this matter. In his book, *The Medical Language of St. Luke* (1882), W. K. Hobart made a comparative study of the language of Luke-Acts and the works of several physicians of the ancient Greek world. He concluded that Luke did indeed employ a great many medical terms, and suggested that this fact demonstrated medical training. But, more recent study has shown that the vast majority of terms regarded as medical appear also in writers of antiquity who had no medical training. So the evidence of Luke-Acts does not demand that the author be a physician, yet it remains true that there are touches here and there which are highly congenial to this conclusion (see Lk 8:43 and 22:51 for Lucan distinctives).

From the fact that the "we" feature of the narrative is discontinued after the account of the founding of the church at Philippi, a reasonable conclusion can be drawn that Luke stayed in that city to shepherd the company of new believers. If so, he deserves to be thought of not alone as a physician and an author but as a preacher and pastor. Christianity meant more to him than his chosen profession. For further discussion of authorship, see the section on the historical worth of Acts.

SOURCES

One can do no better than to cite the conclusion of a noted scholar who has delved deeply into this subject. Jacques Dupont states:

> Despite the most careful and detailed research, it has not been possible to define any of the sources used by the author of Acts in a way which will meet with widespread agreement among the critics. . . . We find traces

15

of rewriting, cases of juxtaposition, even of insertion of different materials one in the other. There are so many indications which set us on the track of pre-existing sources. We seize a link, which is very clear; we try to follow the source from which it comes and, almost immediately, it becomes lost and disappears, whereas other links present themselves, just as clear and just as disappointing. This can be explained by the literary work of the author: he is not satisfied with transcribing his sources, he rewrites the text by putting the imprint of his vocabulary and his style everywhere.[1]

LANGUAGE

Research is demonstrating that although Luke wrote in Greek, there was considerable Semitic influence at work behind this Hellenistic medium, whether in the area of vocabulary or syntax. The theory of C. C. Torrey, that behind the first half of Acts is an Aramaic document rendered into Greek rather literally, has not found favor. All agree that there is evidence of the influence of the Septuagint (Greek translation of the Old Testament) on Acts, but if this were all, no problem would exist, for Septuagintal influence is plain in Luke's gospel. The problem is to account for non-Septuagintal ingredients of a Semitic sort. It is beginning to be recognized that there are affinities between Luke's diction and that of the Targums and of Qumran materials. But the peculiarity is that Luke did not follow one textual tradition consistently. Wilcox notes that "he seems to have had before him 'ready-made' blocks of material, whose deviation from the Septuagint he did not choose to alter."[2] The whole subject is one of great difficulty, where special expertise is required.[3]

PURPOSE

Luke does not tell us why he wrote this book. The prologue of his gospel deals ostensibly with the period of the life and ministry of Jesus and provides no information about the book of Acts beyond giving assurance that the same careful investigation utilized in gathering data for the writing of the gospel may be expected in connection with any further writing undertaken by the beloved physician. Luke wrote to impart truth rather than to entertain.

Comparison of Acts with the gospel discloses an interest in the secular environment of both of these periods. Christianity is viewed as a part of world history. Jewish and Roman authorities move across the pages of the narrative with considerable frequency.

The two periods are intimately related, as the wording of Acts 1:1 suggests. What Jesus began by His earthly ministry is seen as carried forward through the agency of the Holy Spirit working through the Church. Luke evidently conceived of his own writing as divided into two parts, out of

16

respect to the differing nature of the two periods, yet retaining a sense of unity throughout. That the ministry of Jesus should have no transforming effect on the world was unthinkable; that the Church should spring into being without the background of that ministry was equally unthinkable. Luke undertook to provide a sense of continuity between these two phases in giving us Luke-Acts. The more the two halves are studied as a unity, the clearer will be the picture of Christian beginnings. As the gospel events were the fulfillment of Old Testament prediction, they were in turn the fountainhead of developments in the apostolic age.

With reference to Acts alone, the primary objective is doubtless to relate the story of the rise and progress of the early Church—its dramatic origin in Jerusalem, the city which rejected and crucified Jesus of Nazareth; its gradual spread into Judea, impelled in part by persecution; its bold invasion of Samaria with the Gospel; and its steady expansion into the Gentile world, climaxed by the bringing of the message to Rome, the heart of the empire. Just as Jesus accomplished His mission in the power of the Spirit, so men filled with the same Spirit bore witness to Him and His saving work, not sparing themselves. Luke was especially interested in the mission to the Gentiles. He was bent on commending the Christian faith by narrating its progress in the Greco-Roman world.

But a faithful narration of the Gospel's progress during the first three decades of the Church's life must include some account of the rejection of the message as well as of its reception. Luke sought to show that the same spirit of unbelief and repudiation that marked the reaction of the Jews to Jesus in His lifetime (cf. Lk 4:16-30) manifested itself in the treatment of Christian missionaries. This motif runs all the way through Acts, from chapter four on.

Interwoven in this pattern is a related strand, namely, the problem posed for the Roman authorities by the energetic propagandizing carried on by Christians. Jews were not slow in expressing their displeasure and resentment that Christians, even though they were Jews, should be allowed by Rome to enjoy the protection afforded Judaism as a permitted religion (historically based on Julius Caesar's arrangements with the Jewish nation). Luke took pains to show that whenever Jews brought accusations of disloyalty against the Nazarenes before Roman officials, they got nowhere (18:14-15; 25:25; 26:31). He quoted Paul as denying any offense on his part against the empire (25:8), to which the governor concurred (26:31).

In line with this, the closing paragraph of the book pictures Paul, a prisoner, enjoying full freedom to preach the gospel in the capital itself. By ending his account with the words, "without hindrance," Luke seems to have been making an appeal to Rome to allow this freedom to continue.

It would be a mistake, however, to magnify this purpose by making it primary, for most of Luke's narrative has no direct bearing on contact between representatives of the Gospel and Roman authorities.

Did the purpose of Luke include a thrust at Gnosticism, the heresy that plagued the Church of the early centuries for so long? Some would argue that the author's preoccupation with history is a pointer in this direction, and this may be so, but it is rather disconcerting that he made no reference to this danger. The same might be said of the Johannine writings, but it is certainly much easier to see a warning against Gnosticism there than in the writings of Luke.

Date

After devoting more than seven chapters to the events connected with Paul's arrest and trial, Luke strangely brought his account to a close without indicating the outcome of the case. He was content to say that Paul continued for two years in his own hired quarters and was able to witness to those who came to him (28:30-31). This leads naturally to the supposition that the author terminated his account at this point in order to publish it, probably with the hope that it would be of some help to Paul and to the Christian cause in general. It is hardly satisfactory to conclude that Luke's objective must have been simply to trace the progress of the Gospel from Jerusalem to Rome, so that he could regard his task as completed. Actually, Paul was not the one who first brought the Gospel to Rome, and if his mere arrival was regarded as a fitting climax to the story, why should Luke have bothered to take note of the two years which followed?

The possibility should be granted that the author ran out of room on his writing material and felt that the roll could not well be made larger lest it be too bulky for use. Yet his gospel is somewhat longer than Acts. He may have counted on writing an additional book which would contain information on the trial and the last days of Paul. If so, this plan was not carried out. But all this is conjecture, anyway.

What needs to be recognized is the fact that the many references to Paul's vindication before Roman officials which stand in the book would have no real value, or would at best have antiquarian interest, if the work was published after Nero's persecution of Christians at Rome (A.D. 64). "The only time when the picture of the Roman state's originally friendly attitude toward the Christians would have been worth recalling to people's minds was the time when it was still valid but in danger of being lost. And this means that it was the time of Paul's trial, after he had made an appeal to the court of Caesar."[4]

An early date for Acts is supported by the circumstance that nowhere in this book are there allusions to the writings of Paul. Granted, Luke would

18

not be expected to quote from them in a work of history; yet the complete absence of even the slightest allusion to the apostle's writings suggests that those writings had not yet become the common possession of the churches.

Consideration should be given also to Paul's statement in 20:25 that the Ephesian elders would not see him again. That was his conviction at the time. Yet he did return to Ephesus after release from his first imprisonment (1 Ti 1:3). Had Luke written after this, it is questionable that he would have allowed 20:25 to stand in the record. He was with Paul in Rome after the final visit to Ephesus (2 Ti 4:11), and was doubtless aware of his movements prior to that time.

There have been and still are advocates of a late dating for the book. At one time a second-century setting was popular. Today the interval has been shortened by placing the origin of Acts somewhere near the close of the first century. Support for such a position has been sought in the author's supposed dependence on Josephus, whose *Antiquities* appeared in the year 93. In this work the Jewish historian mentions the abortive revolt of Theudas and then refers to the execution of two sons of Judas the Galilean.[5] In Luke's report of Gamaliel's speech before the Sanhedrin (5:35-39) Theudas's revolt is mentioned first, and then that of Judas (which preceded it chronologically). However the order of these two events in Acts 5 is to be explained, it is incredible that a historian of the caliber of Luke would have read Josephus so carelessly as to think that Judas came after Theudas. Few scholars today hold to his dependence on Josephus' work.

Support for a late dating has been sought in Luke 21:20, where the prophetic language concerning the siege of Jerusalem is construed as a reflection of the actual event, which culminated in the destruction of the city in A.D. 70. On the assumption that Acts was written after the gospel (Ac 1:1), the conclusion is reached that Acts must have been penned later than the fall of Jerusalem. This construction will appeal only to those who are unwilling to accept the possibility of genuine prediction.

In recent years some German scholars have advanced the theory that Luke's work was heavily influenced by the delay in the second coming of Christ. This viewpoint insists that in the earliest days of the Church there was an expectancy that the Lord would return very soon, in line with His predictions, but that with the passage of time it became necessary for the Church to adjust to life in the world and to see its mission of witness as lasting for a considerable time before the end would come. The bearing of this reconstruction on the supposed date of Acts is fairly obvious. While it does not attempt to furnish a precise point for the emergence of this book, the theory requires a considerable period during which

19

this shift operated, and therefore favors a date toward the end of the first century.

While the dating of Acts around A.D. 62 seems the most likely in view of Paul's circumstances, one ought not to exclude the possibility that it appeared some years later, largely because Acts is later than the gospel of Luke, and the gospel seems to show the writer's knowledge of Mark. Luke would then have to be dated before A.D. 60, which many find difficult to accept. But the attempt to relegate Acts to the close of the century has no compelling necessity in its favor.

HISTORICAL WORTH

Luke's interest in placing the rise of Christianity in the setting of the secular world, seen in Luke 3:1-2, is continued in his second volume. He is the only New Testament writer who can be described as a historian. But historian in what sense? Certainly he was not a mere annalist who chronicled names and dates and events. Nor was he a historian in the full modern sense of the word, of whom much interpretation and evaluation are expected along with the recital of facts. Rather, his interest was in setting forth sacred history, saving history, showing how the divine purpose in the world is carried out through Christ and His Spirit-filled followers.

There is an observable difference between the two portions of Acts. In the first half, which centers almost entirely in Palestine and revolves around the Jerusalem church, years of expansion are pressed into a few chapters. The record consists of highlights interspersed with summaries. It is the sort of writing one should expect from a man who was not personally present when the events occurred and was therefore dependent on written or oral sources. Sometimes the sentence structure varies considerably from passages describing events in which Luke was involved. In such instances written sources were probably involved. But Luke also had opportunities to confer with various individuals who belonged to the church in Judea. At Antioch he may have known the Hellenists who founded the congregation in that city. Later on, Barnabas, Silas, and others came from Jerusalem. He himself went to the holy city with Paul (21:17) and must have met many disciples. When Paul was kept a prisoner at Caesarea, Luke had time to consult with Philip, who made his home there (21:8). During this interval he could have interviewed many people in Palestine.

With respect to the second half of the book, the "we" sections attest his presence with Paul and others. For the events that occurred when he was not present, he had opportunity to consult with the apostle at Caesarea, on the journey to Rome, and in the imperial city. We may be sure that his visits with Paul were not taken up with discussions about the weather and politics. Luke doubtless learned much also from Timothy and Titus, Paul's trusted lieutenants. The latter may have been Luke's brother (see 2 Co 8:18; 12:18).[6]

Scholars who are historians have frequently noted how true to life in the first century is the whole panorama of Paul's journeys as they are unfolded in Acts. Greco-Roman culture of the day is faithfully reflected. Ease of travel attests the stability that the Roman peace had brought to the eastern Mediterranean area. Jewish penetration of this Hellenistic world accords with the observations of Jewish and Roman historians of the period concerning their dispersion and with the testimony of archaeological remains. Geographical notes are accurate, as are the references to Roman officials, who are always called by the title appropriate to their position. This would be difficult for a writer who was not contemporary; for the status of provinces, whether imperial or senatorial, sometimes changed, as with Cyprus and Achaia, carrying with the change a shift in the title of the Roman official in charge. Luke knew the correct term to apply to the rulers of Thessalonica (Ac 17:6) and to the town clerk at Ephesus (19:35). The case of the chief official on the island of Malta is of interest, for inscriptions have shown that the proper designation for this man is precisely that which Luke used (28:7).*[7]

Important, too, is the fact that Luke did not idealize the Church. Alongside the reports of bold witnessing and almost fantastic results, of devoted commitment to Christ and unselfish concern for fellow-believers, he set down the evidence of human frailty and failure (chaps. 5 and 6).

But some critics insist that despite these and other clear marks of fidelity to the historical situation, the writer of Acts failed to be convincing in other matters. His failures are used to cast doubt on the Church tradition that Luke, a companion of Paul, could have written the book. Two of the more important areas in question are his presentation of Paul and his reporting of the Jerusalem Council.

Involved in the first item is the assertion that the picture of Paul in Acts differs too widely from that of the Pauline epistles to be credible. For example, Luke made practically nothing of Paul's apostleship, which Paul himself magnified, especially when involved in controversy. He was an apostle not from men nor through a man (Gal 1:1), yet Luke represented the Lord as conveying his call through Ananias (Ac 9:11-16). From Galatians, one receives the clear impression of Paul's strong antagonism toward legalism, yet in Acts he is pictured as circumcising Timothy (16:3), taking vows on himself (18:18; 21:17-26), and in his speeches after being made a prisoner as professing a continuing loyalty to the Pharisaic mode

*For comments on these terms see subsequent discussion on the verses indicated here.

21

of life. In the reports of Paul's preaching in Acts, furthermore, sadly lacking is the strong emphasis on redemption through the cross such as is found in his epistles. From his writings it is evident that Paul had many fears and misgivings as he pursued his task, and also great conflicts within his churches. Of all this the reader of Acts is given no inkling. Toward the end of his stay in the East the apostle made a great effort to rally his churches in support of a fund to be taken to Jerusalem to aid the Christian poor in that area. Luke reported the journey and named Paul's companions who represented the local congregations (20:4ff.), but did not explain the purpose of the trip. Again, whereas Paul had the intention of going to Spain (Ro 15:24, 28), Luke said nothing about this, concentrating simply on the journey to Rome.

It should be noted that many of these considerations involve Luke's silence regarding matters set forth in Paul's letters. Silence is not the same thing as disagreement. As for the mediation of Ananias, it is clear that this man did not appoint Paul to be an apostle nor did he reveal the Gospel to him. Luke's account implies that Paul definitely saw the risen Lord when nearing Damascus (Ac 9:7-8, 17) and therefore stood on an equal footing with those who were apostles before him (cf. 22:14; 26:16). It is with these matters that Paul was concerned in writing Galatians, where he speaks more explicitly than Luke does in Acts. As to the allegation that Luke misrepresented Paul's preaching by failing to make central the saving significance of the cross, it may suffice to point to 20:28, which Luke could have omitted if he had a prejudice against such a doctrine. Also notable is the report of Paul's preaching at Pisidian Antioch, where Jesus is called Saviour (13:23), whose mission made possible a message of salvation (13:26), which is then defined in terms of forgiveness and justification (13:38-39). We can cheerfully grant that Luke did not disclose Paul's feelings or trace his difficulties in the churches he founded. This was not germane to his purpose of describing the spread of the Gospel. Finally, Paul's apparent concessions to legalism in Acts were not out of line with his announced principles (1 Co 9:19-23).

Equally serious is the contention that whereas Luke represented the Jerusalem Council as providing a decisive answer to the circumcision party in the church, Paul's letters indicate that the legalists continued to make trouble for him in his work. Moreover, there is no little difficulty in trying to find a place for the Council in Galatians. The book of Acts notes three visits of Paul to Jerusalem that are pertinent to the problem (9:26-29; 11:30; 15:1-29), whereas only two are mentioned in Galatians (1:18-19; 2:1-10). There is general agreement that Acts 9:26-29 and Galatians 1:18-19 refer to the same visit.

Galatians 2 offers promise of picturing the same events as Acts 15, because many of the same persons are involved, and the issue—whether or not Gentiles must be circumcised in order to be admitted into the Church—is the same. Both passages indicate that Gentiles were declared exempt from this rite (and by implication, from bondage to the Mosaic Law). Yet the accounts are not wholly harmonious, in that Acts pictures a large gathering which included elders and others, whereas Galatians presents a rather private meeting between three Jerusalem apostles (though other figures representing the circumcision party are in the background) and the two representatives from Antioch, Barnabas and Paul. Furthermore, the meeting described in Acts resulted in a decision to send a letter to the Gentile churches where trouble had erupted, stating the verdict of the Council and requesting these believers to be careful to abstain from certain things which were abhorrent to faithful Jews. Of such a decree Galatians has nothing to say.

Because of these difficulties some scholars have turned to equating Galatians 2 with the Acts 11 visit of Barnabas and Paul as a possible solution. This identification would explain handily the absence of the decree from Galatians 2, for the Jerusalem Council had not yet been convened. Furthermore, it seems likely that Paul's statement in Galatians 1:20 committed him to include every visit which he made to Jerusalem up to the time of writing, so the famine visit would have to be included in his narrative. Finally, this solution seems to be favored by Paul's statement that he went up to Jerusalem in accordance with revelation (Gal 2:2), since the Acts account informs us that it was Agabus the prophet's revelation about an approaching famine that led the Antioch church to send relief to Judea by the hands of Barnabas and Paul. Perhaps Galatians 2:10 could be said to glance at the same item, for it calls attention to the needs of the poor.

It has to be granted that this identification has its own crop of disadvantages. The occasion of the visit had nothing to do with a doctrinal crisis, and it is not clear that the two emissaries met with any apostles (Luke mentions only elders), who were often out of the city engaged in evangelistic work.

Furthermore, chronology is against the identification. The famine visit cannot be put later than the year 46, when the famine was at its height. Subtracting 14 (Gal 2:1) plus 3 (Gal 1:18) from 46, one arrives at the year 29 for Paul's conversion, obviously too early. Even if both figures in Galatians are calculated on the basis that a part of a year was counted as a full year, this alters the conversion date only to 31, which is still too early, being only a year after Pentecost.

Galatians 1:20 should not be pressed to mean that Paul was solemnly swearing to record every visit he made to Jerusalem, since the issue is not Jerusalem but contact with the apostles, as is clear from his account of his first visit. Likewise the allusion to revelation is not weighty, since the kind of revelation Paul had in mind in Galatians, as chapter 1 makes clear, is not that which comes through man but directly from the Lord. Furthermore, it would be strange for the leaders in Jerusalem to make the request concerning the poor noted in Galatians 2:10 if in fact Barnabas and Paul had just brought a generous offering from Antioch for this very purpose.

Finally, the prominence of Paul in Galatians 2:1-10 does not fit well into the Acts 11 visit. Barnabas is mentioned only at the close of the passage (Gal 2:9). It was during the first missionary journey that the leadership of Barnabas was supplanted by that of Paul. Galatians 2:1-10 clearly reflects this shift, but on the identification of this passage with the occasion of the famine visit the prominence of Paul does not ring true to the actual situation, since no missionary journey had yet been undertaken by the two men.

The problem is admittedly difficult, some would say even insoluble. But it seems that the identification of Galatians 2 and Acts 15 ought not to be abandoned. Since Paul's account has in the background the presence of those who would have liked to have Titus circumcised, a larger assembly may well be implied. Paul was content merely to emphasize that phase of the Council which brought the leading figures into conference. Omission of any reference by Paul to the decree is quite in keeping with his character. When dealing with some of the same practical issues in the Corinthian church he chose to bypass any reference to the Council decree in favor of instructing the church on his own apostolic authority and along lines of spiritual principle.

In comparing what Paul and Luke have written, it should be borne in mind that men who agree in general outlook may still vary from one another in emphasis. In dealing with the Council, Luke was concerned with the peace and progress of the church, but Paul was more concerned with the theological issue of the truth of the Gospel (Gal 2:5). Luke did not cite further Judaizing activity against Paul, probably for the reason that such activity came after the founding of the churches rather than in connection with their establishment, so that it was outside the scope of the task which the writer had set for himself. It is fairly apparent from Acts 21:20-21 that Luke was not uninformed about the persistent propaganda of the legalists against Paul.

Admittedly the writer of Acts did not tell us all we would like to know about the early days of the Church, but what he has told us is of tremendous importance. It is rather paradoxical that some scholars who approach Acts with a Christian background have been extremely critical about Luke's accuracy as a historian, whereas professional historians have tended to be high in their praise of his work. A representative of the latter group has gone on record in these words: "For Acts the confirmation of historicity is overwhelming . . . any attempt to reject its basic historicity even in matters of detail must now appear absurd. Roman historians have long taken it for granted."[8]

One of the most notable features of the study of Acts in recent years is a lessened concern over historical matters and a growing interest in assessing Luke as a theologian. This tendency, strongly marked in the work of Dibelius, has been taken up by Conzelmann and by Haenchen (see bibliography). For a survey of this trend and an evaluation of its strengths and weaknesses, the reader would do well to consult I. Howard Marshall's volume, *Luke: Historian and Theologian*. The author points out that both aspects need to be held in balance and that a trustworthy, historical base is the necessary foundation on which to erect theological interpretation.

THEOLOGY

Since doctrinal teaching is hardly to be expected in the course of historical narrative, it is necessary to look mainly to the speeches contained in Acts for this information. Divergent views have been entertained about their nature and value, with conservative scholars maintaining that although they are not necessarily verbatim reports of what was said on the various occasions, they are nevertheless trustworthy.

However, the approach associated with the name of Martin Dibelius (*Studies in the Acts of the Apostles*) regards them as free compositions by Luke, who shaped their content and is therefore to be considered a theologian more than a historian. This means that the speeches are considered as really directed to Luke's audience several decades after the time of the events described in the book. It is alleged that Luke was simply following the custom of those days, a practice that went back to the Greek historian Thucydides, who confessed that it was hard to retain speeches in the mind word for word, whether he had heard them himself or had a report on them from others, so he had to settle for the following procedure: "My habit has been to make the speakers say what was in my opinion demanded of them by the various occasions, of course adhering as closely as possible to the general sense of what they really said."[9]

This is rather different from relying on the imagination. Indeed, the leading Greek and Roman historians repudiated the manufacturing of speeches. Luke's proven accuracy at many points where he can be tested gives confidence that he would have used all possible means to arrive at a faithful report of the sermons and other addresses which he included in his account. As a Christian he must have had a special concern to honor the truth. It will be noted that nearly all the speeches mention the resurrection of Christ, and several of them make it the principal theme. This is understandable in the setting of the years immediately following the death and resurrection of Jesus, but it is not at all clear that it was the major topic of concern for the Church near the close of the first century, when Dibelius and others assume Luke wrote. Furthermore, it is difficult to think that Luke could have been greatly influenced by Greek models since these do not include the missionary sermon, which is the principal type in the Acts.

In view of Luke's familiarity with the Septuagint, the influence of the Old Testament upon his thinking and workmanship should not be overlooked or underestimated. It is probable, Bertil Gärtner thinks, that Jewish historiography had a greater effect on Luke's methodology than anything of Greek origin.[10] Speeches in many Old Testament passages can be demonstrated to rest on tradition faithfully preserved and highly valued. There is no good reason for doubting that similar factors lie back of Luke's reports of sermons in Acts. In regard to the examples of early apostolic preaching after the resurrection, Bo Reicke observes, "Because of their primitive Christology (e g., Jesus is called *pais*), it is reasonable to look upon these speeches as conforming to a real tradition, and not as later constructions of Luke."[11]

Turning to the theology reflected in the sermons, we note that in discourses addressed to Jews the general procedure was to accent the faithfulness of God in fulfilling the promises made through the prophets by bringing Jesus the Christ into the world, by raising Him from the dead when His nation rejected Him, and by sending the Spirit. The speech of Stephen (chap. 7) and of Paul (chap. 13) are especially full in recounting the Old Testament background for the new age of the Gospel. On the other hand, in addresses to Gentiles there is no specific appeal to the Old Testament but rather appeal to the creation and the providential care exercised by God toward His creatures (chaps. 14, 17).

Concerning the person and work of Jesus, the following items are to be noted: His humanity (2:22; 17:31; also the allusion in 10:41); His dignity as the Son of God (9:20; cf. 13:33); His position as sent of God (3:20, 26; 13:23); His anointing by the Spirit (10:38); His identity as God's Servant (3:13, 26; 4:27, 30); His position as Leader (5:31; cf. 3:15); and His fulfillment of the promise of the Christ (8:5; 17:3; 18:5; cf. 4:26). He is identified as Jesus Christ (2:38); Christ Jesus (24:24); Lord Jesus (4:33; 7:59); Lord Jesus Christ (11:17; 28:31); Lord of all (10:36); the rejected stone (4:11); Saviour (5:31; 13:23; cf. 4:12; 16:31); the Deliverer from sin (3:26; 10:43; 13:38-39; cf. 20:28); the One raised from the dead (2:32; 4:10; 13:30; 17:31); the Righteous One (7:52; 22:14); the exalted One (1:10; 2:33); the returning One (1:11; 3:20); and the Judge of mankind (17:31).

Naturally one does not expect to find in a book such as Acts the same full, rich Christology that meets us in the epistles of Peter and Paul and in Hebrews. There is nothing about preexistence except what is implied in His being sent of God. The theme of Christ's redeeming work is not greatly developed, and beyond what is hinted in 9:5 there is nothing about union with Him as the portion of believers. What stands out is the exaltation of the once rejected Saviour and the revelation of His spiritual presence, energy, and authority exercised in the Church through the Spirit.

The doctrine of the Holy Spirit attains great prominence in Acts, in contrast to the gospels. There He is seen almost entirely in connection with the person of Christ (the Holy Spirit was "not yet," as far as believers were concerned), but in Acts He is the portion of the Church. He was described by the risen Lord as the promise of the Father (1:4; cf. Lk 24:49), and from the very moment of His coming He revealed Himself as the Spirit of power, as in our Lord's ministry (Lk 4:14). The men whom Jesus had called and trained, who had been so timid and uncertain of themselves, were now cogent in thought and bold in speech. Provincial in their Jewish outlook, they became willing to include Gentiles in the scope of their ministry as the Spirit enlarged their vision. Jesus' prediction that He would prove to be their Counselor was abundantly fulfilled. These witnesses for Christ learned that the Spirit sustained them, giving courage to their hearts and readiness of speech to their tongues (Ac 4:13), as Jesus had promised (Lk 12:11-12). The missionary operation of the Church is seen as under His control (Ac 8:29; 10:19; 13:2, 4; 16:6-7). At turning points in the story, He manifested Himself in outward and observable effects which call attention to the reality of the spiritual realm (2:2; 8:17-18; 10:44-46; 19:6).

In summary, the ingredients for a formulation of a doctrine of the Trinity are present in Acts, but none takes shape. This was not intended to be a treatise on theology.

Similarly, Luke was too busy describing the progress of the Church to theologize about it. He was content to note the rise of congregations here and there. Only rarely did he use the singular form to designate the Church at large (9:31; cf. 20:28). Baptism is often cited as the rite by which one is received into the church, but faith (including repentance) is the condition for salvation (2:38, 44; 16:31). The Lord's Supper is not mentioned as a rite but is probably referred to occasionally (2:42; 20:7).

Other items that characterized the life and ministry of the Church (items prominent in the gospel of Luke also) are prayer; the performing of miracles, especially healings; and the experience of angelic visitations (12:7; 27:23).

Finally, we discover that eschatology is not ignored, although it can hardly be said to have great prominence. Christ's return is put in the forefront of the book as a promise (1:11) and had a place in the preaching of

Peter (3:19-20), as the Day of Judgment had in the preaching of Paul (17:31).

Despite all that the book of Acts contains of a theological nature, it should be evident that not all of Christian truth is set forth here. It was not in the purpose of God that the total framework of theology should be communicated at the very beginning of the Church's existence, but rather should be unfolded gradually to meet the specific needs of an expanding and experiencing organism.

QUMRAN INFLUENCE

This community, which was in existence at the time of the rise of the Church in Jerusalem and was located only a few miles away near the Dead Sea, had certain features which bear sufficient resemblance to those of the early Church to suggest some relationship. These "men of the new covenant" were Jews of the Essene type, who had withdrawn from the mainstream of Jewish life as a protest against its corruption. They were especially hostile toward the priestly caste who controlled the Temple. At many points the Qumran community differed substantially from the early Church in Jerusalem, but our concern is to evaluate the elements of possible connection.

For one thing, both groups were known as "the Way," a term that occurs in Acts 9:2 and several other passages. The problem is to know whether both strands go back independently to Isaiah 40:3 for the usage, or whether the Christian use goes back to Qumran influence. Another point of comparison is the communal type of life found in both groups, represented in meals and the pooling of possessions. There is considerable similarity here, although the right of private ownership of property and goods was denied to Qumran members, whereas the sharing in the Jerusalem Church was on a voluntary basis and was exercised as need arose. Of special interest is the use of the term *the multitude* as descriptive of the congregation (Acts 6:2, 5). That this usage should appear also in the Qumran literature as a technical term for the group as convened is a striking phenomenon.

It is quite possible that in these and in some other respects an influence on Jewish Christianity in its earlier stages is to be traced. But this influence was largely peripheral. Faith in Christ as the fulfillment of the hopes of Israel differentiated the Church sharply from this sect of current Judaism that centered its attention on the Mosaic Law.

THE TEXT

It is in Acts that the so-called Western text comes into special prominence. This type of text is old and widespread, which makes the term

28

Western rather inappropriate. Its chief feature is the inclusion of traditional material, some of which may provide valuable information. At times this text type is guilty of omissions also. These features are best explained on the theory that the Western text came into being at an early time, when there was little attempt at regulation or the fixing of a standard text. The chief witnesses for this type of text are Codex Bezae (D) and several manuscripts of the Old Latin Version. Some of the more interesting of the Western readings will be noted in the commentary. The King James Version has a few Western readings (8:37; 9:5b-6a; 24:6b-8a; 28:16 in part; 28:29), but modern translations are free from these additions, since they render a text superior to that which was available to the 1611 translators.

Although J. H. Ropes, in an extensive study of the text of Acts, found little to convince him that there was any theological point of view reflected in the distinctive readings of the Western text in this book,[12] a later investigator, Eldon J. Epp, has found considerable evidence of an anti-Jewish bias in such readings, since they come down heavily on Jewish guilt in rejecting Jesus, in opposing the apostles, and in failing to receive the Gospel.[13] Agreeing basically with this analysis, C. K. Barrett nevertheless finds in the Western text something that is even more characteristic—its tendency to exaggerate. "The editor does not so much introduce new tendencies into Acts as make clearer and more emphatic tendencies that were already there."[14]

CHRONOLOGY

Luke furnished little help for dating the events he described, though occasional time-notices are given, especially in relation to Paul's activities. The generally accepted date for the beginning of the Church is A.D. 30. Certain events can be dated with some precision by means of information from secular sources of the period. One such is the death of Herod Agrippa I in the year 44; another is the proconsulship of Gallio in Achaia, which apparently began in the summer of 51; a third is the ascension of Festus as governor of Judea, concerning which the ancient testimony is somewhat conflicting, but which probably occurred in 59. By using the data of Acts and the Pauline epistles, it is possible to proceed from these fixed points and achieve at least approximate results for the time of Paul's conversion and missionary journeys, the council at Jerusalem, Paul's arrest and arrival at Rome, and other events.

Acts 18:12 seems to imply that shortly after the coming of Gallio to Corinth the Jews appeared before him to accuse Paul. Since 18:11 indicates that the apostle had been in the city for eighteen months, his arrival can be safely put at the end of 49 or beginning of 50. This accords with the information that on arrival at Corinth the apostle took up residence with

Aquila and Priscilla, who had recently come from Rome due to the expulsion of Jews by the emperor Claudius, an event known to have occurred in 49. The apostle's sojourn in Philippi, Thessalonica, Berea, and Athens was brief, so the last few months of 49 probably sufficed for these ministries. Prior to that he was in Asia Minor (Ac 16) for the spring and summer of that year (on the presumption that he commenced his second missionary journey in the spring, the natural time for starting a campaign).

Prior to this journey the apostle attended the council at Jerusalem, which may tentatively be placed early in 49. Before going to Jerusalem he was occupied, along with Barnabas, in evangelizing Cyprus and southern Galatia, a journey that may well have covered most of 47 and 48. Earlier he spent a year in Antioch ministering to the church (Ac 11:26), which accounts for the year 46. Lying back of that is a period of undetermined length spent in the regions of Syria and Cilicia (9:30; 11:25; cf. Gal 1:21). Its duration can be estimated only after an attempt is made to fix the date of Paul's conversion.

Paul's own account includes two time notices (Gal 1:18; 2:1). On the assumption that the periods of three and fourteen years are intended to be sequential, and on the assumption that the second visit to Jerusalem is to be identified with the Jerusalem Council meeting of Acts 15, which has been assigned to the year 49, one arrives at a date of 32 (49 minus 17) for the conversion of the apostle. It is impossible to check this by the data in the early chapters of Acts since time notices are lacking, but the impression made by the narrative on many students (e.g., T. W. Manson and George Ogg) is that the interval from Pentecost to the death of Stephen was rather brief. Some, however, prefer to date the conversion a year or two later. This variation affects in turn the determination of the time spent by Paul in Tarsus and vicinity before going to Antioch, but that period can be roughly estimated as covering eight to ten years.

Now it is expedient to return to the Gallio date and use it as a point of departure for dating events in the latter part of Paul's life. Luke tells us that following the Gallio incident the apostle remained in Corinth for many days (Ac 18:18). This rather indefinite expression may mean no more than that he stayed long enough to avoid suspicion that he was running away from the possibility of further persecution. A brief stop in Ephesus followed, then what appears to have been a somewhat hurried journey to the south, including Caesarea and Jerusalem, ending with a return to Antioch. Again the Lucan narrative is indefinite, stating that Paul spent some time there before making his way back to Ephesus by way of interior Asia Minor. Possibly he spent the winter of 52 in Antioch, arriving at Ephesus in the spring of 53 to begin his longest ministry in one place. The apostle spoke of it as spanning three years (20:31). This figure embraces three months spent in the synagogue (19:8), two years at the school of Tyrannus (19:10) and "a while" (19:22) between this period and his departure from the city.

Presumably it was late in 56 when he arrived in Corinth to spend the winter (1 Co 16:6), which in turn places his final visit to Jerusalem and his arrest in the spring of 57. The period of detention under Felix lasted two years (Ac 24:27). Since the journey to Rome fell in the winter, Paul's arrival at Rome presumably occurred in the spring of 60. Luke observed that he was kept under house arrest for two more years (28:30), which brings the conclusion of the narrative to the year 62.

The question of the apostle's release and subsequent labor, possibly in the East as well as in Spain, is much debated, but there is general agreement as to his martyrdom in 64, the year of the great fire in Rome, even though Eusebius in his *Chronicon* put it in the thirteenth year of Nero (67) and Jerome in his *De Viris Illustribus* still later (68), near the end of Nero's reign. The date of 64 is based in part on the testimony of Clement of Rome who placed the death of Peter and Paul in the imperial city at a time when many other believers were martyred.[15] The only time known prior to Clement when this could have taken place is in the reign of Nero. Clinching testimony comes from Tacitus, who told of the great fire which swept Rome in the summer of 64 and the suspicion that Nero himself had set it.[16] To avert suspicion, the emperor blamed the Christians and had many of them put to death. The close agreement between Clement and Tacitus makes it reasonably certain that the year 64 marked the close of the life of Paul.

VALUE

This book serves as a bridge between the gospels and the epistles. In the gospels the Church is present only as a prediction made by the Saviour. In the epistles the Church is an accomplished fact, fairly widely distributed around the eastern Mediterranean basin. It is from Acts that we acquire needed information on how the Church arose and grew and spread.

In a narrower sense, Acts constitutes a helpful introduction to the epistles of Paul, telling us the circumstances surrounding the founding of most of the churches to which he wrote letters.

Acts is especially pertinent to the present day, for the Church in our time is faced with somewhat the same conditions as confronted the infant Christian community. In the Western world Christians are becoming more and more a minority in the population and are subject to pressures because of unwillingness to conform to some features of modern secular life. Less and less is the Church able to claim government patronage or protection.

31

Under such circumstances the Church cannot afford to neglect the message of this book.

From start to finish the thrust of Acts is missionary. Significantly, its close is abrupt, as though to tell the reader that what Paul was doing in Rome, under conditions not wholly ideal, continues to be the task of all later generations of believers. The unfinished book underscores the unfinished task.

PART I

THE CHURCH AT JERUSALEM–
1:1–8:3

In this section Luke was intent on describing the origin of the Church, relating it to Jesus' ministry and the work of the Holy Spirit. The apostles are the principal human figures. This early phase is restricted to primitive Jewish Christianity and developments in the Jerusalem area. Its content includes sermons, summary statements of the growth of the Christian community, glimpses of spiritual and social life, and intimations of the opposition stirred up in official Jewish circles by the apostolic proclamation that Jesus of Nazareth had been raised from the dead by the power of God.

A. Preparation—1:1-26

INSTEAD OF PLUNGING into the history of the Church immediately by describing what occurred on the day of Pentecost, Luke sketched the background for that event. He had constructed his gospel in somewhat the same way, not starting directly with the birth of Jesus but dealing with the story of John the Baptist as an introduction.

1. JESUS' MINISTRY AND ASCENSION—1:1-11

In this period the risen Lord had contact only with His followers (cf. Mt 23:39). It was a time of fellowship, of instruction, and of adjustment on the part of the disciples for the work which lay ahead of them.

> **1:1** The first account I composed, Theophilus, about all that Jesus began to do and teach,
>
> **2** until the day when He was taken up, after He had by the Holy Spirit given orders to the apostles whom He had chosen.
>
> **3** To these He also presented Himself alive, after His suffering, by many convincing proofs, appearing to them over *a period of* forty days, and speaking of the concerns of the kingdom of God.
>
> **4** And gathering them together, He commanded them not to leave Jerusalem, but to wait for what the Father had promised, "Which," *He said*, "you heard of from Me;
>
> **5** for John baptized with water, but you shall be baptized with the Holy Spirit not many days from now."
>
> **6** And so when they had come together, they were asking Him, saying, "Lord, is it at this time You are restoring the kingdom to Israel?"
>
> **7** He said to them, "It is not for you to know times or epochs which the Father has fixed by His own authority;
>
> **8** but you shall receive power when the Holy Spirit has come upon you; and you shall be My witnesses both in Jerusalem, and in all Judea and Samaria, and even to the remotest part of the earth."
>
> **9** And after He had said these things, He was lifted up while they were looking on, and a cloud received Him out of their sight.
>
> **10** And as they were gazing intently into the sky while He was departing, behold, two men in white clothing stood beside them;
>
> **11** and they also said, "Men of Galilee, why do you stand looking into the sky? This Jesus, who has been taken up from you into heaven, will come in just the same way as you have watched Him go into heaven."

1:1. "The first account" is a reference to the gospel according to Luke. Similarly the Jewish historian Josephus, in Book 2 of his work *Against Apion*, made reference to "the former book" (Book 1). Since the ancients used *first* at times when strict grammatical usage called for *former*, Luke's wording is hardly a sufficient basis for assuming that he planned to write a third volume.

It is reasonably certain, in line with the dedicatory custom of the time, that a real person is intended by the name "Theophilus." In view of the title "most excellent" given to him in Luke 1:3, it is probable that he belonged to the nobility. Possibly he was a Roman official (cf. Ac 26:25). Whether he was a confessed believer is not certain. Luke 1:4 seems to favor this verdict, especially if Luke meant to say that he was instructed, or even catechized, concerning Christian truth. On the other hand, the verb can be rendered "informed," which does not necessarily indicate that he was a believer. The title is dropped at the beginning of Acts, which some interpret as an indication that in the interval between the writing of the two books he became a Christian, warranting a more informal approach by the writer.

"All that Jesus began to do and teach" is Luke's way of summarizing the main lines of Jesus' earthly ministry as enshrined in his gospel. "Began" is the troublesome word here. While it could mean that He acted and taught "from the beginning," more likely it is intended to suggest the thought that after the ascension the Lord continued to make His power felt on earth by these means. This is agreeable to certain passages in the gospels (Mt 28:18-20; Jn 14:12-14). It finds support also in Acts, where the Lord Jesus is represented as intervening in developments on earth such as the coming of the Holy Spirit (2:33; see Jn 16:7); in Peter's use of the keys of the Kingdom (Ac 2, 10; see Mt 16:18-19); and in the conversion of Saul (Ac 9:15) and visions granted to him (18:9; 23:11). Paul expressly attributed the miracles of his missionary career to Christ (Ro 15:18-19).

That Jesus continued to "teach" presents a difficulty in that His ethical teaching, such as is contained in the Sermon on the Mount, is not reproduced in Acts. However, the teaching which He gave to His disciples about His death and resurrection has a prominent place in most of the sermons Luke reports. The ethical teaching may have been shared with converts (Ac 2:42).

1:2. Luke used the same verb "taken up," in verses 11 and 22, and the noun form in Luke 9:51. The ascension is noted here as the event which terminated the Saviour's earthly ministry, but the description of it is reserved to verse 9. "Orders" is similarly an anticipation of verse 8 (cf. Lk 24:47-48), and doubtless of verse 4 also.

The choosing of "the apostles" (Lk 6:12-16) had momentous consequences for the future. These men had authority from Jesus to preach and teach, to perform miracles, and to guide converts. It was "by the Holy Spirit" that the Lord now outlined their task more specifically. Though the Spirit had not yet been bestowed publicly (v. 5), He had been communicated to this select company on the evening of resurrection day (Jn 20:22). Because of this the words of Jesus were more meaningful and powerful in their impact than in the precrucifixion period, when the disciples had been prone to argue and to doubt.

1:3. This is our one source of information concerning the interval between the resurrection and the ascension. No such interval is stated in Luke 24, but it would be precarious to assume that when Luke wrote his gospel he thought the resurrection and ascension took place on the same day. He probably had Mark's account for reference, where the promise is given of appearances in Galilee (Mk 16:7). Acts 1 seems intended to enlarge and clarify the rather summary narrative of Luke 24, and this in several particulars. We know from the gospels that the postresurrection appearances were sporadic. Jesus came and went during this period.

In his gospel, Luke included "many . . . proofs"—Jesus' self-disclosure to the Emmaus pair (Lk 24:31); to Simon (Lk 24:34); and to the eleven, when He showed His hands and feet, invited touch, and proceeded to eat in their presence (Lk 24:36-43).

"Speaking of the kingdom of God" summarizes Jesus' verbal communication to His followers. Judging from verse 6, the teaching did not deal with the future aspect of the Kingdom; otherwise the disciples would not have queried Him with the kind of question they posed. Once again, Luke 24 provides necessary guidance, informing us that after the resurrection Jesus was primarily occupied with explaining His mission in the light of the Old Testament (Lk 24:25, 44-47). The Kingdom, or rule, of God, as used in Acts, seems virtually to be a term for the Gospel viewed in relation to the overall plan of God (8:12; 19:8; 20:25; 28:23, 31). Only in 14:22 is the eschatological aspect given any specific prominence. One has only to refer to Matthew 16:18-19 to realize how closely intertwined are the Church and the Kingdom.

It is notable that the teaching of Jesus here is not described in detail. If Luke had been interested in using his imagination, he could have inserted something about the divine purpose regarding the Gentiles, for example, that could in turn have helped the Church in dealing with this problem later on (chaps. 10-11, 15); or he could have given instruction on church organization. The sacred historian needs to be judged by what he did not say as well as by what he included.[1]

1:4. There is considerable uncertainty regarding the translation of the phrase, "And gathering them together." The expression would ordinarily mean to assemble or congregate, referring to the action of a group, whereas here the action is attributed to Jesus. An alternative rendering is "eating with them," based on the supposition that embedded in the word is the Greek term for salt. The etymology is precarious, but some favor this translation because in two other passages Luke refers to the fact that Jesus ate with his disciples following the resurrection (Lk 24:43; Ac 10:41). A few manuscripts have a form which differs in only one letter from that which most of the others attest. This reading yields the rendering "staying with them," without implying permanence in the relationship. Everything considered, this may well be the most satisfactory solution of a problem that is widely acknowledged to be very difficult.

It was during the period that Jesus was staying (if only intermittently) with His disciples that He commanded them not to leave Jerusalem but to await "what the Father had promised" (see Lk 24:49). We can understand why the disciples would be inclined to leave Jerusalem, for this was the city which had slain their leader. Besides, their homes were far away in Galilee. In fact, their presence in the city at this time cannot be understood apart from obedience to the command of the risen Lord.[2] In the wisdom of God, the Spirit was to manifest Himself at the very place where Jesus was rejected. If the Gospel could make its way there in the power of the Spirit, it could go anywhere in triumph.

The description of the Spirit as "what the Father had promised" goes back to Luke 24:49 and also finds its rationale in the teaching of Jesus on the eve of the crucifixion (Jn 14:16, 26; 15:26). Clearly it was not enough that the disciples had spent three years with Jesus and had been under His instruction. They needed the wisdom and power of the Spirit of God, and were sufficiently chastened by past failures to recognize their need.

1:5. The truth contained here is a decisive one for the Christian era. Up to this time, baptism both with water at the hands of John and with the Holy Spirit had been the experience only of Jesus, not of the eleven (Lk 3:21-22). Though their baptism by John is not recorded, it may be assumed, since many of them had been John's disciples. Now Jesus indicated that these men would share in the Spirit. He did not add that He himself would baptize them with the Spirit, which the Baptist had affirmed (Lk 3:16 and parallels), but this may well be implied in the passive form of the verb. The apostles were the nucleus of the Church, and as such had to possess the Spirit, for this is the indispensable token of belonging to Christ (Ro 8:9; 1 Co 12:13). What the effect would be on the lives of the disciples is not stated, but it comes out in verse 8 (cf. Lk 4:1, 14). For an echo of verse 5 in the experience of Peter, see Acts 11:16.

Just as water baptism is a once-for-all matter, so is baptism with the Spirit. Because of the peculiar historical position of the eleven, they were believers for some time before being baptized with the Spirit; but this is not the norm for this age. Only very special considerations in the life of the early Church dictated delay in the giving of the Spirit (8:12, 15-16).

1:6. "When they had come together" implies a somewhat later occasion and confirms what the gospels make clear—that the Lord's postresurrection appearances were followed by disappearances. The meeting now to be considered was the final one, on which the ascension occurred, and the place was near Bethany (Lk 24:50-51).

Instead of questioning the Lord about the Spirit and what His coming would mean for them, the disciples revived the viewpoint which had been rampant among them even when Jesus was going up to Jerusalem to suffer. The popular expectation and hope was that He would institute the Kingdom at that time (Lk 19:11). In this expectation the disciples shared, despite several intimations from Jesus that He was going to Jerusalem to suffer and die (Mk 10:32-40). To them the thought of death for the Messiah was intolerable, so the words of Jesus were not taken literally. But now that He had risen from the dead, surely that display of power (so they thought) warranted the conclusion that He could restore the Kingdom to Israel. It seemed to them altogether natural. God's chosen people had been trodden down by alien nations for too long. "Restoring," to them, meant the reviving of Israel's independence and glory, with the period of David and Solomon as the model. It is possible that the disciples misunderstood the significance of "what the Father had promised," thinking it applied to the Davidic covenant (cf. Lk 1:32-33).

1:7. Jesus' response questioned the timeliness of this hope. Its realization belongs to the secret, hidden things that are the property of the Father alone (cf. Mk 13:32). "Times" is a strictly chronological word, whereas "epochs" includes the character and circumstances of the times. The two terms are combined again in 1 Thessalonians 5:1.

1:8. But there was something which the disciples could know, and this belonged to the present rather than to some uncertain time in the future. As already indicated, only a few days would elapse before the Spirit would come upon them (v. 5), with resultant "power" to make them effective witnesses for their Master. This would mark the final phase of their preparation for service in His name. The power lay in the person of the Spirit rather than in some sort of spiritual energy He might release to them. The correlation of Spirit and power was notable in the ministry of John the Baptist (Lk 1:15-17) and of Jesus (Lk 4:14; cf. Ac 10:38). That this enduement was not confined to the apostles is apparent from what is said later on of Stephen (Ac 6:5, 8).

"Witness" is related to the old verb *to wit*, that is, "to know." Consequently, a witness is one who is able to give testimony based on knowledge (cf. Is 43:10-12). One must know Christ in order to bear witness to Him. An unbeliever, no matter how much he might have seen and heard Him, cannot qualify. The resurrection was a key element in this testimony (Ac 1:22), and only believers had seen the risen Lord.

Was "You shall be My witnesses" prophecy or command? Surely both. As prophecy the disciples could count on its realization; as command they were bound to sense their responsibility to make themselves obediently available. Implied in our Lord's words is the duty to make Him their message. To preach the Good News of the Gospel and to preach Christ amount to the same thing (see 8:5, 12).

The place where the witness was to be exercised is comprehended in four terms which represent more specific direction than that given in Luke 24:47, and which geographically involve moving out from a center to the circumference, as ripples from a pebble dropped into a pond. The same terms may be viewed according to the degree of spiritual preparation found in these places. In Jerusalem and Judea Judaism held sway, and it rested on the revealed religion of the Old Testament. Samaria enshrined a religion partly true and partly false, a confused mixture (Jn 4:22). The remotest part of the earth speaks of the unenlightened condition of paganism and heathenism, with false notions of God corrupting the ideals and life of society.

Each of these four areas contained its peculiar challenge to the disciples. Jerusalem had the blood of prophets on its hands (Mt 23:37), and now it had added the blood of Jesus of Nazareth. Would the disciples be expected to follow in His train (Mt 16:21, 24-25)? Judea was the home of Judas Iscariot, the man of Kerioth, the betrayer. The prospect of going there was not a welcome one. Samaria, with its traditional hostility toward Jews, was not likely to be hospitable to the followers of One to whom it had refused the rights of a traveler (Lk 9:51-56). The remotest part of the earth was the home of the Gentiles (Is 49:6), whose spiritual and moral uncleanness drew from Jews the epithet *dogs.*

But the disciples were now to be the witnesses of One who had wept over Jerusalem, One who had already taught in all Judea (Lk 23:5), One who had felt that He must pass through Samaria rather than avoid it (Jn 4:4), One who had welcomed the faith of Gentiles and responded to it (Mt 8:5-13; 15:21-28). "The remotest part of the earth" answers to "all the nations" (Lk 24:47; cf. Is 49:6).

Notable is the absence of Galilee from the places indicated by our Lord. He evidently counted on the willingness of His disciples to spread the good tidings in their native place, and so it came to pass (Ac 9:31). However, there is a possibility that "all Judea" is an expression intended to include Galilee, since there are examples where Judea seems to have this comprehensive meaning, notably in the Lucan writings. Especially significant are Luke 23:5 and Acts 10:37.

1:9. With the giving of this final charge, Jesus was ready to be "lifted up." This is one of several terms used for the ascension. In Luke 24:50 it is used of the raising of the hands of the Lord in blessing as He departed from His own. The disciples "were looking on." At other appearances the risen Lord had slipped away after disclosing Himself (Lk 24:31), but this time there was a gradual, stately departure from the earthly scene. The "cloud" is often associated in Scripture with revelations of the Deity, serving to emphasize the dignity and mystery of the divine person (Ex 19:16; Dan 7:13; Lk 9:34).

The ascension has very little place in the gospel records, leading to the observation, "The Ascension apparently did not lie within the proper scope of the Gospels, as seen in their genuine texts: its true place was at the head of the Acts of the Apostles, as the preparation for the Day of Pentecost, and thus the beginning of the history of the Church."[3] This event was the logical sequel to the resurrection of the heavenly Man. It provided the basis for the presentation of the present life and ministry He carries on in heaven, as set forth in the epistle to the Hebrews; and it accorded with the promise of His return, in line with Acts 1:11. It is the exalted Christ who sends the Spirit, and by that same Spirit He, though physically absent, is present dynamically in the lives of His own.

1:10. Straining to keep the Lord in their vision as long as possible, the disciples kept their eyes riveted on Him. The spell was broken by the sudden appearance of "two men" in white. That they were angels is evident both from their appearance and from their message. Other passages describe angels as men (Ac 10:3, 30; Rev 21:17). Such messengers of God are represented as serving also at the annunciation of the incarnation (Lk 1:26), at the birth of Jesus (Lk 2:9, 13), at the temptation (Mt 4:11), and at the resurrection (Lk 24:4).

1:11. "Men of Galilee" agrees with the gospel records. The only probable exception, Judas, was no longer one of their company. If there was a gentle rebuke in the question addressed to them, it merely prepared the way for a message of comforting assurance to the effect that the departing Saviour would someday return. "This Jesus"—the human name, serving to emphasize the abiding humanity of the One who had taken to Himself human nature—"will come in just the same way." This cannot be a reference to the occurrence at Pentecost, the Lord's coming through the Spirit. A personal, visible return was promised, but there was no word added to indicate that these men would be alive to see Him. This event will complete the Lord's relationship to earth; the birth called for the death, the death for the resurrection, the resurrection for the ascension, and the ascension for the return. Can there be any doubt that the earth is the divinely intended center of the universe? The ascension was the acknowledgment by the Father of the finished work of the Son. It set the stage for the sending of the Spirit. Taken with the truth set forth in 1:1, it implies a continuing concern for this world, which is made explicit by 1:11.

2. DAYS OF WAITING—1:12-14

This was a period of ten days, since forty days had passed (*Pentecost* means "fifty"). It was a time of waiting but not of inactivity, for the group was much in prayer.

> **1:12**   Then they returned to Jerusalem from the mount called Olivet, which is near Jerusalem, a Sabbath day's journey away.
> **13**   And when they had entered, they went up to the upper room, where they were staying; that is, Peter and John and James and Andrew, Philip and Thomas, Bartholomew and Matthew, James *the son* of Alphaeus, and Simon the Zealot, and Judas *the son* of James.
> **14**   These all with one mind were continually devoting themselves to prayer, along with *the* women, and Mary the Mother of Jesus, and with His brothers.

1:12. The site of the ascension was apparently the ridge of "the mount called Olivet," famous for its olive groves. "A Sabbath day's journey" was the limit of time allowed by Jewish custom for travel on the Sabbath—a little over half a mile. Luke did not say that the disciples made this short trip on the Sabbath; he was merely noting the distance. According to Luke 24:52 the return to the city was made with great joy, inspired doubtless by the promise of the Lord's return.

1:13. The disciples' destination was "the upper room." Since the definite article is used, this suggests a well-known place, one which they had occupied before. A possibility is the large upper room where Jesus had kept the Passover with His disciples (Lk 22:12), even though a different Greek word (meaning "above the ground level") is used in the latter passage. "Staying" is sometimes used of temporary residence, which fits the present situation.

Luke 24:53 makes no mention of the upper room but concentrates on the public worship in which the disciples participated in the Temple. In Acts 1:13-14 the concern is to picture the activity of Jesus' followers when they were in their own company. Similar alternation between public and private activities is noted in later passages (2:46; 5:42).

The eleven disciples are named at this point (each of the synoptic gospels has a list also). Peter's name stands first, as in all the other accounts. Of considerable interest is the fact that Luke put John next, whereas in his gospel he assigned him fourth place. The shift prepares the reader for the several occasions in Acts when John appears as Peter's partner in the work (3:1; 4:13; 8:14).

1:14. In the relative seclusion of the upper room the apostles were joined by certain "women," no doubt those who had accompanied Jesus from Galilee and were present at the crucifixion and at the empty tomb (Mk 15:40-41; 16:1). Special note is taken of the presence of "Mary the mother of Jesus" and "His brothers." Their names are given in Matthew 13:55. The Lord's appearance to James (1 Co 15:7) may have been influential in bringing the rest of the family to faith (cf. Jn 7:5). Without straining, the word "brothers" (*brethren* is only an alternative rendering) is broad enough to include the sisters. There were at least three of them, all unnamed (Mt 13:56). The presence of Mary and of other women makes this the more plausible.

It was important that the family of Jesus should be found in the company of believers from the start. As descendants of David, their participation and leadership "was a visible sign of the connection between the new community and the old."[4] The apostle Paul testified to their activity in Christian witness at a later time (1 Co 9:5). There is little ground for seeing a reference to them in John 20:17, where the disciples are naturally in view.

The entire company, united as never before by a common devotion to Jesus the Christ, gave themselves to "prayer." Did they remember that Jesus was in prayer when the Spirit came upon Him (Lk 3:21-22)? Perhaps they recalled the promise that the Father would give the Spirit to those who ask Him (Lk 11:13), but they were under no command to pray thus. Jesus had announced the coming of the Spirit, in emphatic terms, as near at hand. However, the events of recent days had been so momentous that the thought of being caught up into the plan of God at this strategic juncture of history was overwhelming. Who was sufficient for these things? They turned instinctively to God in prayer.

3. APPOINTMENT OF MATTHIAS—1:15-26

The group did not remain in prayer continuously, for this spiritual exercise made them aware of practical needs that had to be met. Prayer gave them insight concerning a specific problem within their ranks.

> **1:15** And at this time Peter stood up in the midst of the brethren (a gathering of about one hundred and twenty persons was there together), and said,
> **16** "Brethren, the Scripture had to be fulfilled, which the Holy Spirit foretold by the mouth of David concerning Judas, who became a guide to those who arrested Jesus.

43

17 "For he was counted among us, and received his portion in this ministry."

18 (Now this man acquired a field with the price of his wickedness; and falling headlong, he burst open in the middle and all his bowels gushed out.

19 And it became known to all who were living in Jerusalem; so that in their own language that field was called Hakeldama, that is, Field of Blood).

20 "For it is written in the book of Psalms,

'LET HIS HOMESTEAD BE MADE DESOLATE,
AND LET NO MAN DWELL IN IT;'

and,

'HIS OFFICE LET ANOTHER MAN TAKE.'

21 "It is therefore necessary that of the men who have accompanied us all the time that the Lord Jesus went in and out among us—

22 beginning with the baptism of John, until the day that He was taken up from us—one of these should become a witness with us of His resurrection."

23 And they put forward two men, Joseph called Barsabbas (who was also called Justus), and Matthias.

24 And they prayed, and said, "Thou, Lord, who knowest the hearts of all men, show which one of these two Thou hast chosen

25 to occupy this ministry and apostleship from which Judas turned aside to go to his own place."

26 And they drew lots for them, and the lot fell to Matthias; and he was numbered with the eleven apostles.

1:15. During the ten-day period others joined the group until it increased to around "one hundred and twenty" persons.* Nicodemus and Joseph of Arimathea may have cast in their lot with them. The Emmaus pair are possibilities, as are some if not all of the seventy whom the Lord had sent before Him on the final journey to Jerusalem (Lk 10:1). Could Martha, Mary, and Lazarus have remained aloof? Even so the number is not as great as the five hundred to whom the Lord appeared at one time (1 Co 15:6).

Who was to take the leadership of this company? There was no immediate need for supervising corporate prayer, but now the group faced a problem requiring deliberation. The twelve had suffered a loss through the defection of Judas, and a replacement had to be found for him.

"Peter stood up." He was a man of ready speech and bold action, but

---

*Bo Reicke calls attention to the fact that in Jewish practice a town congregation had to have this many persons in order to be able to elect members to the Sanhedrin ("The Constitution of the Primitive Church in the Light of Jewish Documents," in *The Scrolls and the New Testament,* ed. Krister Stendahl, pp. 145-46). Since Acts 1 is concerned with an election, Luke may have been intent on making clear that the procedure followed was regular.

after his denial of his Lord he could assert himself only because of forgiveness (as indicated in Lk 24:34) and reinstatement graciously granted to him in the presence of his brethren (Jn 21:15-19). He began at once to exercise his authority to shepherd the flock, even as in due course he would be ready to open the door of faith to unbelievers at Pentecost (see Mt 16:19). "In the midst of the brethren" is a reference to the whole company. Jesus had anticipated this by His own usage. (Mt 12:50; Jn 20:17).

1:16-17. Peter indicated at once that he had been to school with the risen Lord, who had talked much about the fulfillment of Scripture in connection with His death and resurrection. One can almost imagine hearing Jesus speak in Peter's words, "the Scripture had to be fulfilled" (cf. Lk 24:44). The apostle had learned also to give the Holy Spirit recognition as the ultimate Author, the One who spoke through David (cf. 2 Pe 1:21). Furthermore, his ability to find Judas alluded to in the Old Testament was no doubt prompted by the fact that on two occasions when our Lord spoke of Judas' failure, He had noted that thereby Scripture had been fulfilled (Jn 13:18; 17:12). But Peter's choice of Scripture passages was not the same as that of his Master, since he was concerned most of all with the position that Judas had abdicated by his betrayal of the Lord (see Ac 1:17).

Before quoting Scripture he made a simple identifying comment about this man, calling him "a guide to those who arrested Jesus." It would have been in order to call attention to his sin more directly, but Peter seems to have been anxious to avoid harsh, judgmental language. After all, he himself had failed the Lord miserably that same night and had been humbled by his failure. One can detect a tinge of sadness and nostalgia in his further comment about this man. The betrayer had shared in the apostolic office, yet had proved unworthy of it.

1:18-19. This portion is properly set apart by a parenthesis, for it was not a part of Peter's speech but rather Luke's own account of what happened to Judas following the betrayal. The inclusion of this material is the more appropriate because Luke's gospel has nothing about Judas after his part in the arrest of Jesus. Likely he gleaned this information through contact with one or more persons from the Jerusalem church.

Some difficulties appear as this account is compared with that in Matthew 27:3-10. Luke says that Judas bought a field with his ill-gotten gain, whereas Matthew indicates that the Sanhedrin bought it as a place in which to bury strangers. If they bought it in his name, seeing the money was his, both accounts become reasonably harmonious. The other problem is that Matthew's account states that Judas took his own life by hanging himself, whereas Luke pictures a fall resulting in a rupture of Judas' body at the middle. The standard explanation of this apparent discrepancy is the assumption that the noose used by Judas broke, resulting in a fatal fall, perhaps on a sharp object such as a stake or jagged stone. The incident accounts for the name given to the plot of ground, namely, "Field of Blood." Thus Luke made clear the meaning of the Aramaic *Hakeldama* for the benefit of Gentile readers.

Now we come to the two citations from the Psalms that Peter makes use of in connection with Judas.

1:20. Among the psalms regarded by the early Church as Messianic is the sixty-ninth, which is ascribed to David and recites a series of afflictions at the hands of his enemies, and his prayers to God for aid. Its applicability to the sufferings of Christ (e.g., v. 21, in the light of Jn 19:28-30) may go back to our Lord's teaching after the resurrection (Lk 24:44). Quoted from the LXX with minor changes, Psalm 69:25 is here applied to Judas. The traitor's place was left empty. This was both a judgment upon him and a tacit acknowledgment that the vacancy cried out for someone to fill it.

The warrant for replacement is found in Psalm 109:8, quoted from the LXX: "his office let another man take." Even apart from Scripture's sanction, the body of believers must have felt the logical necessity for a successor to Judas. The number twelve was highly symbolic, due to its correspondence to the number of the tribes of Israel, and consequently served to express the idea of the Church as the new Israel, or people of God, the faithful remnant of a largely unbelieving nation. The word "office" is literally "bishopric," but there is no warrant for concluding that a term used in a quotation was intended to point to an episcopal structure in the organization of the early Church. Also, it is patent that the reason for choosing a replacement for Judas was not his death but his defection. There is no support here for the doctrine of apostolic succession.

1:21-22. Here Peter laid down the qualifications for the man who was to succeed Judas in the apostolate. The main objective was to have someone who could be "a witness . . . of His resurrection." Already there was an awareness that the proclamation of the twelve would magnify the resurrection, and the sermons in Acts reveal the correctness of this appraisal. To be a witness of the resurrection did not mean that one must have seen Jesus emerge from the tomb, for no human eye saw Him at that moment, but rather must have seen Him alive from the dead and enjoyed fellowship with Him.

But it was also deemed important that this person should have been among the followers of Jesus from the beginning of His ministry, which was marked in a general way by "the baptism of John." According to Mark 1:1-15 this was the beginning of the Gospel. This qualification meant that such a man would have the advantage of having heard the Lord speak on many occasions and having watched Him perform His mighty works of help and healing. In short, he would have all the qualifications of the eleven, apart from actual call to apostleship by the Lord and the special instruction Jesus had given to this restricted group. This passage confirms the accuracy of the presentation in John 1, where initial contact between Jesus and certain of His disciples is tied in with the ministry of John the Baptist.

1:23-26. In the phrase, "And they put forward two men," some manuscripts of the Western text have *he* (Peter) instead of "they." But the latter reading is more likely, especially since exactly this procedure was followed in choosing the seven (6:3). The Church made the selection. In the case before us, only one man was to be chosen, and there were two who possessed the necessary qualifications. The brothers of Jesus were present, but they had been unbelievers during His ministry.

It was a solemn occasion, a time for seeking divine wisdom. The brethren knew the men involved, but only the Lord knew their "hearts." His wisdom was needed, so His help was invoked. "Lord" could be God the Father here, in agreement with 2:39; 3:19 and other passages. It is probably a reference to the Lord Jesus, however, because the words "Thou hast chosen" recall the fact that it was He who had chosen the twelve. The man chosen would fulfill Judas's abandoned "ministry and apostleship" (v. 25). The order of events suggests that the actual service involved, with the sacrifices that would be entailed, was given primary consideration, while honorific position was secondary. The final mention of Judas agrees with Christ's verdict—"son of perdition" (Jn 17:12). He was never a regenerated man (Jn 13:10-11). Membership in a Christian group and even active service therein (Judas was treasurer) do not guarantee that one truly belongs to Christ.

"They drew lots for them." Of the various methods of drawing lots, the one probably used on this occasion was to mark stones for identification, then shake them in a vessel before shaking them out. Matthias was the choice, and he was forthwith "numbered with the eleven apostles."

Various objections to this incident have been raised by those who judge that a mistake was made. For one thing, was it right to use the lot, an Old Testament practice, when the new age of the Gospel had dawned? The practice, however, was not regarded in Old Testament days as a matter of luck or magic. Men might propose, but only God could dispose (cf. Pr 16:33). It should be noted that the Holy Spirit had not yet come, so resort to the ancient method is quite understandable. The brethren themselves had no doubt that the Lord had revealed His will. A second objection, that Matthias is not heard of again, while true enough, does not mean that God

47

refused to honor the choice, for silence cloaks the personal activities of almost all the apostles in the ensuing history. Again, fault is found on the ground that the divine choice was Saul of Tarsus. It is quite apparent, however, that Saul could not meet the qualifications laid down. In addition, his apostleship, which was not from men nor through a man (Gal 1:1), was of a special, independent type. He knew he was of equal rank with the original apostles, but he did not classify himself with them (1 Co 15:11).

One should observe that the selection of Matthias was made after prayer. The will of God was earnestly sought. To rule out Matthias is to call in question the efficacy of divine guidance through waiting on God. There is a possibility that some who were not present could have met the qualifications (1 Co 15:6), but if so, their failure to be present on these crucial days of waiting ruled them out.

B. Birth—2:1-47

THE MATERIALS of Acts 2 fall readily into three parts: the coming of the Spirit, with powerful effects on the disciples which in turn brought excitement and bewilderment to the inhabitants of Jerusalem; the sermon of Peter, which began with an explanation of the strange phenomena just witnessed by the people, continued with an exposition of what God had done through Jesus of Nazareth, and concluded with an appeal for repentance and a promise of acceptance with God sealed by the reception of the Spirit; and a statement of the results of Pentecost in terms of the growth of the Church, its daily activities, and the effect upon the populace.

1. THE SPIRIT'S MANIFESTATION—2:1-13

Jesus' word about the promise of the Father (1:4-5) was now fulfilled. The coming of the Spirit to His followers was the necessary condition for reaching those who were not yet believers (Jn 16:7-8).

> **2:1** And when the day of Pentecost had come, they were all together in one place.
>
> **2** And suddenly there came from heaven a noise like a violent, rushing wind, and it filled the whole house where they were sitting.
>
> **3** And there appeared to them tongues as of fire distributing themselves, and they rested on each one of them.
>
> **4** And they were all filled with the Holy Spirit and began to speak with other tongues, as the Spirit was giving them utterance.
>
> **5** Now there were Jews living in Jerusalem, devout men, from every nation under heaven.
>
> **6** And when this sound occurred, the multitude came together, and were bewildered, because they were each one hearing them speak in his own language.
>
> **7** And they were amazed and marvelled, saying, "Why, are not all these who are speaking Galileans?
>
> **8** "And how is it that we each hear *them* in our own language to which we were born?
>
> **9** "Parthians and Medes and Elamites, and residents of Mesopotamia, Judea and Cappadocia, Pontus and Asia,
>
> **10** Phrygia and Pamphylia, Egypt and the districts of Libya around Cyrene, and visitors from Rome, both Jews and proselytes,

11 Cretans and Arabs—we hear them in our *own* tongues speaking of the mighty deeds of God."

12 And they continued in amazement and great perplexity, saying to one another, "What does this mean?"

13 But others were mocking and saying, "They are full of sweet wine."

2:1. "The day of Pentecost" marked one of the three major festivals of the Jews (the other two being Passover and the Feast of Tabernacles). It had the name *Pentecost* (the Greek word for *fiftieth*) because it fell on the fiftieth day after the Sabbath of Passover (Lev 23:15). Occasionally the word appears in the intertestamental literature (2 Mac 12:32; Tobit 2:1), but the usual Old Testament term is *Feast of Weeks* (Ex 34:22, where it is called also "the first fruits of wheat harvest"). This term, "first fruits," is especially significant, for it hints at the truth that the thousands who came to Christ on that day are to be viewed as the first fruits of a much greater harvest. A Jew could hardly avoid making such an association. On the basis of Leviticus 23:15, which states that the seven full weeks were to be counted after the Sabbath, Pentecost fell on the first day of the week, providing a link with the resurrection of Christ, which also occurred on the first day of the week (Lk 24:1-7).

It seems strange that there is no explanation of Pentecost in the epistles. However, the sole reference (1 Co 16:8) may be significant, for the very fact that Paul was writing to Gentiles and used a term for a Jewish feast without a word of explanation seems to indicate that his readers had been instructed in its theological importance.

"They were all together." It is not clear whether the "all" is intended to refer to the total number of 120 (1:15) or to the twelve apostles. Since the latter group has just been mentioned in the preceding verse, and since the apostles alone are mentioned in the following narrative (2:14, 42), it may well be that they are in view here. On the other hand, it is difficult to think of the remainder of the whole company as passed by in the Spirit's visitation, since they were believers. If those who responded to Peter's message received the Spirit (2:38), surely the same would be true of those who had been waiting for His coming. Yet reception of the Spirit did not necessarily involve the special manifestations that are mentioned in connection with the twelve.

"In one place" is made more precise in verse 2, where the "house" is mentioned (cf. 1:13). Presumably the group moved from the house to some larger area when people began to be attracted to the spot. The Temple offered adequate space, and its consecrated status made it the appropriate setting for explaining what had happened.

2:2. Luke was careful to say that the "noise" was like that of a strong wind, but he avoided saying that a wind was blowing. The word more

50

often means "breath" than "wind." It was the noise which filled the house, not wind. A connection may be seen here with Ezekiel 37:1-14, the episode of the dry bones, where the Spirit is mentioned along with a noise and breath. The symbolism fits well into the concept of the new creation (cf. Jn 3:7-8, where wind illustrates the mysterious operation of the Spirit in effecting the new birth).

2:3. A second token of the Spirit's presence was the appearance of tongues, distributed so as to rest on each of those present, which most naturally includes the others as well as the twelve (cf. 1:15; 2:17-18). In some way these resembled "fire," and as such could be intended to express the presence and involvement of God (cf. Ex 3:2; 19:18; 1 Ki 18:38-39; Eze 1:27). More than that, the fire can be considered the fulfillment of the prediction of John the Baptist that Jesus would baptize with the Holy Spirit and fire (Lk 3:16).

But why the tongues? The most natural explanation is that they symbolized the element of speech, of communication of the Gospel. By the Spirit's impulsion the apostles would be able to make known the message of salvation. The tongues had their unity in the one Spirit, but as "distributing themselves" they pointed to the individualizing of the Spirit's bestowal (cf. 1 Co 12:11). "They rested on each one." This agrees with our Lord's advance announcements about the Spirit's relation to the disciples—an abiding presence (Jn 14:16-17).

The two signs—one of sound for the ear, the other of sight for the eye—recall the scene of Jesus' baptism, when the voice came from heaven and the Spirit was manifested in bodily form (Lk 3:22). The immediate effect of the two phenomena was to make clear to the twelve that God was beginning to work. What had been promised by the Father was being realized. The fulfillment was too external, too realistic to be discounted and written off as imagination. They all had seen and heard.

2:4. Following the outward tokens came the inward reality, "they were all filled with the Holy Spirit." This was something new in Israel, for visitations of the Spirit hitherto had been selective (cf. Nu 11:26-29). There was no suggestion at Pentecost that the objective of the experience was mystic contemplation; it was "utterance." The Spirit has many functions, but the Pentecostal emphasis fell on communication. Jesus had promised a baptism with the Spirit (Ac 1:5).

In reporting the event, Luke used the term "filled" rather than *baptized*, for this was the actual effect. *Baptism* is the objective term, the theological reality, the Godward aspect of the matter. *Filling* is the manward, subjective aspect. *Filling* and *baptism* are not completely synonymous terms. *Baptism* is appropriate for the initial gift of the Spirit (1:5; 11:16-17), for it marks the beginning of a new relationship. Like water baptism, it belongs to Christian beginnings and is not repeatable (cf. 1 Co 12:13; see also the discussion of the apostles' situation regarding baptism, under Ac 1:5). One who has been baptized with the Spirit may be filled, not merely once (4:8) but again and again (4:31; Eph 5:18). But no one is reported to have been baptized with the Spirit more than once.

They "began to speak with other tongues." This is declared to be a supernatural phenomenon, for it was done "as the Spirit was giving them utterance." The sort of thing that took place in the congregation at Corinth is called glossolalia (speaking in a tongue) and refers to ecstatic utterance which required another gift of the Spirit, interpretation of the tongue, in order to make it intelligible to others. Since it could be exercised privately (1 Co 14:28) and in connection with prayer (1 Co 14:14), it was related to the worship of God. But at Pentecost there was no interpretation by the apostles or others. The tongues were not ecstatic utterances but the languages of men (Ac 2:6, 11; cf. 1 Co 13:1). The charge of drunkenness (2:13) need not connote an ecstatic state but rather reflect the joy and freedom of speech enjoyed by the participants.

The hearers understood that the apostles were uttering the mighty deeds of God (v. 11). This special feature of understandable speech in relation to the tongues at Pentecost is apparently connected with the presence of people from many nations (v. 5). It was to a certain extent a prophecy that the Gospel would be made known to men everywhere by the enablement of the Spirit (cf. 1:8). This makes irrelevant the claim that Aramaic and Greek would have been sufficient for communicating with the audience on this occasion, so that other languages were unnecessary.

In the other two instances of speaking in tongues reported by Luke (10:46; 19:6) this feature of intelligible speech is not present. Speaking in tongues, in the technical sense of glossolalia, is said to be concomitant of a highly emotional state; yet the curious thing is that at Pentecost, with the promise of the Spirit's coming followed by the days of waiting and praying as a background, Spirit-filled men spoke in intelligible speech. At Caesarea, on the other hand, there seems to have been much less emotional build-up, yet there was glossolalia, and at Ephesus there was probably even less excitement, yet there was glossolalia again. The element of mystery connected with the Spirit's operations is ever to be reckoned with.

2:5. Two questions must be raised here. One is a problem of text, for some manuscript testimony omits the word "Jews." Could this word be a scribal addition based on its occurrence in verse 14 (somewhat disguised by the translation, "men of Judea")? And would it be justified to go a step further and take the following phrase, "devout men, from every nation under heaven," as including Gentiles who were showing their interest in the Jewish religion by their attendance at the feast? Unquestionably Gentiles could attend (Jn 12:20). However, proselytes are mentioned in verse 10, which strongly suggests that the rest were not. Furthermore, the word "devout" (used again in 8:2; 22:12) is not the term for Gentiles who had adopted the Jewish faith but describes people who were pious and reverent. The conclusion to be drawn, then, is that the vast majority of those present were Jews by race as well as by religion.

But a second question arises. Were these men permanent residents of Jerusalem, or were they in the city for a limited time, after which they expected to return to their places of residence in the Dispersion? The evidence seems somewhat conflicting, for the list includes "visitors from Rome" (v. 10) and yet the word translated "living" and "live" (vv. 5, 14) suggests permanent abode. Many times in Acts Luke used it of residents of a community (1:19-20; 2:9; 4:16; 13:27). Presumably he was thoroughly familiar with the difference between this word and the term for "sojourner" (Lk 24:18). The safest way to handle this difficult question is to conclude that at the very least these men had spent some time in Jerusalem, probably having come for Passover and remaining for the Feast of Weeks. That the converts of that day continued in Jerusalem for a considerable period thereafter appears decisively settled by Acts 2:42. Possibly some of Peter's audience had returned to Jerusalem from the Dispersion in order to spend their last days on the beloved soil of the Holy Land. Some may have resorted there for study (cf. 22:3).

They were a group providentially prepared for the hearing of the Gospel, for they were familiar with the ministry of Jesus (2:22) and presumably had been in Jerusalem at the time of the crucifixion and had heard reports about the resurrection. Furthermore, being devout men, they could be appealed to on the basis of the Scriptures.

The sweeping nature of Luke's language, "every nation under heaven," could be intended to suggest, when taken with the mention of tongues, that Pentecost represented a reversal of the confusion of tongues experienced at Babel (Gen 11:1-9). Though diverse languages continue to exist, those who speak them can find their unity and harmony in Christ.

Some scholars allege that Pentecost was observed as a memorial of the giving of the Law at Sinai. In this case, the birthday of the Church could be thought of as marked by a new and gracious revelation of God, with emphasis on His saving act in Christ. Rabbinic testimony to this conception of Pentecost in late Judaism begins early in the second century A.D. There is some evidence, however, that in Jewish circles represented by the *Book of Jubilees,* and in the Qumran community, the association of Pentecost with the giving of the Law is pre-Christian.[1]

2:6. As a siren attracts a crowd on a busy street, the sound of many voices brought the milling "multitude" together. By this time, presumably, the disciples had left the upper room and were making their way to the Temple. "Bewildered" suggests in the original a combination of confusion and excitement. The content of the speaking is not stated here, but is reserved to verse 11.

2:7-8. The amazement was due to the fact that they were hearing "Galileans" speak in their own languages. It is hazardous to conclude that, since the word for "language" (v. 6) is *dialect,* the amazement stemmed from the ability to reproduce even local linguistic peculiarities. Luke previously used the word in connection with Aramaic (1:19). The *koine,* or Hellenistic type of Greek, in its full designation, is the koine dialect, which shows how broad the use of the term *dialect* could be in the Greek tongue. "Language" is the proper translation in our passage.

2:9-11. Jerusalem, mother of all Jewry, drew her sons from around the civilized world, where they had been dispersed due to the captivity of their ancestors or voluntary emigration for economic advantage. In a general way the list proceeds from east to west, though Cretans and Arabians disturb this pattern.* Mesopotamia, Asia (the province), Egypt, and Rome had large concentrations of Jewish residents. Rather strangely, Greece and Syria are not included.

Especially vexing is the inclusion of Judea, since it is out of place geographically. Various suggestions have been made as to what the original wording may have been ("Armenia," "Syria," "India," are some). Perhaps "Judea" was introduced into the text by an early scribe who was influenced by the opening words of Peter's speech (v. 14). On the other hand, it may refer to a district north of Antioch, which has recently become known through a few inscriptions in Phoenician with some Aramaic mixture.

"Visitors from Rome" is ambiguous since the word *Rome* does not occur here, but rather *Romans,* which elsewhere in Acts means Roman citizens. If the NASB rendering is accepted, it opens the possibility that these visitors eventually returned to Rome and became the founders of the church there. It is uncertain whether "Jews and proselytes" is intended to apply only to Romans or whether it should be referred to the entire list. Since proselytes (Gentile converts to Judaism) were certainly to be found in many places, the latter view is the more probable.

"The mighty deeds of God" (cf. Lk 1:49) are not defined. Luke's source of information may not have included anything precise at this point. But

---

*B. M. Metzger notes that it was not uncommon among the ancients to regard lands and regions as placed under the dominion of heavenly bodies. But his comparison of Luke's catalog with that of Paul Alexandrinus reveals such disparity as to raise serious doubts in his mind that Luke shared this conception ("Ancient Astrological Geography and Acts 2:9-11," in *Apostolic History and the Gospel,* ed. W. Ward Gasque and R. P. Martin, pp. 123-33).

it is wholly natural to conclude that the gift of the Messiah and the succeeding gift of the Holy Spirit occupied a central place among these works.

2:12-13. The mood of amazement continued (cf. v. 7), with the sense of wonder gradually shifting to perplexity. Such strange things cried out for an explanation.

Some went beyond questioning and ventured an answer. The apostles must have been intoxicated, "filled with sweet wine." (The KJV has "new wine," but the more strict rendering is "sweet wine"; the grape harvest, which would provide new wine, came later in the year, associated with the Feast of Tabernacles). The verdict was given in a jesting spirit, but it revealed an underlying attitude of unbelief, for the apostles were speaking of the mighty deeds of God. Luke caught the frame of mind by using the word "mocking." It would be difficult to say whether the reaction of this portion of the crowd was called forth by the joyous bearing of the apostles or by their readiness of speech or both. One wonders also if the claim of drunkenness was associated with a similar jibe at Jesus (Lk 7:34).

2. PETER'S SERMON—2:14-40

This consisted of explanation of the apostles' conduct, first negatively, and then positively (vv. 14-21); proclamation of the Christ-event by touching lightly on Jesus' ministry and death, and dwelling at length on His resurrection and exaltation to God's right hand as Lord and Christ (vv. 22-36); and exhortation, calling for a response to the preaching in terms of repentance and reception of Christ, which would in turn bring the gift of the Spirit (vv. 37-40).

> **2:14** But Peter, taking his stand with the eleven, raised his voice and declared to them: "Men of Judea, and all you who live in Jerusalem, let this be known to you, and give heed to my words.
>
> **15** "For these men are not drunk, as you suppose, for it is *only* the third hour of the day;
>
> **16** but this is what was spoken of through the prophet Joel:
>
> **17** 'AND IT SHALL BE IN THE LAST DAYS, GOD SAYS,
> THAT I WILL POUR FORTH OF MY SPIRIT UPON ALL MANKIND;
> AND YOUR SONS AND YOUR DAUGHTERS SHALL PROPHESY,
> AND YOUR YOUNG MEN SHALL SEE VISIONS,
> AND YOUR OLD MEN SHALL DREAM DREAMS;
>
> **18** 'EVEN UPON MY BONDSLAVES, BOTH MEN AND WOMEN,
> I WILL IN THOSE DAYS POUR FORTH OF MY SPIRIT
> And they shall prophesy.
>
> **19** 'AND I WILL GRANT WONDERS IN THE SKY ABOVE,
> AND SIGNS ON THE EARTH BENEATH,
> BLOOD, AND FIRE, AND VAPOR OF SMOKE.

20 'The sun shall be turned into darkness,
And the moon into blood,
Before the great and glorious day of the Lord shall come.

21 'And it shall be, that every one who calls on the name of the Lord shall be saved.'

22 "Men of Israel, listen to these words: Jesus the Nazarene, a man attested to you by God with miracles and wonders and signs which God performed through Him in your midst, just as you yourselves know—

23 this *Man*, delivered up by the predetermined plan and foreknowledge of God, you nailed to a cross by the hands of godless men and put *Him* to death.

24 "And God raised Him up again, putting an end to the agony of death, since it was impossible for Him to be held in its power.

25 "For David says of Him,
'I was always beholding the Lord in my presence;
For He is at my right hand, that I may not be shaken.

26 'Therefore my heart was glad and my tongue exulted;
Moreover my flesh also will abide in hope;

27 'Because thou wilt not abandon my soul to Hades,
Nor allow Thy Holy One to undergo decay.

28 'Thou hast made known to me the ways of life;
Thou wilt make me full of gladness with thy presence.'

29 "Brethren, I may confidently say to you regarding the patriarch David that he both died and was buried, and his tomb is with us to this day.

30 "And so, because he was a prophet, and knew that God had sworn to him with an oath to seat *one* of his descendants upon his throne,

31 he looked ahead and spoke of the resurrection of the Christ, that He was neither abandoned to Hades, nor did His flesh suffer decay.

32 "This Jesus God raised up again, to which we are all witnesses.

33 "Therefore having been exalted to the right hand of God, and having received from the Father the promise of the Holy Spirit, He has poured forth this which you both see and hear.

34 "For it was not David who ascended into heaven, but he himself says:
'The Lord said to My lord,
"Sit at My right hand,

35 Until I make Thine enemies a footstool for Thy feet."'

36 "Therefore let all the house of Israel know for certain that God has made Him both Lord and Christ—this Jesus whom you crucified."

37 Now when they heard *this*, they were pierced to the heart, and said to Peter and the rest of the apostles, "Brethren, what shall we do?"

38 And Peter *said* to them, "Repent, and let each of you be baptized in the name of Jesus Christ for the forgiveness of your sins; and you shall receive the gift of the Holy Spirit.

39 "For the promise is for you and your children, and for all who are far off, as many as the Lord our God shall call to Himself."

40 And with many other words he solemnly testified and kept on exhorting them, saying, "Be saved from this perverse generation!"

2:14-15. Peter's leadership, already demonstrated in the company of believers (1:15), was now exhibited in a public situation. The apostles were not scattered through the crowd, but remained together as a unit, conscious that they were a chosen band with a mission to their own people. *To stand* was a favorite verb with Luke, used to express the grasping of a strategic moment for addressing others (Lk 19:8, marg; Ac 17:22; 27:21). As this word portrays the manner of a speaker, the word "declared" suggests weighty utterance rather than a speech of trivialities (cf. 26:25).

There is no suggestion here of the continued use of tongues. As to whether Peter spoke in Aramaic or Greek, a study of the text for clues is rather indecisive, so a decision is determined by the length of time the hearers had been in Jerusalem. Recent arrivals would probably have been more familiar with Greek than with the language of their fathers, but the longer the duration of their stay the greater would be their familiarity with Aramaic. It is worth recalling that when Paul addressed the mob in the Temple area, also at the time of Pentecost (20:16), he spoke in the national language (22:2, where "Hebrew" probably means Aramaic, which was in common use at the time in Palestine).

Peter's initial task was to refute the slanderous charge that the apostles were "drunk." That was comparatively easy, since "the third hour of the day" was not the time people became inebriated (cf. 1 Th 5:7). It was a case of spiritual intoxication, as he went on to explain (v. 17). Three times in Scripture a contrast is stated between using wine and being filled with the Spirit. The other two instances are Luke 1:15 and Ephesians 5:18. A certain similarity exists between the drunken man and the Spirit-filled man, for both are carried out of themselves into an abnormal sense of freedom and expressiveness. But beyond this all is contrast, for the results in one case are not fruitful of good as they are when the Spirit is controlling.

2:16-21. Since Peter's audience was made up of Jews and proselytes, it was useful to quote Scripture to establish the meaning of what had just happened. While the quotation from Joel 2:28-32 is essentially the LXX text, there are certain changes, the most important being "in the last days" as a substitution for "after these things," to make clear the eschatological bearing of the passage, its applicability to the beginning of the Messianic age (cf. Heb 1:2). "This is what was spoken of through the prophet Joel" is a correlating of prediction with event, a practice learned at Jesus' feet (Lk 24:44-46) and used by Him in His preaching (Lk 4:16-30). The word "this" picks up the "this" in the question of the crowd (v. 12). Men of Israel should not have been wholly taken aback by the phenomenon of Pentecost, seeing this event had been predicted by one of their own prophets.

"I will pour forth of My Spirit" employs the language of effusion common in reference to the Spirit (v. 33; Is 32:15; Ro 5:5) and prepares one for the concept of the fullness of the Spirit.

"All mankind" seems to be defined by what follows: old and young, women as well as men. This makes it reasonably certain that the whole company of 120, which included women, received the Spirit at Pentecost.

"Shall prophesy" means not "to predict" but "to declare the counsel of God" under the immediate influence of the Spirit. Where glossolalia was involved, prophecy was sharply distinguished from it (1 Co 14:2-5). But at Pentecost, where the apostles spoke in languages that were known, they could be said to have prophesied (Ac 2:11). "Visions" and "dreams" were common means of communicating revelation, especially in the Old Testament. Visions are referred to rather frequently in Acts (9:10; 10:3, 17; 16:9; 18:9; cf. 23:11). In each case the vision had a definite bearing on the progress of the divine program.

It cannot be ascertained whether those " 'Wonders . . . and signs' " noted in the text were thought to have some relation to the portents that occurred at the crucifixion (Mt 27:45, 51-53). The sequence given in the Olivet discourse is the proclamation of the Gospel; the Tribulation; and the return of the Son of Man, preceded by upheavals in the realm of nature (Mt 24:14, 21, 29-30). It was taught in the prophets that the "day of the Lord" was a time of judgment and also of deliverance. In fact, in the Joel passage, the word "saved" (Ac 2:21) could well be rendered "delivered" when its original setting is regarded. In the context of Pentecost it referred to salvation unto eternal life (cf. Ro 10:13), although it included salvation from the threat of judgment (cf. Ac 2:40).

In summary, prophecy had indicated the outpouring of the Spirit in connection with the Day of the Lord, the time of divine manifestation. Pentecost was a clear indication that the Messianic age had dawned. Its consummation, whether near or remote, was rendered certain. Peter did not enlarge on this phase of prophecy. As H. N. Ridderbos says, with reference to the early Christians in general, "It was simply because what had *already happened* was of such immense importance to them that their attention was focused less upon the expected consummation than upon the fulfillment which had already begun."[2]

2:22-23. "Men of Israel" confirms what has already been noted, that Peter's audience was made up of Jews (cf. v. 14). It is at this point that the sermon proper begins, hence the renewed address.

Nothing had been said about "Jesus the Nazarene" up to this time, but here He, rather than the Spirit, was immediately placed in the forefront. Peter began by calling Jesus a "man" (v. 22) and concluded by calling Him Lord and Christ (v. 36). By using the word "attested," the speaker made it plain that this was no ordinary Man; He had been sent of God. Since Jesus Himself had not shied away from certifying His divine mission by His works (Lk 4:18-21; Jn 5:36), Peter could the more boldly call attention to the "miracles and wonders and signs."

The first word calls attention to the power of God at work. The second term views the miracles as demonstrations that appeal to the senses, creating wonder and awe. As signs, the works underline the message that is communicated to the discerning through what occurs. It is the spiritual interpretation of the occurrence and as such makes appeal to faith. In view of the fact that the audience was made up largely of men of Judea and Jerusalem, the observation, "in your midst," tends to confirm what the fourth gospel maintains, namely, that Jesus performed mighty works in that area (Jn 2:23; 5:1-9; 9:1-7; 11:1-44). "As you yourselves know," even the enemies of our Lord were obliged to acknowledge that He did mighty works (Mk 3:22; Jn 11:47). It is notable that Peter did not call attention to what Jesus said. This would be more appropriate for converts to the faith. Salvation comes not through what Jesus said but through what He did. Peter quickly passed to this, calling attention to His death (v. 23). Statements of the *kerygma*, or Gospel message, often enough have nothing to say about the ministry, but begin with a reference to the death of Christ (5:30-32; 1 Co 15:1-8).

"Delivered up . . . of God, you nailed to a cross" tersely summarizes the Godward and manward aspects of the crucifixion. God's purpose was declared in the prophetic Scriptures (Is 53:10), accepted by Jesus as His role (Mk 10:45) and maintained in the teaching of the Church. It was understood by the Christian community at Jerusalem (Ac 4:28), but Jews had found it hard to accept before the event (Mt 16:21-23; Jn 12:34). The Romans had put Jesus to death, but the major share of blame rested with the Jewish nation. By its refusal to accept Him (Jn 1:11) and by its acquiescence in the scheming of its leaders to turn Him over to the Roman governor, it had condemned Him to this shameful death. Peter continued to level the accusation "you nailed to a cross" at his audiences (3:15; 4:10; 5:30; 10:39) and found no one able to offer a rebuttal (5:28). Full recognition was given to the part played by the Romans—"godless men"— but the very description of them implies deeper guilt for the Jews, because they had the Law of God, which made known His sovereign will.

2:24-32. The God who was active in the ministry of Jesus (v. 22) and proceeded according to plan in the death of His Son, asserted Himself also in the next step of redemption history. "God raised Him up again," a grand reversal of the human verdict regarding Jesus (cf. Lk 3:22). "Putting an end to the agony of death," curiously, uses the word for the pains of a woman in travail. Jesus indeed had experienced pain in anticipation of His death, since He had predicted it, and He had had the terrible pain and distress of the crucifixion. But these pains came to an end and were succeeded by resurrection life (paralleling birth in human experience).

"It was impossible for Him to be held in its power." Why was it impossible? Because Jesus had no personal sin which would warrant a continuation under the power of death, the executor of sin. Once He had met the judgment of a righteous God against a sinful race by laying down His own infinitely valuable life, there was no basis on which He could rightly be held by death. Furthermore, the resurrection was the clear demonstration that His sacrificial death on behalf of sinners had been accepted by God. The whole plan of redemption called for His risen life to be imparted to those who come to Him by faith. Finally, Scripture had to be fulfilled. David had foretold the resurrection in Psalm 16, from which Peter proceeded to quote. The psalmist had spoken better than he knew. His own desire to escape the hold of death ("Hades" means the unseen realm) prophetically guaranteed the deliverance of God's Anointed. Whatever desire to escape death David may have had, this was not his fortune. But David's greater Son triumphed over the grave; His flesh did not suffer "decay." He is now in the presence of God.

In Acts 13:35-36 we find Paul using a portion of the same psalm and applying it to Jesus as Peter did. David died, but Jesus the Christ survived death. Evidently the use of the psalm early became a part of the Christian arsenal of Old Testament proof texts that could be applied to the Lord Jesus (recall Paul's teaching that the resurrection was according to Scripture [1 Co 15:4]). This is readily understandable if the Saviour, after His resurrection, directed His disciples to this psalm (see Lk 24:44).

Peter went on to point out that whereas the casual reader might assume that David had been speaking of himself, his death voided any such simple conclusion. It must be understood that he was a "prophet." One would not readily gather this from the Old Testament, for David depended on prophets for counsel. God did not give the so-called Davidic covenant to David directly but through Nathan the prophet (2 Sam 7). His prophetic powers came out, however, in the psalms, where from time to time he spoke of the future and of God's Anointed.

An example of this is Psalm 16. It was recognized in Israel that "God had sworn to him with an oath" (v. 30; Ps 132:11) concerning the perpetuity of his house. His "throne" would not lack one to sit upon it. Had not God reiterated His promise in recent days (Lk 1:32-33)? In the last analysis, an enduring throne called for a deathless occupant. So David really "looked ahead and spoke of the resurrection of the Christ." Only Christ has a truly indestructible life (Heb 7:16). He was in the tomb, but his flesh did not suffer decay. In support of the argument from fulfilled prophecy, Peter adduced the personal witness of the apostles and possibly others who had seen Jesus alive from the dead (cf. Ac 3:15; 4:20; 5:32; 10:39, 41).

Looking back for a moment, it can be readily seen that Peter devoted far more attention to the resurrection than to the death of Christ, and in dealing with the latter he did not state its purpose. His main thrust was to convince his hearers of the resurrection. The sin problem could be dealt with later (v. 38).

2:33-35. "Therefore having been exalted to the right hand of God" notes a major result of the resurrection. In His risen state, the Lord Jesus did not belong any longer in this sin-ridden world. His place was at the right hand of the Majesty on high. This was one of the glories that belonged to Him as a result of His humiliation and suffering (1 Pe 1:11).

Peter's hearers had not seen the ascension any more than they had seen the Lord after His resurrection. How then could they be convinced that He was not only risen but also was now in glory? First, by the gift of the Spirit which came from Him. Could a dead man do that? The people had seen the powerful manifestations of the Spirit that very day. Jesus the Lord had the authority to dispense the Spirit. But further, Scripture had anticipated the exaltation as well as the resurrection. David was appealed to once more. David had not "ascended into heaven," as surely as he had not risen from the dead, so what he said on this point in Psalm 110:1 must apply to another. The discussion between Jesus and the Pharisees on this psalm indicates that both parties took it to be Messianic (Mt 22:41-46). There is an obvious distinction between the persons called "Lord," for one speaks to the other. The two words for *Lord* are different in the Hebrew, the first pointing to the Lord God, the second to God's Anointed, the One who is called His Son in Psalm 2:7.

"Sit at My right hand" marks the completion of Jesus' mission on earth and is the divine recognition of it (Heb 1:3). It also points forward to the return in glory, as the "until" of verse 35 indicates (cf. 3:21). There is a work of judgment reserved for that future day. Meanwhile the Son of God will be reaping the fruit of His redemptive mission through the working of His Spirit in the world from which He has departed.

2:36. By virtue of resurrection and exaltation, God has made the very Jesus whom the nation had crucified "both Lord and Christ." This raises the question whether Jesus is properly viewed as Lord and Christ prior to the resurrection. It is clear that Peter did not intend to restrict the use of

61

the titles in this fashion, for according to his own statement a bit later, it was the Christ of God who suffered (3:18), and this was in line with Jesus' teaching (Lk 24:46), with Peter's confession and Jesus' acceptance of it (Mt 16:16-17), and with the Saviour's affirmation before the high priest and the Council (Mk 14:62). So it is reasonable to conclude that Jesus was Lord and Christ during the ministry, but that the resurrection and ascension put the application of these titles to His person beyond dispute. Before this time they were used sparingly. The marvel of the Son of God among the sons of men was too great, too mysterious, too overwhelming to be flashed on the scene at once. The awareness had to come gradually. So it was that the title *Lord* was used only occasionally of Jesus in the gospels until the resurrection. Help on this problem can be derived also from Romans 1:4, where it is stated that this same Person was marked off as Son of God with power by the resurrection. The preceding verse makes it clear that He was the Son of God prior to the resurrection, but that event lent a powerful attestation to his Sonship. Doubtless Acts 2:36 should be understood in the same way. What was true of His person essentially, but was only dimly perceived before, was now known demonstrably.

2:37. Peter's speech revealed how thoroughly the word of Jesus was fulfilled in respect to the teaching ministry of the Spirit in the lives of the apostles (Jn 16:12-13). Now it was to be seen also how His prediction about the Spirit's ministry in convicting the world of sin, righteousness, and judgment (Jn 16:8-10) was vindicated. This was apparent in the sphere of sin. The audience had previously not believed in Jesus as their Messiah, and this was their chief sin. Peter accused them of the sin of crucifying the One who fulfilled the promises. Jesus' word regarding righteousness was fulfilled also, and in line with it we find Peter placing great emphasis on the return of the Son to the Father. The judgment aspect of which Jesus spoke is reflected here in the warning to the hearers that they should save themselves from a nation displeasing to God and ripe for judgment (v. 40).

"They were pierced to the heart," the conviction went deep. To think that they had been guilty of rejecting their Messiah! It is difficult for a Gentile to appreciate how great must have been the sense of shame and sorrow. What a blunder! (See Isaiah 53; Zechariah 12:10; and 1 Timothy 1:13, 15 taken with Acts 9:4.) Hence the outcry, "What shall we do?" (cf. Ac 16:30).

2:38. "Repent, and let each of you be baptized" sounds like a repetition of the summons of John the Baptist to his audiences (Lk 3:3). But something distinctively new was added—"in the name of Jesus Christ." It was on the basis of the name (the person and the worth) of Christ, as already expounded by Peter, acknowledged in baptism, that people could expect forgiveness of sins. As the sign and seal of their acceptance before God in His Son, they would receive "the gift of the Holy Spirit" (cf. Eph 1:13-14). Nothing is said here about the gifts of the Spirit. The Spirit Himself is the great gift in which all lesser gifts are contained.

It would be a mistake to conclude that the Spirit was automatically bestowed because people submitted to baptism. This rite was administered in response to repentance, which includes faith (Ac 2:41, 44). Baptism is a means of making confession of allegiance to Christ (Ro 10:9-10). It is clear from Acts 8:15-16 that water baptism was not in itself the key to receiving the Spirit. Repentance and a believing heart provided the necessary preparation. One might insist that Acts 1:5 does not make room for water baptism at all. This was true in the case of the apostles, but they were a special class. Having received the baptism of John, in all likelihood, and having the qualification of faith, plus years spent in following Jesus, they were fit candidates for the reception of the Spirit. Acts 2:38 presents the normal pattern for obtaining the Spirit (10:44-48 involves a special situation which, together with the Samaritan episode, must be left for later examination).

2:39. "The promise" presumably refers to the gift of the Holy Spirit, but this as conditioned on repentance and faith. Its blessings are not withheld from the "children." This is in line with the covenant promise to Abraham (Gen 17:7).

"All who are far off" could refer to other Jews in the Dispersion, perhaps with a glance at Isaiah 57:19. But a few years later Paul used the phrase of Gentiles, who are contrasted with those who are near, namely, the Jewish people (Eph 2:17), and Peter may have used it in the same way. The question is bound up with the early Christian understanding of the Joel prophecy. Since Paul quoted Joel 2:32 as applicable to Gentiles as well as to Jews (Ro 10:13), it is possible that Peter understood it in the same way. He may have universalized "all flesh" also, in which case "all who are far off" could readily be assumed to be Gentiles.

The promise is related to the divine "call," which was a familiar thought to Peter's audience from its frequent use in the Old Testament. Israel was a called, i.e., chosen nation, the peculiar people of God. Now, there seems to be a hint of an extended family in terms of the New Covenant, embracing Gentiles as well as the children of Israel. Its application would appear presently as the Gospel was taken to Caesarea, Antioch, and other Gentile communities.

2:40. It is made plain here that Peter had more to say on this occasion than is reported. "Testified" suggests a further witness of a strong and penetrating nature, whereas "exhorting" indicates repeated appeals to come to the point of decision. That decision involved separation from a "perverse generation" (cf. Lk 11:29) which had taken upon itself the blood of the Crucified (Mt 27:25). It involved identification with the new people of God who called on Him through the name of Jesus Christ.

3. CONVERTS—2:41-47

A brief summary is provided of the life of the Christian community following Pentecost. The little band found its numbers swelled immediately by the response to Peter's preaching. Wonders and signs brought favor with the people throughout the city, and among believers there was instruction and growth, the sharing of possessions, and continual praise to God.

> 2:41 So then, those who had received his word were baptized; and there were added that day about three thousand souls.
> 42 And they were continually devoting themselves to the apostles' teaching and to fellowship, to the breaking of bread and to prayer.
> 43 And everyone kept feeling a sense of awe; and many wonders and signs were taking place through the apostles.
> 44 And all those who had believed were together, and had all things in common;
> 45 and they *began* selling their property and possessions, and were sharing them with all, as anyone might have need.
> 46 And day by day continuing with one mind in the temple, and breaking bread from house to house, they were taking their meals together with gladness and sincerity of heart,
> 47 praising God, and having favor with all the people. And the Lord was adding to their number day by day those who were being saved.

2:41. "Three thousand" people were "baptized" that day and took their places among the disciples as believers. The number may well exceed the total number of Jesus' true disciples during the days of His flesh (cf. 1 Co 15:6). The Temple area, especially the court of the Gentiles, was commodious, able to contain around 200,000 people. If only a quarter of this total constituted Peter's audience (more would have made hearing very difficult), the figure of three thousand is not astonishing, for, as noted earlier, this was a prepared audience consisting of devout men who were familiar with the Scriptures and who had been in the city during the agonizing period of the crucifixion. Added to all this was the power of the Spirit at work in Peter's message.

A question could be ventured here as to whether such success does not tend to give the Spirit greater stature than Christ Himself possesses. This possibility is negated by the very nature of the Spirit's work, which is intended to glorify the Son by bearing testimony to Him (we have observed that Peter made only passing reference to the Spirit at the beginning and the end of his address, but made Christ his theme). Furthermore, Acts 1:1 is a warning not to forget that the Spirit's activity is to be viewed as the continuing work of the Lord Jesus.

2:42. The converts were "continually devoting themselves to the apostles' teaching." What a large church to shepherd! Yet it had twelve pastors and teachers. If some of the people returned to the lands of their birth, they did not do so immediately. They needed instruction. There is general agreement today that the early Church had not only a kerygma, or Gospel proclamation to the unsaved (most of the ingredients of which can be gleaned from the Pentecost sermon), but also a rather well-defined pattern of instruction for new converts. This is in view in the word "teaching," which is a synonym for the apostolic tradition handed down in the Church.

Unfortunately Luke did not provide information about its content. But this may be reconstructed with a fair degree of probability. It must have included the high points of Jesus' life and work; His ethical teaching, such as is enshrined in the Sermon on the Mount; an appreciation of the Old Testament prophetic background for His ministry, such as He imparted to the eleven after the resurrection; a digest of obligations toward one another, especially in the family relationship, and toward those outside the fold; and a warning about the possibility of persecution and the inroads of false teaching. Since these converts were Jews, much could be assumed from their background. What they needed was insight into the epochal character of the new age into which they had entered because of Christ's finished work and the advent of the Spirit. The commandments of Jesus must have been given special prominence (Mt 28:20). In later times catechetical instruction preceded baptism as a condition for acceptance into the Church. It was especially necessary for those who came out of paganism.[3]

"Fellowship" is hardly to be thought of as a substitute for *church*, or even as a reference to the sharing of goods (v. 44). Rather, the act of sharing possessions was a practical demonstration of a more fundamental fellowship of a spiritual nature. Fellowship was the reality of the unity of faith and love and joy that characterized these early believers. In the structure of the sentence the word is not intended to imply that this was the apostles' fellowship to which others were admitted. It was instead the fellowship of the Spirit in which all alike participate (cf. 2 Co 13:14). Since the converts had formerly lived in diverse parts of the earth, their genuine fellowship augured well for the unity of the Church in days to come, when still greater diversity would prove no bar to oneness in Christ.

"The breaking of bread" is probably something different from what is mentioned in verse 46. In that verse ordinary meals are in view, whereas in this instance the close association with prayers suggests a sacramental function. But if the Lord's Supper is intended, why does the terminology not include the wine, as in the account of the Last Supper in the upper room? Probably because the renewed association with the Saviour after His resurrection involved the breaking of bread (Lk 24:30). It became a kind of shorthand way of speaking of the Lord's Supper (cf. Ac 20:7), as is true today in some circles. Possibly there was a common meal which preceded the solemn observance of the sacrament. At least we have evidence for this in the Corinthian church (1 Co 11:20-34). *Agape* is the term given to this common meal, since it was thought of as a love-feast (see Jude 12).

The word "prayer" almost certainly refers to seasons of prayer in which believers alone participated, and so is to be distinguished from attendance on the hours of prayer in the Temple (cf. 3:1). The apostles and their associates had already discovered the importance of waiting on God together (1:14).

2:43. Jesus had promised that the disciples would do the works which He had done (Jn 14:12). Luke was content to note that the apostles wrought "many wonders and signs." One of these was especially notable in its results and on this account is related in detail (3:1-8), but the continuing occurrence of such things helped to maintain an atmosphere of fear, or "awe," among the people. That God was at work could not be doubted. Was the Day of the Lord about to break upon them? The manifestation of the Spirit and the substantial number of converts made at Pentecost must have brought considerable soul searching to the population of Jerusalem.

2:44-45. "And all those who had believed were together." This does not mean that the saints lived in the same quarter of Jerusalem. They were not a separate community in that sense. However, they were together as much as possible for instruction, fellowship, and worship. This togetherness prompted the result stated, namely, that they "had all things in common." This was not a forsaking of the principle of private ownership, since the disposal and distribution of their possessions was occasioned "as anyone might have need." When the need became known, action was taken based on loving concern (cf. 1 Jn 3:17). So the Christian society differed from that of Qumran, where the pooling of resources was obligatory when one was taken into the group.

The assumption of some scholars, that this picture presented by Luke is not historical but rather based on his own concern for the poor (judging from the prominence given to them in his gospel), is ill-founded. If Luke inserted this element into his record of the early Jerusalem church, he could be expected to have mentioned it in connection with other churches, but this he did not do. Cessation of the practice of a community of goods was probably due to the gradual diminution of resources, a process hastened by persecution. It also received a jolt due to flagrant perversion of its whole spirit and purpose (chap. 5).

2:46-47. By frequenting "the temple" and mingling with other worshipers, the believers made it plain that they were not seeking a break with the religion of the Jews. It should be recalled here that our Lord, despite His differences with the spiritual leaders of the nation, did not forsake the Temple, which He spoke of as His Father's house. Judaism had several sects with their special emphases, and all were free to use the Temple. Even Gentiles could use it in part. If the Christians had withdrawn from the Temple, the task of reaching their Jewish brethren with the Gospel would have been rendered difficult if not impossible. But as it was, they continued "having favor with all the people." It is likely that a favorite spot for coming together was Solomon's portico (3:11).

Believers alternated between the Temple and their homes, where they took their meals in an atmosphere of joy and mutual helpfulness, grateful to God for His blessings. The Mosaic Law had directed that Pentecost should be a time of gladness and sharing the bounty God had bestowed on His people (Deu 16:10-11). It is not surprising that the inhabitants of Jerusalem were impressed. Such a life-style was contagious, possessing evangelizing power. People continued to be "saved" daily (note the correlation between vv. 46 and 47 on the basis of the phrase "day by day"). When the church is truly Christian in its day-to-day life and activity, it is a growing church.

Since those who were healed of physical ills could be said to be saved, or made whole (4:9 in the case of the lame man), the question may be raised whether "those who were being saved" were the beneficiaries of healing, since the wonders and signs noted in verse 43 must have included many such cases. But with regard to joining the Christian community, being saved would much more naturally relate to their spiritual than to their physical condition, especially since "the Lord was adding" these people. After all, the three thousand who responded at Pentecost are noted for their faith rather than for being the recipients of healing, about which the record is silent.

There is nothing here to suggest that the increase was due to more public preaching. While the possibility of such preaching must be granted, the more likely explanation for the growth of the Church at this stage was the transformation observable in the three thousand. The impact of the few at Pentecost had broadened and become the impact of the many.

C. Growth of the Church—3:1—4:37

THIS GROWTH began on the day of Pentecost, but it continued without abatement for some time, spurred on especially by the notable miracle of the healing of the lame man (4:3-4, 21-22) and aided by the boldness of the apostles (4:13, 31) and the healthy, happy condition of the Church in general (4:32-35). The authorities' attempt to curb the testimony only made believers more determined to fulfill their task.

1. MIRACLE—3:1-10

The story follows closely the pattern of the accounts of healing miracles in the gospels—a description of the circumstances surrounding the contact between healer and healed, the nature of the infirmity, the request for help, the act of healing, the demonstration of bodily (or mental) soundness, and the impression made on bystanders.

> **3:1** Now Peter and John were going up to the temple at the ninth *hour*, the hour of prayer.
> **2** And a certain man who had been lame from his mother's womb was being carried along, whom they used to set down every day at the gate of the temple which is called Beautiful, in order to beg alms of those who were entering the temple.
> **3** And when he saw Peter and John about to go into the temple, he *began* asking to receive alms.
> **4** And Peter, along with John, fixed his gaze upon him and said, "Look at us!"
> **5** And he *began* to give them his attention, expecting to receive something from them.
> **6** But Peter said, "I do not possess silver and gold, but what I do have I give to you: In the name of Jesus Christ the Nazarene—walk!"
> **7** And seizing him by the right hand, he raised him up; and immediately his feet and his ankles were strengthened.
> **8** And with a leap, he stood upright and *began* to walk; and he entered the temple with them, walking and leaping and praising God.
> **9** And all the people saw him walking and praising God;
> **10** and they were taking note of him as being the one who used to sit at the Beautiful Gate of the temple to *beg* alms, and they were filled with wonder and amazement at what had happened to him.

3:1-3. "Peter and John" had a friendship which reached back several years and continued through these days in Jerusalem. The two men, along with their brothers, had been partners in the fishing business (Lk 5:10). They had belonged to the inner circle of three among the disciples of Jesus (Lk 9:28), who entrusted to them the preparation of the feast in the upper room (Lk 22:8). They had shared the agony of Peter's denial of the Lord (Jn 18:15-17) and the marvel of the empty tomb (Jn 20:2-8). For them the risen Lord had had a special word regarding the future (Jn 21:18-22). By going about together they honored the two-by-two procedure set by Jesus for His disciples (Mk 6:7; cf. Lk 10:1). Here in the book of Acts John maintains a role that is secondary and silent except for some corroboration of Peter's testimony (4:13, 19; 8:14-23).

"Going up to the temple" is in line with the previous notice that believers frequented this spot (2:46). "The hour of prayer" is designated as the "ninth" hour. The principal feature of the daily routine of the Temple was the offering of the morning and evening sacrifice, at which time incense was burned to symbolize the ascending prayers of the gathered worshipers (cf. Lk 1:9-10). The ninth hour was three o'clock in the afternoon. These two periods of prayer, the one shortly after dawn and the other in midafternoon, were kept by godly Jews and even by God-fearing Gentiles far from the holy city, as in the case of Cornelius (10:30). A third period for prayer at the Temple was observed at sunset, but the other two occasions were more prominent (Dan 6:10 does not fit into this pattern, for it is not related to the Temple worship).

The central figure in this episode was a man "lame from birth." He was somewhat more fortunate than the invalid whom our Lord healed in Jerusalem (Jn 5:7) in that he had friends to place him daily before one of the gates of the inner Temple area. Possibly he had heard the Lord teach during holy week in Solomon's portico, which was not far from the gate called Beautiful, the scene of the miracle. It is thought that this gate opened onto the court of the women, which in turn led to the inner court surrounding the Temple building proper. Less likely is the identification with the Golden Gate in the outer wall near the northeastern corner of the temple area. It was to the court of the women that worshipers made their way morning and afternoon for the seasons of prayer.

He was there "to beg alms." Ideally there should have been no poverty in the land of Israel (Deu 15:4), since obedience to God's will carried with it assurance of the supply of temporal needs; but realistically, the poor were a factor in the society at all periods (Deu 15:11; Mk 14:7). It is hard to think of this lame man as already a member of the Christian community, since his needs would have been cared for (2:45).

He was shrewd enough to know where to take up his post, for people could not worship God restfully if they carried with them into the Temple the image of a helpless man whom they had passed by. As friends were in the process of placing him in his accustomed spot, Peter and John came along on their way to prayer.

3:4. Peter "fixed his gaze upon him." The idea conveyed is of looking with fixity and intensity at an object (cf. 1:10; 23:1). His attentiveness may have been in unconscious imitation of his Lord, who on one occasion had spotted a lame man and proceeded to minister to him (Jn 5:6). The command, "Look at us!" seems to have been designed to awaken a sense of expectation.

3:5-6. Responding with fixed "attention," the lame man showed his hope that some unusual generosity might be extended to him. Cruel disappointment would have followed had Peter stopped with the words, "I do not possess silver and gold." The truth was, he had something infinitely better to give—a soundness of limb that the unfortunate had never known. There is a discernible tension between "Look at us!" and "in the name of Jesus Christ the Nazarene." In himself Peter had no more power to bestow healing than he had money in his wallet.

Incidentally, it is to Peter's credit that he had no money, for it shows that he had not dipped into the common treasury which had been established (2:44). In view of the sin of Judas, those who had been his associates could only look on such an act of pilfering with horror. Another aspect of the story is that Peter was going into the house of God for worship without any money (the court of the women, whither he was bound, contained the Temple treasury). He seemed to know that true worship is not identical with the presentation of gifts (cf. Mt 2:11).

The moment had come for action, and "the name of Jesus Christ" proved efficacious for the miracle that was needed. It was by His authority that the good deed was accomplished (cf. Lk 10:17). Was there any special significance in linking Jesus with Nazareth? It was sufficiently well-known that this was His home, so such information was hardly needed. Noting the frequent use of this appendage in postresurrection settings, C. F. D. Moule suggests, "This seems to reflect an awareness of his continuity with the Jesus of history."[1]

3:7-8. To encourage the lame man to act on his command to walk, Peter extended his "right hand" and lifted him to his feet. Luke the physician was interested in calling attention to the instantaneous impartation of strength provided for the portions of the body that needed it. With a leaping motion the man tested his feet and found them able to sustain his weight, whereupon he began to take steps and entered the Temple with his benefactors, unable to restrain his exhilaration. He expressed his elation by "leaping" about as he gave praise to God for the deliverance from his infirmity. He recognized that Peter and John were only instruments in the hand of God to effect his healing. That he became a believer through this experience may safely be assumed.

3:9-10. There could be no question in the minds of the people as to the reality of the miracle, for they recognized the familiar figure that had sat for so long in the same spot. Verification was much easier than in the case of the man born blind, whose recovered sight seemed to transform his appearance completely (Jn 9:9). The popular reaction to the lame man's restoration was "wonder and amazement." What seemingly could never have happened had occurred, and the credit was to be ascribed to Jesus of Nazareth, the despised and rejected One. Surely there was food for thought here.

2. MESSAGE—3:11-26

Whereas in the Pentecost sermon the great proof of the claims of Jesus was His resurrection, here the emphasis falls on the demonstration of His person through a miracle which, wrought in His name, revealed the power of His risen life. Peter's first task in addressing the gathered multitude was to provide sufficient background concerning Him to give an explanation for the miracle. With this established, he proceeded to explain what the mission of the Christ could mean to Israel if only the people would respond to Him in faith.

> **3:11** And while he was clinging to Peter and John, all the people ran together to them at the so-called portico of Solomon, full of amazement.
>
> **12** But when Peter saw *this*, he replied to the people, "Men of Israel, why do you marvel at this, or why do you gaze at us, as if by our own power or piety we had made him walk?
>
> **13** "The God of Abraham, Isaac, and Jacob, the God of our fathers, has glorified His Servant Jesus, *the one* whom you delivered up, and disowned in the presence of Pilate, when he had decided to release Him.
>
> **14** "But you disowned the Holy and Righteous One, and asked for a murderer to be granted to you,
>
> **15** but put to death the Prince of life, *the one* whom God raised from the dead,—*a fact* to which we are witnesses.
>
> **16** "And on the basis of faith in His name, *it is* the name of Jesus which has strengthened this man whom you see and know; and the faith which *comes* through Him has given him this perfect health in the presence of you all.
>
> **17** "And now, brethren, I know that you acted in ignorance, just as your rulers did also.
>
> **18** "But the things which God announced beforehand by the mouth of all the prophets, that His Christ should suffer, He has thus fulfilled.

71

19 "Repent therefore and return, that your sins may be wiped away, in order that times of refreshing may come from the presence of the Lord;

20 and that He may send Jesus, the Christ appointed for you,

21 whom heaven must receive until *the* period of restoration of all things, about which God spoke by the mouth of His holy prophets from ancient time.

22 "Moses said, 'THE LORD GOD SHALL RAISE UP FOR YOU A PROPHET LIKE ME FROM YOUR BRETHREN; TO HIM YOU SHALL GIVE HEED IN EVERY-THING HE SAYS TO YOU.

23 'AND IT SHALL BE THAT EVERY SOUL THAT DOES NOT HEED THAT PROPHET SHALL BE UTTERLY DESTROYED FROM AMONG THE PEOPLE.'

24 "And likewise, all the prophets who have spoken, from Samuel and *his* successors onward, also announced these days.

25 "And it is you who are the sons of the prophets, and of the covenant which God made with your fathers, saying to Abraham, 'AND IN YOUR SEED ALL THE FAMILIES OF THE EARTH SHALL BE BLESSED.'

26 "For you first, God raised up His Servant, and sent Him to bless you by turning every one *of you* from your wicked ways."

3:11-12. Even after they emerged from the Temple service the healed man clung to the apostles out of sheer joy and gratitude. By this time the people were in a mood of excitement as they moved toward that portion of the outer court, on the eastern side, known as the portico of Solomon. It is likely that prior to this time believers had become accustomed to congregating in this area. Probably most of the people who had observed the hour of prayer stayed for a time to hear what the apostles would say about the miracle. To this astounded assembly Peter addressed first of all a rebuke, for the crowd was staring at the apostles as though the two had some hidden source of magic or some inherent power that enabled them to perform miracles. (Paul encountered a somewhat similar reaction after healing a cripple at Lystra [14:11-18].) But neither their "power" nor their "piety" was the true explanation.

3:13-16. Instead of simply stating that God had performed the miracle, Peter prefaced his explanation (v. 16) with the background for the release of divine power (vv. 13-15). For such an audience it was wise to begin with God, whom Peter identified as "the God of Abraham, Isaac, and Jacob." The title goes back to Exodus 3:6 and emerges on especially solemn or important occasions (1 Ki 18:36; 1 Ch 29:18). Its thrust is to underscore the covenant faithfulness of God. In line with the promises made to the fathers, God "glorified His Servant Jesus."

"Servant" is the first of several distinctive terms for the Lord Jesus Christ which appear in this sermon. The Greek word is *pais*, which is used in the LXX in Isaiah 52:13 to render the Hebrew *ebed* at the commencement of a passage that runs through chapter 53. The LXX translators should have used it also in 53:11, where the word occurs again in the Hebrew, but they misconstrued the meaning. Since Peter at this point stressed the glorification, then went on immediately to speak of Jesus' death, and since glorification as well as death is part of the presentation in Isaiah (52:13; 53:12), the concept of the suffering Servant was likely in his thought. What renders this more certain is the identification of the Servant with Jesus by Philip, another member of the Jerusalem church, when he dealt with the Ethiopian eunuch (8:30-35). Evidently this interpretation of Isaiah 53 was held by the Jerusalem church and in fact seems not to have taken hold elsewhere. At any rate, the only other occurrences of *pais* with reference to the Lord Jesus are confined to the early chapters of Acts (3:26; 4:27, 30). It is not surprising, however, that in his first epistle, especially in 2:23-24, the apostle Peter should again make use of the Servant motif.

God's appraisal of His Servant was vastly different from that of the nation which "delivered up" the One whom He had sent. This term *delivered* up is used twice in the LXX text of Isaiah 53:12. In the New Testament it serves to describe the act of the Father in giving His Son to die for the sins of men (Ro 8:32), of the Son in giving Himself (Gal 2:20), of Judas in betraying Him (Lk 22:21), of the Council in handing Him over to Pilate (Mk 15:1), and of Pilate in surrendering Him to the will of His accusers (Lk 23:25). Similarity of action may conceal a great difference in motive. Peter charged his audience with complicity in the death of Jesus, for although the Sanhedrin had delivered Him to Pilate, the representatives of the people supported the demand for His death. Theirs was the special responsibility for having put pressure on Pilate when he had been inclined to release the prisoner (Lk 23:4, 15-16, 20, 22). They had denied Jesus in the presence of the governor, preferring that a murderer be released to them (Lk 23:18). They would not have Him as their King (Jn 19:15).

Peter could hardly take on his lips the word "disowned," in reference to their sin, without feeling pain over his own, even though his denial had involved not rejection but disloyalty. Peter had claimed that he did not know Jesus; the Jews had refused to acknowledge Him as their Messiah. Men may deny a statement and think little of it, but to deny a Person who claimed, with the proper credentials, to be sent of God as the Saviour and Lord of men involves a sin of inestimable magnitude (Mt 10:33). It amounts to making God a liar (1 Jn 2:22; 5:10).

Peter used a double title here for Jesus, one which presented a strong contrast to "murderer"—"the Holy and Righteous One." This description was clearly intended as a Messianic title. Neither term appears to have been much used outside the early Jerusalem church. "Holy" may owe something to its occurrence in Psalm 16, which Peter had quoted in his Pentecost message (2:27), but this was not the first time he had employed it of his Lord (cf. Jn 6:69). The term "Righteous One" emerges again on the lips of Stephen in a context similar to that of 3:14, when he spoke of an unjust and murderous throng taking the life of Jesus (7:52). The remaining example is Ananias's use of the term in speaking of Jesus to Saul of Tarsus (22:14).

If it is correct to assign to Isaiah 53 the source of the use of "Servant" in this sermon, the possibility is strong that the same Old Testament influence may account for the use of "Righteous One" (Is 53:11). Its use by the centurion at the cross (Lk 23:47, [margin]), however gratifying, is not sufficient basis for the adoption of the title by the Church.

Peter achieved a startling contrast when he charged his audience with having killed "the Prince of life" (v. 15). How incongruous! It is improbable that the thought behind this title is the initial communication of life to men (Jn 1:3-4), since the association is rather with the resurrection life of Jesus (cf. Jn 14:19), as indeed the present verse suggests as it continues, "whom God raised from the dead."

The word rendered "Prince" is found in three other passages (Ac 5:31; Heb 2:10; 12:2), and has also been translated "Author," "Leader," "Pioneer," and "Originator." Its use in Hebrews raises the question of relationship and suggests the distinct possibility that the writer of that epistle may have been rather well acquainted with the outlook of the early Palestinian Church. The idea conveyed by the word is that of a champion whose victory involves those whom he represents (cf. 1 Sa 17:8-9). C. F. D. Moule makes the observation that this is one place at which the early Jerusalem church possessed a concept of Christology somewhat akin to that of Paul, who emphasized so much the corporate relationship between Christ and those who belong to Him.[2] Peter and his associates were "witnesses" (v. 15), not of the resurrection event itself (seen by no mortal) but of the resurrection fact (cf. 10:41).

Finally Peter was ready to speak of the miracle that had his audience agog with excitement. The ultimate explanation for the cure lay in the "name" of Jesus, which is full of power—not in a magical sense, but as summing up who and what He is. But even this reservoir of power flows into human life only as it is tapped by "faith in His name." This involves trusting in Jesus as the Son of God and Saviour of men (cf. Jn 1:12). If the lame man had not exercised faith in Jesus and had instead resisted the use of His name by Peter (v. 6), he would not have been healed. To call upon the name of the Lord brings salvation, for it means calling upon the Lord Himself (Ro 10:13).

3:17-21. Peter handled his audience with gentleness, for which his opening word, "brethren," was a fitting preparation. Having charged them in strong language with the death of Jesus, he now sought to mitigate their wrong as much as he could. The crime was committed "in ignorance" (cf. 13:27; Jn 8:19; 1 Co 2:8). Here we are probably confronted with an Old Testament conception, for in Israel sins were classified as done in ignorance or done with a high hand (Num 15:27-31). The man who gathered sticks on the Sabbath flaunted the law and found no mercy (Num 15:32-36). Proof that the term *ignorance* was interpreted liberally may be seen in the case of David's sin (2 Sa 12:13-14). Saul of Tarsus received mercy because he acted ignorantly in unbelief when he persecuted the Church (1 Ti 1:13).

The Jews should have known that God was sending them a Messiah who would "suffer," since He had foretold it through "all the prophets." As Jesus said on more than one occasion, the leaders of His people did not know the Scriptures (Jn 5:39; Mt 22:29). Peter himself had not been able to accept the idea of a suffering Messiah, even from the lips of the Master (Mt 16:21-22), and on this very account he felt compassion for his hearers and desired for them the insight he had come to possess concerning the prophetic word (cf. 1 Pe 1:11).

It is somewhat disconcerting to read that "all the prophets" foretold a suffering Messiah. True, the prophets are referred to in Luke 24:44-46 as predicting a suffering Messiah. But it is hard for us to find this strain in many places as we read the prophets today. The clearest pronouncement on the suffering aspect is found in the Servant passages of Isaiah. Since these found their fulfillment in the person of One who was also the Christ, the liberty was taken to speak of a suffering Messiah (and not simply of a suffering Servant). The word "all" remains as a stumbling block. Is this a case of hyperbole, or is there more in the prophets than we have been able to see? "He has thus fulfilled," that is to say, God brought to pass the death of Jesus in the manner indicated, through suffering wrought by the action of men. One pathway of hope lay before the guilty ones, and Peter was quick to point it out.

Peter exhorted his audience, "Repent therefore and return." If repentance was in order in the preaching of John the Baptist and of Jesus, how much more now, in view of a crucifixion inflicted by human passion and unbelief. The Lord's word to Peter, that he would turn again after his denial (Lk 22:32), was now held out by the apostle to those who may yet find mercy with God. Their "sins"—not only of rejection and crucifixion, but all others—"may be wiped away" (cf. Is 43:25; 44:22). The figure of speech involves the erasure of a writing, in this case a record of sins committed (cf. Col 2:14).

Repentance and forgiveness would clear the way for "times of refreshing." Seasons of refreshing and renewal are not to be thought of as a present respite from the labors and sorrows of life, as in Matthew 11:28-30, but as the hoped-for day of the return of the Messiah (cf. Mt 23:37-39). The source of the refreshing is the presence of the Lord, who in this passage is God the Father. The ascended Lord Jesus is with Him in glory, whence He will return. The Lucan writings afford many examples of *Lord* being used of the Lord God (e.g., Lk 1:46, 66; 2:15; Ac 1:24; 4:24). Jesus will bring from the Father's presence the time of renewal and blessing when He returns.

He is "the Christ appointed" for His people. More may be involved here than meets the eye, for the word "appointed" has a prefix, a preposition meaning "beforehand," which appears also in verse 18. This raises the possibility that we have here a hint of the preexistence of the One whose first coming is history and whose second coming is being seen in prospect.

"Heaven" has been the abode of the Messiah since the ascension, but "until" is a reminder of the promise of His return (cf. 1:11), which is the time for the "restoration of all things" in accordance with what has been prophesied. The pattern of thought here bears a close resemblance to what our Lord talked about when He anticipated the *palingenesia,* or re-generation, of the present order in connection with His return in glory (Mt 19:28). This theme looms large indeed in the writings of the prophets.

3:22-23. Having spoken of the prophets, Peter then went back to cite the testimony of Moses, regarded by the Jews as the greatest of the prophets.[*] He was the one who had foretold the coming of a prophet like himself who would speak the words of God and who must be heeded (Deu 18:15, 18). While Peter did not in so many words identify this Prophet with Jesus, his intention is evident from the movement of thought and also from verse 26, where "raised up" looks back to the same expression in verse 22. In this context the verb "raise up" does not allude to resurrection but to emergence on the plane of history (other examples in Acts occur at 5:36-37; 7:18; 20:30).

The fact that Stephen alluded to the same passage in Deuteronomy (Ac 7:37) makes it clear that the early Church was aware of this prediction as pointing to Christ. That Judaism looked for a prophet like Moses can be seen from John 1:21; 6:14. This was a strong feature of the Samaritan religion also.[†] A trace of the Samaritan expectation seems to

---

[*]Philo not only calls him "the greatest and most perfect of men" (*De Vita Mosis* 1:1), but in dealing with him as a prophet, in the words of H. A. Wolfson, makes him "a prophet according to the wider sense which that term has in Scripture, namely, a prophet who by virtue of his being a prophet is also priest and lawgiver" (*Philo* [Cambridge, Mass.: Harvard U., 1948], 2:18).
[†]The Samaritans believed, "Moses' soul returned to God at his death and he was to be reborn as Taheb for the restoration" (John Macdonald, *The Theology of the Samaritans,* p. 443).

emerge in John 4:25. In recent times it has been learned that the Qumran community also had such an expectation of an eschatological prophet based on the Deuteronomy passage. Luke's point is not that Jesus was a prophet (this was freely granted on all sides during His ministry) but that He was that particular Prophet for whom many were looking in that day as the One whose appearance would herald the consummation. The ancient prophecy had warned that unwillingness to heed this prophet would mean destruction (Ac 3:23). As a sidelight, we should recall that at the transfiguration the heavenly voice bade the disciples give heed to the Son (Lk 9:35). He is the Prophet par excellence.

3:24. Not only the unique prophet Moses but the whole order of prophets, beginning with Samuel, who was both judge and prophet, "announced these days." The reference seems to be to the times of refreshing mentioned in verse 19, and this agrees with the fact that the great burden of the prophets was the proclamation of the Messianic Kingdom.

3:25-26. The conclusion of the address was intended to bring encouragement, for the hearers were descendants of the prophets and should have taken seriously their predictions. They were also the beneficiaries of the covenant God had made with Abraham. As his posterity, they could enter into the blessing of the covenant for themselves and receive forgiveness of their "wicked ways." God had "raised up" (sent) His Servant Jesus "first" to Israel. This was to be expected, for God could not ignore His covenant (cf. Ro 1:16). It agrees with our Lord's insistence on restricting His ministry to His own people Israel (Mt 15:24). Yet His openness to the needs of Gentiles and His responsiveness to their faith (Mt 8:13; 15:28) demonstrated that there was room for Gentiles in the divine plan. Scripture presents the prospect that through a believing Israel "all the families of the earth" can and will be blessed (Gen 12:3). This, to a degree, actually took place as the history in the book of Acts unfolds, for it was through believing Jews that Gentiles heard of the Lord Jesus and entered into the blessings of the covenant. Paul foresaw a day when this divine purpose will be fully realized (Ro 11:11-12).

Anton Fridrichsen summarizes the thrust of the sermon as a whole by saying,

> Peter interprets the significance of the resurrection of Jesus from a Jewish point of view: "God, having raised up his servant, sent him to you first" (3:26). The resurrection of Jesus from the dead means that he is now, as the heavenly Messiah of Israel, ruling over the new-covenant people consisting of those Jews who believed in him. The way of salvation is open to all children of Abraham; one has only to believe in Jesus as the crucified and exalted Messiah. This form of gospel is all through based upon the priority of Israel as the covenant-people of the world; they are the people

of prophecy now experiencing its fulfillment. It is a typical gospel of the circumcision.[3]

One need only add that it is not exclusively Jewish, for all the families of the earth are seen as the ultimate recipients of blessing.

3. OPPOSITION—4:1-22

THIS SECTION has three successive developments: the arrest of Peter and John by Jewish authorities and their overnight imprisonment (vv. 1-4); the hearing before the Sanhedrin the following morning, featuring Peter's speech (vv. 5-12); and the deliberations of the Council, leading to the decision to release the apostles but also to forbid further preaching in the name of Jesus (vv. 13-22).

> **4:1** And as they were speaking to the people, the priests and the captain of the temple *guard,* and the Sadducees, came upon them,
> **2** being greatly disturbed because they were teaching the people and proclaiming in Jesus the resurrection from the dead.
> **3** And they laid hands on them, and put them in jail until the next day, for it was already evening.
> **4** But many of those who had heard the message believed; and the number of the men came to be about five thousand.

4:1-2. The phrase, "As they were speaking to the people," leads to two conclusions: John joined Peter in addressing the throng that had gathered, and much more was said on this occasion than is contained in 3:12-26.

The apostles were interrupted by the arrival of certain dignitaries from the Sanhedrin. Luke delighted to use the verb meaning "to come upon," especially in the sense of a sudden and unexpected arrival (cf. Lk 2:9; Ac 17:5). Drawn by the report of a large concourse of people in the Temple area, this investigating group consisted of "priests" and "Sadducees," accompanied by "the captain of the temple guard." This officer was second only to the high priest in authority. Under him were men who supervised the guards of the Temple treasures and the gatemen. In other words, he commanded the Temple police force. His presence on this occasion heralded an arrest.

The priests were likely chief priests (some manuscripts have the word) since they, rather than ordinary priests, had a place in the Council. However, it is possible that some of the officiating priests joined the investigating party because of concern that the afternoon worship period had been somewhat disturbed.

The Sadducees constituted one of the sects into which current Judaism was divided. Differing from the Pharisees in that they refused to sanction the oral traditions that had grown up around the interpretation of the Mosaic Law, these men jealously guarded the ancient right of the priests to teach the Law as well as to supervise the worship in the house of God. Due to historical trends during the intertestamental period, they were drawn increasingly into the political arena, since there was no king in Israel, and by the time of Christ they had found it expedient to keep on good terms with the Romans (Jn 11:48). They manifested little interest in Jesus until it appeared that He might turn out to be a revolutionary leader whose movement would bring reprisal from Rome. Joining hands with the opposition party, the Pharisees, they engineered the death of Jesus.

Their reason for visiting the Temple courts on this day was that they were "greatly disturbed" over two things. For one, the apostles "were teaching the people." After all, these were rude Galileans, unschooled in the Law. To be sure, Jesus had taught there, but He had had such ability that men instinctively called him Rabbi. It was galling to have to put up with the attempt of His disciples to assume a similar role.

But more than that, the Sadducees were inflamed because the two men were "proclaiming in Jesus the resurrection from the dead." It was bad enough to have people preaching the doctrine of resurrection, something the Sadducees did not accept, presumably because it did not seem to be in the Pentateuch, which they ranked higher than the rest of the Old Testament as the foundation of all else (23:8). But to preach resurrection in the case of Jesus, whom they had condemned to death, was doubly offensive. Months before, it had been the resurrection of Lazarus which had stirred them up against Jesus (Jn 11:45-53; 12:9-11). Now the report of the resurrection of Jesus Himself was beginning to haunt them and make them uneasy. But it is reasonably certain that their religious views, even on resurrection, were less vital to them than their political well-being. They feared any disturbance among the people that threatened to upset the status quo and bring Roman intervention.

4:3-4. "They laid hands on them." No delay is indicated, nor is there any evidence of resistance either by the apostles or by the people on their behalf. An attempt to arrest Jesus in the Temple had failed when the officers had been overawed by His teaching (Jn 7:32, 45-46), but on this occasion their superiors were in action, men who would not be denied. Because it was now "evening," probably three hours or so after the hour of prayer, it was not possible to have a meeting of the Council; so the prisoners were placed in custody overnight with a view to placing them before that body the next morning. The crowd could readily be persuaded to leave, for it was time to close the Temple gates anyway.

Then, or later on, the apostles learned that their testimony in the Temple had not been in vain, for "many" in their audience "believed." These additions brought the total of believing "men" (there were women also) to "about five thousand." This does not mean that an additional two thousand were converted that afternoon, for believers were being added from day to day ever since Pentecost (2:47). It is not possible to know how many days had intervened.

This figure of five thousand has been questioned on the ground that Paul had no such success in his efforts to evangelize his own people. But the conditions were by no means the same. By the time Paul was carrying on his work, official Judaism had arrayed itself against the sect of the Nazarenes; but at this early period in Jerusalem no official action had been taken, and there was a great wave of popular support for the apostles, aided by their works of mercy among the masses (cf. 2:43). All this was changed after the death of Stephen.

> **4:5**   And it came about on the next day, that their rulers and elders and scribes were gathered together in Jerusalem;
> **6**   and Annas the high priest *was there*, and Caiaphas and John and Alexander, and all who were of high-priestly descent.
> **7**   And when they had placed them in the center, they *began to* inquire, "By what power, or in what name, have you done this?"
> **8**   Then Peter, filled with the Holy Spirit, said to them, "Rulers and elders of the people,
> **9**   if we are on trial today for a benefit done to a sick man, as to how this man has been made well,
> **10**   let it be known to all of you, and to all the people of Israel, that by the name of Jesus Christ the Nazarene, whom you crucified, whom God raised from the dead—by this *name* this man stands here before you in good health.
> **11**   "He is the STONE WHICH WAS REJECTED BY YOU, THE BUILDERS, *but* WHICH BECAME THE VERY CORNER *stone.*
> **12**   "And there is salvation in no one else; for there is no other name under heaven that has been given among men, by which we must be saved."

4:5-6. During the night, while Peter and John were kept in prison, word went out to the members of the Sanhedrin to be ready to meet "on the next day." This was the highest court in the land, having had its origin, so far as is known, in the *Gerousia,* or senate, which functioned in Maccabean times. Its membership was drawn from the two leading parties, Sadducees and Pharisees, and totaled seventy men (cf. Num 11:16-17) in addition to the high priest, who presided over the body.

Luke's description of the court has some interesting features. He revealed his detachment as a Gentile by speaking of "their" rulers (cf. "their" language in 1:19). Three elements among the members are noted: "rulers and elders and scribes." The first group can safely be identified with the chief priests or ex-high priests. Elders were representatives of the people and were probably for the most part Pharisees. Scribes were men with rabbinical training who attached themselves both to the Pharisees and to the Sadducees as experts in the Law.

Certain individuals are mentioned also because of their prominence. Annas is called "the high priest." He had been high priest for several years but was removed by the Roman procurator in A.D. 15. It is likely that the Jewish people still regarded him as the legitimate holder of the office, which according to the Law was for life. In addition, he continued to exert influence through five sons, one grandson, and his son-in-law Caiaphas, who was the actual incumbent at the time. In Luke's gospel the two men, probably out of deference to popular sentiment, are presented as sharing the office (Lk 3:2; cf. Jn 18:13). "John" may be Jonathan, one of the sons of Annas (Codex Bezae has this reading). Of Alexander nothing is known. "All who were of high-priestly descent" included five or six families, the priestly aristocracy from which high priests were selected in this period.

Luke's source of information for this narrative could have been the apostle John, provided he can be identified with "the other disciple" who was known to the high priest (Jn 18:16).

4:7-12. The two apostles were placed "in the center," where they could be readily seen and heard (the Sanhedrin sat in a semicircle). This was the first occasion when the prediction of Jesus that His followers would be delivered up to councils (Mk 13:9) was fulfilled. Perhaps they recalled His further remark that the purpose behind such a situation was that they might bear testimony before them. At any rate, when the two were interrogated as to the "power" and the "name" (authority) by which they had been acting (cf. Lk 20:1-2), Peter was enabled to reply because he was "filled with the Holy Spirit," as Jesus had promised (Mk 13:11).

There was no thought of using guarded language that might make their lot easier. Peter came right to the point, appearing to rejoice that he had such an audience through which, in a sense, he was making his message known to all the people of Israel (cf. Paul's attitude in a similar situation, which gave him a sounding board for reaching the Gentiles, 2 Ti 4:17). As to the miracle itself, he was content to remind his hearers that it was a "benefit," so there should have been no ground for complaint. As to the source of the power behind the miracle, the answer was Jesus Christ of Nazareth, for the One who went about doing good was still at work through His own (Ac 1:1).

Peter could have stopped there and received only a mild reaction to his testimony, for other miracles had been wrought in recent days in Jerusalem without inciting the wrath of the authorities (2:43). But the urge to bear a testimony to his Lord before the rulers of his people was irresistible. He might not have another opportunity. So on he went, disregarding the consequences to himself. His judges had "crucified" the Saviour, but they had not thereby brought His career to an ignominious close, as they had supposed, for God had "raised" Him "from the dead." Neither here nor in the Pentecost address did Peter mention the empty tomb. As a mere fact, this phenomenon was open to more than one possible interpretation. What mattered supremely was the confidence that Jesus was alive, to which the apostles could bear witness because of their contact with Him. The healing of the cripple was a demonstration of the reality and power of His risen life.

But rather than continue to talk about the man who had been healed, Peter returned to the themes of the death and resurrection of Jesus. For this purpose he made use of Psalm 118:22. The form of the quotation is notable in two respects. First, it differs from the LXX, to which Luke usually adhered rather closely in his quotations. "Stone" stands here in the nominative rather than in the accusative case, which may indicate that Luke was drawing on *testimonia*, that is, groupings of Scripture passages to serve as proof texts for various Christian themes, especially in relation to Jesus as the Messiah. Such *testimonia* would naturally use the nominative. Second, Luke identified the builders as "you," the men in front of Peter, making an addition to the passage.

The thrust of the verse used by Peter is clear. It contains on the one hand an indictment of Israel's leaders as rejecters of the Lord Jesus, and on the other hand a vindication of His claims by God's action in raising Him from the dead. The leaders are viewed as builders looking for just the right stone with which to complete the edifice of Judaism by satisfying the nation's Messianic hopes. They had scornfully rejected God's Man as not meeting their requirements, and did it by inflicting on Him a shameful and violent death. God had answered by raising up His Son and making Him the "cornerstone." This truth renders futile all attempts to find the origin of the Church at some point in the pre-cross ministry of Jesus (except by way of prediction), for the Church was founded on a rejected and resurrected Saviour.

"Cornerstone" is somewhat hard to define. Literally it is "head of the corner," and was applied by Jesus to Himself in a parabolic setting of rejection (Lk 20:17) and implied vindication. The term is certainly intended to suggest importance and honor. "The Crucified is the rejected stone which in the resurrection is made by God the chief corner-stone in the heavenly sanctuary (Acts 4:11), to be manifested as such in the *parousia.*"[1]

Peter did not pursue the line of thought expressed by Jesus in Luke 20:18, with its threat of judgment, though he touched on it in 1 Peter 2:7-8. The reason for his reserve is hardly timidity or fear, but rather his desire to stress the positive value of Christ the stone, as the One in whom salvation is to be found (v. 12).

Salvation in the Lord God is set forth in a refrain that occurs three times in the very psalm Peter was using (Ps 118:14, 21, 28 in the LXX). Salvation was the supreme concern of this prince of apostles (Ac 2:40; 5:31; 15:11; cf. 1 Pe 1:5, 9-10). It is found exclusively in Christ and "no one else," and it is an imperative need for sinful men (they "must be saved"). What had happened to the physical condition of the cripple, in that he had been made whole (literally, saved) was a parable for the healing of the whole man by the power of Christ.

> **4:13** Now as they observed the confidence of Peter and John, and understood that they were uneducated and untrained men, they were marveling, and *began* to recognize them as having been with Jesus.
>
> **14** And seeing the man who had been healed standing with them, they had nothing to say in reply.
>
> **15** But when they had ordered them to go aside out of the Council, they *began* to confer with one another,
>
> **16** saying, "What shall we do with these men? For the fact that a noteworthy miracle has taken place through them is apparent to all who live in Jerusalem, and we cannot deny it.
>
> **17** "But in order that it may not spread any further among the people, let us warn them to speak no more to any man in this name."
>
> **18** And when they had summoned them, they commanded them not to speak or teach at all in the name of Jesus.
>
> **19** But Peter and John answered and said to them, "Whether it is right in the sight of God to give heed to you rather than to God, you be the judge;
>
> **20** for we cannot stop speaking what we have seen and heard."
>
> **21** And when they had threatened them further, they let them go (finding no basis on which they might punish them) on account of the people, because they were all glorifying God for what had happened;
>
> **22** for the man was more than forty years old on whom this miracle of healing had been performed.

4:13. It is likely that Peter's words were seconded if not supplemented by John. As they listened, the members of the Sanhedrin took note of the "confidence" of the two men. The word carries the idea of expressing oneself without holding anything back (which has an interesting implication in such a passage as Hebrews 4:16). When the Council coupled this observation with another, the fact that the two men before them were "uneducated" and untrained," the result was astonishment. The two things did not seem to hang together—the apostles' utter freedom in speaking and their lack of schooling (not general education so much as that which the scribes enjoyed [Jn 7:15]); plus their provincial character, lacking through inexperience the urbanity and poise necessary to command the attention of this august body.

Gradually the truth dawned on them. They "began to recognize" them as having been with Jesus. There is no thought here to the effect that the disciples had been waiting on the Lord Jesus in prayer and had thereby gained in boldness, however true that may have been. Rather, the dignitaries of the Council finally recalled having seen them before, possibly in the court of the high priest's house after the arrest of the Master in the garden (Jn 18:15) if not during Jesus' daily teaching in the Temple (Lk 22:53). That night Peter had been the target of jesting by guards and maids, so that he had ended up in confusion and denial, leaving the premises in tears. John had remained silent on that occasion. Now these two were fearless in the presence of national leaders, refusing to be browbeaten. How could this be?

The unwelcome truth began to steal over the minds of the judges. Jesus also had been uneducated (Jn 7:15) but was adept in handling Scripture. He, too, had belonged to the backwoods country of Galilee (cf. Jn 1:46), yet He had won the favor of the people. This thorn in their sides had finally been removed, to their great relief. But now it appeared that Jesus had succeeded in reproducing Himself in His disciples. Could they ever truly be rid of Him?

4:14. For the moment the Council was nonplussed. No objection could be raised against the miracle, for the formerly lame man had accompanied the apostles into the council chamber, a silent testimony to the power of God and the efficacy of the name of Jesus.

4:15-17. What was needed was time and privacy for consultation. To that end the apostles were removed while the members conferred with one another. The sentiment commonly expressed was one of frustration, strikingly similar to the mood shown by the same body after the resurrection of Lazarus (Jn 11:47-48). They were not prepared to make themselves appear foolish in the eyes of the people by denying the miracle. But they had to do something "in order that it may not spread any further."

What was "it" that could not be voiced by troubled men? Grammar may dictate that the antecedent is "sign" (v. 16), but by this time virtually the entire city had heard about the healing. Clearly what the Council had in mind was to block further teaching about Jesus and the resurrection. It

85

was the speaking that was considered dangerous. Nothing was said about curtailing the working of miracles.

4:18-22. The restriction covered both preaching and teaching—all public utterance similar to what the apostles had been giving since Pentecost. Actually, if the language be pressed, even personal conversation on the subject was ruled out (v. 17).

If the Council had hoped to shut the mouths of these simple but eloquent men, they were immediately disillusioned. The answer of Peter and John was polite but firm. These men who had pronounced the dictum were judges. Appropriately, the apostles asked them to "judge" whether it would be right before God for them to obey the prohibition or to heed the command of God, which was the basis for their insistence on declaring what they had "seen and heard" (the risen and exalted Lord, the descending Spirit, and the power of God at work in the bodies and souls of men).

It was an embarrassing moment. No wonder the Council made no attempt to answer beyond repeating the warning to maintain silence, adding threats should the ban be ignored. This gave them an excuse to apprehend the apostles again in case their edict was disobeyed. There the matter rested, and since there was no ground on which Peter and John could rightly be detained, and in view of the popular sentiment in their favor, they were allowed to depart. Jerusalem was filled with praise to God for the manifestation of His goodness and power in the healing of the cripple who had endured over forty years of handicap and deprivation.

4. CONFIRMATION—4:23-31

Released from custody, Peter and John sought the fellowship and counsel of the apostolic company. Through united prayer and a fresh visitation of the Spirit all were reinforced in their purpose to continue their witness despite the warning of the Sanhedrin.

4:23 And when they had been released, they went to their own *companions*, and reported all that the chief priests and the elders had said to them.

24 And when they heard *this*, they lifted their voice to God with one accord and said, "O Lord, it is Thou who DIDST MAKE THE HEAVEN AND THE EARTH AND THE SEA, AND ALL THAT IS IN THEM,

25 who by the Holy Spirit, *through* the mouth of our father David Thy servant, didst say,

'WHY DID THE GENTILES RAGE,
AND THE PEOPLES DEVISE FUTILE THINGS?

26 'THE KINGS OF THE EARTH TOOK THEIR STAND,
AND THE RULERS WERE GATHERED TOGETHER,
AGAINST THE LORD, AND AGAINST HIS CHRIST.'

27 "For truly in this city there were gathered together against Thy holy Servant Jesus, whom Thou didst anoint, both Herod and Pontius Pilate, along with the Gentiles and the peoples of Israel,
28 to do whatever Thy hand and Thy purpose predestined to occur.
29 "And now, Lord, take note of their threats, and grant that Thy bond-servants may speak Thy word with all confidence,
30 while Thou dost extend Thy hand to heal, and signs and wonders take place through the name of Thy holy Servant Jesus."
31 And when they had prayed, the place where they had gathered together was shaken, and they were all filled with the Holy Spirit, and *began* to speak the word of God with boldness.

4:23. "They went to their own companions." The Greek simply has "to their own" (cf. 24:23). John 13:1 represents a close parallel since it involves the twelve. Clearly a small company is in view here, in contrast to the larger circle of believers in verse 32. The new policy adopted by the Sanhedrin would affect these leaders in a special way. They would be under close observation. So it was important that they should confer and pray and present a solid front to the authorities, indicated as "the chief priests and the elders."

This is the first time chief priests are mentioned in Acts (although some manuscripts have the word in 4:1), but the expression is well known from its use in the gospels. It creates difficulty, however, for the word "chief priest" in the original is identical with *high priest*. It would only add to the confusion if the plural form were translated "high priests" wherever it occurs. After considerable research, J. Jeremias concluded that these men must be differentiated from the ordinary priests who ministered in the Temple. "The chief priests permanently employed at the Temple formed a definite body who had jurisdiction over the priesthood and whose members had seats and votes on the council."[2] This group included the current high priest, the captain of the Temple (4:1), the Temple overseer, and several treasurers.[3] As Acts 4:6 suggests, these men belonged to the priestly aristocracy. The older view, set forth by E. Schürer,[4] that "chief priests" indicated members of the high-priestly families, is no longer widely accepted as adequate.[5]

No mention is made here in verse 23 of scribes (in contrast to v. 5). They probably did not take an active part, since the case did not involve interpretation of the Law.

4:24-26. Luke does not report any discussion among the apostles, but seems to say that the account of Peter and John led to a spontaneous outburst of united prayer. "Lord" translates a word used also at the opening of Simeon's prayer (Lk 2:29). It is sometimes rendered "Master" (2 Ti 2:21; Jude 4). Here it is followed by praise of God for His creative majesty

(v. 24) and also for His activity in human affairs (vv. 25-26). "He does according to His will in the host of heaven and among the inhabitants of the earth" (Dan 4:35). Having been made keenly aware in recent days of the relevance of certain Scriptures to their own time, the apostolic company turned readily to the second psalm as fitting their circumstances. The portion quoted emphasizes the vanity of the effort of the Gentile nations to free themselves from divine control, and the futility of their rebellion "against the Lord and against His Christ" (anointed One, Messiah).

This is an instance in which "Lord" refers to God the Father. The distinction of persons (cf. Ps. 110:1) was readily seized upon by the early Church, no doubt under the direct tutelage of the risen Lord (Lk 24:44) as warranting the identification of the anointed One with their Lord and Master. The expression "His Christ" is the pointed reminder that at this early stage in the life of the Church *Christ* was not yet used as a name (as it is frequently in the epistles) but was still a title.

4:27-28. Tokens of the fulfillment of the psalm are now spelled out. Here Jesus is spoken of as God's "holy Servant." Peter had already used the expression in his second sermon (3:13, 26), but now we are made aware that this was a familiar way of speaking of Jesus, one in which others shared.

Noting the close conjunction of "Servant" and "Christ" in 4:26-27, Richard Longenecker writes,

> [This] indicates that the earliest appreciation of Jesus as the Suffering Servant was inextricably tied up with the conviction regarding Jesus as the Messiah. While, therefore, a suffering servant interpretation of Jesus' ministry ultimately stemmed from Jesus himself, it seems to have been only established in the church's consciousness on the basis of conviction regarding his messiahship.[6]

"Whom Thou didst anoint" probably means the same as in 10:38, where the baptism of Jesus is indicated, the occasion when He received the endorsement of the Father and the enduement with the Spirit. As the anointed One, Jesus is the Messiah; as the Servant, He is the Saviour. In this spontaneous expression of the apostles' awareness of the dignity of their Lord there is recognition both of His office and of His redeeming work.

Now the rulers who opposed God and His program, indefinite in the psalm, were specified in terms of recent events. Herod Antipas, though technically a tetrarch, could be called king by courtesy (Mk 6:14), answering to the language of the psalm. Luke was the only evangelist to mention Herod in connection with the trial of Jesus (Lk 23:6-12). He seemed to have had special information regarding his court (Lk 8:3; Ac 13:1). In the person of Pilate the Church found a fulfillment of the reference to "rulers." In terms of the Roman soldiers, "Gentiles" were present and involved, as were "the peoples of Israel" through their various tribal representatives at Jerusalem during the Passover. What had been done in concert by the will of man was now understood as a working out of the divine purpose (cf. 2:23). The futility of human opposition to God is never seen to better advantage than when it serves to implement His plan.

4:29-30. The prayer turned to the present situation of the Church— "Lord, take note of their threats." These "threats" must be related to the warning given by the Sanhedrin (v. 18). Though Psalm 2 warned of wrath and destruction upon the enemies of God and His Anointed, in this prayer there was no petition for reprisal, nor even a request to be spared the rigors of persecution. The servant is not greater than his Lord (Jn 15:20). All that was sought was divine restraint so that testimony to the Saviour could continue. For themselves, the followers of the Lord asked for "confidence," or boldness, such as Peter and John had displayed (Ac 4:13) in proclaiming the Word.

One other petition was voiced, the plea that God would continue to show forth His "signs and wonders," especially the manifestation of His power to heal. The two things—boldness in preaching and the divine working through healing—had been the pattern thus far (chap. 3). If only the human boldness were to remain visible, the impression could be created that God was withholding His blessing (cf. Heb 2:3-4).

4:31. The answer came quickly, first in the form of a physical sign, the shaking of the building where the company was gathered (cf. 16:25-26), and then in a renewed filling with the Spirit as the means of boldness in testimony (cf. 4:8, 13; Jn 15:26-27). The group lost no time in acting on this fresh manifestation of divine power by bearing effective witness to the Lord Jesus.

5. STATE OF THE CHURCH—4:32-37

Here emphasis rests on the spiritual accord and mutual consideration that prompted to unusual generosity in providing for the material needs of the Church.

> **4:32** And the congregation of those who believed were of one heart and soul; and not one *of them* claimed that anything belonging to him was his own; but all things were common property to them.
>
> **33** And with great power the apostles were giving witness to the resurrection of the Lord Jesus, and abundant grace was upon them all.
>
> **34** For there was not a needy person among them, for all who were owners of lands or houses would sell them and bring the proceeds of the sales,

35 and lay them at the apostles' feet; and they would be distributed to each, as any had need.

36 And Joseph, a Levite of Cyprian birth, who was also called Barnabas by the apostles (which translated means, Son of Encouragement),

37 and who owned a tract of land, sold it and brought the money and laid it at the apostles' feet.

4:32-35. Luke makes it clear that the willingness to share possessions was based on a powerful sense of unity ("one heart and soul"). This provided the inspiration for refusing to insist on the right to retain what one had received by inheritance or toil. It was not a matter of legislation, as in the Qumran community, where sharing of goods was imposed on its members. According to the Qumran sect such renunciation was necessary in order to purify the mind in the truth of God.[7] With the Christian community, however, the sharing was not a means to the end of personal edification but rather was the expression of the love of the Spirit, to use Paul's phrase (Ro 15:30; cf. Gal 5:22). It was also in line with the teaching of Jesus (Mk 10:21).

Right in the midst of this description, as though to emphasize that the maintenance of the group was not the primary consideration, attention is called to the public witness borne by the apostles to "the resurrection of the Lord Jesus." Above all, this was a witnessing community, and for this reason enjoyed "abundant grace" from the Lord.

Returning to a description of the community of goods, Luke adds the information that the common fund, out of which means were provided for the needy, was built up by the voluntary sale of "lands" and "houses." This meant that eventually the resources of the more affluent members would be drained, and the common fund would have to be replenished from other sources or be abandoned. But the Church, caught up in the enthusiasm of sacrificial giving, was content to leave the future with God. The poverty of the Jerusalem congregation is noted a few years later (Gal 2:10). This condition existed not only in time of famine (11:27-30) but as a chronic state calling for help from the Gentile churches (24:17; cf. Ro 15:26).

The very fact that benefactors brought the proceeds of their sales and deposited them with the apostles demonstrates the comprehensive role of leadership maintained by these men. Besides preaching to the unsaved and teaching believers, they assumed general oversight of the church's affairs. As the saints increased in number, the responsibility of overseeing the common fund became too great, and a change had to be made (6:1-6). But for the present the apostles continued to supervise the distribution of relief, which was a daily responsibility (6:1).

4:36-37. Unexpectedly, in the midst of this general description of the

Church's means of subsistence, Luke introduces an individual and furnishes certain items of information about him. This is the historian's way of alerting the reader to the fact that this man, Barnabas, was destined to play a large part in the unfolding story of the spread of the Christian faith. There are two dozen references to him in Acts alone. He is described as a good man, full of the Holy Spirit and faith (11:24). That goodness included generosity. Barnabas was eager to help the church on a later occasion also (11:27-30). When his own resources were largely depleted he was ready cheerfully to work for his living while preaching the Gospel rather than depend on others, and may even have inspired Paul to adopt the same pattern (1 Co 9:6). He lived by the principle of the name he bore (*Barnabas* means encouragement). Luke notes that this name was bestowed on him by the apostles, indicative of the esteem in which he was held.

Barnabas's possession of a piece of property seems to violate the ancient prohibition affecting Levites (Num 18:24) and priests (Num 18:20). But even by the time of Jeremiah this was not strictly maintained (Jer 1:1; 32:6-15).

Being a native of Cyprus, Barnabas was a Hellenistic Jew, as was Paul, so it is not surprising that later he took a leading role in missionary endeavor beyond the borders of Palestine.

D. Problems—5:1—8:3

THE PROBLEMS were both internal and external. Within the church distress was occasioned by the dishonesty of two people (5:1-11) and by the growing difficulty of caring for the needy (6:1-7). From the outside, pressure was mounting in the form of persecution directed at the apostles (5:12-42), and then at the church (8:1-3), growing out of Stephen's preaching and martyrdom (6:8—7:60).

1. ANANIAS AND SAPPHIRA—5:1-11

The connection with the previous paragraph is close, for the subject is the same, but there is also sharp contrast. Unity was temporarily disturbed, and joy was dimmed as divine judgment was meted out to a husband and wife.

5:1 But a certain man named Ananias, with his wife Sapphira, sold a piece of property,

2 and kept back *some* of the price for himself, with his wife's full knowledge, and bringing a portion of it, he laid it at the apostles' feet.

3 But Peter said, "Ananias, why has Satan filled your heart to lie to the Holy Spirit, and to keep back *some* of the price of the land?

4 "While it remained *unsold,* did it not remain your own? And after it was sold, was it not under your control? Why is it that you have conceived this deed in your heart? You have not lied to men, but to God."

5 And as he heard these words, Ananias fell down and breathed his last; and great fear came upon all who heard of it.

6 And the young men arose and covered him up, and after carrying him out, they buried him.

7 Now there elapsed an interval of about three hours, and his wife came in, not knowing what had happened.

8 And Peter responded to her, "Tell me whether you sold the land for such and such a price?" And she said, "Yes, that was the price."

9 Then Peter *said* to her, "Why is it that you have agreed together to put the Spirit of the Lord to the test? Behold, the feet of those who have buried your husband are at the door, and they shall carry you out *as well.*"

10 And she fell immediately at his feet, and breathed her last; and the young men came in and found her dead, and they carried her out and buried her beside her husband.

11 And great fear came upon the whole church, and upon all who heard of these things.

5:1-4. The change of atmosphere is heralded by the opening word, "But." Ananias was of a different caliber than Barnabas. Probably it was the desire for recognition from the apostles and the church that led to the concocting of a plan, shared by his wife Sapphira, whereby Ananias hoped to gain a reputation as a generous man. The plan was simple, namely, to sell a piece of property and ostensibly bring the amount received to the apostles, but in actuality to hold back a portion of the total for personal use. No fault would have been found had he brought part of the sale price rather than the whole amount, if the facts in the matter had been made known; but he made it appear that the entire sum was being given, as in the case of Barnabas. There was an intention to make the element of sacrifice appear greater than it actually was. This was hypocrisy.

Peter's question, "Why has Satan filled your heart to lie to the Holy Spirit?" clearly implies that it was the responsibility of Ananias to resist the solicitation of the evil one (cf. 1 Pe 5:8-9). Most New Testament references to Satan's activity relate to saints rather than to the unbelieving world. Peter himself had become the tool of Satan on one occasion (Mt 16:23). It was a source of grief to him that so early in the life of the Church Satan had been successful in making damaging inroads. Presumably Ananias was not conscious of having lied to the Holy Spirit; but this was the reality, since the Spirit was in actual control of the Church, empowering its witness and fostering its loving benevolence. Both were now endangered by this sin of dishonesty, for the Spirit was grieved (Eph 4:30) and unable to grant His blessing until this affair was cleared up.

What is involved here in lying to the Holy Spirit? No help can be gained by referring to the unpardonable sin (described as blasphemy against the Spirit [Mk 3:29]) and assuming from the death of these offenders that they must have been unsaved people masquerading as saints. This was not a case of blasphemy but of lying. There is no sound reason for questioning the redeemed status of the pair. Believers are capable of lying (Col 3:9). Chastening of God's people can be unto death (1 Co 11:30, and possibly 5:5). The lie to God the Spirit was so much greater than the attempted deception of the church that Peter could say, "You have not lied to men, but to God." Yet the whole affair had been motivated by a desire to appear in a good light before men! Relation to God must be kept in its primary place as the key to right relations with one's fellows.

5:5-6. Peter's words were the death knell for Ananias. The suddenness and severity of the punishment brought "fear" upon everyone who learned of the episode. God had revealed Himself as a consuming fire (Heb 12:29). Burial was immediately carried out by certain "young men" who were available for service but were not an official body within the church (cf. 1 Pe 5:5). If we ask why the penalty was so severe, surely the explanation lies at least partially in the necessity of reminding the church that believers were not to trifle with the things of God. A rough parallel may be seen in the death of Achan (Jos 7), which also was occasioned by involvement in financial scandal.

5:7-11. Unaware of what had overtaken her husband, Sapphira came home (had she been out spending some of the money kept back from the sale?) only to discover that she was a widow. Worse than that, her complicity in the plot to deceive the church was about to bring her to the grave along with her husband, as Peter's searching examination brought to light her guilt. Impressive is the amount of space devoted to this incident. Perhaps a key to the understanding of its importance lies in Luke's repeated observation that "fear" came on everyone, including "the whole church." God was teaching His people that sin among the saints is no light matter. He can use only those who are honest with Him as well as with the brethren.

The drastic nature of the divine intervention is in contrast to the milder treatment of offenders at Qumran: "If there be found in the community a man who consciously lies in the matter of (his) wealth, he is to be regarded as outside the state of purity entailed by membership, and he is to be mulcted of one fourth of his food ration."[1] After the death of Ananias and Sapphira, a Jerusalemite would think twice before professing faith in Christ in order to share in the common fund of the church.

Two lessons emerge from this incident. One is the fact that the Church is not perfect, not even when it is standing in the shadow of Pentecostal blessing. Spurgeon is reputed to have counseled a man seeking his help in finding a perfect group of God's people that if he found one he should not join it, for if he did it would no longer be perfect. The other lesson is the reminder that the God of the Bible intends to judge sin. He has done it at the cross; He does it among His people; and He will do it at the last day when unbelievers stand before Him.

In bringing this story to a close Luke mentions the "church" for the first time, having been content up to this point to indicate the group as believers (2:44; 4:4, 32). The freer use of the word *church* from this point on (there are twenty-three occurrences in Acts) may indicate a growing self-consciousness on the part of the Christian community as to its distinctive nature and place in the world.

2. PERSECUTION OF THE APOSTLES—5:12-42

The first paragraph is transitional, summarizing the aggressive ministry of preaching and healing which brought the leaders of the Jerusalem church to the attention of the authorities once more. Luke's method in the early chapters of Acts is to present alternating pictures of the Church alone and of the Church in contact with the world of unbelievers. The scheme is quite apparent: the focus is on believers in chapter 1, followed by Peter's challenge to the Pentecost throng in 2:1-41; believers are noted again in 2:42-47, then further confrontation with unbelievers as a result of the miracle of the healing of the lame man in 3:1—4:22; once more there is a section depicting the life of the Church in 4:23—5:11, followed by an account of further contact with those outside and the opposition that developed in 5:12-42. The same twofold pattern persists into Acts 6.

Verses 12-16. The continued growth of the church is noted. Here the emphasis is on the mighty works of the apostles rather than on preaching, although public testimony must have accompanied the miracles by way of explanation. Purged of sin within its ranks, the church once more enjoyed the prospering of God.

> **5:12** And at the hands of the apostles many signs and wonders were taking place among the people; and they were all with one accord in Solomon's portico.
>
> **13** But none of the rest dared to associate with them; however, the people held them in high esteem.
>
> **14** And all the more believers in the Lord, multitudes of men and women, were constantly added to *their number;*
>
> **15** to such an extent that they even carried the sick out into the streets, and laid them on cots and pallets, so that when Peter came by, at least his shadow might fall on any one of them.
>
> **16** And also the people from the cities in the vicinity of Jerusalem were coming together, bringing people who were sick or afflicted with unclean spirits; and they were all being healed.

5:12-16. With a grievous offense judged and the church purified, God was once more pleased to grant various "signs and wonders" in abundance through the apostles. This was one of the distinctives of the men appointed and trained by the Saviour (Jn 14:12), and in the early days of the Church's life miracles seem to have been performed by them alone (2:43; 4:22, 30; 5:12); but with the appointment of the seven the privilege became shared with this group, at least with Stephen (6:8) and Philip (8:6, 13). Later still, Paul and Barnabas exercised this function (14:3; 15:12). It would be hazardous to insist that no others participated, but from Luke's account it is evident that the working of miracles was vested mainly in the leaders of the church and helped to accredit them as Christ's representatives. Paul could refer to signs as marking him off from others as a true apostle of Jesus Christ (2 Co 12:12). It seems that the healings took place in the Temple, for Luke informs us that the apostles were frequenting Solomon's portico, a colonnaded area along the east side of the enclosure, where Jesus had resorted for teaching (Jn 10:23).

What follows appears to involve a contradiction, namely, that the people kept their distance out of fear, unwilling to identify with them, yet "multitudes" were added to the Lord. But those who were moved by fear need not be thought of as the people, but rather the saints. Only the apostles are singled out as being in Solomon's portico. "The rest," who held back from joining them, could be a reference to believers who had been awed by what had happened through the instrumentality of Peter in the Ananias incident (in Acts 17:9 "the others" indicates believers rather than outsiders). Then follows Luke's comment that the people generally "held them," that is, the apostles, "in high esteem." This is understandable in the light of the miracles that were taking place (v. 12; cf. 4:21). So the group was made up of apostles, the rest of the believers, the admiring people, and the new converts made at this time. These included "women," some of whom would soon have to pay a price for their adherence to the faith.

The healing activity of the apostles was not confined to the Temple but took place here and there throughout the city. Luke seems to say that it was the new believers who desired help for their loved ones and brought them into the streets in the hope that Peter's shadow might fall on them and bring relief (cf. Lk 8:43-44; Ac 19:12). Public interest was mounting to a high pitch. For the first time notice was taken of the arrival of people from outside the city, bringing their loved ones for healing. History was repeating itself (Mt 4:24), and the way was being prepared for the advance of the Gospel into Judea (Ac 9:31; cf. 1:8).

The summary which concludes here does not contain any mention of apostolic proclamation of the Gospel, concentrating as it does on the healing ministry; yet the addition of multitudes to the Church certainly implies fidelity in preaching the Word.

Verses 17-32. The reaction of official Judaism to all this activity of the apostles is strikingly similar to what has been noted in regard to Acts 3 and 4. One can retrace the same cycle—healing, preaching, popular response, then the attempt of the authorities to intervene by suppression, leading in turn to the apostles' further testimony to the religious hierarchy.

    5:17 But the high priest rose up, along with all his associates (that is the sect of the Sadducees), and they were filled with jealousy;

    18 and they laid hands on the apostles, and put them in a public jail.

    19 But an angel of the Lord during the night opened the gates of the prison, and taking them out he said,

    20 "Go your way, stand and speak to the people in the temple the whole message of this Life."

    21 And upon hearing *this,* they entered into the temple about daybreak, and *began* to teach. Now when the high priest and his associates had come, they called the Council together, even all the Senate of the sons of Israel, and sent *orders* to the prison house for them to be brought.

22 But the officers who came did not find them in the prison; and they returned, and reported back,

23 saying, "We found the prison house locked quite securely and the guards standing at the doors; but when we had opened up, we found no one inside."

24 Now when the captain of the temple *guard* and the chief priests heard these words, they were greatly perplexed about them as to what would come of this.

25 But someone came and reported to them, "Behold, the men whom you put in prison are standing in the temple and teaching the people!"

26 Then the captain went along with the officers and *proceeded* to bring them *back* without violence; (for they were afraid of the people, lest they should be stoned).

27 And when they had brought them, they stood them before the Council. And the high priest questioned them,

28 saying, "We gave you strict orders not to continue teaching in this name, and behold, you have filled Jerusalem with your teaching, and intend to bring this man's blood upon us."

29 But Peter and the apostles answered and said, "We must obey God rather than men.

30 "The God of our fathers raised up Jesus, whom you had put to death by hanging Him on a cross.

31 "He is the one whom God exalted to His right hand as a Prince and a Savior, to grant repentance to Israel, and forgiveness of sins.

32 "And we are witnesses of these things; and *so is* the Holy Spirit, whom God has given to those who obey Him."

5:17-21a. This new wave of opposition, like the former (4:1), stemmed from the Sadducees, who were dominant in the Sanhedrin and operated in response to the high priest, who was one of themselves. Anger at the preaching of the resurrection of Christ had previously spurred them to try to curtail the Christian movement, but now an additional factor is mentioned, their "jealousy" of the apostles. To think that these common men had the temerity to ignore the orders of their superiors and were enjoying ever greater support from the people! This was getting to be unbearable. One senses here an echo of the frustration of these leaders at an earlier time, when the resurrection of Lazarus had created great enthusiasm on behalf of Jesus (Jn 11:47-48). The fear of a revolutionary movement at that time may now have been revived. If so, it only demonstrated how completely the Sadducees misunderstood both Jesus and His followers.

Formerly they had arrested Peter and John; now they put the whole apostolic company in prison overnight. But "an angel of the Lord" proved to be their deliverer (cf. Heb 1:14). Peter could look back on this as a dress rehearsal for his own escape at a later time (12:7-11). Luke the historian has much to relate about angels in connection with Christ and His Church, evidently accepting at face value this element of early Christian tradition and giving it a prominent place. While it is true that the word for "angel" can also mean "messenger" and indicate a human being, this is rare; it is wholly unlikely in the present instance, where the full description "angel of the Lord" emphasizes a celestial origin and dignity.

Acting in the Lord's name, the angel directed the apostles to resume their preaching in the Temple. When God sets before His servants an open door, no man can shut it (Rev 3:8). The message to be given concerned "this Life," a suitable term for salvation in Christ, the Prince of life (Ac 3:15). It bears comparison with "this Way" in 22:4.

5:21b-26. The design of God was totally different from that of the Sanhedrin. Whereas the latter planned by prison and further threatening to intimidate the followers of the Lord Jesus, God wrought to discomfit the rulers and to show them that the proclamation was to continue with His blessing.

The situation called for a meeting of the nation's highest tribunal, and the high priest duly summoned the Council and all the Senate of the people. At first glance this seems to indicate two separate bodies meeting in combined session. But the Senate, or *gerousia,* was the original title of Israel's council of elders in the intertestamental period (cf. Ex 12:21, LXX), and Luke may have been intent simply on identifying the two. This is feasible grammatically, since the conjunction often translated "and" can also be rendered "even," as it is here, when the context makes this suitable (cf. "that is, the full senate of the Israelite nation," NEB).

Officers were sent to fetch the imprisoned apostles (cf. Jn 7:32). They returned empty-handed, reporting that the prison was empty despite the presence of guards in their usual positions. There are unanswered questions here. Were no other prisoners being kept at this time? Had the crime rate dropped to nothing because of the preaching of the Gospel? Or had other prisoners gone out along with the apostles? Or had the apostles been kept in a separate area?

The situation was naturally disquieting to the Council, now thoroughly bewildered by this fresh turn of events. Especially concerned was "the captain of the temple guard." This man was no petty officer. He belonged to the priestly aristocracy; he was second in authority to the high priest, and could minister on the Day of Atonement in his place if necessary. As chief of police in the Temple area, he had power to make arrests by means of the Levite police under his jurisdiction.[2] When word reached the Sanhedrin that the missing prisoners were only a short distance away in the Temple, engaged in teaching the people, the captain joined his subordinates in seeking out their quarry. The popular esteem enjoyed by the apostles dictated persuasion rather than force, but there was no resistance of any kind on the part of men who trusted God to work out their predicament to His glory.

5:27-32. When brought before the Council for questioning, the apostles were content to state their defense in terms of fidelity to God. They were merely doing what He had commanded them.

The high priest opened the questioning with a reminder that the Sanhedrin had issued strict orders not to teach in this name, a reference to the ban placed on Peter and John (4:18). His complaint that the apostles had so completely ignored the order as to fill Jerusalem with their teaching is an unwilling confession of the widespread impact of Christian testimony on the city during a brief period. In the high priest's remarks no more respect is shown to the Lord Jesus than was accorded Him during His ministry. By avoiding direct reference to Him, choosing to speak of "this name," "this man," he was perpetuating the practice attested by the gospels (Jn 9:16, 24, 29; 11:47; 18:30, 40; 19:12; cf. Mt 27:63), a practice largely followed by Jews in later centuries. The reference to the "blood" of Jesus finds its explanation in Matthew 27:24-25. It is quite apparent from the high priest's complaint that he was on the defensive, not knowing how to deal with a situation which was getting out of hand.

Seconded by the other apostles, Peter took exactly the same position he had voiced on the earlier occasion (4:19-20). When one is under orders from God, he cannot obey contrary orders from men. This principle was so deeply imbedded in the history of Israel (e.g., Moses versus Pharaoh, Daniel versus the king of Babylon) that the Council could not question its validity. With this in view, it is no surprise that obedience should hold an important place in the teaching of Peter's first epistle (1:2, 14, 22; 3:1, 6; 4:17).

By referring to God as "the God of our fathers," Peter seemed intent on suggesting that the great interventions the Almighty made during Old Testament days had simply prepared the way for this climactic development of the sending of the Lord Jesus as Saviour of His people. In fact, the same terms "raised" and "Savior" are used in the LXX of Judges 2:18; 3:9. This leads to the likely conclusion that "raised up" (v. 30) is not an allusion to resurrection, which Peter was apparently including in the exaltation of Jesus, but to the emergence of Jesus in the arena of history (he used the same approach in 3:26, in line with 3:22).

Peter followed his characteristic method of contrasting the adverse human reception of Jesus with God's vindication of Him. The word for "cross" is literally "tree," another Petrine feature (10:39; 1 Pe 2:24). As exalted to the right hand of God, the Lord Jesus is described as "Prince," or Leader (*archēgos*), and "Savior." The former term occurs also in 3:15. Christ has opened the door of salvation, making full provision for those who follow Him by faith. "Savior," as a term, is little used in the gospels (Lk 2:11; Jn 4:42), but Jesus Himself was fully aware of His saving mission (Lk 19:10).

Only after His resurrection did the awareness of His Saviourhood blossom forth into full recognition, for only then did the whole sweep of the divine purpose which centered in Him come into focus. Peter summed up what His saving work was intended to mean for Israel: "repentance" and "forgiveness of sins." These had been coupled in Peter's public preaching (2:38; 3:19). The sin which especially called for repentance was the rejection of Jesus as God's appointed Saviour.

The apostle concluded by saying, "And we are witnesses of these things." He and his companions were not expounding some new philosophy of their own devising. On the contrary, they were simply passing on to others what they knew to be true.

The Greek for "things" can also mean "words" (so used in 5:20), but here the term is employed with reference to the death and resurrection of the Lord Jesus. The apostles' witness was aided by that of the Holy Spirit, hence the boldness with which they had been able to speak (cf. Jn 15:26-27).

Verses 33-42. Just when it seemed that the apostles' boldness in addressing the Sanhedrin might cost them their lives, God brought to their aid an unexpected advocate, from within the ranks of the Council itself, who pleaded successfully for a policy of moderation.

> **5:33** But when they heard this, they were cut to the quick and were intending to slay them.
>
> **34** But a certain Pharisee named Gamaliel, a teacher of the Law, respected by all the people, stood up in the Council and gave orders to put the men outside for a short time.
>
> **35** And he said to them, "Men of Israel, take care what you propose to do with these men.
>
> **36** "For sometime ago Theudas rose up, claiming to be somebody; and a group of about four hundred men joined up with him. And he was slain; and all who followed him were dispersed and came to nothing.
>
> **37** "After this man Judas of Galilee rose up in the days of the census, and drew away *some* people after him; he too perished, and all those who followed him were scattered.
>
> **38** "And so in the present case, I say to you, stay away from these men and let them alone, for if this plan of action should be of men, it will be overthrown;
>
> **39** but if it is of God, you will not be able to overthrow them; or else you may even be found fighting against God."

40 And they took his advice; and after calling the apostles in, they flogged them and ordered them to speak no more in the name of Jesus, and *then* released them.

41 So they went on their way from the presence of the Council, rejoicing that they had been considered worthy to suffer shame for *His* name.

42 And every day, in the temple and from house to house, they kept right on teaching and preaching Jesus *as* the Christ.

5:33-39. The threat of the use of violent measures against the apostles was very real when Peter finished speaking, but a more moderate attitude was taken after hearing Gamaliel's counsel.

The Council members were enraged ("cut to the quick," literally, "sawn through") and ready to kill the apostles. This is psychologically understandable, for the high priest had alluded to the death of Jesus in such a way as to intimate that leaders of the Jews were highly sensitive to the charge that they were responsible for that death. For Peter to ignore the protest and reiterate his charge (v. 30) was more than they could bear. Their strong reaction may be taken as an indirect admission of guilt.

At this juncture the providence of God brought forward a Pharisee to quiet the rage of the Sadducees and throttle their murderous intent. (Later on, this same tension between the two parties was a means of deliverance for Paul [23:6-10].) Gamaliel, a distinguished teacher, was the man under whom Paul studied in his early days (22:3). Ordering the removal of the apostles, he launched on a very frank talk with his associates, urging caution and moderation and warning against usurping the prerogative of God Himself by passing hasty judgment on a movement which, for all they knew, might be an instrument in the hands of the Almighty.

His counsel was typically Pharisaic. The same scrupulosity which led the Pharisees to almost fanatical devotion to Levitical purity (to be sure they had done enough, they should plan to do more than enough in order to be on the safe side) caused them to be careful in the administration of justice. For instance, instead of giving forty stripes in a beating, they would settle for thirty-nine lest by miscount they should happen to give too many and so become guilty of undue severity (2 Co 11:24).

Gamaliel's thesis was that movements of a revolutionary nature, when inspired merely by human desire and effort, have a way of coming to nought. He offered two illustrations, and doubtless could have furnished more (cf. 21:38). It was a restless age, with many Messianic pretenders seeking a following. The first case was that of a certain Theudas, whose small force of four hundred men was readily dispersed when he himself lost his life. Josephus mentions a man of this name,[3] an impostor who persuaded many to take their possessions and follow him to the Jordan, evidently posing as a second Moses who would part the waters and lead them out to a place where they would be free from Roman domination. By acting quickly, the procurator Fadus intercepted the people, killed many, and took numerous prisoners. Theudas himself was executed.

Was this the same man to whom Gamaliel was referring? It is doubtful, for the regime of Fadus belonged to a period approximately a decade later than the time of Gamaliel's speech. Furthermore, to assume that Luke got his information from Josephus rather than from some source contemporary with the events of this chapter is precarious; the Jewish historian indicated that many people were involved, as well as their possessions, whereas Luke stated that a relatively small number were with Theudas. Also, Luke was precise in saying that this man was prior to Judas, whom he cited as Gamaliel's second illustration. It is hard to believe that a historian of Luke's stature would reverse the order of two events that had happened a generation removed from each other. So, even though *Theudas* was not a common name (Josephus has no other in his history), it is probable that the Theudas of Luke's account was a different person than the one named by Josephus.

The second example was not as felicitous as the first in supporting Gamaliel's thesis, for the truth of the matter is that, whereas Judas the Galilean "perished," the Zealot movement which he had spawned was growing all the time, and in another generation would lead the nation over the precipice in a disastrous war with Rome. The revolt of Judas stemmed from his opposition to the "census," which gave the Romans information on the wealth of their subjects and led to the imposition of burdensome taxes. To hold, as some scholars do, that Luke was merely putting words in the mouth of Gamaliel, since he had no way of knowing what the rabbin actually said, runs into a snag by the very fact that when Luke wrote Acts, around thirty years after this gathering of the Council, it would have been perfectly clear to him and to everybody else that the Zealot movement had *not* come to nothing—it was growing in strength.

Despite some deficiency in his presentation, Gamaliel had a restraining effect on his peers, especially by his parting observation that in dealing harshly with the apostles they might be found "fighting against" God. This possibility was frightening to a pious Israelite. When Saul of Tarsus found that in his case it was an actuality (because of his persecuting the Church of God), he was broken and repentant (26:14; 1 Ti 1:13-15).

The fact that Gamaliel successfully resisted the policy of the Sadducees meant that the Jewish leadership was divided on the issue of persecuting the Church, for the Pharisees naturally lined up behind Gamaliel. This guaranteed a period of freedom from pressure for the growing Church until new issues were raised by the preaching of Stephen (chaps. 6-7).

5:40-42. The Council did not see fit to follow Gamaliel's advice com-

pletely, for he counseled that they let the apostles alone. But t[...]
off their anger and frustration toward God's servants by a be[...]
stern warning to stop their public speaking in the name of [...]
apostles went forth nursing their bruises but rejoicing at the privilege of
suffering for the name of Christ. This was in line with the teaching of the
Lord Jesus (Mt 5:11-12), and it must have been experienced over and over
in the days of the early Church (e.g., Ac 16:23-25; cf. 1 Pe 4:12-16).

Unconcerned about what might happen to them for disobeying the
orders of the Sanhedrin, the apostles went right back to their work of
"teaching and preaching," making known Jesus as the Christ (cf. Ac
2:36). They had already received a demonstration of God's protection,
and they realized that their support from the people would make it difficult for the Sanhedrin to carry out any official persecution on a major scale.

The construction of the closing verse of the chapter should be noted. In
all probability the order of the words "teaching" and "preaching" is reversed from the normal order (teaching being more appropriate for the
ministry "from house to house" and preaching for the proclamation "in the
temple" (cf. 2:46). The gatherings in the Temple would naturally have
been addressed by the apostles, with believers supporting by their presence
and personal work among the listeners as opportunity afforded. The meetings at home set the pattern found both in Acts and in the epistles, namely,
the church in the house. Here Christian fellowship found expression, and
instruction in the things of God was carried forward on a more or less
methodical basis (cf. 2:42). Doubtless such gatherings were open to interested neighbors (cf. 1 Co 14:23) and became an instrument for evangelism. The children of believers also would be welcome.

3. CARE OF THE NEEDY—6:1-7

In this picture of the church at Jerusalem there is described an important
administrative development which averted a breach in the unity of the
Lord's people and actually contributed to the further growth of the Christian community.

> **6:1** Now at this time while the disciples were increasing *in number*,
> a complaint arose on the part of the Hellenistic *Jews* against the *native*
> Hebrews, because their widows were being overlooked in the daily serving
> *of food.*
>
> **2** And the twelve summoned the congregation of the disciples and
> said, "It is not desirable for us to neglect the word of God in order to
> serve tables.
>
> **3** "But select from among you, brethren, seven men of good reputa-
> tion, full of the Spirit and of wisdom, whom we may put in charge of this
> task.

4 "But we will devote ourselves to prayer, and to the ministry of the word."

5 And the statement found approval with the whole congregation; and they chose Stephen, a man full of faith and of the Holy Spirit, and Philip, Prochorus, Nicanor, Timon, Parmenas and Nicolas, a proselyte from Antioch.

6 And these they brought before the apostles; and after praying, they laid their hands on them.

7 And the word of God kept on spreading; and the number of the disciples continued to increase greatly in Jerusalem, and a great many of the priests were becoming obedient to the faith.

6:1. "At this time" establishes only a loose connection with the foregoing events. Luke provided no precise time notices in this portion of his narrative, but the interval between Pentecost and this episode was probably quite brief.

The increase in the number of disciples posed a problem, since some were not self-supporting. Particularly acute was the need of the "widows." Historically, Israel had to be reminded from time to time of its obligation to care for these, along with orphans (Deu 14:29; 24:19; 26:12; Is 1:17; Zec 7:10). It was a blemish on the record of some Pharisees that they took advantage of them and dispossessed them (Lk 20:47). The early Church's concern for this group was confirmed by James, who included in his definition of true religion the care of widows and orphans (Ja 1:27). In time, within the church an order of widows developed, consisting of the more elderly, who were cared for by the congregation and in turn performed various services according to their abilites (1 Ti 5:3-10).

Theoretically, Christian widows might have been eligible for help by the Jewish authorities, but this was probably increasingly difficult to receive, as the gulf between Christian and non-Christian Jews widened. Furthermore, the church itself would not encourage this practice, for failure to care for its own members would place a stigma on this new movement in Israel.

A "daily serving" is mentioned, undoubtedly of food, in view of the mention of tables (v. 2). Probably the apostles took the funds brought to them (4:35) and in person or through helpers bought the provisions that were distributed. With the increase in numbers the arrangement became steadily more unwieldy, with the result that some of the widows, especially those of the Hellenists, "were being overlooked." There is nothing to suggest that the neglect was intentional. As noted under 2:42, this sharing was a practical application of the spiritual fellowship of the church, so that any breakdown of the material aspect would be likely to have unfortunate effects on spiritual rapport. So the apostles were doubly concerned.

How were the "Hellenistic Jews" (simply "Hellenists" in the original) and the "Hebrews" to be distinguished? Luke gives no explanation. The most obvious distinction lies in the terms themselves—a difference in language. The one group used Greek, the other Hebrew or Aramaic. Both groups were Israelites rather than Gentiles. If the Hellenists were Gentiles, they must have been proselytes to the Jewish faith before becoming believers in Jesus (cf. v. 5). Otherwise there would have been added antagonism from the synagogue toward the Nazarenes, of which Luke says nothing. Furthermore, the difficulty felt by many in the Jerusalem church over admitting Gentiles without circumcision (11:1-18; 15:5) would be strange indeed if that congregation had already received a company of Gentiles into its fellowship.

For understanding the status of the Hellenists it is well to go back to Pentecost. Many of those who listened to Peter and became believers had come to Jerusalem from areas of the Dispersion where Greek was spoken. These Jews had their own synagogue arrangements (6:9). It would be wholly natural for such people, after becoming disciples, to maintain a special relationship with one another within the unity of the whole church. "They most probably established their own house-congregations in which they made use of the Greek language, the LXX, and the traditions related to it as they once did in the Diaspora synagogue."[4]

The notion that the "Hebrews" were of Samaritan stock and were a minority group in the church as well as the Hellenists is improbable, for in that case the assumption would have to be made that the Hebrews were in charge of the distribution, for the murmuring was against them, whereas actually the operation was carried on under the direction of the twelve.

Language was not the only distinguishing factor of the two groups, for if Stephen was truly representative of the Hellenists' viewpoint, they had reservations about the Temple which were not shared by the Hebrew brethren. As a result they became the target of a violent persecution following Stephen's death. But we need not conclude that the Hellenists were influenced by Qumran and its estrangement from the Temple.[5]

6:2-4. To meet the crisis concerning the widows, the apostles "summoned the congregation." It was an indication of the spiritual soundness of the church that the situation was faced publicly and immediately with a view to removing the grievance. The apostles suggested that the smoother operation of the current system would require them to give more time and attention to it, which would mean that they could not properly fulfill their primary task of preaching and teaching "the word of God." This was a sacrifice they were not prepared to make; it would mean putting secondary things first. As appointees of the Head of the Church, they took the initiative in directing the congregation to a solution, namely, to

105

select "seven men" to supervise the distribution. Congregational participation was honored within the framework of apostolic administration.

It was expedient to remind the people that certain qualifications ought
to be kept in mind in selecting those who were to serve. These were three
in number: ethical, having a good testimony because of sterling character
and conduct; spiritual, full of the Spirit; and practical, possessing the wisdom to manage this operation.

The apostles were relieved at the prospect that they could henceforth
devote themselves "to prayer, and to the ministry of the word." For them,
the trouble in the church was a blessing in disguise. By including prayer,
they hinted that this was a time-consuming exercise and one which was
indispensable to effective ministry.

It is of some interest that the same word for "ministry" (*diakonia*) is
applied both to the care of physical needs (v. 1) and to the communication
of God's truth (v. 4). Both elements had an important place in the ministry of Jesus. A church dedicated to the continuation of that ministry
(1:1) could not afford to slight either aspect.

6:5-6. In listing the seven, Luke anticipated Stephen's prominence in
the continuing narrative by naming him first and adding the description,
"full of faith and of the Holy Spirit" (cf. 6:10; 7:55). He had the supernatural equipment for miraculous works and for dynamic preaching; again
Luke seemed to be anticipating Stephen's service beyond his duties as
one of the Seven.

Philip is named next, and he too figured in Gospel outreach as the one
who brought the message to Samaria (8:5). Next to nothing is known of
the other men. Nicolas was thought by some of the early Fathers to have
been the founder of the Nicolaitans (Rev 2:6, 15), but the supposition is
tenuous. By noting that he was a proselyte of Antioch, Luke, with an eye
on later missionary developments, may have been hinting at the prominence to be achieved by Antioch and the part of the Hellenists in bringing
the Gospel to that area (11:19-20). There may also be a hint that Luke
himself belonged to Antioch (see comment on 11:28).

It should be observed that all of the seven bore Greek names. While
this does not prove all were Hellenists, members of the complaining group
(for the apostles Andrew and Philip had Greek names and were Hebraists),
yet this conclusion is quite possible. If this was the case, the Hebrew segment showed real grace in selecting men to serve who belonged to the
aggrieved minority. Luke did not call them deacons, a term which came
into use at a somewhat later time (Phil 1:1; 1 Ti 3:8-13).

The meaning of the second "they" in verse 6 is debatable. It could refer
to the congregation or to the apostles. If the former, there is no change of
subject, which means that the people chose the men, prayed, and set them

apart by the laying on of their hands, thus making them their representatives. But the decisive factor appears to be the word of the apostles to the effect that they themselves would set the appointees over this task.[6] If the men chosen were set apart by the apostles, the laying on of hands would signify that the seven would be doing their work under the authority of the apostles. Implied also is the pledge of the apostles to stand behind the appointees and support them in every possible way (cf. 13:3). Clearly the purpose of the rite in this instance was not the communication of the Holy Spirit (8:17), for the possession of the Spirit in fullness was a qualification for the selection of the seven (6:3) and is explicitly noted in the case of Stephen (v. 5).

Nothing more is reported about the seven as a group. Presumably their task was taken over by the elders (11:30) after the Hellenists were driven out in the coming persecution (8:1).

6:7. This summary statement seems intended to suggest that the adjustment of the problem of the widows brought renewed blessing to the believing community. "The word of God kept on spreading" is a shorthand way of saying that the influence of the Gospel was expanding (cf. 12:24; 19:20). As a result, the number of disciples in Jerusalem was greatly augmented. The three thousand converts (2:41) had increased to five thousand men (4:4). Luke's further statements (5:14; 6:1, 7) are not specific, but in a general way indicate further growth.

J. Jeremias has carefully estimated the population of Jerusalem at this period between 25,000 and 30,000, not counting some 18,000 priests and Levites.[7] At festival times the number of people in and around the city was greatly increased. It is probable that believers in Jesus represented about one-fifth of the population of the city at the time of Stephen, only to be diminished by persecution shortly after. This shrinkage was balanced by increase in other places (9:31).

The "priests" who were identifying with the faith at this time were not of the Sadducean aristocracy (we have no record of a Sadducee becoming a believer) but were ordinary priests of a truly pious spirit, such as the father of John the Baptist (Lk 1:6). Doubtless they had heard Peter and others bearing witness in the Temple courts and were greatly impressed. They must have known of the attempts of the Sanhedrin to stop the apostolic testimony and were aware of their ineffectiveness. They saw the hand of God at work in their midst. Since believers were permitted to use the Temple, there is no reason to think that these converted priests were excluded from the priesthood. However, if Luke's notice of them is intended to suggest that they were influenced by Stephen, who is mentioned next, these priests would likely have been prepared to give up their priestly service voluntarily.

107

4. PERSECUTION OF STEPHEN—6:8—7:60

THE SUMMARY ACCOUNT of Stephen's public ministry of preaching and debating reveals a man peculiarly gifted and empowered. His very success prompted his opponents to instigate false charges against him supported by false witnesses. Even in the presence of the Council Stephen maintained his fearless, searching exposure of the unbelief of Judaism, resulting in his martyrdom.

· *Verses 8-15.* The background for Stephen's speech before the Council is presented by Luke in terms of both miracle and the spoken word. In the various factors involved—the dual ministry, the inability of his adversaries to match him in debate, the resort to false witnesses, the arrest and appearance before the Sanhedrin—one notices a striking parallel to the experience of our Lord.

6:8 And Stephen, full of grace and power, was performing great wonders and signs among the people.

9 But some men from what was called the Synagogue of the Freedmen, *including* both Cyrenians and Alexandrians, and some from Cilicia and Asia, rose up and argued with Stephen.

10 And *yet* they were unable to cope with the wisdom and the Spirit with which he was speaking.

11 Then they secretly induced men to say, "We have heard him speak blasphemous words against Moses and *against* God."

12 And they stirred up the people, the elders and the scribes, and they came upon him and dragged him away, and brought him before the Council.

13 And they put forward false witnesses who said, "This man incessantly speaks against this holy place, and the Law;

14 for we have heard him say that this Nazarene, Jesus, will destroy this place and alter the customs which Moses handed down to us."

15 And fixing their gaze on him, all who were in the Council saw his face like the face of an angel.

6:8-10. In addition to his service on behalf of the needy, about which nothing specific is said, Stephen went on to engage in a dual ministry of miracle working and witnessing. Many today have reversed the pattern by diminishing their emphasis on Gospel testimony in favor of social service.

It would be totally wrong to hold that the seven were emerging as a rival group to the apostles and that miracles were counted on as substantiating their right to leadership on a par with the men chosen by the Lord in the days of His flesh. There is no evidence of any such tension (cf. 8:14). "Grace and power" are coupled here as in the ministry of the apostles (4:33).

The general description of Stephen resembles that of Jesus in Luke 24:19. His faith (v. 5) enabled him to lay hold of divine grace, which in turn released the power of God in the performance of mighty works. This brought him to the attention of Hellenists who were not believers but were passionately devoted to Judaism.

Nothing precise is indicated as to the substance of the debates which followed in the synagogue. Whereas the Temple was devoted to worship (though teaching could be carried on in its courts) the synagogue was dedicated to instruction, and this often led to discussion. Some uncertainty attaches to Luke's reference to the synagogue in this instance. Did he mean that all the groups named shared one building, or that each of the five groups had its own, or that the number of buildings lay somewhere between these extremes?

The first option is the most probable. Jeremias identifies this synagogue with one discovered on Ophel, the southern portion of the Temple mount, early in this century.[1] He notes that a guesthouse and baths were attached. Jews of the Dispersion gathered here, their diverse geographical origins proving no hindrance to the cultivation of their common interests. On the other hand, a case can be made for two synagogues, based on a repetition of "some" before mention of Cilicia and Asia, two areas that belong to Asia Minor and are geographically remote from the North African districts. The Freedmen have often been identified as descendants of the Jews who were taken to Rome by Pompey as captives of war about 60 B.C., but Sherwin-White doubts that after such a long interval their descendants would be thus classified.[2]

Especially interesting is the mention of those Hellenists who came from Cilicia. There is a possibility that Saul of Tarsus (21:39) may have been one of those who confronted Stephen and, like his fellows, found himself unable to withstand the "wisdom" of this Spirit-filled man. Stephen's capability fit in remarkably with a prediction of Jesus regarding His persecuted followers, "It will lead to an opportunity for your testimony. So make up your minds not to prepare beforehand to defend yourselves; for I will give you utterance and wisdom which none of your opponents will be able to resist or refute" (Lk 21:13-15; cf. Mt 10:19-20). The spiritual gifts exercised by Stephen agree closely with those enumerated in 1 Corinthians 12:8-9.

6:11-15. Defeated in argument, the unbelieving Hellenists prevailed on certain individuals to circulate reports that they had heard Stephen "speak blasphemous words against Moses and against God." The language is vague, but the charges were sufficiently inflammatory to excite "the people" as well as their leaders, both "the elders and the scribes."

The people have already been mentioned as those among whom Stephen had been doing mighty works (v. 8). Up to this time the population of the city, generally speaking, had been favorable to the followers of Jesus, and this had deterred the authorities from taking harsh measures against those who were preaching Christ publicly. But now the ominous rumor that Stephen was disloyal to what Jews held most dear was bringing a swift reversal of popular sentiment.

The Hellenists took note of this shift and turned it to their advantage by making bold to seize Stephen and bring him before the Council. Their "false witnesses" were on hand to state their allegations. Now the charges became more specific. The claim that Stephen had spoken against God became the assertion that he had been speaking against "this holy place," namely, the Temple. The charge of blasphemy against Moses was now formulated as speaking against "the Law." Finally the accusations became still more explicit. The witnesses were prepared to assert that they had heard Stephen make the claim that Jesus of Nazareth would destroy the Temple.

Here one detects an echo of the Master's trial, when other false witnesses asserted that they had heard Him say, "I will destroy this temple made with hands, and in three days I will build another made without hands" (Mk 14:58). This was a distortion of what Jesus had declared on this subject (Jn 2:19). Never had He predicted that He would destroy the Temple in Jerusalem, though He had predicted its destruction (Mk 13:2), which came to pass in the war with Rome. Likely Stephen had declared the truth of the new creation based on the resurrection of the Lord Jesus. In the new order the physical Temple had no function to fulfill (Jn 4:21).

The other great bulwark of Judaism, the Mosaic Law, was likewise affected by the work of Jesus Christ. Stephen seems to have perceived what Paul later emphatically declared, that no one could be justified by the Law. Though Jesus lived under the Law and denied that He had come to destroy it, He saw that His own mission would fulfill the Law (Mt 5:17-18), and He Himself would become the law of His people, living and not static. Any change in the "customs" (the totality of the Mosaic legislation) which Moses had delivered, the prophets had applied, and tradition had amplified, was regarded as the rankest heresy by those who had not learned to look beyond Moses to Christ.

When the false witnesses had finished their tirade, all eyes gravitated to

Stephen to see what his reaction would be. What they saw was a man with face aglow, for the false testimony had brought to Stephen the realization that he was following in the succession of his Lord, being tried before the same tribunal, his words twisted as were those of Jesus, and with the multitude crying out for his blood. The Spirit of glory was indeed resting on him, betokening the presence of God. Criticism and opposition could not destroy his composure any more than it did Jesus'. His face was radiant, like that of an angel (cf. Judg 13:6; Lk 9:26).

Chapter 7, verses 1-8. Some introductory observations should be made before examining Stephen's address to the Council, which fills most of this chapter. For one thing, this is the longest of the speeches given in Acts, which probably indicates that Luke attached considerable importance to its content and to the whole situation in which Stephen was involved. The address differs from those which have been included so far, in that Christ is not prominent, being introduced only at the end (v. 52) and then not by name (cf. a somewhat similar situation in chap. 17). Furthermore, His resurrection, which had been the burden of Peter's sermons, is not mentioned at all.

Luke's interest in Stephen was probably due to his grasp of the strategic fact that this man emerged just as the Church was being called on to undertake a new stage of its mission to the world, the Samaritan advance, which was an intermediate step between Jewish and Gentile Christianity. Stephen was hardly removed from the scene by death when Philip carried the Gospel to Samaria (8:1-5). The address preserved for us contains certain evidences of Samaritan influence, particularly with reference to the Temple, making probable the conclusion that Stephen was fully aware that if the young Church did not assume a different stance toward the Temple than that which current Judaism had, it could not hope to succeed in winning the Samaritans to Christ.[3]

It should be noted that Stephen did not attempt to meet the charges raised against him by direct and detailed refutation. In fact, he did not mount a defense in the technical sense, for he was less interested in clearing himself than in declaring the truth so as to reach the consciences of his hearers. He had almost nothing to say about the Law; and with respect to the Temple, to which he devoted more attention, he did not discuss the allegation stated by the false witnesses (6:14).

His methodology was to sketch the history of his people from Abraham down to the days of David and Solomon, noting that divine revelation was not restricted to the land of Israel (it came in Mesopotamia, Egypt, and the wilderness) or to the Temple. Interwoven with these motifs was the failure of Israel to respond to God in faith and obedience (somewhat after the pattern of Ps 78). The address came to a sudden climax in the assertion that this rebelliousness had manifested itself most fatally in the rejection of God's supreme disclosure in the righteous One. Yet the way had been prepared for this final accusation by the allusions to the rejection of Joseph by his brothers (v. 9) and of Moses by Israel (vv. 23-29, 39).

The first eight verses are devoted to Abraham. Stephen launched into this discourse immediately after the opening question from the high priest, who presumably was Caiaphas, the man who had presided over the Sanhedrin's trial of Jesus. The chief items stressed were that God's dealings with Abraham had started not in Canaan but in Mesopotamia, and that even in Canaan he had lived as a pilgrim, yet enjoyed a covenant relationship with the Almighty.

> 7:1 And the high priest said, "Are these things so?"
>
> 2 And he said, "Hear me, brethren and fathers! The God of glory appeared to our father Abraham when he was in Mesopotamia, before he lived in Haran,
>
> 3 AND SAID TO HIM, 'DEPART FROM YOUR COUNTRY AND YOUR RELATIVES, AND COME INTO THE LAND THAT I WILL SHOW YOU.'
>
> 4 "Then he departed from the land of the Chaldeans, and settled in Haran. And from there, after his father died, God removed him into this country in which you are now living.
>
> 5 "And He gave him no inheritance in it, not even a foot of ground; and *yet*, even when he had no child, He promised that HE WOULD GIVE IT TO HIM AS A POSSESSION, AND TO HIS OFFSPRING AFTER HIM.
>
> 6 "But God spoke to this effect, that HIS OFFSPRING WOULD BE ALIENS IN A FOREIGN LAND, AND THAT THEY WOULD BE ENSLAVED AND MISTREATED FOR FOUR HUNDRED YEARS.
>
> 7 "'AND WHATEVER NATION TO WHICH THEY SHALL BE IN BONDAGE I MYSELF WILL JUDGE,' said God, 'AND AFTER THAT THEY WILL COME OUT AND SERVE ME IN THIS PLACE.'
>
> 8 "And He gave him the covenant of circumcision; and so *Abraham* became the father of Isaac, and circumcised him on the eighth day; and Isaac *became the father of* Jacob, and Jacob *of* the twelve patriarchs.

7:2. "Brethren and fathers!" was the same form of address used by Paul in speaking to the throng in the Temple (22:1). Stephen shared the legacy of Israel's history with his audience. He was no Samaritan, as some have thought.[4] His opening thrust was the reminder that God had begun His dealings with the father of the Hebrew people when he had lived in a foreign land, thus making the point that the divine presence was not restricted to the land of Israel.

A reader of Genesis 12 would naturally assume that God's command to depart came to Abram in Haran, which is mentioned at the close of the preceding chapter. In stating that the divine revelation came "before he lived in Haran," Stephen was following Jewish tradition.[5] (The translators of the KJV had this in mind when they used *had said* rather than *said* in Genesis 12:1.) Even before touching on the place of revelation, Stephen noted the quality of it by observing that the *shekinah* which appeared on Mount Sinai and later engulfed the shrine of the tabernacle was already anticipated in God's disclosure to the patriarch Abraham, and this outside the land, apart from the tabernacle, long before the Law was given.

7:3-5. Following the will of God may involve great sacrifices. In this case it meant separation from land and kindred. The life of faith is a pilgrim life (cf. Heb 11:13-16). Close at hand was the moment when believers in Jerusalem would be leaving land and kindred because of the Gospel (Ac 8:1; 11:19).

Stephen did not attempt to account for the period of residence in Haran before the journey to Canaan was resumed. The mention of the death of Abram's father, Terah, at this point has led some interpreters to conclude that Terah had been opposed to going any farther than Haran, and his son had bided his time until the father died. Some of his relatives remained in Haran (Gen 24).

Abram's adopted country is curiously described as "this country in which you are now living." Why did Stephen say "you" rather than *we*? This is too slender a basis on which to claim that by dissociating himself from his hearers Stephen was admitting he was not a Jew. Probably all that was intended was a pointed reminder to his audience that if they wished to boast about being Abraham's descendants, they should be grateful for their forefather's faith and not settle down too securely in their land, as though it were their fixed inheritance. Special emphasis was put on the fact that Abraham was not permitted to own even "a foot of ground," though he walked up and down in it. Stephen was speaking of the early years of nomadic wandering rather than of the more settled period when Abraham purchased a burying place from the Hittites (Gen 23). Passing notice was taken of the twofold promise to the patriarch regarding the land and offspring. His posterity would inherit the land in which he lived as a pilgrim. Abraham had had to believe God for both provisions, for in those early years he was without a son.

7:6-8. Prior to the enjoyment of the land as their home, Abraham's descendants would have to be tested in the furnace of affliction "in a foreign land." This experience was often referred to by Moses and the prophets, along with the deliverance wrought by God, as the background for the emergence of Israel as a nation and as the chosen people. Even so, some preferred Egypt with its bondage to the prospect of Canaan with the difficulties of arrival and acquisition (vv. 39-40). "Four hundred years," being a round number, agrees with the time notice in Genesis 15:13. More precise is the figure of four hundred and thirty years given in Exodus 12:40.

Paul used the latter reckoning (Gal 3:17) but spreads out the interval to make it commence with God's promise of offspring to Abraham.

In quoting from Genesis 15 the promise of God to restore Abraham's posterity to their "place" in Canaan, Stephen added an item apparently taken from Exodus 3:12 (it is not in Genesis 15), that there Israel would "serve" God.

"The covenant of circumcision" was given to Abraham (Gen 17), the man of faith (note how Paul handled this in Ro 4:11), a point which needed emphasizing because the Jews had come to associate circumcision more with Moses and the Law than with Abraham (Jn 7:22-23).

Verses 9-16. Having mentioned "the twelve patriarchs," Stephen now singled out one of these sons of Jacob for detailed comment, and this for several reasons. As with Abraham, so with Joseph, God manifested His presence outside the land of Canaan. The bad treatment he received from his brothers served to foreshadow the rejection of the Lord Jesus by His own, even as his forgiveness of his brothers was a foretaste of the readiness of the Saviour to forgive the imposition of death on the cross (Lk 23:34).

> **7:9** "And the patriarchs BECAME JEALOUS OF JOSEPH AND SOLD HIM INTO EGYPT. And *yet* God WAS WITH HIM,
>
> **10** and rescued him from all his afflictions, and GRANTED HIM FAVOR and wisdom IN THE SIGHT OF PHARAOH, KING OF EGYPT; AND HE MADE HIM GOVERNOR OVER EGYPT AND ALL HIS HOUSEHOLD.
>
> **11** "Now A FAMINE CAME OVER ALL EGYPT AND CANAAN, and great affliction *with it;* and our fathers could find no food.
>
> **12** "But WHEN JACOB HEARD THAT THERE WAS GRAIN IN EGYPT, he sent our fathers *there* the first time.
>
> **13** "And on the second *visit* Joseph made himself known to his brothers, and Joseph's family was disclosed to Pharaoh.
>
> **14** "And Joseph sent *word* and invited Jacob his father and all his relatives to come to him, seventy-five persons *in all.*
>
> **15** "And Jacob WENT DOWN TO EGYPT AND *there* PASSED AWAY, he and our fathers.
>
> **16** "And *from there* they were removed to Shechem, and laid in the tomb which Abraham had purchased for a sum of money from the sons of Hamor in Shechem.

7:9-10. Joseph's early days at home are passed by with only a brief notice. Because his brothers were "jealous" of him (Gen 37:11), they sold him into Egypt. The same chapter emphasizes that the jealousy deepened into hatred. But "God was with him." This was evident in Joseph's prospering as Potiphar's right-hand man and in his successful resistance of temptation in the household of his master. His "afflictions" suffered in prison (cf. Ps 105:18) were not an indication that God had deserted him, for they befell him because of his righteous stand and were followed by a display of God's favor when He rescued His servant from these distresses and gave him "favor and wisdom" in the eyes of Pharaoh. The wisdom enabled him to interpret the sovereign's dreams and later to set forth a plan for sustaining life during the seven years of famine that he predicted. This brought him into acceptance and led to his exaltation next to Pharaoh (Gen 41:39-40).

7:11-13. The famine which Joseph had predicted came in due course and was felt not only in Egypt but in Canaan. It proved to be a providential means of bringing Joseph's brethren to Egypt in search of grain and thereby into his presence. On their "second visit" Joseph made himself known to them in a highly emotional scene (Gen 45:1-4). This reconciliation was followed by a favorable reaction on the part of Pharaoh, paving the way for the settlement of the whole clan in Egypt.

7:14-16. In his latter years in Egypt Joseph was surrounded by all his kindred whom he had sheltered and cared for, "seventy-five persons." Stephen was using the LXX text, as he did throughout and as a Hellenist would be expected to do. The LXX differs at this point (Gen 46:27) from the Hebrew, which reads "seventy." The LXX figure was apparently calculated by including Joseph's posterity (cf. Gen 50:23).

In what follows, Stephen was concerned with the death of the patriarchs. Curiously, he made Shechem the burial place, although it was well-known that Jacob was buried with Abraham at Machpelah near Hebron (see the fairly lengthy account in Gen 50:4-13). Further, it was Jacob, not Abraham, who purchased land from the sons of Hamor in Shechem (Gen 33:19). Possibly, in the rapidity of his summary of the patriarchs' demise, Stephen ran together two events which were separated in time and place—the burial of Jacob in the Hebron area, and that of Joseph at Shechem. That no alteration was made by Luke or anyone else to bring the statements into conformity with Genesis speaks well for the accuracy with which the speech of Stephen was transmitted and later recorded by Luke. Bearing in mind that the section before us concerns Joseph primarily, it is natural to suppose that his burial, which occurred at Shechem, was chiefly in the mind of the speaker.

Stephen's mention of Shechem was probably not casual but deliberate. This was the great center of Samaritan life, and nearby stood the Samaritan temple on Mount Gerizim, a rival of the Temple at Jerusalem, which was destroyed by the Hasmonean John Hyrcanus approximately a century and a half before Stephen's time. This event deepened the hostility which had existed since the days of the restoration from Babylonian captivity, when the Samaritans were refused any participation in the rebuilding of the Temple at Jerusalem, and soon thereafter built their own. Added to

115

this was the reproach presented by the mixed origin of the Samaritans to a Jewish generation sensitive to this matter (Ezra 9:10).

The rift had existed in Jesus' day (Lk 9:52-53; Jn 4:9, 20), and He had done much to heal it by mingling with Samaritans and ministering to their needs (Lk 17:15-16), and by including a Samaritan in His teaching (Lk 10:29-37). It seems that He paid a price for this (Jn 8:48).

Luke himself doubtless had an interest in these neglected people. He had already reported the inclusion of Samaria in Jesus' commission (Ac 1:8) and now, with the evangelization of Samaria near at hand, he was careful to include this note about Shechem in Stephen's speech. A rigid Jew might want to forget the patriarchal contacts with Shechem, but Stephen would not permit that. To mention Shechem was almost the equivalent of calling attention to Samaria.

Verses 17-22. Here begins the great central section of the address, the portion which is concerned with Moses (vv. 17-43). The first three verses are transitional, and the remainder of the paragraph deals with his birth and early years.

> **7:17** "But as the time of the promise was approaching which God had assured to Abraham, the people increased and multiplied in Egypt,
>
> **18** until THERE AROSE ANOTHER KING OVER EGYPT WHO KNEW NOTHING ABOUT JOSEPH.
>
> **19** "It was he who took shrewd advantage of our race, and mistreated our fathers so that they would expose their infants and they would not survive.
>
> **20** "And it was at this time that Moses was born; and he was lovely in the sight of God; and he was nurtured three months in his father's home.
>
> **21** "And after he had been exposed, Pharaoh's daughter took him away, and nurtured him as her own son.
>
> **22** "And Moses was educated in all the learning of the Egyptians, and he was a man of power in words and deeds.

7:17-19. The descendants of Abraham enjoyed a prosperous period during which their numbers increased greatly, an increase which finally troubled the Egyptians. An alien people within the land could join forces with an invader and turn on their benefactors. By playing up this fear, Egypt's king was able to make slaves of the Hebrews (Ex 1:8-11). Even so, their numbers continued to grow (Ex 1:12), so inhumanity was added to oppression by compelling the Hebrews to "expose their infants" (confined to the male children, according to Exodus 1:15-16).

Infanticide was a common method of limiting population growth even at the beginning of the Christian era.[6] Probably the memory of this enforced limitation during the days in Egypt helped to create a distinct hatred for this practice among the Israelites, and this, together with the biblical teaching on the sacredness of human life, caused the astounding growth of the nation from what some estimate to have been a few hundred thousand at the time of the Babylonian captivity[7] to perhaps some seven million in and out of Palestine in the days of the early Church. The one man Abraham ("father of a multitude")had indeed become a host.

7:20-22. What an unfavorable time in which to be born! Yet such was God's plan for Moses. The child was "lovely," which made his abandonment all the more painful for the loving parents, though they did it in faith (Heb 11:23). This word "lovely" merits attention. Its original meaning was "pertaining to the city," and since the city was, at least ideally, a place of beauty where man's skill in design and craftsmanship could be displayed to best advantage, the term took on this additional meaning. In somewhat the same way, *urban* provided the foundation for *urbane,* the former relating to the environment and the latter emphasizing the personal qualities suitable to such an environment.

Whereas Hebrews 11:23 accents parental feeling for the babe, Stephen's address had in view the divine estimation—"lovely" before God. This knowledge of the divine attitude derives from what happened when the child became a man who had an important niche in God's plan. The sparing of the little life was in keeping with His purpose.

Not only did Pharaoh's daughter save the infant, she adopted him. Her identity remains obscure. Josephus called her Thermuthis, but other ancient writers gave different names. The account of Josephus runs as follows:

> Such was the child whom Thermuthis adopted as her son, being blessed with no offspring of her own. Now one day she brought Moses to her father and showed him to him, and told him how she had been mindful for the succession, were it God's will to grant her no child of her own, by bringing up a boy of divine beauty and generous spirit, and by what a miracle she had received him of the river's bounty, 'and methought,' she said, 'to make him my child and heir to thy kingdom.' With these words she laid the babe in her father's arms; and he took and clasped him affectionately to his breast and, to please his daughter, placed his diadem upon his head. But Moses tore it off and flung it to the ground, in mere childishness, and trampled it under foot; and this was taken as an omen of evil import to the kingdom.[8]

No figure in the history of Israel has been given the attention bestowed on Moses. The seven-volume work by Louis Ginzberg, *The Legends of the Jews,* supplies an abundance of legendary material for various phases of his life. Due to his place in the royal family, Moses as a lad was provided with the best education Egypt could offer. His curriculum was "all the learning of the Egyptians." Exodus omits this phase of Moses' preparation, but Jewish tradition magnified it. Philo declared that teachers were summoned from far and near, including Greece and Assyria.[9] In much the same way as the apocryphal gospels make the boy Jesus uniquely precocious, Philo pictured Moses as propounding problems which his teachers could not readily solve.

The description of him as "a man of power in words and deeds" carries us into Moses' young manhood and may reflect Jewish tradition. His own self-estimate was somewhat different after his initial failure and flight from Egypt, compounded by isolation in Midian (Ex 4:10). Stephen's description bears a marked resemblance to what is said of Jesus in Luke 24:19.

Verses 23-29. Here we are taken from Moses' youth to his mature years. Stephen divided the life into three segments of forty years each, so these are the middle years of Moses. It was in this period that he made an abortive attempt to identify with his people and become their deliverer. Due to his rashness he ended up a lonely figure in Midian.

7:23 "But when he was approaching the age of forty, it entered his mind to visit his brethren, the sons of Israel.

24 "And when he saw one *of them* being treated unjustly, he defended him and took vengeance for the oppressed by striking down the Egyptian.

25 "And he supposed that his brethren understood that God was granting them deliverance through him; but they did not understand.

26 "And on the following day he appeared to them as they were fighting together, and he tried to reconcile them in peace, saying, 'Men, you are brethren, why do you injure one another?'

27 "BUT THE ONE WHO WAS INJURING HIS NEIGHBOR pushed him away, saying, 'WHO MADE YOU A RULER AND JUDGE OVER US?

28 'YOU DO NOT MEAN TO KILL ME AS YOU KILLED THE EGYPTIAN YESTERDAY, DO YOU?'

29 "AND AT THIS REMARK MOSES FLED, AND BECAME AN ALIEN IN THE LAND OF MIDIAN, where he became the father of two sons.

7:23-29. "It entered his mind to visit his brethren" is put in stronger language in the parallel passage in Hebrews 11:24-25, where it is recorded that Moses had come to a decision to cast his lot with Israel, though they were slaves. This meant renunciation of his claim to the throne and the whole prospect of a comfortable life in Egypt. He was prepared to suffer with his people. As the saying goes, "Blood is thicker than water."

Seizing an opportunity to intervene on behalf of a Hebrew who was being mistreated by a taskmaster, he thought that this would be a kind of signal for an uprising, which he would be happy to lead. But it was an unrealistic dream, and it became a near disaster for himself when he ended up by killing the Egyptian. He had not learned to match bravery with self-control. God was unwilling to entrust the leadership of His people to one who was not yet fit to lead. The evidence for his unfitness lies in the fact that he was not penitent over the murder he had committed but was back the next day trying to persuade the Hebrews that he was their captain by posing as intermediary between two of their number who were quarreling.

The rebuff he received, plus the awareness that the killing was now public knowledge, determined his next step. He became an exile, an "alien" in the land of Midian, unwanted, it seems, by Egyptians and Hebrews alike. But God still had plans for his life. Meanwhile he married in the land of Midian and had two sons, Gershom and Eliezer, who were numbered among the Levites (1 Ch 23:14-15).

Verses 30-34. These verses constitute an account of God's revelation to Moses at the burning bush.

> **7:30** "And after forty years had passed, AN ANGEL APPEARED TO HIM IN THE WILDERNESS OF MOUNT Sinai, IN THE FLAME OF A BURNING THORN BUSH.
>
> **31** "And when Moses saw it, he *began* to marvel at the sight; and as he approached to look *more* closely, there came the voice of the Lord:
>
> **32** 'I AM THE GOD OF YOUR FATHERS, THE GOD OF ABRAHAM AND ISAAC AND JACOB.' And Moses shook *with fear* and would not venture to look.
>
> **33** "BUT THE LORD SAID TO HIM, 'TAKE OFF THE SANDALS FROM YOUR FEET, FOR THE PLACE ON WHICH YOU ARE STANDING IS HOLY GROUND.
>
> **34** 'I HAVE CERTAINLY SEEN THE OPPRESSION OF MY PEOPLE IN EGYPT, AND HAVE HEARD THEIR GROANS, AND I HAVE COME DOWN TO DELIVER THEM; COME NOW, AND I WILL SEND YOU TO EGYPT.'

7:30-34. What Moses had sought and failed to achieve on his own became his by divine appointment at the burning bush (Ex 3). Meanwhile, forty years had passed, during which time he kept the sheep of his father-in-law (Ex 3:1). Suddenly the monotony of his pastoral life was shattered by the appearance of "an angel." He became aware that he was in contact with the heavenly world. This prepared the way for "the voice of the Lord" announcing that He was the God of the fathers of Moses, hinting that the present revelation was bound up with the covenant promises made to these patriarchs.

The command to remove his shoes because he was standing on "holy ground" was significant for Stephen's purpose, because it underscored the truth that God is free to reveal Himself wherever He is pleased to do so; and this place was well outside the so-called holy land (cf. Ac 7:2). God's time had come to deliver His people from affliction (cf. Gen 15:13-16), and He proposed to make Moses His instrument in restoring them to the promised land. This servant of God, chastened by his failure and the price he had paid for it for forty years, was now almost as reluctant to lead as he had formerly been rash (Ex 4:1-17).

Verses 35-43. Two main thoughts dominate this passage. One is the success of Moses, under God, in effecting the deliverance of Israel from Egypt and transmitting to them the Law (vv. 35-38). The other is the failure of the people to respond to Moses and their disregard of the Law he brought to them, thus meriting their ultimate removal from the land which the Lord had promised to them (vv. 39-43).

7:35 "This Moses whom they disowned, saying, 'WHO MADE YOU A RULER AND A JUDGE?' is the one whom God sent *to be* both a ruler and a deliverer with the help of the angel who appeared to him in the thorn bush.

36 "This man led them out, performing wonders and signs in the land of Egypt and in the Red Sea and in the wilderness for forty years.

37 "This is the Moses who said to the sons of Israel, 'GOD SHALL RAISE UP FOR YOU A PROPHET LIKE ME FROM YOUR BRETHREN.'

38 "This is the one who was in the congregation in the wilderness together with the angel who was speaking to him on Mount Sinai, and *who was* with our fathers; and he received living oracles to pass on to you.

39 "And our fathers were unwilling to be obedient to him, but repudiated him and in their hearts turned back to Egypt,

40 SAYING TO AARON, 'MAKE FOR US GODS WHO WILL GO BEFORE US; FOR THIS MOSES WHO LED US OUT OF THE LAND OF EGYPT—WE DO NOT KNOW WHAT HAPPENED TO HIM'.

41 "And at that time they made a calf and brought a sacrifice to the idols, and were rejoicing in the works of their hands.

42 "But God turned away and delivered them up to serve the host of heaven; as it is written in the book of the prophets, 'IT WAS NOT TO ME THAT YOU OFFERED VICTIMS AND SACRIFICES FORTY YEARS IN THE WILDERNESS, WAS IT, O HOUSE OF ISRAEL?

43 'YOU ALSO TOOK ALONG THE TABERNACLE OF MOLOCH AND THE STAR OF THE GOD ROMPHA, THE IMAGES WHICH YOU MADE TO WORSHIP THEM. I ALSO WILL REMOVE YOU BEYOND BABYLON.'

7:35-38. The very man whom Israel had refused became God's chosen instrument. Implicit here is the contrast drawn on a higher level with reference to Jesus of Nazareth at the close of the address (v. 52). Whereas Israel would not have Moses at the beginning as "ruler" and "judge" (cf. v. 27), God not only made him such but also set him apart as the "deliverer" of Israel from bondage (v. 35). Here again, one with discernment could be expected to draw the parallel with the two separate missions of Jesus, one as Saviour, the other as Ruler and Judge. As deliverer, Moses performed his work in three places and over a span of forty years (v. 36).

Turning from what Moses had accomplished, Stephen spoke of what he had received from God—approbation for his exercise of the office of "prophet," to such an extent that the prophet who was to come (Deu

18:15, 18; cf. Jn 1:21, 25; Ac 3:22-23) was foretold as being like him, having a unique relationship to God not enjoyed by the prophets as a whole. The Lord God was accustomed to speak to Moses face to face, as a man speaks to his friend (Ex 33:11).

This promise of a Prophet to come was the only Messianic prediction acknowledged by the Samaritans (they accepted only the Pentateuch as Scripture, and even this they altered here and there to give warrant for their position and beliefs). Gradually the Samaritans came to think of the passage as teaching that Moses would reappear and act as the *Taheb* (restorer) who would restore the theocracy and the worship of God in its purity. A curious circumstance is that the Samaritan Pentateuch has the passage about the prophet to come not only in Deuteronomy 18 but also inserted into the text of Exodus 20 in connection with the giving of the Law.[10] Scharlemann concludes, "There can be little doubt, therefore, that Stephen is here echoing a Samaritan context dealing with the revelation on Mount Sinai."[11]

Continuing the description of Moses and his work, Stephen noted that he was "in the congregation in the wilderness." The rendering "church" in the KJV is unfortunate, in view of the proper reservation of the word for the New Testament body of God's people (Mt 16:18) and the fact that in no instance does the KJV render *ekklēsia* in this manner in the Old Testament, where it occurs dozens of times in the LXX as the translation of several Hebrew terms.

It is not said that Moses was *over* the congregation (cf. Heb 3:5-6), for these were the days of the theocracy. In line with this, Moses was kept in touch with God through "the angel" of the Lord, who gave assurance of the divine presence and enablement. Perhaps a hint was intended also of the participation of angels in the giving of the Law (cf. v. 53).

It is to this subject that Stephen referred next, describing the Law as "living oracles" (v. 38). By the word "oracles" the divine origin of the Law is affirmed. But how are we to understanding "living"? If the purpose was to emphasize that the Law should engage the life of God's people (Deu 32:47), the Jews—especially the Pharisees—could affirm that they had made the Law exactly that. More likely, however, is the thought that obedience to the Law was the way to life, whereas disobedience brought death (Deu 30:19). Paul was prepared to acknowledge that the Law, ideally considered, pointed to life, though in actuality it brought death (Ro 7:10). Similarly Stephen held that the Law had been divinely given and had supernatural authority. He differed from his audience regarding the tenure of the Law and its power to save.

7:39-43. Having touched on the benevolent purpose of the Law, Stephen elaborated the failure of the nation Israel under it, both at the time it was given and in later days. He returned to this theme at the very close of his speech (v. 53).

Israel's rejection of Moses and of the Law were intimately connected (vv. 39-41). When "in their hearts" the people "turned back" to Egypt they showed a hankering after the idol worship of that land, and a repudiation of Moses' leadership. They rejected his espousal of a God who could not be seen and who warned them not to approach the mount where the Law was delivered. Moses had made himself invisible to the people by his trek up into Mount Sinai, and the people concluded that he was probably gone for good. Their request of Aaron, second in command, was not that he should lead them in the place of Moses, but that he should make gods to go before them. This was blatant idolatry, and it reared its ugly head again in the days of the Divided Kingdom (1 Ki 12:28). The godly remnant, however, never ceased to look on it as a reproach (Neh 9:18; Ps 106:19-22).

The lure of idolatry lies in the fact that an object is provided which appeals to the senses and removes the seeming unreality of a purely spiritual approach to the Deity. But however high the motive, the tendency is to make the physical object the recipient of worship rather than merely a means to the end of honoring the invisible God. In the light of the express prohibition of the Law, it is clearly contrary to the divine will. The deleterious effect on character and life is only too apparent in the subsequent history of Israel. "Such as thou makest thy God, such wilt thou make thyself."[12]

Part of the gratification of idolatry is the feeling of having contributed something to the worship rather than being utterly dependent on God. This is brought out in the observation that the people "were rejoicing in the works of their hands." They had contributed the gold, and the calf had been shaped by human skill (Ex 32:2-4). That which God ordains is often described as made without hands (Mk 14:58; 2 Co 5:1; Col 2:11).

The transgression proved costly to Israel (vv. 42-43), for it increased the desire for false worship, on account of which God allowed the captivity many years later. He "delivered them up" to forms of worship they preferred. This is judicial language such as that used by Paul in Romans 1:24, 26, 28, where the theme is basically the same as here.

Israel was particularly attracted to the adoration of "the host of heaven" (astral deities). To support this statement, Stephen quoted from Amos 5:25-27. The opening question seems at first glance to suggest that Israel did not offer sacrifices to God during the wilderness wanderings. Such offerings are mentioned in the Pentateuch (Ex 24:4-5; Num 7), and without any suggestion that they were unacceptable. But the references are scanty, hinting that possibly the people as a whole neglected them, as they did circumcision (Jos 5:5). Another possibility is that they went through the motions of sacrifice, much as their descendants did (Is 1:11-13), which was only a formal obedience lacking true purpose and desire to honor God. As time went on, the people became more addicted to an alien worship, that of the host of heaven. The two deities mentioned here were astral— Moloch, the god of the Ammonites, was also known as the Venus Star;[13] *Rompha* (or *Rephan*) is the Babylonian name for Saturn. In the Hebrew and LXX texts of Amos we read "Damascus" rather than "Babylon," for Amos was referring to the exile of the northern kingdom. But because Stephen was talking to men of Judah, he took the liberty of substituting "Babylon," the place of captivity for the southern kingdom. Judah's offense in the realm of astral worship is noted more frequently than Israel's (2 Ki 21:3, 5; 23:5; Jer 8:2; 19:13; Zep 1:5).

Verses 44-50. This passage describes the transition from the tabernacle to the Temple of Solomon.

> **7:44** "Our fathers had the tabernacle of testimony in the wilderness, just as He who spoke to Moses directed *him* to make it according to the pattern which he had seen.
>
> **45** "And having received it in their turn, our fathers brought it in with Joshua upon dispossessing the nations whom God drove out before our fathers, until the time of David.
>
> **46** "And *David* found favor in God's sight, and asked that he might find a dwelling place for the God of Jacob.
>
> **47** "But it was Solomon who built a house for Him.
>
> **48** "However, the Most High does not dwell in *houses* made by *human* hands; as the prophet says:
>
> **49** 'HEAVEN IS MY THRONE,
> AND EARTH IS THE FOOTSTOOL OF MY FEET;
> WHAT KIND OF HOUSE WILL YOU BUILD FOR ME?
>   says the Lord;
> OR WHAT PLACE IS THERE FOR MY REPOSE?
>
> **50** 'WAS IT NOT MY HAND WHICH MADE ALL THESE THINGS?'

7:44-50. Instead of recounting the history of Judah following the captivity, Stephen drew a contrast between the tabernacle and the Temple, and to this extent gave some attention to the charge that he had spoken against the holy place (6:13). The tabernacle had the distinction of being constructed in accordance wtih a divinely given pattern (v. 44; Ex 25:40; Heb. 8:5). It was eminently suitable to the period spent "in the wilderness," since its various parts could be detached and carried to the next encampment and there assembled. During the conquest of Canaan it symbolized the presence and conquering might of Israel's God.

A change came with David, who felt grieved that whereas he dwelt in

123

a house of cedar, the Ark of the Lord continued to be under a tent (2 Sa 7:2). David's desire to build a house for the Lord was not granted, but the privilege was given to his son Solomon (2 Sa 7:12-13).

It is true that the initiative for the erection of the Temple came not from a divine directive but from David's desire. God did not require it (2 Sa 7:5-7), yet He permitted it to be erected and gave it His blessing by filling it with the *shekinah* of His presence (1 Ki 8:10-11). Solomon, indeed, indicated that the Lord had commended David for the desire to build a house for His worship (1 Ki 8:18). Stephen seemed intent on emphasizing that God cannot be confined to a house "made by human hands" (cf. "hands" in v. 41), a truth which Solomon recognized when he dedicated the Temple (1 Ki 8:27).

To reinforce his point, Stephen quoted Scripture again, this time Isaiah 66:1-2. In view of the fact that heaven is God's throne and earth His footstool, the Almighty can ask the question, "What . . . house will you build for me?" The words apparently refer to the erection of a Temple after the exile. "He is the Being who filleth all, the Creator, and therefore the possessor, of the universe; and if men think to do Him a service by building Him a temple, and forget His infinite majesty in their concern for their own contemptible fabric, He wants no temple at all."[14]

One can see something of a parallel between the problem presented by sacrifices (v. 42) and that which the Temple posed. Both could be abused by serving to exalt man rather than the Lord.

Was Stephen maintaining that the erection of the Temple was wrong, an act of rebellion and pride, and that only the tabernacle represented the will of God? Or was he intent on pointing out that by magnifying the Temple and its cultus, the Jewish nation in his time had made the Temple almost an end in itself and were glorying in it rather than in the God for whose sake it was constructed?

The answer is not easy. If we had a digest of Stephen's discussions in the synagogue, light would be thrown on this question. To appeal to the Qumran community and its opposition to the Temple is not particularly helpful, since the opposition was not to the temple per se but to the corruption of the priesthood that controlled it. If Stephen was influenced by the attitude and teaching of Jesus (something that can be neither affirmed nor denied) it is difficult to see how he could reject the Temple entirely, seeing that Jesus regarded it as His Father's house and a place of prayer, not only for the Jews but for all nations (Mk 11:17). Our Lord's attitude was reflected in the cleansing of the Temple at the beginning of Holy Week. If He repudiated the Temple, why had He bothered to cleanse it? It is rather hard to accept the idea that Stephen rejected the Temple and did so on the authority of Jesus, when the apostles, who were under the teaching of our Lord, continued to make use of the Temple and to regard it as the house of God.

Of some relevance, perhaps, is the fact that the writer of the epistle to the Hebrews made frequent reference to the tabernacle but did not mention the Temple. The motive for this choice may well have been that the tabernacle suggested movement, going along with God under His direction, whereas the Temple was static and served to symbolize a certain satisfaction in the status quo that made the nation unresponsive to further revelation, especially that which came in the person of God's Son. He was the new temple made without hands (Jn 2:19, 21), into which believers are incorporated as living stones (1 Co 3:16; 1 Pe 2:4-5). So the Jerusalem Temple was not intended to be permanent. Such concepts may well have been shared by Stephen.

Verses 51-53. The speaker turned from his résumé of Israel's history to a charge that his audience and the nation were perpetuating the sins and failures of their ancestors.

> **7:51** "You men who are stiff-necked and uncircumcised in heart and ears are always resisting the Holy Spirit; you are doing just as your fathers did.
>
> **52** "Which one of the prophets did your fathers not persecute? And they killed those who had previously announced the coming of the Righteous One, whose betrayers and murderers you have now become;
>
> **53** you who received the law as ordained by angels, and *yet* did not keep it."

7:51-53. Coming to the close of his address (he may have planned to say more but was interrupted) Stephen was prophetlike in the directness and severity of his accusations. He described his hearers as "stiffnecked" people, as God had done in the case of Israel at Mount Sinai (Ex 33:3, 5, marg.). This national characteristic had been present all along ("always resisting the Holy Spirit"). The proneness to rebel against God manifested itself in the persecution of "the prophets," as Jesus had charged (Mt 23:37; Lk 11:47-48). He Himself had experienced the enmity of the Jewish leaders, meeting death at their hands (cf. 1 Th 2:15).

Stephen did not shrink from accusing the Sanhedrin of direct responsibility for handing over Jesus to death and thereby becoming His murderers. He used even stronger language than Peter had employed (Ac 3:13-15). He, like Peter, called Jesus "the Righteous One." This act of rejection was the crowning offense, and it was in line with the failure to keep "the law" which came from God rather than from human wisdom and authority, as attested by the mediation of "angels" in connection with its delivery to Israel (cf. Heb 2:2). That very Law had prohibited murder in general. How much more heinous was the crime of murdering the Son of God!

Possibly Stephen intended to mention the resurrection as the divine reversal of the human action, as Peter was accustomed to do, but his strong language so inflamed his hearers that further discourse was rendered impossible.

Verses 54-60. The martyrdom of Stephen is reported as coming immediately after his address before the Council.

> **7:54** Now when they heard this, they were cut to the quick, and they *began* gnashing their teeth at him.
> **55** But being full of the Holy Spirit, he gazed intently into heaven and saw the glory of God, and Jesus standing at the right hand of God;
> **56** and he said, "Behold, I see the heavens opened up and the Son of Man standing at the right hand of God."
> **57** But they cried out with a loud voice, and covered their ears, and they rushed upon him with one impulse.
> **58** And when they had driven him out of the city, they *began* stoning *him,* and the witnesses laid aside their robes at the feet of a young man named Saul.
> **59** And they went on stoning Stephen as he called upon *the Lord* and said, "Lord Jesus, receive my spirit!"
> **60** And falling on his knees, he cried out with a loud voice, "Lord, do not hold this sin against them!" And having said this, he fell asleep.

7:54. The words of Stephen, especially at the close, filled his hearers with rage. There was no atmosphere of calm in which his statements could be discussed. This man had been ostensibly put on the stand to defend himself, and he had chosen not to do this but rather to turn the tables by bringing charges against the leaders of Israel. It was intolerable to them, and they beset him on every side to silence him once and for all.

7:55-56. "Full of the Holy Spirit" (cf. 6:5), his source of wisdom and strength, Stephen was caught up in the ecstasy of the privilege of bearing witness to his Lord. Enraptured, he gazed into heaven and saw "the glory of God," that glory which had ceased to fill the earthly sanctuary (Eze 11:22-23) but which did not fail to betoken the presence of God in the heavenly sanctuary (Rev 21:22-23).

The vision of glory included "Jesus standing at the right hand of God." This implies the resurrection and ascension. Usually Jesus is represented as seated there (Lk 22:69; Ac 2:33-34; Heb 1:3, 13). Stephen commented on the standing posture as he went on to identify Jesus as "the Son of Man." A twofold problem presents itself here: the posture of Jesus and the use of the title *Son of Man.* In the gospels that title is used only by

Jesus for Himself (it does not occur in the epistles). These two items can be considered together.

The standing posture is hardly to be explained as indicating that the Son of Man was on the point of returning to earth as Judge, for that did not happen. Quite naturally the standing can be looked on as the welcome of Jesus for the spirit of the martyr. Yet this will not explain the extraordinary use of the title "Son of Man." A variation of this is the idea that the universal aspect of the last day when the Son of Man comes is here individualized to express the hope of the believer. "Only dying Stephen was in position to see the coming Son of man. It was at the 'last day,' in the hour of death, that the Son of man would be seen. . . . Only Stephen qualifies, as a dying Christian, for an individual *parousia* of the Son of man."[15]

A possible objection to this viewpoint of Barrett is that the typical way of describing Christian death is to make it a departure to be with Christ (e.g., Phil 1:23) rather than as an advancing of the Lord to meet His own (the typical way of setting forth the eschatological appearing). It would be hard to find a passage to support Barrett's formulation. Some have taken John 14:3 in this sense, but the interpretation is doubtful. A different solution to the problem presented by the text is to see in the combination of standing and the use of the title "Son of Man" an indication that the Lord was here taking the position of witness and vindicator on behalf of His servant.

> In short, this is a double trial scene, exactly as in the scene in which Jesus witnessed a good confession before Pontius Pilate (I Tim. 6:13) or before the Sanhedrin: just as there Christ is condemned by the human court but declares that the Son of Man will thenceforth be exalted with the clouds and vindicated, so here Stephen is condemned and put to death, but in the heavenly court, where the books have been opened, this member of the Son of Man community is already being vindicated by the head of that community—*the* Son of Man *par excellence;* and as Stephen's witness confessed Christ before men, so Christ is standing to confess him before the angels of God. It is the more significant, if so, that the martyr with his dying words begs the heavenly court for mercy towards those against whom he is vindicated.[16]

7:57-58. Despite the judicial setting, a tumult broke out as men rushed toward the prisoner, screaming at him and holding their ears so as to hear no more from his lips, that he might know they regarded his words as blasphemy. In the eyes of the Jews, Stephen's closing words about Jesus as the Son of Man involved a claim that Jesus supported him in his stand. Very well, they would see to it that Stephen should have the same fate as the Nazarene. Both of them were iconoclasts meriting death. The probable explanation for this unseemly conduct is that others were present besides the Sanhedrin, according to the custom which permitted outsiders, especially students, to stand at the rear of the room.[17] Punishment followed the pattern laid down in Leviticus 24:11, 14. That the stoning was a matter of official decision and not simply mob action seems indicated by the prominence of "witnesses" in the actual stoning.

There may be a certain awkwardness in holding that the Sanhedrin acted on its own initiative in this instance, when our sources indicate that it was not free to do so in the case of Jesus, for whose condemnation Pilate's consent was required (Jn 18:31). But the situation had probably changed by Stephen's time, if his death can be put in the year 36 or later. Reicke notes that Vitellius, the imperial legate from 35 to 37, had a lenient attitude toward the Jews. To gain their good will he deposed Pilate, whom they detested, and replaced Caiaphas with a strong high priest named Jonathan. At the same time Vitellius restored the high priestly vestments to the custody of the high priest (they had been kept in Roman hands). "The high priest did not bother to have his decision ratified by the procurator, but rather let the stoning and persecution go ahead without consulting the Roman authorities."[18]

On the other hand, if it could be demonstrated that the stoning occurred prior to A.D. 36, this solution can no longer be relied on. But even so, as Sherwin-White observes, "It is possible that the Sanhedrin, which before the Herodian period had been the sovereign court of Judaea, tried to exercise its full power whenever there was a chance of doing so unchecked."[19]

The witnesses, in order to be able the better to cast the first stones, as the Law prescribed (Lev 24:14; Deu 13:9-10), removed their outer garments and placed them "at the feet of a young man named Saul." This was a convenient way for Luke to call attention to a figure who would dominate much of the remaining narrative of the book.

Was more intended? Was Luke saying that in the providence of God the mantle of Stephen was falling on Saul? Those who think so are prone to go further and suggest that Stephen's Hellenistic outlook must have made him eager to take the Gospel to the Gentiles, and though prevented by death from doing so, his desire was destined to be realized through Saul after his conversion.

But one looks in vain for evidence that Stephen had the vision of reaching out to the Gentile world. As far as the evidence goes, he was concerned for the mission of the Church to his own people and also to the Samaritans, but nothing more. True enough, it was a group of Hellenists who began the Gentile work in Antioch (Ac 11:19-20), but any connection with Stephen has to be read into the text. The mention of Saul at this point in the narrative is mainly to prepare the reader for his prominence in the persecution which broke out after Stephen's death.

7:59-60. Two things are noted about the manner of the death of the first martyr, and both of them link him with the Master. "Lord Jesus, receive my spirit" recalls the prayer of Jesus to the Father, "Into Thy hands I commit My spirit" (Lk 23:46). Also, in asking the Lord not to hold this sin of murder against those who put him to death, Stephen seemed to echo the request of Jesus that the Father would forgive those who had a part in bringing about His crucifixion (Lk 23:34). The similarity does not stop with these two items, for there are more. Stephen wrought wonders and signs, his words could not be refuted, he was filled with the Spirit, and he died under a charge of blasphemy.

His last thought and his last plea were for others, and then without a word he "fell asleep," the term for Christian death (1 Th 4:15), an expression which should not be understood as suggesting the sleep of the soul (cf 2 Co 5:8; Phil 1:23).

5. PERSECUTION OF THE CHURCH—8:1-3

Previous efforts to suppress the followers of Jesus had been confined to the beating and imprisonment of apostles. Now for the first time the rank and file began to pay the price of discipleship.

> **8:1** And Saul was in hearty agreement with putting him to death.
>
> And on that day a great persecution arose against the church in Jerusalem; and they were all scattered throughout the regions of Judea and Samaria, except the apostles.
>
> **2** And *some* devout men buried Stephen, and made loud lamentation over him.
>
> **3** But Saul *began* ravaging the church, entering house after house; and dragging off men and women, he would put them in prison.

8:1. The mention of Saul as being "in hearty agreement" with the action taken against Stephen helps to interpret the item about him in 7:58, which otherwise might be taken as mere happenstance. This second statement is the bridge between 7:58 and 8:3. Saul was in complete accord with those who put Stephen to death, as he later acknowledged (22:20). It was not simply passive consent, but rather active approval (cf. the use of the word in Ro 1:32). Doubtless Saul swung into action without delay, heading up the persecution.

The KJV rendering, "at that time," is too general. Rather, it was "on that day" that the campaign was launched against the Jerusalem church. Luke seems to say that *all* believers were scattered abroad with the exception of the apostles. But this can hardly be taken strictly, since many were detained and imprisoned. This is an example of hyperbole which is not uncommon in Scripture when emphasis is desired (e.g., Mk 1:5). It is probable that the brunt of persecution was borne by the Hellenists, those who were closely attached to Stephen. Their use of the Greek language would help to identify them.

Those who escaped are described as scattered throughout the regions of "Judea and Samaria." Luke could have used a general term for scattering but chose instead to use a word which means to scatter as seed is scattered on the ground. This suggests that as the episode was viewed in retrospect by the Church, it was seen as a providential event to facilitate the mission set before His followers by the risen Lord (1:8). The people went as missionaries more than as refugees.

Why, then, did the apostles not take the lead in this exodus? Why did they remain in the city? The very fact that they were able to do so without being arrested indicates that the fury of the persecution was not directed primarily toward the "Hebrews" (6:1) who (in contrast to Stephen) had continued to make use of the temple and maintain the customs of the Law. No doubt these leaders felt that for the time being they should stay in the city to shepherd those who escaped detention and to provide a center of control for the now enlarging sphere of the Church (Judea and Samaria). It would be a mistake to conclude that the persecution meant a permanent wiping out or withdrawal of the entire Hellenist segment of the Jerusalem church. A sufficient refutation is the fact that this church sent Barnabas, a Hellenist, to assist the Antioch church (11:22).

8:2-3. The decision of the Sanhedrin was not universally popular, as evidenced by the fact that "devout men" came forward to bury Stephen and to make lamentation over him. While it is not impossible that some of these were believers, the previous use of the word *devout*, for those who had listened to Peter's Pentecost sermon and were therefore not at that time believers, suggests that these men did not belong to the Church. There is a certain parallel with the situation of Jesus, when He was lamented by women of the city as He was led out to be crucified (Lk 23:27).

But Saul was not inclined to any such show of regret. His whole energy was thrown into the task of destroying the Church if he could. The expression "ravaging" occurs only here in the New Testament, though much the same idea is conveyed in Galatians 1:13, 23 by a different verb. In view of the use of the imperfect tense in all these passages, it is probable that the so-called conative force of the tense is called for here. In other words, Saul kept trying to destroy the Church but was unsuccessful. It proved indestructible (Mt 16:18). The persecutor's activity is more fully described in his speech before Agrippa (26:9-11), where he stated that his authority was given to him by the chief priests and that when some of his victims were put to death his vote helped to condemn them.

Notable is the fact that up until the Stephen episode, opposition had come to the apostles from the Sadducees, who resented the preaching of the resurrection. But now that Stephen had spoken out on the Temple and the Law, the Pharisees had been enlisted as persecutors. Such was Saul of Tarsus (Phil 3:5-6). The counsel of Gamaliel (Ac 5:38-39) was regarded as no longer relevant, since the issue had been shifted by Stephen's speech.

PART II

THE CHURCH IN JUDEA, SAMARIA, AND SYRIA–8:4–12:25

Up to this point in the narrative the proclamation of the Gospel has been largely confined to Jerusalem. We have seen people from the surrounding territory come to the city, especially to bring their sick for healing (5:16), but no information has been given about any effort to reach out into Judea. The risen Lord's final command called for a witness to Him in all Judea and Samaria (1:8). Having noted summarily the general dispersion of believers throughout these districts due to persecution (8:1), Luke now concentrates on the Samaritan mission (8:5-25), then returns to describe further ministry through Peter in Judea (9:32–11:18).

But he also has in mind the forward thrust of the Church, for which this intermediate stage was a preparation. This is reflected in the account of Philip's meeting with the Ethiopian eunuch, possibly the first missionary encounter on the African continent (8:26-40). It is apparent also in the report of the activity of certain Hellenists who ministered along the Phoenician coast and then began to preach to Gentiles in Syrian Antioch, which became the major missionary base for outreach to Gentiles farther removed (11:19-26). An even more evident token that Luke is looking ahead to the second half of his account is his description of the conversion and early labors of Saul, the man who was destined above all others to be God's instrument in penetrating to the regions beyond (9:1-30).

A. PHILIP AT SAMARIA—8:4-25

AT ONCE the narrative becomes more detailed, suggesting that Luke was concerned to describe the witness of the Church rather than to go into particulars of its trials and tribulations.

8:4 Therefore, those who had been scattered went about preaching the word.

5 And Philip went down to the city of Samaria and *began* proclaiming Christ to them.

6 And the multitudes with one accord were giving attention to what was said by Philip, as they heard and saw the signs which he was performing.

7 For *in the case of* many who had unclean spirits, they were coming out *of them* shouting with a loud voice; and many who had been paralyzed and lame were healed.

8 And there was much rejoicing in that city.

9 Now there was a certain man named Simon, who formerly was practicing magic in the city, and astonishing the people of Samaria, claiming to be someone great;

10 and they all, from smallest to greatest, were giving attention to him, saying, "This man is what is called the Great Power of God."

11 And they were giving him attention because he had for a long time astonished them with his magic arts.

12 But when they believed Philip preaching the good news about the kingdom of God and the name of Jesus Christ, they were being baptized, men and women alike.

13 And even Simon himself believed; and after being baptized, he continued on with Philip; and as he observed signs and great miracles taking place, he was constantly amazed.

14 Now when the apostles in Jerusalem heard that Samaria had received the word of God, they sent them Peter and John,

15 who came down and prayed for them, that they might receive the Holy Spirit.

16 For He had not yet fallen upon any of them; they had simply been baptized in the name of the Lord Jesus.

17 Then they *began* laying their hands on them, and they were receiving the Holy Spirit.

18 Now when Simon saw that the Spirit was bestowed through the laying on of the apostles' hands, he offered them money,

135

19 saying, "Give this authority to me as well, so that everyone on whom I lay my hands may receive the Holy Spirit."

20 But Peter said to him, "May your silver perish with you, because you thought you could obtain the gift of God with money!

21 "You have no part or portion in this matter, for your heart is not right before God.

22 "Therefore repent of this wickedness of yours, and pray the Lord that if possible, the intention of your heart may be forgiven you.

23 "For I see that you are in the gall of bitterness and in the bondage of iniquity."

24 But Simon answered and said, "Pray to the Lord for me yourselves, so that nothing of what you have said may come upon me."

25 And so, when they had solemnly testified and spoken the word of the Lord, they started back to Jerusalem, and were preaching the gospel to many villages of the Samaritans.

8:4-8. At this point the historian repeats the fact of dispersion of believers from Jerusalem before concentrating on one area, Samaria. Possibly there was a conscious comparison with the well-known Jewish Dispersion, when men of Israel penetrated many lands where they lived and worked, retaining their religion and customs in the midst of a pagan population. Now another dispersion was developing, having much in common with its Jewish counterpart, yet distinguished by faith in Jesus of Nazareth as Saviour and Lord (cf. 1 Pe 1:1). While the Jewish Dispersion was to a limited extent missionary in character, the Christian dispersion was much more so. The prime objective was "preaching the word." This activity is strongly emphasized throughout the chapter (8:4, 12, 25, 35, 40). Though preaching doubtless continued in Jerusalem, little is said about it (9:28-29). While the city remained the home of the mother church, the theater of action that Luke was concerned to report lay beyond its limits.

With Stephen gone, Philip came to the fore as the leader in carrying the Gospel to Samaria. He has been noted as a member of the seven (6:5). Eventually he became known as Philip the evangelist (21:8). Jesus had included Samaria in His commission (1:8) and had prepared the way by His own ministry in this area (Jn 4).

The exact location of Philip's labors is not certain, for the manuscript testimony is divided, some having the reading "the city," others "a city" (of Samaria). The former reading, despite having witnesses of good quality, is probably to be rejected here, since the old capital no longer existed. Herod the Great had rebuilt the city, calling it Sebaste in honor of Augustus (the new name is the Greek equivalent of the Latin Augustus). It is unlikely that Luke would go back to the old term if he meant to designate the district's leading city. Gitta is a possibility, since this was the birthplace of Simon Magus, who is mentioned later in the chapter.

Philip's message centered in "Christ" (literally, "the Messiah"). This means he identified Jesus of Nazareth as fulfilling the promises of the coming of God's anointed One for whom the Samaritans were looking (Jn 4:25, 29).

Philip's impact was twofold, through the spoken word and through the signs wrought before the people. As a result, they gave "attention" to him when he preached, the very thing they had been doing in the case of Simon (v. 11). That charlatan was now faced with a serious rival. If no miracles had been performed by Philip, the superstitious Samaritans could easily have concluded that he represented something inferior to Simon. The signs were those which were characteristic of Jesus' ministry and reproduced in the experience of the early Church's witness (3:1-10; 5:16; 9:33-34). Little is recorded of mighty works wrought by Jesus among the Samaritans (Lk 17:11-19 is an exception). But now these neglected people were given an opportunity equal to that which the Jews had enjoyed. The mission produced "much rejoicing."

8:9-13. The section describes Simon's first contact with the Christian message and his reaction to it. Early Christian literature has considerable to relate about a man of this name who was alleged to oppose Peter in the city of Rome, seeking to lead people astray by his diabolically inspired deeds.[1] Simon practiced "magic," the most degraded form of religion in the Hellenistic age. (We encounter it again in 13:6 and 19:19.) The Samaritans were open to such influence because of their background, for they were a mixed people both racially and religiously. It is recorded of them, "They feared the LORD and served their own gods, according to the custom of the nations from among whom they had been carried away" (2 Ki 17:33).

The people were amazed at Simon's pretensions, for he announced himself as "someone great" and backed it up by a display of magic. In the original there is a possible play on words between "practicing magic" and the word "great." The wise men of the nativity story (Mt 2) are called magi, but there is no basis for concluding that they resorted to magic. Their skills were of a higher order and not intended to deceive. To the Samaritans, Simon appeared as one deserving of reverence for his supernatural demonstrations. So they called him "the Great Power of God." The word *power* was much used in antiquity, sometimes as a synonym for Deity (Mk 14:62). Philo used the term in the plural to denote the intermediaries through whom God worked in creating and sustaining the world.

Simon had had things going his way until the preaching of Philip introduced a power more potent and blessed than any he could muster (cf. the magicians of Egypt in relation to Moses, Ex 8:18-19). Philip's preaching

137

centered not only on the person of Christ but also on the Good News of the Kingdom of God (cf. 1:3). He was concerned to set forth God's sovereign plan, which included the universal emphasis of salvation as opposed to an exclusively Jewish message (cf. Jn 4:42).

Among those who responded was Simon. He both "believed" and was "baptized." After having amazed others, he himself could not help being amazed at the miracles he saw being performed before his eyes. The question as to whether or not he was a genuine believer must await the further developments in the story, but it is well to reflect that Scripture sometimes cites as belief that which the context deplores as quite inadequate (e.g., Jn 2:23-25). What is emphasized is the open-eyed wonder of one who was intent on studying Philip and his work, willing to be an apprentice in the hope of ultimately being a master.

8:14-25. The church at Jerusalem learned of the success of the Samaritan mission before long and moved to welcome the new believers into the fellowship. It is doubtless significant that "the apostles" as a body (cf. 8:1) sent the two men of their number who had been most prominent in the work of the Lord since Pentecost (3:1; 4:13, 19). This is the last appearance of John in Acts, but Peter continues to be prominent in chapters 9-12, 15. The fact that he was sent to Samaria suggests that he had no preeminence of position, despite his leadership in the church.

The mission had the blessing of God, as evidenced by the giving of the Holy Spirit, after their prayer, to the converts at Samaria. In the case of these new believers, the rite of baptism had been performed, but the Spirit had not been bestowed (contrast 2:38; 10:44). The translation, "they *began* laying their hands on them," is awkward. This inceptive use of the imperfect is less likely than the iterative, which would describe the action as being repeated as the apostles moved from one to the other (cf. the use in Lk 9:16).

So far as the book of Acts is concerned, no inflexible pattern for the reception of the Spirit is discernible, though usually the experience of the saints must have been that the Spirit came as the seal of faith (19:2; Eph 1:13). That the Samaritans received the Spirit was clear evidence that God had accepted them as well as Jewish believers. This was calculated to remove any sense of inferiority and to encourage them to feel their oneness with others in the body of Christ. The delay in granting the Spirit as well as the conveyance of the Spirit through apostles from the Jerusalem church was a warning that there must be no thought of perpetuating the old antagonism between Jews and Samaritans within the church (cf. Jn 4:22). There was not to be a separate Samaritan church.

Regarding the Samaritan situation, G. W. H. Lampe writes,

We must bear in mind, once again, that for St. Luke the Spirit's primary work is the furtherance of the Church's world-wide mission. . . . It may not be too much to assert that this event is meant to demonstrate that a new nucleus of the missionary Church has been established, and to suggest that Luke's readers are intended to infer that the Gospel proceeded to radiate outwards from this new center of the Spirit's mission.[2]

Simon was an attentive observer of what happened when the apostles prayed and laid their hands on believers. Evidently there were some outward tokens which accompanied the gift of the Spirit, perhaps such as are noted in 19:6. Simon was intrigued. Here was a power he longed to possess for himself, thinking it would add to his stock in trade and increase his prestige. He was quite prepared to pay for it. The term *simony*, which was common in the medieval church for the purchase of ecclesiastical offices, stems from this incident.

Peter was so shocked that he reacted with severity. Was he thinking of Judas when he said, "May your silver perish with you" (v. 20; cf. 1:18)? Money has no more to do with the gift of the Spirit than with the gift of eternal life. Peter's remarks to Simon may not be sufficiently clear to determine whether the apostle held him to be a child of God who sadly needed correction and illumination or considered him unregenerate. "Perish" is a strong word, as is the statement, "For I see that you are in the gall of bitterness and in the bondage of iniquity" (v. 23). On the other hand, the admonition that Simon had "no part or portion" in this matter bears a striking resemblance to what the Lord said when Peter resisted Jesus' attempt to wash his feet (Jn 13:8). On that occasion Peter was sorely mistaken but did not lack faith.

Peter's reference to forgiveness as the pressing need for Simon can be taken either way, as something every sinner needs in coming to God or as a fresh experience of divine grace for an erring believer. This much is clear: throughout the report of this incident there is a complete lack of spiritual perception on Simon's part, and little if any recognition of wrongdoing against the Lord. The fear of punishment is very much like the attitude of Cain, essentially self-centered.

Their mission ended, Peter and John made their way unhurriedly back to Jerusalem (v. 25). Their recent experience encouraged them to minister in other Samaritan communities. What a change from the day when John had been prepared to call down fire from heaven on a Samaritan village which had refused hospitality to Jesus (Lk 9:51-55)!

B. PHILIP AND THE ETHIOPIAN—8:26-40

Hardly had the Gospel reached Samaria, than by a great leap it jumped to the uttermost part, in this instance to the continent of Africa. For all we know, there may have been other contacts with travelers from afar that resulted in the spread of the faith to remote places. Luke was content to relate this one example.

> **8:26** But an angel of the Lord spoke to Philip saying, "Arise and go south to the road that descends from Jerusalem to Gaza." (This is a desert *road.*)
>
> **27** And he arose and went; and behold, there was an Ethiopian eunuch, a court official of Candace, queen of the Ethiopians, who was in charge of all her treasure; and he had come to Jerusalem to worship.
>
> **28** And he was returning and sitting in his chariot, and was reading the prophet Isaiah.
>
> **29** And the Spirit said to Philip, "Go up and join this chariot."
>
> **30** And when Philip had run up, he heard him reading Isaiah the prophet, and said, "Do you understand what you are reading?"
>
> **31** And he said, "Well, how could I, unless someone guides me?" And he invited Philip to come up and sit with him.
>
> **32** Now the passage of Scripture which he was reading was this:
>
> "HE WAS LED AS A SHEEP TO SLAUGHTER;
>
> AND AS A LAMB BEFORE ITS SHEARER IS SILENT,
>
> SO HE DOES NOT OPEN HIS MOUTH.
>
> **33** "IN HUMILIATION HIS JUDGMENT WAS TAKEN AWAY;
>
> WHO SHALL RELATE HIS GENERATION?
>
> FOR HIS LIFE IS REMOVED FROM THE EARTH."
>
> **34** And the eunuch answered Philip and said, "Please *tell me*, of whom does the prophet say this? Of himself, or of someone else?"
>
> **35** And Philip opened his mouth, and beginning from this Scripture he preached Jesus to him.
>
> **36** And as they went along the road they came to some water; and the eunuch said, "Look! Water! What prevents me from being baptized?"
>
> **37**°
>
> **38** And he ordered the chariot to stop; and they both went down into the water, Philip as well as the eunuch; and he baptized him.
>
> **39** And when they came up out of the water, the Spirit of the Lord snatched Philip away; and the eunuch saw him no more, but went on his way rejoicing.
>
> **40** But Philip found himself at Azotus; and as he passed through he kept preaching the gospel to all the cities, until he came to Caesarea.

8:26. Guidance came to the early Church at times through "an angel of the Lord" (cf. 5:19-20). The message was clear, and the command uncontested. Philip must leave Samaria, but he was leaving behind him men and women who now had the Spirit to enable them to grow and be strong

---

°Verse 37 lacks sufficient authority to include it in the text. It reads as follows: "And Philip said, 'If you believe with all your heart, you may.' And he answered and said, 'I believe that Jesus is the Son of God.'"

in the Lord. They could take up the task of witnessing where Philip laid it down. Human wisdom might reason that it was a mistake to leave a thriving work, especially since no intimation was given as to the scope of the new theater of action (contrast 23:11). As it turned out, the witness was given to one man, yet he was a potential witness to many in his own land. God's thoughts and ways are often not ours, but they are always vindicated.

The direction given pointed Philip to the south, to the road from Jerusalem to Gaza. Judging from verse 40, it is probable that God's servant made his journey to a point somewhere near Gaza rather than in the Jerusalem area. Some have called in question the description of this line of travel as a desert road. It certainly is less true of the area between Jerusalem and Gaza than between Gaza and Egypt. But often, especially in the gospels, the word *desert* does not mean wasteland or a sandy area but rather a place without human habitation. Philip was to meet this man in a lonely spot where nothing would distract from the communication of the message.

Another solution to the problem has been proposed, namely, that "desert," in this instance, has the force of *deserted* and refers to the old Gaza which had lain in ruins since it was destroyed by Alexander the Great. The new Gaza was on the coast, some two miles away. Since the word "this" could refer to Gaza as well as to "road," and since the directions given to Philip would then be quite explicit, this interpretation should not be lightly dismissed, although verse 36, with its mention of the road, may be said to favor the former view.

8:27-28. In spite of being uninformed as to the reason for the journey, Philip "arose and went." This implicit obedience recalls that of Abraham when he was given a most difficult command (Gen 22:3). It is in contrast with Peter's attitude toward an unwelcome order from the Lord (10:14). Faith in God calls for a readiness to trust in His wisdom and does not demand an explanation.

Attention shifts to the man whom Philip was about to meet, a stranger from Ethiopia. In ancient times, this term indicated a large territory lying directly south of Egypt, hence to be distinguished from modern Ethiopia located to the southeast. This man was an "official" of the court of Candace,† the queen (more accurately, the queen mother) of the land, and was her leading financial officer. Incidentally, there is a play on words here, as "treasure" in the original closely resembles the word *Gaza*.

Another item of information is provided—this individual was a "eunuch." It is well-known that in the Orient eunuchs were placed in charge of the

†*Candace* is a title (cf. *Pharaoh*) rather than a personal name.

141

harems (Est 2:3). They also sometimes rose to positions of prominence in the government, as in this case. His rank may have given him a certain amount of freedom of movement, accounting for his visit to Jerusalem.

He had come to "worship," which raises a question as to his status. That he was a convert to Judaism (a proselyte) is unlikely, since the Law excluded eunuchs from the congregation of Israel (Deu 23:1). But if he was a God-fearer he could take his place with other Gentiles in the court reserved for them (1 Ki 8:41-43; Mk 11:17). We read of Greeks coming to Jerusalem to worship during our Lord's ministry (Jn 12:20).

Worth observing is the timing of the encounter with Philip—he was "returning" from his visit to the holy city. On his way there he would likely have been annoyed at any interruption, since he was bent on fulfilling a sacred pilgrimage. But now that his mission was over and his heart was as needy as ever, conditions were ripe for the introduction of the Gospel (cf. the strategy of Jesus recorded in Jn 7:37).

The visitor was taking home with him as a memento a scroll of the prophet Isaiah in the LXX, as indicated by the fact that the words quoted correspond with this version more closely than with the Hebrew text. The eunuch was probably reading aloud, since he did not reread the passage before asking an explanation of it from Philip. The matter is made certain in verse 30.

8:29-31. With the Spirit prompting him, Philip mustered sufficient boldness to intercept the chariot and engage the occupant in conversation. Apparently the eunuch was quite preoccupied with his reading, not noticing the stranger until he was questioned as to what he was reading, or more exactly, as to his understanding of it. The interruption was received kindly, and the response was a veiled invitation to Philip to serve as interpreter of the Scripture involved. At last the reason for this long trip to the south was beginning to unfold. The meeting, the reading, the precise passage being read—all this loomed as providential. Philip's pounding heart was not due entirely to running as he mounted the chariot and took his seat beside the eunuch.

8:32-35. In his reading the Ethiopian had come to the high point of Isaiah (chap. 53), with its mysterious words about the Servant of the Lord and what was to happen to Him. He was puzzled about the identification of this figure. This is not surprising in view of the variety of interpretations which have been put forward: Israel the nation, Israel the remnant, and the personal Servant of the Lord. The eunuch felt sure that the prophecy concerned an individual, but was unable to fix his identity.

What an embarrassment it would have been for Philip to admit that he shared the eunuch's perplexity. That he was able to proclaim Christ from this passage shows that already within the Church there was an understanding of its interpretation. All that is necessary is to move back through our Lord's teaching about Himself from the prophets after the resurrection (Lk 24:25-27, 44) to His earlier predictions concerning His death, couched in the language of this chapter from Isaiah (Mk 10:45; Lk 22:37). Unquestionably Jesus had identified Himself and His mission with the unnamed Servant of Isaiah 53 and other passages. That Philip "preached Jesus" makes it certain that the person of our Lord was included along with His work.

What is not wholly clear is the phrase, "beginning from this Scripture." Are we to understand that Philip used other portions of the chapter and perhaps other prophets in addition to Isaiah, or that he proceeded immediately to a recital of fulfillment in terms of the ministry of Jesus culminating in His death and resurrection? In this story we find a classic illustration of the truth affirmed in 1 Peter 1:10-12, that the same Spirit who provided the message to the prophets concerning the sufferings of the Christ and the glories to follow guides and illumines those who make use of the prophecies in preaching the Gospel. It is not at all unlikely that Philip went on down the chapter to include the truths that the Servant bore the sins of many and was rewarded (a hint of the resurrection).

8:36-40. Although no statement is recorded to the effect that Philip went on to state that faith in God's Servant was essential for salvation, the narrative implies this. The eunuch's request for baptism rested on his understanding that in this act he would be confessing his faith as well as repentance for his sins (cf. 2:38; 8:12).

Quite early in the transmission of the text an effort was made to clarify this matter, with the result that manuscripts of the Western text add a statement making faith requisite. We may assume that when this scribal addition originated, sometime fairly early in the second century, this sort of a response was commonly made by the candidate for baptism.

During the conversation the chariot had been rolling along on its way toward Africa, but now the eunuch ordered a halt, that he might be baptized in the water he had glimpsed near the road. Philip was pleased to comply with the request, evidently satisfied as to the genuineness of the eunuch's faith.

The association of the two was abruptly terminated as they emerged from the water, for the Spirit removed Philip from the scene (cf. 1 Ki 18:12). "Snatched" is the same Greek word that Paul used for the rapture of the saints when the Lord comes again (1 Th 4:17). Apparently the disappearance of the messenger of Christ did not disconcert the new convert or make him doubt the reality of the experience which had come to him, for he "went on his way rejoicing" (cf. 8:8).

We can only speculate about Philip's reaction to the mission which had

143

taken him from crowded Samaria to a lonely road in the south. Perhaps, as with others since his time, he thought in terms of fulfillment of the psalmist's words, "Ethiopia will quickly stretch out her hands to God" (Ps 68:31).

Commentators have noted a certain similarity between the experience of Philip and that of Elijah, especially in respect to sudden appearance and disappearance and the fact that such removal is attributed to the Spirit of the Lord (cf. 1 Ki 18:12; 2 Ki 2:16). As for Philip, he ended up at Azotus, the Ashdod of the Old Testament, a city on the coastal plain some twenty miles north of Gaza. He seems to have interpreted his arrival there as an indication that he was not to return to Samaria, but should bear witness in the area. So he pursued a northerly course, preaching as he went, "in all the cities." This would include Joppa, farther up the coast, and possibly Lydda also, which was somewhat inland. It is conceivable, therefore, that Philip laid the foundation for Peter's ministry in these places (9:32-43). His travels ended when he reached Caesarea, but not his preaching. Here he settled and raised a family which shared in ministry along with him (21:8-9).

It may seem strange that he was not called on to bring the Gospel to Cornelius, the centurion of Caesarea (10:1), who was instructed to send to Joppa for Peter. Philip was not slighted. It was simply a case that required the fulfillment of the divine purpose that the one to whom the keys of the Kingdom had been given (Mt 16:19) should open the door of faith to the Gentiles as he had done at Pentecost for the Jews (Ac 15:7).

Saul's Conversion and Early Labors—9:1-31

THREE ACCOUNTS of the conversion are recorded by Luke. The one immediately before us is the historian's own narrative, no doubt based on information supplied by Paul himself. It emphasizes the role of Ananias. In the second account (chap. 22) Paul addressed hostile Jews and sought to present his experience as above all a divine intervention in his life to which he bowed in obedience. The third account is also Paul's, but this time spoken in the presence of Festus and Agrippa (chap. 26), omitting all reference to Ananias and majoring instead on Paul's commission to go to the Gentiles.

At the very least one must say that the inclusion of three accounts of Saul's conversion is an indication of the importance Luke attached to this event. The one who was turned to Christ on the Damascus road was destined to be the leading instrument of the risen Lord in extending the Gospel beyond the bounds of Palestine to remote places and to Gentiles as well as Jews. Paul is the key figure in most of the remaining narrative of Acts.

Verses 1-2. This transitional section deals with Saul's persecuting activity and is a continuation of what has been related in 8:1-3.

> **9:1** Now Saul, still breathing threats and murder against the disciples of the Lord, went to the high priest,
> **2** and asked for letters from him to the synagogues at Damascus, so that if he found any belonging to the Way, both men and women, he might bring them bound to Jerusalem.

9:1. Not satisfied with what he had done to terrorize the church in Jerusalem, Saul began to look farther afield, with his ferocity unabated. Not content with using "threats," he resorted to "murder," not by his own hand but in the sense described in 26:10. Luke might well have hesitated to use such strong language of one who had become his friend and companion had not Paul pictured himself in the same light: "I used to persecute the church of God beyond measure, and tried to destroy it" (Gal 1:13; cf. Ac 26:11).

How is this to be explained, especially in one who was a Pharisee schooled in the necessity of caution in executing punishment (see comments on 5:33-39)? The pupil (22:3) had parted company with his teacher.

Whatever difference in temperament may have existed between the two will not suffice to explain the devastating rampage of this wolf of Benjamin (Gen 49:27). Some scholars are content to hold that Saul was bitter because in his eyes Jesus of Nazareth was a pretender, an impostor who thought of Himself as the Messiah and made dupes out of His followers. But this is not sufficient to explain the vehemence of the persecutor.

Saul was deeply devoted to Judaism, a fact which he mentioned in conjunction with his attacks on the Church (Gal 1:14). At the heart of Judaism stood the Torah, which Saul sensed was in jeopardy since the campaign launched by Stephen against the Law (6:13). This ardent Jew had organized his life around the Torah, and felt he was blameless respecting its demands (Phil 3:6). His zeal for the Law explains his zeal in persecuting the Church. The one had to go if the other was to stand.[1] So he was willing to put to death as well as to prosecute the followers of Jesus.

He could point to precedents for this. Others had been zealous for the Law and willing to resort to violence, sometimes with divine approval. When Antiochus Epiphanes was bent on destroying the religious life of the Jews, Mattathias and his sons took up the sword to defend their Jewish heritage after Mattathias had slain a fellow-Jew who was prepared to lead in a pagan sacrifice (1 Mac 2:23-28). Significant is the language Mattathias used in urging others to take the same stand: "Whosoever is zealous for the law . . . let him come forth after me." This recalls Galatians 1:14 and Philippians 3:6. Mattathias was able to defend his conduct on the basis of Old Testament examples, including Phinehas, who had won the commendation of the Lord for smiting the errant Israelite and his Midianite consort (Num 25:6-13) and Elijah, who slew the prophets of Baal for leading Israel astray (1 Ki 18:40). The zeal for the Lord and His Law on the part of these worthies is underscored by Mattathias (1 Mac 2:50-58).

Closer to Saul's time, some Pharisees had taken up arms to get rid of Herod the Great for what they regarded as impious acts.[2] Saul had ample precedent.

9:2. The persecutor was aware that if he hoped to stamp out the Church, he must follow believers wherever they went, including those who had fled Jerusalem in recent days. So he secured letters from the high priest to the synagogues at Damascus which stated his identity and gave him authority to deal with the disciples.* This ancient city had several

---

*A problem presents itself here. Would Rome permit such a persecution as Saul conducted? Rome gave the Church protection from the Jews on various occasions, as Luke relates later on. It is possible that at the time when Saul went to Damascus the city was under the control of Aretas IV, ruler of the Nabatean empire (Arabian in constituency). This kingdom had not been subdued by Rome. To gain favor with the Jews, who were also anti-Roman in their feelings, Aretas may have permitted the Sanhedrin to exercise authority in this distant city. See W. L. Knox, *St. Paul and the Church of Jerusalem*, p. 53, n. 20; p. 59, n. 47.

synagogues, and Saul was reasonably certain that they harbored some followers of Jesus. His procedure would be to apprehend all whom he could lay hands on and return them to Jerusalem for action by the Sanhedrin.

There is no clear basis here for insisting that Saul, highly trained in Judaism and zealous for its traditions, must have been a member of the nation's supreme Council. As Bruce points out,[3] Saul's youth (Ac 7:58) would likely exclude him from such a body of elders (for further discussion see under 26:10). What is clearly implied here is the recognition of the Sanhedrin's authority by Jews even outside the bounds of Palestine (cf. 1 Mac 15:15-21). Evident also is the fact that believers in Jesus still frequented the synagogues—much as early disciples in Jerusalem, the apostles included, had felt free to make use of the Temple.

That they had their own gatherings in addition may be regarded as certain. But from the standpoint of the Jewish authorities, they were still within the fold of Judaism and known as the sect of the Nazarenes (24:5). As such, they were subject to correction and discipline in the hope of changing their thinking. They needed to be brought into line and made "regular" again. It is instructive to note that Paul himself, as a Christian, was disciplined by the synagogue on several occasions (2 Co 11:24), which implies that he was regarded as still within the ranks of the chosen people. And Paul was not averse to being considered so, since it kept open for him the door of access to his nation as a witness for Christ. He could be driven out of a synagogue or out of a town, but there is no indication of excommunication or any attempt along this line (cf. 28:17-20).

The term *Nazarene* is not used in the present passage. Instead, believers are described as belonging to "the Way," which was an early designation they gave to their own group. It was devoid of the derogation attached to "the sect of the Nazarenes" (24:14). Whether or not it owed its origin to the claim of Jesus to be "the way" (Jn 14:6) cannot be determined. What is clear is that this group was asserting that it possessed the secret of salvation and life in an absolute sense. Christianity was not regarded as one way among many possible choices.

Verses 3-9. Here the conversion of Saul is recounted objectively, with no attempt to diagnose the thoughts that coursed through the persecutor's mind.

> **9:3** And it came about that as he journeyed, he was approaching Damascus, and suddenly a light from heaven flashed around him;
> **4** and he fell to the ground, and heard a voice saying to him, "Saul, Saul, why are you persecuting Me?"
> **5** And he said, "Who art Thou, Lord?" And He *said*, "I am Jesus whom you are persecuting,

147

6 but rise, and enter the city, and it shall be told you what you must do."

7 And the men who traveled with him stood speechless, hearing the voice, but seeing no one.

8 And Saul got up from the ground, and though his eyes were open, he could see nothing; and leading him by the hand, they brought him into Damascus.

9 And he was three days without sight, and neither ate nor drank.

9:3-6. This great event of conversion, or better, of being laid hold of by the Lord (Phil 3:12), occurred when Saul's journey was almost completed. It is vain to conjecture, as some have done, that on the way he had been thinking seriously about his own spiritual state in the light of what he knew about Jesus and His claims, with a growing uneasiness and lack of self-confidence, until finally he capitulated and looked away to Jesus, thus effecting an inner change or conversion. From all we know of this man, he was likely anticipating, with pent-up feeling, purging from the synagogues of Damascus those who confessed their faith in Jesus of Nazareth. Paul's own writings give no justification for imagining a psychological build-up of self-distrust combined with misgivings about the rightfulness of his course as a persecutor. The change which occurred that day was initiated not from within but from without.

"Suddenly a light from heaven flashed around him." To a Jew, the combination of a "light" of great intensity with a "voice" was calculated to bring awareness that a divine revelation was taking place (Ex 3:2, 4-5; Mt 17:2, 5). The message was for him: "Saul, Saul, why are you persecuting Me?" The Lord deliberately identified Himself with His Church, a truth which became deeply ingrained in Paul as he grew in understanding of its meaning (e.g., 1 Co 12:12).

For the moment he was nonplussed, because he had thought of his persecuting activity as directed simply against men and women. This fact, however, does not warrant rendering his response, as Goodspeed does, "Who are you, sir?" Granted, *kyrios* is capable of this pedestrian meaning, especially as people meet for the first time (Jn 4:11); but in this case, in view of the light and the voice, the word had a numinous significance. Saul knew he was in the presence of a supernatural manifestation, but he could not yet cope with it, and his question reflects his bewilderment. That very bewilderment underscores the likelihood that he had not been thinking about the Lord Jesus along the way. Suddenly he had to think about Him and communicate with Him.

Enlightenment about the source of the heavenly voice came quickly. "I am Jesus whom you are persecuting." The use of the human name rather than a divine title put everything into focus for Saul. Jesus of Nazareth was alive. His disciples had been right after all in proclaiming His resurrection from the dead. What the arguments of Stephen and others could not do, this Christophany, graciously given to the persecutor, accomplished without deliberation or debate. Everything was suddenly in right perspective. The one whom he had called Lord out of deference, lest he offend the Deity or His messenger, was now seen to be Lord indeed (cf. 2:36).

It was His prerogative to command, which He did at once, telling Saul to rise and go into the city, promising that there the next step would be made known to him. The city, of course, was Damascus. In writing to the Galatians Paul incidentally confirmed the location of his conversion experience (Gal 1:17). All the New Testament references to Damascus have to do with his conversion or early activity at this spot.

"And it shall be told you what you must do" might seem to suggest that Saul would have the Gospel explained to him by someone and on this basis would be able to make his decision. If this were so, it would contradict Paul's own statement that the Gospel he preached did not come to him from man or by human instruction, but rather through a revelation of Jesus Christ (Gal 1:12). But in neither Acts 9, 22, nor 26 is there anything to indicate that men imparted the knowledge of the Gospel to him. He was helped by Ananias—greeted, delivered from his blindness, baptized, and received into the fellowship of believers—but by his own statement, it was God who had been pleased to reveal His Son in him (Gal 1:15-16).

9:7-9. Set forth here are the effect of the confrontation on Saul and the involvement of his companions. The men who journeyed with him are described as "hearing the voice, but seeing no one." A problem is created by the fact that in 22:9, in some versions (e.g., KJV, RSV), it is stated that those who were with Saul did not hear the voice of the one who spoke to him. At least two attempts have been made to resolve the difficulty. One is to note that although the verb "hear" is the same in the two passages, it is followed by the genitive case in 9:7 and by the accusative case in 22:9. Some Greek scholars take the position that the genitive denotes merely the physical sensation (sound), whereas the accusative conveys the idea of hearing with comprehension. This distinction is based on classical Greek usage. However, a study of the data in Epictetus and in the LXX, both of which fall in the period of Hellenistic Greek as does the New Testament, has called in question this distinction for New Testament times.[4]

A different tack is taken by F. F. Bruce, who writes regarding 9:7, "Luke may very well mean here that it was Paul's voice that his companions heard, although they could neither see nor hear the person whom he appeared to be addressing."[5] This is ingenious, but it is hardly natural to refer "the voice" (used without any qualification) to Saul in a situation dominated by the communication of the Lord to him. In the parallel passage (22:9) the voice clearly belongs to the Lord Jesus.

The former solution is still the more likely. An echo of 9:7, it may be, occurs in connection with the death of Polycarp in the second century. "Now when Polycarp entered into the arena there came a voice from heaven: 'Be strong, Polycarp, and play the man.' And no one saw the speaker, but our friends who were there heard the voice."[6]

By saying that the men saw no one (22:9 simply notes that they saw the light) Luke seems to imply by contrast that Saul did. Other passages state with sufficient clarity that he saw the Lord (9:17; 22:14; 26:16). Paul based his apostleship on this fact (1 Co 9:1; 15:8-9). Both items—the hearing of the voice by others and the seeing of the Lord by Paul—help to establish the fact that the conversion was effected by something objective rather than by an internal process in the persecutor. The blindness he suffered points to the same conclusion (cf. Ac 22:11).

Helpless because of his blindness and humbled by the realization that in his misguided zeal he had been guilty of attacking the very congregation of God, the true Israel (Gal 1:13), and of wounding the exalted Lord (Ac 9:4), Paul was assisted to quarters in the city. There he remained quiet, spending three days in fasting, pondering recent events, and praying (cf. v. 11). His life had reached a crisis point. What lay before him? He had no means of knowing.

Verses 10-19a. The significance of this section, so far as Saul and Christ are concerned, is well expressed by R. B. Rackham: "He is crucified with Christ, and the three days of darkness are like the three days in the tomb. But on the third day with Christ he rises from the dead in baptism; after this he is filled with the Holy Ghost—his Pentecost."[7]

> **9:10** Now there was a certain disciple at Damascus, named Ananias; and the Lord said to him in a vision, "Ananias." And he said, "Behold, *here am* I, Lord."
>
> **11** And the Lord *said* to him, "Arise and go to the street called Straight, and inquire at the house of Judas for a man from Tarsus named Saul, for behold, he is praying,
>
> **12** and he has seen in a vision a man named Ananias come in and lay his hands on him, so that he might regain his sight."
>
> **13** But Ananias answered, "Lord, I have heard from many about this man, how much harm he did to Thy saints at Jerusalem;
>
> **14** and here he has authority from the chief priests to bind all who call upon Thy name."
>
> **15** But the Lord said to him, "Go, for he is a chosen instrument of

Mine, to bear My name before the Gentiles and kings and the sons of Israel;

16 for I will show him how much he must suffer for My name's sake."

17 And Ananias departed and entered the house, and after laying his hands on him said, "Brother Saul, the Lord Jesus, who appeared to you on the road by which you were coming, has sent me so that you may regain your sight, and be filled with the Holy Spirit."

18 And immediately there fell from his eyes something like scales, and he regained his sight, and he arose and was baptized;

19a and he took food and was strengthened.

9:10-12. Though the words of the risen Lord to Saul about what would happen to him in Damascus (v. 6) were vague enough to keep him in suspense, they contained a promise. To fulfill it, the Lord selected a messenger among the believers in Damascus, appearing to Ananias in a vision. Judging from what is said about him in 22:12, namely, his devotion to the Law and his good standing with the Jewish community, he was not a Hellenist who had fled from Jerusalem but one who had been settled in Damascus for some time. He was a man of different stamp from the individual of the same name who had disturbed the church at Jerusalem (chap. 5)—even as Judas, the man to whose home he was sent, was of higher caliber than the betrayer of Jesus; and Saul, to whom Ananias was called to minister, was vastly superior to Saul the king of Israel.

Ananias was directed to go to "the street called Straight." H. V. Morton, noting that this street was a mile long, observes, "It was so named because, like the main streets of nearly all the great Hellenistic cities, it ran straight as an arrow from one end of the city to the other."[8]

Saul is designated as "a man from Tarsus." This is the first of five references in Acts to the city, all of them relating to Saul. Perhaps as old as Damascus, it was the capital of the province of Cilicia. On the basis of Galatians 1:15, Sir William Ramsay contended that the divine preparation of the human vessel must have included the environment, and that on the basis of available knowledge of this place there was no other spot in the ancient world which could have prepared Saul equally well.[9] It was here that he had spent his early years before going to Jerusalem for training in Judaism (22:3).

By granting a "vision" to Saul, in which he perceived Ananias coming in to lay hands on him for the recovery of his sight, and then by informing Ananias of this fact, the Lord made it difficult for the latter to refuse the commission of being His messenger. To be sure, there was a measure of protest, but it was quickly overcome.

9:13-16. The protest was natural, in view of all that Ananias knew of Saul and in view of his lack of information about his conversion. "Many"

151

people had told him of the terrible inroads Saul had made on the church at Jerusalem. Some had doubtless been eyewitnesses of his ruthlessness before taking flight to Damascus. Ananias was well informed about Saul, knowing even of his mission to Damascus. How he had received this information is uncertain. Possibly he had received letters from people in Jerusalem, or first-hand reports from some who had left the city just ahead of Saul and his party, or even some word from those who had accompanied Saul and now felt free to divulge the purpose of the trip in view of what had happened to their leader. It is a testimony to the courage of Ananias that despite the threat of persecution he did not panic and resort to flight. His objections were not answered directly but were silenced by a word of command—"Go."

To leave the matter there would have meant sending Ananias on his way still filled with misgiving, so the Lord shared with His servant the importance of Saul in His plans for the future progress of the Gospel: "He is a chosen instrument of Mine." The word rendered "instrument" more often occurs in the sense of "vessel," especially when it refers to a material receptacle. In the Old Testament it was sometimes used, in a metaphorical sense, of Israel (Ho 8:8; cf. Jer 18:1-11) or of an individual (Ps 31: 12). This sense is strong in Paul's writings. The idea of inherent weakness which must be transcended by divine power is prominent in 2 Corinthians 4:7 and may be latent in the passage before us. Saul, despite his apparent unsuitability due to his past conduct, would prove to be a potent instrument for the Lord as he submitted his life to be used by Him.

The figure of the vessel is carried forward in the statement of the Lord's purpose, "to bear My name." Saul would be His personal representative wherever he went. The "Gentiles" are named first as a special sphere of ministry. No conflict with Romans 1:16 is involved, for there the apostle was speaking in general terms of the historic fact that the Gospel had been given first to the covenant people (cf. 3:26). But as the remainder of Acts shows, the Gentiles were to be the main object of Paul's labors. "Kings," including Agrippa and Caesar, come into prominence after his arrest. Other rulers were the Roman governors Felix and Festus. "The sons of Israel" were not forgotten, and they remained close to the apostle's heart throughout his ministry (Ro 9:1-3; 10:1). Through his use of the synagogue for testimony, Paul was able to reach both Jew and Gentile at the same time on numerous occasions.

By way of conclusion, the privilege of being Christ's representative was balanced by the announcement that Saul must "suffer" much for the Lord's sake. There is no hint here or elsewhere that the former persecutor must now endure suffering because he had inflicted so much of it on the saints. It was not because of them, but for the Lord's sake (Ac 9:16). Saul would enter into fellowship with the sufferings of Christ (Phil 3:10). This became a distinguishing mark of his service and of his apostleship, one which would-be apostles were unable to match (2 Co 11:22-27). However, it should not be thought that Saul was to be in this respect unique among the Lord's true servants (Mt 10:16-25; Jn 15:20-21).

9:17-19a. The first act of Ananias on entering Judas's house was to lay his hands on Saul. In the initial sense, this pertained to the healing of the blindness (cf. Ac 28:8), but it had relevance also to the filling with the Spirit that is noted here (cf. 8:17). The commission of verse 15 would have had little meaning apart from the divine enablement to fulfill it.

Since Ananias was not an official of the church, Saul was not put in the position of being subordinated to a "higher-up." No doubt the hands were gently applied, but what reassured Saul more than this was the opening word, "Brother" Saul. To be counted as a brother in Christ after his attempts to ruin the Church must have suffused his soul with astonishment and joy. What a blessed introduction to Christian fellowship! No word of reproach for his persecuting activities, only a hearty welcome into the fold.

Saul responded by being baptized and then eating a meal, which broke his fast. The spiritual took precedence over the physical. Whether he was filled with the Spirit in connection with his baptism or prior to it is of little moment, since Acts provides examples of both sequences (2:38; 10:44). A sidelight here is the observation that baptism was administered by a layman, without any question as to its validity.

A comparison of the words of Ananias to Saul with what the Lord had disclosed to him concerning Saul's future is instructive. Ananias had nothing to say about the suffering in store for him. After all, the Lord Jesus had indicated that *He* would unfold this to Saul (v. 16).

Verses 19b-25. The compact narrative is about evenly divided between a recital of Saul's mission in Damascus and of his escape from those who sought his life.

> 9:19b Now for several days he was with the disciples who were at Damascus,
> 20 and immediately he *began* to proclaim Jesus in the synagogues, saying, "He is the Son of God."
> 21 And all those hearing him continued to be amazed, and were saying, "Is this not he who in Jerusalem destroyed those who called on this name, and *who* had come here for the purpose of bringing them bound before the chief priests?"
> 22 But Saul kept increasing in strength and confounding the Jews who lived at Damascus by proving that this *Jesus* is the Christ.

23 And when many days had elapsed, the Jews plotted together to do away with him,

24 but their plot became known to Saul. And they were also watching the gates day and night so that they might put him to death;

25 but his disciples took him by night, and let him down through *an opening in* the wall, lowering him in a basket.

9:19b-22. Almost overnight the persecutor became the preacher, building up the faith which formerly he had sought to destroy (cf. Gal 1:23). One receives the impression that for "several days" Saul was content to bask in the delight of the new fellowship "with the disciples," in which case "immediately" (v. 20), in connection with the commencement of preaching, involves something of an interval, in contrast to the "immediately" of verse 18. But by temperament as well as by reason of his dedication to the Lord, he was eager to confess his newly found faith, and the synagogues of the city provided the platform he needed. What he had expected to make the scene of interrogation and possibly the application of third degree tactics (v. 2) was now a forum for his proclamation of the Gospel. No wonder those who heard him were "amazed."

The Christian Jews must have shared this amazement. God had done a marvelous thing. Not only had He demonstrated care for His own by halting the persecution on their very doorstep, but in the process He had gained for Himself a herald of the message of grace. Men would have counted it a great thing if the hand of God had rewarded the persecutor by striking him dead (cf. 12:1, 23). But to salvage the opponent and enlist him on behalf of the cause was a far greater victory.

Saul's message is gathered up in two statements, both centered on the Lord Jesus. One is the declaration that He is the Son of God (v. 20), the other that He is the Christ, the Messiah (v. 22). The same combination is found in Peter's confession (Mt 16:16) and in the statement of purpose behind the writing of John's gospel (Jn 20:31). The concept of the Lord Jesus as the Son of God continued to be central to Paul's Christology, as can be ascertained from Romans 1:3-4 (cf. Ac 13:33). It had been prominent in the teaching of Jesus Himself (Mt 11:27) and basic to Mark's presentation of His person (Mk 1:1). What had been true before the resurrection was more evident as true after the resurrection, and Saul had very recently been in touch with the risen One. The title *Son of God* must have been highly meaningful to him and also intelligible to his audiences (cf. Ps 2:7; Lk 3:22; Ac 13:33).

Saul's immense learning in the fields of Scripture and Jewish tradition, now set on fire by his conversion, proved too much for any who ventured to contend with him. He made a convincing presentation by yoking prediction to fulfillment in reference to the Messiahship of Jesus. This continued to be his synagogue approach (17:3; 18:5), and it was shared by Apollos (18:28). Peter used the method also (2:36), taking it over from the Master (Lk 24:44-46).

Luke says nothing in this account about Saul's departure from Damascus for Arabia and his return to the city (cf. Gal 1:17). From his omission of this journey one may perhaps conclude that the major purpose of this trip (which need not have taken him far, since the kingdom of Aretas was directly east of the city) was not to evangelize but to meditate on what had been revealed to him. This is agreeable to the Galatian context. At the same time, it is hard to picture this man refraining from preaching for any great length of time. Other factors may have operated, such as the desire to spare the saints in Damascus from persecution which was being stirred up against him in the city because of his outspoken testimony.

9:23-25. The final stage of Saul's stay in Damascus is pictured here. The persecutor became the persecuted; the hunter became the hunted. A ministry of "many days" was now coming to a head, with the opposition becoming organized and determined. In writing to the Galatians, Paul indicated a three-year period between his conversion and his first journey to Jerusalem (Gal 1:15-18), but there is no indication as to how much of this period was spent in Damascus and how much in Arabia. The sojourn in the latter place may well have been brief.

At any rate, the Jews in Damascus made their plans to get rid of Saul. This was the first of many attempts on his life after becoming a believer. Another was made in Jerusalem shortly after this (Ac 9:29). Others occurred at Corinth (20:3), at Ephesus (20:19; cf. Ro 16:4), at Jerusalem in connection with his final visit (23:21), and when he was at Caesarea (25:3). No wonder he could write of "dangers from *my* countrymen" (2 Co 11:26). That he was able to travel and preach with this kind of pressure on him much of the time is an indication that he had committed his life completely to the Lord and was trusting Him for safekeeping.

This protection was worked out in various ways—by the help which his Roman citizenship provided (e.g., Ac 25:11), by division among his adversaries (23:6-10), but mainly by the assistance of fellow believers. On this occasion, "his disciples" managed under cover of darkness to lower him through an opening in a Christian's house abutting the city wall, or more properly, built into the wall (cf. Jos 2:15).

Paul referred to this incident later on (2 Co 11:32-33), adding the information that the ethnarch under Aretas the king was involved in the effort to seize him. This may indicate that he had offended the Arabs during his stay in their territory, perhaps by his witness for Christ. Or it may be that the Arabs felt it was to their advantage to cooperate with the Jews who were trying to apprehend him. There is even a possibility that the Romans, in a gesture of good will toward the Nabataeans, had restored Arabian control over Damascus, the emperor Gaius being eager to placate Aretas, who had been the target of a military campaign planned by emperor Tiberius, Gaius' predecessor.[10] Saul had a capacity for making bitter enemies as well as firm friends.

It should not escape our notice that those who helped him are called "his disciples" (the only time this expression occurs). The word *disciple* is prominent in the gospels and Acts, but fails to appear at all in the remainder of the New Testament, being replaced by such terms as *saints, believers,* and *brethren.*

Verses 26-31. The scene changes to Jerusalem and Saul's first contact with the church there. After only a few days it proved expedient to depart, as strong opposition developed. With the departure, an era of peace came for the church in Palestine.

> **9:26** And when he had come to Jerusalem, he was trying to associate with the disciples; and they were all afraid of him, not believing that he was a disciple.
>
> **27** But Barnabas took hold of him and brought him to the apostles and described to them how he had seen the Lord on the road, and that He had talked to him, and how at Damascus he had spoken out boldly in the name of Jesus.
>
> **28** And he was with them moving about freely in Jerusalem, speaking out boldly in the name of the Lord.
>
> **29** And he was talking and arguing with the Hellenistic *Jews;* but they were attempting to put him to death.
>
> **30** But when the brethren learned *of it,* they brought him down to Caesarea and sent him away to Tarsus.
>
> **31** So the church throughout all Judea and Galilee and Samaria enjoyed peace, being built up; and, going on in the fear of the Lord and in the comfort of the Holy Spirit, it continued to increase.

9:26-28. Quite naturally, no indication is given of any contact between Saul and the Sanhedrin after his arrival in Jerusalem. His life was in a different orbit now. The members of the Council knew what had happened, and they would have liked to forget all about Saul if they could.

Even on the part of the disciples there was a measure of hostility, or at least of suspicion (cf. the reaction of Ananias, v. 13). Doubtless there had been some reports from Damascus about the conversion of Saul, but it was felt that this might be a trick, that the archpersecutor had decided that he could do more damage by becoming a wolf in sheep's clothing. The very fact that he seemed to be trying so hard to be accepted at Jerusalem could have confirmed their suspicions. Apparently he had come without any written commendation from the brethren in Damascus.

Hungering for Christian fellowship, Saul must have been on the brink of despair. Then he found in the church one man of influence who recognized his sincerity and accepted at face value his account of his experience with the risen Lord and his testimony at Damascus. Barnabas was never more truly "a son of encouragement" (4:36) than on this occasion. By taking Saul first to the apostles and persuading them, he was able to break down the suspicion of the church as a whole. Apparently the new arrival made himself at home with the leaders of the church and joined them in public testimony.

From Galatians 1:18 it is evident that Saul had a special purpose in going to Jerusalem at this time. He wanted to become acquainted with Peter, and was able to spend fifteen days in his company as his guest. At that time he also had contact with James the Lord's brother (Gal 1:19). Consequently Luke's statement about the apostles (Ac 9:27) should not be thought of as meaning that the entire group was on hand. Doubtless most of them were out shepherding the churches of Judea, which had recently felt the bruising effect of persecution. Paul's statement that he remained unknown by sight to the Judean churches (Gal 1:22) confirms that he remained in Jerusalem.†

Little imagination is required to appreciate what this visit meant to Saul. From James he was able to learn much about the early life of Jesus at Nazareth. The two could rejoice together over what the resurrection had made possible in the life of each of them. From Peter must have come many a helpful account of how the Lord had ministered to the multitude and how He had taught His disciples. This fortnight left him rich with memories he would treasure in days to come.

9:29-30. Saul was not content to remain only in the company of believers. Drawn irresistibly to the synagogue where he had heard Stephen declare his faith, he now picked up the torch and entered into dialogue with the Hellenistic Jews. He had no greater success, apparently, than Stephen had enjoyed. Probably the pattern was repeated—inability to answer the messenger of Christ brought a determination to silence him by death (cf. 6:9-12). This happened within a few days' time (Gal 1:18).

Word of the contemplated attempts on his life came to the attention of the leaders of the church, who acted swiftly to get Saul out of the city. The Lord's warning to him at this time (22:17-18) must have gone far to make him willing to leave. Furthermore, he did not care to be responsible for a fresh wave of persecution for the church such as he himself

---

†The expression "moving about freely" is literally "going in and out." But this need not have involved leaving the city. The idiom simply expresses movement. Luke distinctly states that this activity took place in Jerusalem. For another example of this idiom see 1:21.

had instigated (8:3). His stay in Jerusalem ended on the same note as his sojourn in Damascus. Boldness in witness had nearly cost him his life for a second time.

Friends accompanied him as far as Caesarea (was there contact with Philip there?), then he proceeded on his own to Tarsus, his boyhood home. It is possible that he had not been there for a good many years, in view of his time of study in Jerusalem, where he had a sister (23:16). For ten years or so, a veil of silence descended over Saul's career, to be lifted when he reappeared as a leader in the church at Antioch (11:25-26). However, his own statement suggests that he did not confine his residence wholly to Tarsus, but was active in Christian work throughout Syria and Cilicia (Gal 1:21).

9:31. In this summary Luke notes the peace then pervading the church in Palestine. The point of "so" is to remind the reader of the great contrast between this state of quiet and the turmoil caused by persecution.

Saul's conversion was the primary factor in the change. Another was the shift in the political situation. Vitellius, the imperial legate in Syria from A.D. 35 to 37, had installed a certain Jonathan as high priest in Jerusalem. He became so independent and aggressive that Vitellius, when visiting Jerusalem in 37, removed him from office and appointed his brother Theophilus in his place. At the same time, word came of the death of Tiberius and the succession of Gaius (Caligula) as emperor. "The new emperor was as famous for his adherence to Hellenism as his predecessor was for his opposition to it, and so a reverse was to be expected for the recently kindled flame of Judaism."[11] The restricting of official Jewish influence would naturally be felt by the church in terms of greater security and freedom to expand.

This summary verse is of interest also because of its use of the word *ekklēsia* (church). Although the plural form is found here in many manuscripts, those of superior quality have the singular, suggesting the concept of the Church universal as contrasted with the local sense of the word (e.g., 8:1). That is, the church in Palestine is viewed as a whole rather than as separate congregations. The three districts named, Judea, Galilee, and Samaria, comprised the whole country west of the Jordan.

Two general observations are made about the state of the church. First, it was being "built up," with this edification being recognized in the lives of God-fearing believers. This was a time of spiritual growth. Second, under the comfort and encouragement of the Holy Spirit there was a reaching out to minister the Gospel to others, so that the church "continued to increase."

The mention of Galilee is a reminder that Luke has not narrated the circumstances under which the witness to Jesus reached the Saviour's native territory after Pentecost. The eleven, being Galilean themselves, could not have been expected to rest easily as long as this area remained unevangelized. Probably the five hundred to whom the Lord appeared after His resurrection (1 Co 15:6), presumably in Galilee (cf. Mt 28:16-17), took an active part in witnessing to this area.

D. PETER'S MINISTRY—9:32—11:18

THAT AN INTIMATE CONNECTION exists between this section and the fore-going is evident. Saul's conversion has been recounted, including his commission to go to the Gentiles, but the story of that task has not yet been taken up. The telling of it must wait until the narration of Peter's mission to Cornelius, which provided the opening wedge of the campaign to reach the Gentiles, a campaign which Saul was to prosecute with vigor and magnificent leadership.

1. AT LYDDA AND JOPPA—9:32-43

Much of Peter's itinerating activity in Judea is passed by with merely a hint as to how extensive it was—"all those parts"—in order to describe that portion which led him to Joppa and ultimately to Caesarea.

9:32 Now it came about that as Peter was traveling through all *those parts,* he came down also to the saints who lived at Lydda.

33 And there he found a certain man named Aeneas, who had been bedridden eight years, for he was paralyzed.

34 And Peter said to him, "Aeneas, Jesus Christ heals you; arise, and make your bed." And immediately he arose.

35 And all who lived at Lydda and Sharon saw him, and they turned to the Lord.

36 Now in Joppa there was a certain disciple named Tabitha (which translated *in Greek* is called Dorcas); this woman was abounding with deeds of kindness and charity, which she continually did.

37 And it came about at that time that she fell sick and died; and when they had washed her body, they laid it in an upper room.

38 And since Lydda was near Joppa, the disciples, having heard that Peter was there, sent two men to him, entreating him, "Do not delay to come to us."

39 And Peter arose and went with them. And when he had come, they brought him into the upper room; and all the widows stood beside him weeping, and showing all the tunics and garments that Dorcas used to make while she was with them.

40 But Peter sent them all out and knelt down and prayed, and turning to the body, he said, "Tabitha, arise." And she opened her eyes, and when she saw Peter, she sat up.

41 And he gave her his hand and raised her up; and calling the saints and widows, he presented her alive.

42 And it became known all over Joppa, and many believed in the Lord.

43 And it came about that he stayed many days in Joppa with a certain tanner, Simon.

9:32-35. Lydda, the Lod of the Old Testament (1 Ch 8:12), stood at the crossroads of two important travel routes, one between Egypt and Babylon, the other between Joppa and Jerusalem. By the time Peter visited the place, a church had already been established, probably the work of Hellenists who had been obliged to leave Jerusalem when persecution broke out there (8:1). A visit by Philip (8:40) is a possibility.

It can be assumed that Peter preached the Word on this occasion, but Luke made no reference to it, concentrating rather on a miracle of healing. Aeneas had been paralyzed for eight years. There is no indication in the gospels that Jesus had visited this area, otherwise Aeneas might have been relieved of his distress long before Peter's coming. But now Jesus *was* there, working through His servant to bring healing.* The effect was similar to the healing of the lame man (chap. 3) in that both were well known, so that the healing created a sensation. A general turning to the Lord resulted, both at Lydda and Sharon. The linking of the two places gives the impression that Sharon was a town, but none is known, so the reference is probably to the maritime plain, especially the southern portion.†

9:36-37. Joppa, now known as Jaffa, was located on the seacoast, about twelve miles from Lydda. It was here that Huram, king of Tyre, brought timber from Lebanon to be carried up to Jerusalem for the building of the temple in Solomon's time (2 Ch 2:11-16). It was here that Jonah took ship to avoid going to Nineveh as the Lord's messenger.

Tabitha (gazelle), or Dorcas (the Greek equivalent), was a "disciple," indicating that the Gospel had reached this spot as well as Lydda (cf. 8:40). Like Martha, she found that her gift lay in the area of physical ministry (cf. "helps" in 1 Co 12:28). Perhaps her sacrificial labors had contributed to a sickness that proved fatal. The body was prepared for burial, but no interment was held, as the sequel explains.

9:38-42. The known presence of Peter a few miles away spurred hope in the minds of the believers, which suggests that news of the healing of Aeneas had reached their city. We may take for granted that they had

*"Jesus Christ *heals* you" does not have the force of "heals at any time" but is an example of a relatively infrequent use of the present tense, meaning in this instance, "here and now heals you."
†The fact that "Sharon" has the definite article, whereas "Lydda" does not, may have been sufficient to convey the idea of a district (cf. *the Sahara, the Sudan*).

faith in the resurrection of Jesus. Reports had come of mighty miracles at Jerusalem, Samaria, and other places. We cannot be sure that there was a report of a raising from the dead (none has been recounted thus far in Acts), but after all, Jesus had raised the dead and had promised that the works which He had done would be carried on by His disciples. So hope burned brightly. As it turned out, Dorcas's situation was like that of Lazarus, who had sickened and died—it was all for the glory of God, leading up to resurrection.

The message that was sent to Peter, "Do not delay to come to us" (v. 38) did not have in view that he would conduct a funeral service. Peter obliged, putting aside all else to go with the two messengers. One can detect here a certain preparation for a like response to another urgent appeal soon to come (10:23).

As Peter arrived at the upper room he was quickly made aware of how great a loss the Christian community had suffered. The widows were there in force, exhibiting the garments that Dorcas had made for them. Similarly, a congregation is apt to remember a man's pastoral ministry, lovingly given in times of need, even more than the sermons he labored to prepare.

But it was not the past which concerned Peter. The lamentation was genuine, but it was a damper. So "Peter sent them all out" (v. 40). Was he recalling what the Lord had done when He raised the daughter of Jairus (Mk 5:40)? Sensing his need of divine power, he "prayed." Had not Jesus, in promising that great works would be done through His disciples, reminded them that whatever they would ask He would perform in answer to prayer (Jn 14:12-14)?

It took faith to turn again to the lifeless "body" and say, "Tabitha, arise." Peter found it natural to use the Aramaic name rather than Dorcas, and the fact that it is so recorded favors the idea that Luke has followed an early source preserved in the Jewish wing of the church. Awakened from the sleep of death, Tabitha sat up. To help her rise from the couch, Peter extended his hand. As Rackham notes, "To have done so before would have made him unclean,"[1] in light of Numbers 19:11.

Now the people who had been barred from the room were invited in to see and greet their friend, "alive" by the power of God. News of the miracle soon spread through the city, with the result that "many believed in the Lord." Nothing is said about the prestige of Peter. He was no Simon Magus (8:9-11).

9:43. Attention is directed to Peter's residence for a time in Joppa. Probably he did not anticipate what his next move was to be. It was a time of waiting for guidance, which came in due course.

Meanwhile his host was another Simon. Being a "tanner," he had likely been shunned by the Jewish community because of his distasteful occupation. Living close by the sea (10:6) served two purposes: plenty of water was available for washing the hides, and the unpleasant odors were not liable to reach people in the city to any great extent.

Simon had already found a welcome among believers, which must have been enhanced by Peter's willingness to abide with him. One may even see in this liberal attitude of readiness to reside with a man who handled unclean animals a preparation in Peter himself for the much larger step he was about to take at Caesarea (10:28).

2. THE WITNESS TO CORNELIUS—10:1-48

Since Luke was not greatly concerned with chronology, we do not have the information necessary to date this incident with any precision. What the writer desired to emphasize is the beginning of testimony to the Gentiles. He had already given considerable attention to the ministry of Philip to an individual of this status, which is a pointer toward the present narrative. But now it was time to set forth the evangelizing of Gentiles in a Palestinian setting. The very fact that Luke narrated the story at some length and then in effect repeated it in Peter's report to the Jerusalem church (chap. 11) clearly indicates its importance in the overall plan of the book.

In view of the large place given to Paul in the Acts, and especially to his work among the Gentiles, grounded in a divine commission (9:15), the placing of Peter in the forefront of this new development demonstrates that the historian was being true to the source material available to him. Luke granted that Peter took the lead at the beginning (cf. 15:7, 14). He had no associate on whom to rely for counsel, so was shut up to the leading of the Spirit. "Peter's position throughout 1-8 is as spokesman and representative of the Twelve, and is quite different in 9-15 where he acts in a personal capacity."[2]

Verses 1-8. Since the Gentiles did not know the Good News, and since the apostle Peter, steeped in Jewish Christianity, was not yet prepared to minister Christ to such people, God had to take the initiative. He had to deal with Peter, but first of all He moved to make Cornelius aware of divine concern for his spiritual state.

> **10:1** Now *there was* a certain man at Caesarea named Cornelius, a centurion of what was called the Italian cohort,
>
> **2** a devout man, and one who feared God with all his household, and gave many alms to the *Jewish* people, and prayed to God continually.
>
> **3** About the ninth hour of the day he clearly saw in a vision an angel of God who had *just* come in to him, and said to him, "Cornelius!"
>
> **4** And fixing his gaze upon him and being much alarmed, he said,

"What is it, Lord?" And he said to him, "Your prayers and alms have ascended as a memorial before God.

5 "And now dispatch *some* men to Joppa, and send for a man *named* Simon, who is also called Peter;

6 he is staying with a certain tanner *named* Simon, whose house is by the sea."

7 And when the angel who was speaking to him had departed, he summoned two of his servants and a devout soldier of those who were in constant attendance upon him,

8 and after he had explained everything to them, he sent them to Joppa.

10:1. Caesarea is the setting (cf. 8:40). This city on the coast was one of the monuments of the building activity of Herod the Great, who revamped the former community known as Strato's Tower and renamed it Caesarea in honor of Augustus. The construction went on for more than a decade and included many magnificent buildings and a harbor which Josephus states to have been larger than the Piraeus which served as the port of Athens. Later on it became the headquarters of Roman procurators who ruled the land in the name of Rome (cf. 23:23-24). Quite naturally Gentiles predominated over Jews in this location. It was here that friction between the two groups sparked the outbreak of the war between the Jews and the Romans which flared in A.D. 66.

Stationed here at the time of our narrative was a "centurion" named Cornelius. A centurion, as the word indicates, was in charge of a hundred men. In this instance they belonged to the Italian Cohort. "His troop . . . belonged to a special group recruited originally in Italy, though it is true that auxiliary units were kept up to strength after their formation by local recruitment."[3]

10:2. Having dealt with the secular status of Cornelius, Luke described his spiritual condition—"a devout man, and one who feared God." At first glance these two statements seem to say about the same thing; but Luke used this word for *devout* only here and in verse 7, and one form of the verb in Paul's Athenian address (17:23). The term as used by Luke may well be intended to indicate, then, a reverent attitude toward God and the supernatural on the part of one who needs further information to bring him to biblical faith.

The second phrase is more precise in its reference, being a technical term for a Gentile who attended the synagogue and to some degree honored Jewish law and custom, but who had not yet been incorporated into the congregation of Israel because he had not accepted circumcision. In the synagogues of the Dispersion this group made up a fairly substantial part of the attendants, sufficient to be recognized by a speaker (cf. 13:16). The God-fearer, then, must be distinguished from the Gentile who was thoroughly absorbed into Judaism and was known as a proselyte (2:10; 6:5; 13:43). The latter were usually harder to reach with the Gospel than God-fearers, for they had committed themselves fully to Judaism, while the God-fearers had not.

Cornelius had the strength of character to influence his entire "household," which may have included a family and certainly included servants and some soldiers in attendance on him (cf. v. 7). This broad significance of *household* is familiar from Philippians 4:22.

The piety of Cornelius extended not only Godward but toward the "people" around him, apparently the Jewish people (cf. 26:17). In helping them with his "alms," he was expressing his thanks for what he had received in the synagogue. The centurion whom Jesus had encountered, whose servant He healed, had been similarly generous toward the Jewish people, even to the extent of building a synagogue for them (Lk 7:5).

It was during the intertestamental period that almsgiving began to be associated with the idea of merit, regarded as able to secure forgiveness of sins for the giver (Tobit 12:9; Ec'us 3:30). It is impossible to say whether Cornelius shared this notion, but the fact that his activity in this realm is favorably noted (v. 4) inclines one to think that he did not consider it as meritorious, but as something his heart inclined him to do. Neither his alms nor his prayers had availed to bring him salvation (11:14)—a reminder that religion, no matter how honestly motivated and how sacrificially carried on, whether by cultus or benevolence, is not able to achieve salvation, which comes only through Christ (4:12). Nevertheless, Cornelius's devotion had great value because it made him a candidate for salvation (v. 4), prompting guidance from heaven to give him the knowledge whereby he could be saved, in line with the truth expressed in Romans 2:6-7.

10:3-6. God's response was not to save Cornelius by fiat, but to show him how he could learn of the appointed way. The ninth hour (3:00 P.M.) was one of the stated periods of prayer observed by the Jews (cf. 3:1) to which Cornelius had conformed his practice. Absorbed in his devotions he found himself experiencing a "vision" which included an angel speaking his name. As with Saul on the Damascus road (9:5), he responded by using the term "Lord," knowing that he must be in divine presence. It was a circumstance that alarmed him, for it might betoken God's displeasure. But his fears were immediately allayed through the message that his devotions and acts of kindness had been noted in heaven.

The vision was tantalizing because it contained directions to send to Joppa for Simon (his surname Peter distinguishes him from the other Simon who was his host) but said nothing about what would be accomplished by such a mission. But Cornelius showed that he was not far from the Kingdom by having a readiness to act without doubting or arguing. The least he could do was to obey the heavenly command.

10:7-8. The response of the centurion was immediate. He did not make the mistake of Naaman and request that some extraordinary thing be done for him (see 2 Ki 5:11), but was content to send as directed. For this purpose he selected two household slaves and a soldier, all of whom presumably shared the pious stance of their leader and lord. Cornelius did not want unsympathetic men for this task, but men akin to him in spirit. To them he imparted a knowledge of the vision he had received and the commission they were to fulfill. Joppa by the sea, some thirty miles to the south, was their destination.

Verses 9-16. The scene shifts to Joppa, where Peter had already spent many days (9:43), apparently not sure what God had in store for him. Now he was to learn afresh that God "works for those who wait for him" (Is 64:4, RSV). His waiting on God in prayer (matching Cornelius) was not in vain but opened up one of the most thrilling chapters of his life.

> **10:9** And on the next day, as they were on their way, and approaching the city, Peter went up on the housetop about the sixth hour to pray.
>
> **10** And he became hungry, and was desiring to eat; but while they were making preparations, he fell into a trance;
>
> **11** and he beheld the sky opened up, and a certain object like a great sheet coming down, lowered by four corners to the ground,
>
> **12** and there were in it all *kinds of* four-footed animals and crawling creatures of the earth and birds of the air.
>
> **13** And a voice came to him, "Arise, Peter, kill and eat!"
>
> **14** But Peter said, "By no means, Lord, for I have never eaten anything unholy and unclean."
>
> **15** And again a voice *came* to him a second time, "What God has cleansed, no *longer* consider unholy."
>
> **16** And this happened three times; and immediately the object was taken up into the sky.

10:9-10. It was on the second day of their journey that the servants of Cornelius found themselves nearing Joppa. Luke, the narrator, had a sense for the dramatic as he pictured the vision about to be given Peter as occurring just before the men arrived.

In Palestine, the housetop was flat and approached by a flight of steps on the outside of the house. Since it was a good spot for reflection or prayer, Peter made his way there to pray at the "sixth hour" (noon). Some evidence exists that godly Israelites had observed this period as well as the morning and evening for prayer (Ps 55:17; Dan 6:10). Hunger asserted itself, which God used to make the forthcoming vision relevant to Peter. "He fell into a trance" (not the same word as "vision" in v. 3 but occurring again in the case of Paul in 22:17), or an ecstatic state, which God induced for His own purposes of revelation and instruction. Consciousness was at least partially suspended (cf. Gen 2:21 LXX).

10:11-12. First of all Peter saw something being let down from the opened sky before his uplifted eyes. It appeared to resemble a "great sheet," held by its four corners so as not to lose what was contained in it. The sheet descended to a point where Peter could readily see the contents. In it were all kinds of animals, including walking, crawling, and flying varieties. For the sequel to have meaning, it is necessary to understand that both clean and unclean animals, in terms of the Levitical code, were present for Peter's inspection.

10:13-16. Unexpectedly the Lord proceeded to instruct Peter by bidding him, "Kill and eat," thereby to satisfy his hunger. Peter replied without hesitation. He must have felt that he was being tested, and it was his nature under such conditions to want to show his loyalty (cf. Mt 26:33). So he protested that nothing unclean had ever entered his mouth. He had been a practicing Jew all his life.

Probably it did not occur to him that he was actually disobeying the Lord, who had just given him a command. At Caesarea Philippi he had disputed with Jesus the necessity for the Lord's going to the cross. Here the issue concerned his own conduct, and he was just as vigorous in his protestation as on the former occasion (Mt 16:22). Probably he had forgotten that Jesus had taught the disciples, "Whatever goes into the man from outside cannot defile him" (Mk 7:18). According to Matthew's account it was Peter himself who had inquired about the meaning of those words (Mt 15:15). Quite likely the editorial note in the parallel passage, Mark 7:19 ("Thus He declared all foods clean"), owes its origin to Peter's experience on the housetop after its significance had dawned upon him. (According to several early Fathers, Mark wrote his gospel as the interpreter of Peter.)

The voice came "a second time" with a final word to settle Peter's complaint. "What God has cleansed, no longer consider unholy." Altogether the vision of the sheet was given "three times," to impress it upon Peter's mind, and then was withdrawn.

Verses 17-23a. Peter's perplexity over what he had seen is understandable in a practicing Jew. He did not yet perceive that the restrictions of the Mosaic Law had been valid while the Law was in force but were not binding when Christ, the end of the Law, had brought that dispensation to a close. As far as foods were concerned, the edict at creation had declared everything that God had made to be good (Gen 1:31). This principle was now reestablished.

The termination of the Law was not recognized by unbelieving Jews and only gradually perceived by Jews who trusted in Christ. It required a period of education to free them from the outlook of years of living under the Levitical code. Even in the post-cross period a Christian Jew such as Peter, now aware of the situation, could be expected to avoid giving offense to a fellow Jew who was not a Christian by refusing to eat "unclean" food when in his company. But the principle of freedom in this area was clearly established (cf. 1 Ti 4:1-5).

> **10:17** Now while Peter was greatly perplexed in mind as to what the vision which he had seen might be, behold, the men who had been sent by Cornelius, having asked directions for Simon's house, appeared at the gate;
>
> **18** and calling out, they were asking whether Simon, who was also called Peter, was staying there.
>
> **19** And while Peter was reflecting on the vision, the Spirit said to him, "Behold, three men are looking for you.
>
> **20** "But arise, go downstairs, and accompany them without misgivings; for I have sent them Myself."
>
> **21** And Peter went down to the men and said, "Behold, I am the one you are looking for; what is the reason for which you have come?"
>
> **22** And they said, "Cornelius, a centurion, a righteous and God-fearing man well spoken of by the entire nation of the Jews, was *divinely* directed by a holy angel to send for you *to come* to his house and hear a message from you."
>
> **23a** And so he invited them in and gave them lodging.

10:17-23a. Peter's reflections on this matter were interrupted by the arrival of the men from Cornelius. The timing was perfect. Their mission would enable Peter to solve his perplexity by substituting unclean men for unclean food in his thinking. The Spirit did not provide the solution by direct revelation, but prompted Peter to go with the men "without misgivings," thus assuring him of God's blessing on the venture (cf. 8:29; Jn 16:13).

"Three" men had come, according to the almost unanimous testimony of the manuscripts. One important witness, Codex Vaticanus, has *two* at this point, possibly due to the reference to two servants in verse 7. But *three* doubtless represents the actual situation, harmonizing with the three-fold disclosure of the vision (v. 16). Peter could hardly have missed this circumstantial agreement in numbers. It enabled him to substitute men for animals, giving point to the whole episode on the housetop.

When Peter greeted the three and asked about the reason for their visit, they responded with restrained pride as they told of their master, Cornelius. One item emerges here which is not openly stated in verses 1 and 2, namely, the high esteem in which Cornelius was held by "the entire nation of the Jews." This exaggeration is pardonable. The statement was indeed true of the Jews in the Caesarea area, as a natural result of his almsgiving to the Jewish people (v. 2).

Cornelius had been "divinely directed" to send for Peter. Every time this verb appears in the New Testament in the passive voice it refers to supernatural guidance (cf. Lk 2:26). This was enough to satisfy Peter. In showing hospitality to the new arrivals he was already manifesting a willingness to have contact with Gentiles, a kind of firstfruits of his full illumination about his forthcoming mission to the house of Cornelius.

Verses 23b-29. This section deals with the arrival at Caesarea and provides the setting for the explanation given by Cornelius.

> **10:23b** And on the next day he arose and went away with them, and some of the brethren from Joppa accompanied him.
> **24** And on the following day he entered Caesarea. Now Cornelius was waiting for them, and had called together his relatives and close friends.
> **25** And when it came about that Peter entered, Cornelius met him, and fell at his feet and worshiped *him.*
> **26** But Peter raised him up, saying, "Stand up; I too am *just* a man."
> **27** And as he talked with him, he entered, and found many people assembled.
> **28** And he said to them, "You yourselves know how unlawful it is for a man who is a Jew to associate with a foreigner or to visit him; and *yet* God has shown me that I should not call any man unholy or unclean.
> **29** "That is why I came without even raising any objection when I was sent for. And so I ask for what reason you have sent for me."

10:23b-29. Peter had been told by the Spirit to go without misgivings, but this did not mean that he should go without foresight. This he exhibited by taking some brethren from Joppa with him, six in number (11:12). The reason for the precaution is fairly evident. As witnesses to what was to transpire at Caesarea they would be able to corroborate Peter's testimony when he was called on to explain the incident to the leaders at Jerusalem (11:1-18). Clearly Peter was aware that his mission at Caesarea might well be a turning point for the Church.

He (some manuscripts say "they") arrived at the destination and found Cornelius "waiting" for them. No doubt he had carefully calculated the time required to make the trip from Joppa and had summoned his relatives and friends accordingly. This man did not question in the least the reality of the vision, nor did he question the certainty that Peter would come. His faith resembled that of the centurion at Capernaum (Mt 8:10).

So great was his gratitude on seeing Peter that he prostrated himself before him. The word "worshiped" is probably too strong a rendering here, for Cornelius, as a faithful attendant at the synagogue, must have known that God alone is worthy of worship. But even the physical prostration was altogether unnecessary, since he was dealing with a "man." Even an angel is not entitled to receive worship (Rev 22:8-9).

On entering the house Peter discovered an assembled company waiting for his arrival. The same unselfishness which characterized Cornelius in his giving of alms had motivated him to share the anticipated blessing of Peter's visit with others.

It was natural that Peter's opening words should set forth the awkwardness of his position and the daring required to set foot in this house filled with Gentiles. Even though his hearers were aware of the exclusivism of the Jews and their avoidance of Gentiles lest defilement should result, Peter felt the need of reminding them of the unusual nature of what was transpiring. Ordinarily a Jew would neither "associate" with a Gentile nor "visit" him. He would have as little to do with him as possible.

This may sound unreasonable since the Jews welcomed Gentiles into the synagogue. But fraternizing with them was a different matter. The explanation takes us back to the return from Babylonian captivity, when the Jews, realizing that too close contact with the nations surrounding Israel had brought their fathers into idolatry and other sins, determined to remain separate from the people of the land (Neh 13:3, 23-27). Business relations with Gentiles were sometimes necessary, but social contacts were frowned on. The Jews felt that they must do everything necessary to retain their own religion and culture apart from Gentile contamination.

However, God had been dealing with Peter. Either before leaving Joppa or on the way, his eyes had been opened to see the meaning of the vision on the housetop, namely, that he should not call any "man" unholy or unclean. The lesson had sunk in. Peter had a freedom he had never known before (cf. 15:7-9). He succumbed on a later occasion to the pressure of Jewish-Christian strictness (Gal 2:11-12), but in principle he recognized that the middle wall of partition between Jew and Gentile had been broken down in Christ (cf. Eph 2:14).

All this time Peter was without clear indication as to what was expected of him at Caesarea. Apparently the conversation with Cornelius at the entrance of the dwelling had not disclosed anything more than what the messengers had told him, that he was to give a message in the centurion's house. By asking why he had been sent for, Peter opened the way for Cornelius to inform the entire group of the background for this gathering.

Verses 30-33. The explanation of Cornelius gives the essentials of God's dealings with him, as recounted at the beginning of the chapter.

10:30   And Cornelius said, "Four days ago to this hour, I was praying in my house during the ninth hour; and behold, a man stood before me in shining garments,

31   and he said, 'Cornelius, your prayer has been heard and your alms have been remembered before God.

32   'Send therefore to Joppa and invite Simon, who is also called Peter, to come to you; he is staying at the house of Simon *the* tanner by the sea.'

33   "And so I sent to you immediately, and you have been kind enough to come. Now then, we are all here present before God to hear all that you have been commanded by the Lord."

10:30-33. Cornelius had a word of commendation for Peter—he had been "kind enough" (literally, "you have done well") "to come." He realized that this represented a new departure for the apostle. Also he encouraged Peter by indicating the mood of expectancy that filled all hearts as they awaited the message. God had been moving both in his life and in Peter's, and it was in keeping with this that he expected Peter to pass on only what he had been "commanded" rather than his own ideas.

Verses 34-43. It was Peter's turn to speak. He must have been overwhelmed as he looked at his hearers, so attentive and expectant, realizing that God was breaking through Jewish prejudice by using him, a Christian Jew, to communicate the Gospel to Gentiles. His message was thoroughly in accord with his own position as one who had known and followed the Lord from earliest days.

10:34   And opening his mouth, Peter said: I most certainly understand *now* that God is not one to show partiality,

35   but in every nation the man who fears Him and does what is right, is welcome to Him.

36   "The word which He sent to the sons of Israel, preaching peace through Jesus Christ (He is Lord of all)—

37   you yourselves know the thing which took place throughout all Judea, starting from Galilee, after the baptism which John proclaimed.

38   *"You know of* Jesus of Nazareth, how God anointed Him with the Holy Spirit and with power, and *how* He went about doing good, and healing all who were oppressed by the devil; for God was with Him.

39   "And we are witnesses of all the things He did both in the land of the Jews and in Jerusalem. And they also put Him to death by hanging Him on a cross.

40   "God raised Him up on the third day, and granted that He should become visible,

41   not to all the people, but to witnesses who were chosen beforehand by God, *that is,* to us, who ate and drank with Him after He arose from the dead.

171

42 "And He ordered us to preach to the people, and solemnly to testify that this is the One who has been appointed by God as Judge of the living and the dead.

43 "Of Him all the prophets bear witness that through His name every one who believes in Him has received forgiveness of sins."

10:34-35. Peter began by commenting on the revolution in his own thinking. He was now in position to "understand" the character and purpose of God in a way he had not perceived before. The uniqueness of the covenant people had blinded him to the breadth of God's operations. Not only had the Abrahamic covenant mentioned all the families of the earth (Gen 12:3), other passages too had cited a gracious purpose toward the nations. But the Jews were so impressed with their distinctiveness as the chosen people that they had relegated others to a subordinate position. So it was a great insight which led Peter to remark that God is without "partiality" (cf. 1 Pe 1:17; Ro 2:11).

The historical priority of the Jew (Ac 3:26; Ro 1:16) does not detract from this great truth. God is prepared to receive those "in every nation" who fear Him and work righteousness, the very things which are noted about Cornelius (10:2; cf. Mt 6:1-2). The meaning is not that such persons are thereby saved (cf. Ac 11:14) but rather are suitable candidates for salvation. Such preparation betokens a spiritual earnestness which will result in faith as the Gospel is heard and received.

10:36-37. "The word" is the message proclaimed by Jesus in the days of His flesh. "Peace" was a keynote of the angelic proclamation at His birth (Lk 2:14) and served to summarize the good news of His mission by which the estrangement between unholy sinners and a righteous God could be reconciled.‡ Probably the Lord Jesus had this in mind as well as physical preservation when He made Himself the key to Jerusalem's peace (Lk 19:42).

Peter had indicated that this message was heralded to "the sons of Israel" (v. 36). Now, as though to anticipate the emphasis of verse 43 with its inclusion of Gentiles, he added almost as an afterthought, "He is the Lord of all." Gentiles as well as Jews have a stake in Him and alike are brought under His sway when they receive the Gospel.

In saying, "You yourselves know the thing which took place," Peter was referring to the Christ event, the breaking in of the Son of God on human life and history. He was able to assume that the story of our Lord's life and work in broad outline did not have to be recounted as something new; for the life, ministry, and death of the Prophet of Nazareth were public knowledge, seeing that these things had not been done in a corner (26:26;

‡For *peace* as virtually a synonym for salvation see Is 52:7.

cf. 2:22). This helps to account for the summary character of the description of the ministry.§

In speaking of all Judea, Peter was using the term in its broadest sense as covering the homeland of the Jews (cf. Lk 23:5). "Starting from Galilee" confirms the representation of the synoptic gospels that Galilee was the place where the ministry began. The time, "after the baptism which John proclaimed," is also in harmony with what the gospels report (Mk 1:1-14).

10:38-41. Making a fresh start, as it were, Peter emphasized that the Good News revolves around "Jesus of Nazareth"; then he highlighted the leading features of the ministry, including the baptism, where "God anointed Him with the Holy Spirit and power" (Lk 3:22; 4:14; Ac 4:27). Jesus Himself affirmed this anointing (Lk 4:18). It signified that He was the Christ (which means, "the anointed One").

The ministry proper is compressed into the two items of "doing good" and delivering people from Satan's power. The former is an apt description of those acts of mercy and compassion which so occupied the Saviour that there was scarcely time to eat. The other aspect seems to refer to the exorcisms, though a wider range could be intended so as to include some healings (cf. Lk 13:16). Success in these activities was due to the fact that "God was with Him" (cf. 2:22). What was implied in the anointing was demonstrated in the mighty works.

Nothing is said about the teaching. For the most part this seems to have been reserved for the instruction of converts (cf. 2:42).

To assure his audience that he was not relying on hearsay in these matters, Peter included the fact that he and others had been witnesses of all that Jesus did throughout the land and then in Jerusalem, concluding with His death on the cross. The value of this death was not declared immediately but was reserved for a later point (v. 43). As in earlier addresses by Peter, the human responsibility for the death was placed in the foreground.

The sequel to the cross was the resurrection "on the third day" (cf. 1 Co 15:4), followed by the appearances (cf. 1 Co 15:5-7). No attempt was made to link the resurrection with Old Testament prophecy, since the audience was made up of Gentiles. Peter freely acknowledged that there was no appearance of the risen Lord to the general public, but only to the chosen few who had been with Him during the course of His ministry, to whom the return from the dead was far more meaningful than it could possibly have been to others. It is here (v. 41) that the word

§In a comparative study of statements of the Gospel found in Paul's epistles, in Acts, and in the synoptic gospels, C. H. Dodd traces the similarity between this address by Peter and the gospel according to Mark (*The Apostolic Preaching and Its Developments* [London: Hodder & Stoughton, 1936]. Once more it is helpful to note the close contact between Peter and Mark as a background for this similarity.

witnesses is used a second time (cf. v. 39) as though to say that of all the things the disciples could attest as witnesses, this stood out as the most important (cf. 1:22).

The mention of eating and drinking with Christ after the resurrection goes beyond what the gospels relate (Lk 21:30, 41-43; Jn 21:13), yet it was a natural thing both as a token of His identity and as an expression of fellowship. There may seem to be here a contradiction with the Master's assertion at the Last Supper that He would not drink again until He drank the wine anew with His own in the Kingdom; but He had been referring to the wine of the Passover, not to drinking of any kind (see Mt 26:29).

10:42-43. In the sequence of statements, the command of the risen Lord to His disciples to preach was naturally taken as a command issued between the resurrection and the ascension. Nothing that fits this exactly is found in the gospels, but we do not have a complete account of what Jesus communicated to His own during the appearances. Such a command is implied in the authority vested in Him by virtue of the resurrection (Mt 28:18).

"The people" were members of the Jewish nation. This observation by Peter could have served in that instance as something of a reason for the delay in reaching Caesarea, a largely Gentile community, with the Gospel. The first obligation of the apostles was to proclaim the message to their own people (3:26).

For the first time in Acts we read of the judging function of the Lord Jesus Christ. Reports of early preaching do not always contain all the elements which belonged to the kerygma, or Gospel proclamation, but this is not an isolated reference (cf. 17:31; 24:25). Mention of "the dead" as well as the living implies the power of the risen Lord to raise unbelievers as well as the saints (24:15). The phrase, "Judge of the living and the dead" is readily recognizable as the source of an article in the Apostles' Creed (the old English *quick* being the equivalent of *living*).

Considerable difficulty surrounds Peter's final Christological statement, the one which claims prophetic anticipation of forgiveness of sins for all who believe in the Lord Jesus. I. Howard Marshall observes,

> At first sight this is a strange statement. Prophecies of forgiveness by the Messiah are hard to find, and the allusion to "all the prophets" seems highly exaggerated (cf. Lk. 24:27). The solution to the problem lies in two statements. First, in the Old Testament forgiveness is associated with the name of Yahweh, "the Lord." It is the prerogative of God; those who seek the Lord find that he will abundantly pardon them (Isa. 55:6f.). Second, the effect of the resurrection is that Jesus is exalted and receives the title of Lord (Acts 2:36). The conclusion is obvious: by virtue of his exaltation Jesus has received the prerogative of God the Lord to dispense

174

forgiveness of sins (cf. perhaps Stephen's prayer, Acts 7:60). What is asserted of God in "all the prophets" can now be asserted of the exalted Jesus.[4]

The statement about the prophets was not out of order in addressing these Gentiles, for at least some of them had frequented the synagogue and were familiar in a general way with the content of Old Testament revelation.

Verses 44-48. The effect of the message on Peter's audience is here spelled out.

> **10:44** While Peter was still speaking these words, the Holy Spirit fell upon all those who were listening to the message.
>
> **45** And all the circumcised believers who had come with Peter were amazed, because the gift of the Holy Spirit had been poured out upon the Gentiles also.
>
> **46** For they were hearing them speaking with tongues and exalting God. Then Peter answered.
>
> **47** "Surely no one can refuse the water for these to be baptized who have received the Holy Spirit just as we *did,* can he?"
>
> **48** And he ordered them to be baptized in the name of Jesus Christ. Then they asked him to stay on for a few days.

10:44-48. The juncture at which "the Holy Spirit fell" on the hearers is significant, for they had just received the assurance that belief in the risen Lord would bring forgiveness of sins. The descent of the Spirit upon the audience was in itself proof that acceptance of the Lord had indeed taken place on the part of the people. God's answer was swift and unmistakable. It was a source of amazement to Peter's companions as they sensed that the Spirit had indeed been poured out, the "speaking with tongues" being evidence. "Exalting God" is a reasonable equivalent of the activity of the apostles in Jerusalem when the Spirit had come upon them (2:11).

What is so striking about the event in the house of Cornelius is that the experience of these Gentiles was recognized to be the same as that of the twelve. They were not treated as had been the Jewish converts on the day of Pentecost, who heard the message, believed, and were baptized before they received the gift of the Spirit (2:38). Nor were they dealt with in the same manner as the believers at Samaria, who had been obliged to wait some time after their baptism for the gift of the Spirit (8:12, 15). These Gentile converts were treated just as the apostles had been treated at Pentecost—the Spirit descended, and they spoke with tongues and magnified God. The granting of this gift of the Spirit to uncircumcised Gentiles who had not yet even been baptized was a powerful demonstra-

175

tion to the church of the acceptability of Gentiles on the basis of faith alone, anticipating the decision of the Jerusalem Council (chap. 15). It amounted to a declaration of the equality of Jew and Gentile in the body of Christ, the Church.

Peter could see no difference between the ministry of the Spirit on this occasion and the ministry to the apostles at the beginning (v. 47; cf. 11:15). Baptism was promptly administered, even though it might have seemed an anticlimax. It was the Lord's command, and it was a means of confessing faith to others. His six companions may have performed the baptisms (cf. 1 Co 1:13-17).

Nothing is said about circumcision. The presumption is that the seal of God was so overwhelming and so final as to overcome doubts on this point. All barriers came down, as evidenced by Peter's acceptance of an invitation to be a house guest for a few days. This implies the eating of food that was not kosher, and in fact it led to a charge of misconduct when he returned to Jerusalem (11:3).

3. REPORT TO THE JERUSALEM CHURCH—11:1-18

The shock of what had occurred at Caesarea was felt in congregations throughout the land and especially in the mother church at Jerusalem. Whatever joy there may have been over the salvation of Gentiles was overshadowed by misgiving, as evidenced by the criticism leveled at Peter when he returned to the holy city. The apostle had anticipated objection and was prepared to meet it. For the time being fears were allayed.

> **11:1** Now the apostles and the brethren who were throughout Judea heard that the Gentiles also had received the word of God.
>
> **2** And when Peter came up to Jerusalem, those who were circumcised took issue with him,
>
> **3** Saying, "You went to uncircumcised men and ate with them."
>
> **4** But Peter began *speaking* and *proceeded* to explain to them in orderly sequence, saying,
>
> **5** "I was in the city of Joppa praying; and in a trance I saw a vision, a certain object coming down like a great sheet lowered by four corners from the sky; and it came right down to me,
>
> **6** and when I had fixed my gaze upon it and was observing it I saw the four-footed animals of the earth and the wild beasts and the crawling creatures and the birds of the air.
>
> **7** "And I also heard a voice saying to me, 'Arise, Peter; kill and eat.'
>
> **8** "But I said, 'By no means, Lord, for nothing unholy or unclean has ever entered my mouth.'
>
> **9** "But a voice from heaven answered a second time, 'What God has cleansed, no longer consider unholy.'

10 "And this happened three times, and everything was drawn back up into the sky.

11 "And behold, at that moment three men appeared before the house in which we were *staying*, having been sent to me from Caesarea.

12 "And the Spirit told me to go with them without misgivings. And these six brethren also went with me, and we entered the man's house.

13 "And he reported to us how he had seen the angel standing in his house, and saying, 'Send to Joppa, and have Simon, who is also called Peter, brought here;

14 and he shall speak words to you by which you will be saved, you and all your household.'

15 "And as I began to speak, the Holy Spirit fell upon them, just as *He did* upon us at the beginning.

16 "And I remembered the word of the Lord, how He used to say, 'John baptized with water, but you shall be baptized with the Holy Spirit.'

17 "If God therefore gave to them the same gift as *He gave* to us also after believing in the Lord Jesus Christ, who was I that I could stand in God's way?"

18 And when they heard this, they quieted down, and glorified God, saying, "Well then, God granted to the Gentiles also the repentance *that leads* to life."

11:1-3. When the news reached them, the apostles were likely scattered in various places, preaching and ministering to the churches of Judea. Word came to "the brethren" as well. Their reaction was probably not greatly different from that of the leaders. There was intense interest but also perplexity and anxiety. "That the Gentiles had received the word of God" may sound commonplace to us, but it was new and strange to the Jewish church. The evangelization of Samaritans had not created a stir, nor had the winning of the Ethiopian eunuch, since he was a solitary case and was on his way out of the land when converted. But now a group of Gentiles had believed. What did this mean for the future of the Church?

On his arrival at Jerusalem Peter was challenged by "those who were circumcised." Ordinarily this description would mean simply Jews, or Jewish Christians if the context called for this sense (cf. 10:45). This may be the meaning here, but there is a strong possibility that the phrase is a bit more precise in this instance, indicating those Christian Jews who were prepared to insist that Gentile converts to the faith must submit to circumcision, in line with practice during Old Testament days. If Luke intended this nuance (and it seems that he did, because all believers in Jerusalem would have been circumcised, and this seems to be a reference to a certain number), the reader is being prepared for his observation in 15:5.

The charge against Peter was not that he preached to Gentiles and per-

177

mitted them to be baptized, but that he had fraternized with uncircumcised men and had gone so far as to eat with them. Peter himself had voiced the Jewish attitude when he began to address the people in Caesarea, and he had only consented to come to them because God had directed him (10:28). These two issues—the reception of Gentiles into the church and having table fellowship with them—were bound up together. If Gentiles were taken into the church without circumcision and then were refused table fellowship on the very ground that they were uncircumcised, the reception would be hollow indeed. Logically it would then be impossible for Gentile believers to sit at the Lord's Table with Jewish believers. The end result would inevitably be two churches rather than one. Paul saw this clearly, and on this account was stirred up by Peter's momentary lack of consistency in the incident at Antioch (Gal 2:11-16).

11:4-17. Peter's answer to the charge of the circumcision group is contained here. It is an answer based not on Scripture or tradition but on recent history, upon the intervention and direction of God Himself. Who could contest such evident leading? The best defense was to relate what had actually happened, and this is what Peter proceeded to do.

His account moved "in orderly sequence," leaving out only details that were not essential, such as his position on the housetop and the time of day. It was important to retain the fact that he had been "praying," waiting upon God. Some details were added, such as the observation that the object being lowered "came right down" to him and that he fixed his gaze on and observed it closely. Thus he had been able to see that the object contained animals of all kinds, not simply those that were clean according to the Law. So his refusal to eat had been grounded on close inspection and the realization that he would be violating the Levitical code by partaking (v. 8).

Peter was careful to note that the divine correction of his refusal had occurred three times, as though to impress on him that what he had done in the past was not a guide in the present situation. The divine command had been unmistakable. To emphasize the striking way in which God had confirmed His command by circumstances, "at that moment" (a time notice absent from chapter 10) three men sent from Cornelius had come to the house. To seal it all, the Spirit had bidden him go with these men without misgivings, thus bolstering his confidence by putting him immediately into contact with Gentiles.

He had been given the foresight to ask certain brethren (Jewish Christians) from Joppa to go with him, so that he could now report, "We entered the man's house." Peter's testimony had the support of men who had been on the spot and had witnessed all that took place at Caesarea (cf. 10:45). They had taken the trouble to come up to Jerusalem with him to give support and corroboration. The Law required only two or three witnesses. To muster "six" can only mean that Peter felt the need of impressing the Jerusalem church with the realization that a new thing had happened and that the facts were beyond challenge.

Included in Peter's report was the information given by Cornelius that an angel had appeared to him and directed him to send to Joppa for Peter. From this the mother church could understand that God had been working in Cornelius' life as well as in Peter's. An important item is added here (not in chapter 10), that God's purpose in all this activity was to bring Cornelius and his household the knowledge of salvation (v. 14).

Still holding to the bare essentials, Peter declared that his message to these Gentiles was not even completed, when "the Holy Spirit fell upon them"—the same Spirit who had bidden him go to Caesarea—as though to emphasize the divine sovereignty at work in welcoming Gentiles into the fold. Peter saw in this bestowal a repetition of what had occurred at Pentecost. It was not necessary to mention the gift of tongues, which would be implied in the very fact that the two incidents were of the same nature. There in the house of Cornelius the words of the risen Lord had flashed into Peter's mind (something not stated in chapter 10) predicting the impending baptism with the Holy Spirit (1:5). Surely it was of the utmost importance that what had been granted to the apostles of the Lord should now be extended to those outside the ranks of Israel. It was "the same gift." God was making no difference between the two groups—marvelous indeed.

"Who was I that I could stand in God's way?" (cf. 5:39). Peter had resisted the command to eat of animals judged by him to be unclean. To resist a second time when the higher reality was being acted out before his eyes would be unthinkable even for a man as stubborn as Peter. God had used the right man to persuade the Jerusalem church. If he was convinced, their opposition could no longer stand.

11:18. With their objections silenced, Peter's audience turned to praise. They were genuinely astonished that God would move in this unprecedented fashion among Gentiles. It was a fresh and mighty revelation of His grace. We are accustomed to think of "repentance" as a humanly inspired act which prepares the soul for faith that leads to "life." But in the last analysis both the possibility and the actuality of this turning away from sin and turning to God is His gracious work (cf. 5:31). It embraces Gentiles as well as the children of Israel (cf. 20:21; 26:20).

This joy in the enlargement of the divine operations unfortunately did not last, or at least did not become the portion of the entire Jerusalem church. Some who were absent that day remained dubious about the

179

extension of the Gospel to Gentiles apart from the demand of circumcision, and perhaps even some who heard Peter were not prepared to endorse a continuing work among Gentiles. They may have thought of the Cornelius episode as a solitary thing which should not be allowed to set a precedent. At any rate, it was from the Jerusalem church that the demand was made later on that such converts be required to accept circumcision and the yoke of the Law (15:1). The maintenance of the Christian faith as a Jewish phenomenon was deemed essential, and this was being imperiled.

It may be significant also that so far as the book of Acts informs us Peter did not continue to work among Gentiles. He was known as the apostle of the circumcision (Gal 2:7-9). Primary leadership for the Gentile mission was to belong to the apostle Paul.

E. The Outreach to Antioch—11:19-30

AT THIS POINT Luke reaches back to the period of Stephen and the dispersion of the Hellenists from Jerusalem (11:19 begins with exactly the same expression as 8:4). This is to bring the reader up to date respecting the missionary activities of this group, especially those who carried the Gospel northward to Phoenicia and Syria, laying the foundation for further advance into Europe. Therefore the passage before us is of crucial importance in the expansion of Christianity and in the plan of the book of Acts.

11:19 So then those who were scattered because of the persecution that arose in connection with Stephen made their way to Phoenicia and Cyprus and Antioch, speaking the word to no one except to Jews alone.

20 But there were some of them, men of Cyprus and Cyrene, who came to Antioch and *began* speaking to the Greeks also, preaching the Lord Jesus.

21 And the hand of the Lord was with them, and a large number who believed turned to the Lord.

22 And the news about them reached the ears of the church at Jerusalem, and they sent Barnabas off to Antioch.

23 Then when he had come and witnessed the grace of God, he rejoiced and *began* to encourage them all with resolute heart to remain *true* to the Lord;

24 for he was a good man, and full of the Holy Spirit and of faith. And considerable numbers were brought to the Lord.

25 And he left for Tarsus to look for Saul;

26 and when he had found him, he brought him to Antioch. And it came about that for an entire year they met with the church, and taught considerable numbers; and the disciples were first called Christians in Antioch.

27 Now at this time some prophets came down from Jerusalem to Antioch.

28 And one of them named Agabus stood up and *began* to indicate by the Spirit that there would certainly be a great famine all over the world. And this took place in the *reign* of Claudius.

29 And in the proportion that any of the disciples had means, each of them determined to send a *contribution* for the relief of the brethren living in Judea.

30 And this they did, sending it in charge of Barnabas and Saul to the elders.

11:19-21. Apparently it was before Peter went to Caesarea that these missionaries had passed through Phoenicia, probably visiting the major centers at Ptolemais, Tyre, and Sidon. References later on to believers at Tyre (21:3) and Ptolemais (21:7) may indicate that churches were established there in connection with this northward expansion. "Cyprus," an important island off the Syrian coast, has been mentioned as the home of Barnabas (4:36) and will figure again in Luke's account of the first missionary journey of Barnabas and Saul (13:4-12). The place named last, Syrian "Antioch," held such great opportunity that there was no further movement into more remote areas at this time.

In all these places the Gospel proclamation was restricted to Jews; but sometime after the witness had begun at Antioch, a change of strategy took place in that some of the Hellenists began to give the word to "Greeks also."* The word "also" requires us to think that those who began a mission to the Greeks did not abandon the attempt to reach the Jews. In all likelihood the word "Greeks" is used as a synonym for *Gentiles* (cf. 14:1; Ro 1:16). In this part of the world *Jew* and *Greek* summarized the population, for ever since the days of Alexander the Great the influence of Greek language and culture had molded the Near East, especially the cities. The Jews, even though they were affected by Hellenization, retained in large measure their own national heritage, which was a combination of religion and culture.

The men who were responsible for this new departure at Antioch had been dispersed, like the others, from Jerusalem. Their original homes had been in Cyprus and the Cyrene area of North Africa (cf. 2:10). There is a distinct possibility that they may have visited Antioch prior to their period of residence in Jerusalem and were aware of the unusual opportunity for evangelism presented by this city.

Antioch was founded by Seleucus, one of the generals of Alexander. Favored by climate and geographical position, it grew rapidly and became the capital of the Seleucid empire. When the Romans came in shortly before the middle of the first century B.C., Pompey made it the capital of the province of Syria. Under the Romans it enjoyed the status of an autonomous city, and its fame increased as a center of commerce and of luxurious living, the third most important city in the empire. The mixed population included a large number of Jews, perhaps twenty-five thousand or more. In such a cosmopolitan atmosphere people learned to live with one another in a spirit of toleration, which is borne out by the fact that Luke recorded no persecution of the church there, either by Jews or pagans.

---

*Some manuscripts have "Hellenists" instead of "Greeks," but this reading cannot stand because of what the context indicates. A contrast is obviously intended with the proclamation to "Jews alone" (v. 19), and Hellenists were Jews.

The unprecedented move to reach the Gentiles met with divine approval, "for the hand of the Lord was with them." Luke used the same expression in connection with the early life of John the Baptist (Lk 1:66). The hand of the Lord was symbolic of divine activity and intervention (4:28, 30; 13:11). Believers in considerable numbers were gathered into the fellowship. As though to underscore the overwhelmingly Gentile character of the church, Luke did not indicate that there was a ministry in any of the synagogues, though verse 19 implies such a ministry at the beginning. For the first time the Christian faith had established itself in one of the major centers of the Roman Empire.

To judge from the deliberate effort of Luke to tie in this mission with the associates of Stephen, as noted above, we are no doubt intended to understand that the outlook of the first martyr—an appreciation of the new revelation in Jesus Christ, transcending alike the Temple and the Law—was to characterize the Antioch church. It would face forward, eager to take a leading role in Christ's victorious march through the world.

11:22-24. Before long the news of the growing work at Antioch came to the Jerusalem church, resulting in the sending of Barnabas to supervise and aid in the ministry. Similar action had been taken in the case of Samaria, except that two apostles had been sent on that occasion (8:14). A further difference emerges in that whereas Peter and John had returned to Jerusalem when their mission was completed, Barnabas stayed on, thus identifying himself permanently with the work among Gentiles. When he visited Jerusalem later (11:30; 15:2) it was not to make a report or give an accounting of his work at Antioch. In Galatians 2:1-10 he appears as the associate of Paul, not as a representative of the Jerusalem congregation. The choice of Barnabas as the one to go to Antioch was singularly fortunate. He was a native of Cyprus (4:36) and as such would have much in common with the men who first sowed the Gospel seed among the Gentiles at Antioch (11:20).

What he saw of the manifest operation of divine "grace" was a source of satisfaction to him. He "rejoiced" to see it, and instead of raising questions about the propriety of evangelizing Gentiles or dwelling on the Law and circumcision, he entered heartily into the work, doing all he could to "encourage" the new converts to continue to be faithful to the Lord. He was living up to his name, "Son of Encouragement" (4:36). It is likely that he sensed the strategic importance of a strong church at Antioch, although he may not have foreseen its full significance as a base for missionary outreach.

Luke was so impressed with the sterling quality of this man that he went out of his way to list some of his qualifications: "a good *man*," marked by integrity and wholesomeness, also "full of the Holy Spirit and of faith," a description that tallies with that of Stephen (6:5). As though to stress the impetus that the presence of Barnabas gave to the work, Luke comments again on the addition of converts. In fact, whereas a goodly number had been brought to faith before his coming (v. 21), now the influx became a host (v. 24).

11:25-26. Apparently it was this great increase that prompted Barnabas to seek help. He thought of Saul, whom he had come to know at Jerusalem several years before (9:27). At that time Saul had needed him. Now he needed Saul. Possibly he had heard from the mouth of Saul that Gentiles had been specifically included in his call (9:15; 22:21).

Leaving Antioch, he set out in person "to look for Saul." The language suggests uncertainty as to his whereabouts (cf. Lk 2:44-45, the only other occurrences of the word). He might have been in Tarsus, where he had gone from Jerusalem years before (9:30) or possibly was laboring in other parts of Cilicia or northern Syria (Gal 1:21-23). Tarsus lay northwest of Antioch and could be reached by sea as well as by land. The latter route would require a journey of over one hundred miles and would consume several days. As he traveled, Barnabas must often have resorted to prayer that God would lead him to Saul and incline his friend to respond favorably to the request he would make.

God was pleased to give success to Barnabas. Doubtless Saul could see for himself that the work he had been doing (passed over by Luke) had prepared him for just such a ministry as Barnabas pictured to him. That Saul had been witnessing mainly to Gentiles during this period of obscurity is attested in 22:21. The rigor of his service is reflected in the variety and intensity of his sufferings (2 Co 11:23-27), many of which must have been experienced in those early years rather than in the period which Luke narrates from this point on.

The two men combined forces to lead the church for "an entire year" in a teaching ministry. This does not mean, of course, that evangelism ceased or even slackened, but that special emphasis was now placed on instruction and growth in the Lord, after the example of the Jerusalem church (2:42) and in obedience to the Lord's command (Mt 28:20). A detail in the narrative at verse 26 reflects this change of emphasis. The expression denoting those who were taught ("considerable numbers") is identical with the description of the converts in verse 24. An earnest effort was made to mature these babes in Christ.

C. H. Dodd ventures the plausible suggestion that the catechetical materials which appear in the Pauline letters, beginning with 1 and 2 Thessalonians, derive principally from the teachings that were used in the Antioch church.[1] Converts from paganism, even more than God-fearers, would need help in understanding the nature of the new life in Christ and its implications for Christian conduct. The temptation to allow themselves to conform to the pagan environment they had known would have to be met by setting forth the obligations of discipleship and the glorious resources of the risen Lord available to them (cf. Phil 4:13).

It was at Antioch that the disciples of Christ were first called "Christians" (v. 26). The contention that this name was given by God through revelation is not well founded, for cases in which the word rendered "called" has this connotation (Mt 2:12, 22; Ac 10:22) are marked by contextual features (such as dreams or instruction) clearly indicating divine activity. Such intimation is lacking here. A strictly parallel example to the one before us is provided by Romans 7:3, "She shall be called an adulteress." In this usage a person (or a group, as at Antioch) is labeled.

The problem centers in finding a suitable source responsible for the naming. Who first described believers in Christ (used as a personal name rather than a title) as Christians? Jews can be ruled out since they refused to concede that Jesus was the Christ (Messiah) whom their nation expected. Believers can be eliminated also, since they had other terms for describing themselves—mainly *disciples, believers, saints,* and *brethren.* By elimination, the responsibility is to be placed on the pagan population of Antioch.

The non-Christian origin of the name is to some extent confirmed by the fact that the two remaining occurrences of the word in the New Testament (Acts 26:28; 1 Pe 4:16) involve its use by outsiders. In line with this we have the remark of Tacitus that Nero, to counter rumors that he himself had set fire to Rome, "falsely accused culprits and subjected to most unusual punishments those whom, hated for their shameful deeds, the populace called Christians."[2]

That the label was first affixed at Antioch makes understandable its use in several of the letters of Ignatius, bishop of Antioch, early in the second century.

A variation from the usual approach to the problem of the origin of the name is provided by H. B. Mattingly.[3] He notes that the word in the original owes its form to the Latin, where it would be written *Christiani*. Positing that it was a popular designation of pagan origin, he understands it to have been coined as a playful take-off in opposition to the coterie of *Augustiani* who surrounded the idolized Nero. The argumentation is ingenious, but the dating (59-60) makes it tenuous. Though Luke did not say that the name was given at the juncture he was describing (in the 40s), that is the impression left with the reader.

The place at which Luke injected his remark, following the account of evangelistic and teaching activity, makes it evident that the new faith made a strong impact on a great city in a comparatively short time. Incidentally, the new name bears testimony to the essentially Gentile complexion of the church, setting the community of believers quite apart from the Judaism with which the people had been familiar for a much longer period. The supposition that the name was given in ridicule is problematical, even though later on it was sometimes used in derision, as in the quotation from Tacitus.

11:27-30. About this time an unexpected opportunity presented itself for the Antioch congregation to express its appreciation to the Jerusalem church for those who had come with the Gospel and with gifts of ministry.

The arrival of "prophets" from Jerusalem manifests the continuing interest of the mother church in the Christian community at Antioch. In his account of the Jerusalem church Luke has not previously mentioned the presence of prophets, though the phenomenon was not unexpected in view of 2:17-18. Such men spoke by revelation from the Spirit (1 Co 14: 29-30), usually in terms of edification and encouragement (1 Co 14:3, 31) and even of fundamental doctrine (Eph 3:4-5). But occasionally, as here, their ministry included prediction. Agabus appears again in such a role (21:10-11).

The Western text of verse 28 states that the prediction occurred "when we were gathered together," indicating Luke's presence. This may reflect a reliable tradition, in which case he may have been a native of Antioch. Probably he was a convert during those early days. One can imagine him sitting under the instruction of Saul and coming to share his deep devotion to Christ and the Christian Gospel. This would help to account for his readiness to travel with his friend on the second missionary journey. Perhaps it was at the urging of the apostle that he was led to prepare an account of Christian beginnings which we know as Acts and to reach even further back to pen one of the synoptic gospels.

It is not possible to substantiate from ancient historians that there was "a great famine all over the world" at this time, as Agabus predicted. However, there were serious shortages from time to time during the reign of "Claudius." One of these is noted by Suetonius, who says, "There was a scarcity of grain because of long-continued droughts."[4] So it is legitimate, as F. F. Bruce observes, to think in terms of dearth at various intervals rather than a single famine.[5] All over the world" means that we cannot limit the deprivation to Palestine, but should think of the Roman Empire as a whole (cf. the use of the same word *oikoumenē* in Lk 2:1).

The mention of Claudius, who reigned from A.D. 41-54, prepares the reader somewhat for the events recorded at the beginning of the next chapter, since he was responsible for putting Herod Agrippa I on his throne in Judea.

Acting on the prophecy and without any request from the Jerusalem church, the saints at Antioch responded beautifully, "each of them" determining to give in proportion to his means. It was democratic, congregational action. How long the gathering of funds went on we are not told. If the plan that Paul used later (1 Co 16:2) was employed here, believers put aside what they could on the first day of the week until such time as an adequate sum was realized. The word "relief" means simply service or ministry and is the same term already used for the daily distribution to the needy at Jerusalem in the early days of the Church (6:1).

The rationale of this gesture of brotherhood could not be better stated than in the words of Paul respecting a later offering from the Gentile churches to the needy of the Jerusalem congregation: "Yes, they were pleased to do so, and they are indebted to them. For if the Gentiles have shared in their spiritual things, they are indebted to minister to them also in material things" (Ro 15:27). Indeed, this experience at Antioch may have been the chief inspiration behind Paul's plan for the later collection. So important was this love gift in the eyes of the Antioch church that they asked Barnabas and Saul, their most prominent leaders, to convey it on their behalf to "the elders" in Jerusalem. The line between the material and the spiritual has at times to be very thinly drawn.

This is the first notice of elders in connection with the Jerusalem congregation. It may indicate two things: that the seven (chap. 6) were no longer functioning because the lack of means had forced the abandonment of the common fund, and that the apostles were perhaps absent from the city ministering to the churches throughout Judea as at an earlier time (cf. 9:27; Gal 1:18-19). Just when elders were appointed in the Jerusalem church is not indicated. The more the apostles were needed in areas outside the city, the more would elders be useful to guide the congregation and provide needed administration. The prophets from Jerusalem must have brought the Antioch church up to date on conditions in the mother church.

The exact time of departure for Jerusalem cannot be fixed, but the great drought can be determined with some precision as falling in the period A.D. 46-47. Since the events of the next chapter belong to the year 44 (the date of the death of Herod), it was likely after his death that the two deputies made their trip, anticipating the worst of the famine condition by their alacrity in bringing relief.

F. Peter's Deliverance and Herod's Demise—12:1-25

At this point Luke picks up the story of Peter once more, relating his imprisonment and miraculous escape, concluding this segment with an account of what happened to his persecutor.

12:1 Now about that time Herod the king laid hands on some who belonged to the church, in order to mistreat them.

2 And he had James the brother of John put to death with a sword.

3 And when he saw that it pleased the Jews, he proceeded to arrest Peter also. Now it was during the days of *the Feast of* Unleavened Bread.

4 And when he had seized him, he put him in prison, delivering him to four squads of soldiers to guard him, intending after the Passover to bring him out before the people.

5 So Peter was kept in the prison, but prayer for him was being made fervently by the church to God.

6 And on the very night when Herod was about to bring him forward, Peter was sleeping between two soldiers, bound with two chains; and guards in front of the door were watching over the prison.

7 And behold, an angel of the Lord suddenly appeared, and a light shone in the cell; and he struck Peter's side and roused him, saying, "Get up quickly." And his chains fell off his hands.

8 And the angel said to him, "Gird yourself and put on your sandals." And he did so. And he said to him, "Wrap your cloak around you and follow me."

9 And he went out and continued to follow, and he did not know that what was being done by the angel was real, but thought he was seeing a vision.

10 And when they had passed the first and second guard, they came to the iron gate that leads into the city, which opened for them by itself; and they went out and went along one street; and immediately the angel departed from him.

11 And when Peter came to himself, he said, "Now I know for sure that the Lord has sent forth His angel and rescued me from the hand of Herod and from all that the Jewish people were expecting."

12 And when he realized *this,* he went to the house of Mary, the mother of John who was also called Mark, where many were gathered together and were praying.

13 And when he knocked at the door of the gate, a servant-girl named Rhoda came to answer.

14 And when she recognized Peter's voice, because of her joy she did not open the gate, but ran in and announced that Peter was standing in front of the gate.

15 And they said to her, "You are out of your mind!" But she kept insisting that it was so. And they kept saying "It is his angel."

16 But Peter continued knocking; and when they had opened, they saw him and were amazed.

17 But motioning to them with his hand to be silent, he described to them how the Lord had led him out of the prison. And he said, "Report these things to James and the brethren." And he departed and went to another place.

18 Now when day came, there was no small disturbance among the soldiers *as to* what could have become of Peter.

19 And when Herod had searched for him and had not found him, he examined the guards and ordered that they be led away *to execution*. And he went down from Judea to Caesarea and was spending time there.

12:1-5. The circumstances surrounding the imprisonment are sketched in simple but dramatic fashion—the power of an earthly monarch pitted against the power of prayer to the Almighty. The Herod of this story was the third ruler by that name to cross the pages of the New Testament: first Herod the Great; then Herod Antipas; and now a grandson of the first Herod, the son of Aristobolus, known as Herod Agrippa I. His youth was spent in Rome, where he cultivated a friendship with Gaius (also known as Caligula), who later became emperor. As a result, Gaius favored him, granting him in A.D. 37 the tetrarchies of Philip, the brother of Antipas, which included districts north and east of Galilee, and of Lysanias in southern Syria (cf. Lk 3:1). In the year 39 Galilee and Perea were added to his realm, and in 41 he was made king of Judea, ruling over a territory approximating in extent that of his grandfather. He made it plain that he would do all in his power to be agreeable to the Jewish people, who responded by according him widespread popularity.

Joachim Jeremias[6] notes an item in the *Antiquities* of Josephus (19.7.4) about a verbal attack on Agrippa by a certain Simon when the king was absent from Jerusalem. The charge was that the king, being unclean, ought to be excluded from the Temple. Jeremias, perhaps incorrectly, interprets this to mean that Agrippa was being accused of being a non-Jew (he was an Idumean, but had some Hasmonean blood) rather than of being ritually unclean. Josephus went on to praise Agrippa for summoning Simon and freely forgiving him this denigration.

As a further indication of the embarrassment felt by Agrippa because of his lineage, which he did not attempt to hide, Jeremias cites a passage in the Mishnah (Sotah 7.8). The custom prevailed, going back to Hasmonean days, when the kingship and the high priesthood were held by one person, that he should read from the Law at the Feast of Tabernacles, seated in the Court of Women. But Agrippa remained standing while reading the Law, out of humility. When he came to the passage which said, "Thou mayest not put a foreigner over thee which is not thy brother" (Deu 17:15), he broke out into tears, whereupon the people cried out, "Our brother art thou! Our brother art thou! Our brother art thou."

Because of his position as king, he felt able to do what no Roman procurator in previous years would have dared to do, namely, attack the Church. Luke speaks of "some" who were his targets, but names only two, both of them apostles. James, the brother of John, and Peter may have been the only members of the twelve in Jerusalem at the time. Jesus had predicted the martyrdom of both men (Mk 10:39; Jn 21:18-19). But it is important to notice that with reference to Peter, Jesus explicitly stated that he would lose his life only when he was old. His time was not yet. James died by "the sword," probably beheaded like John the Baptist. This "pleased the Jews," encouraging Agrippa to "arrest" Peter (the same word is used of the seizure of Jesus in the garden, Lk 22:54).

The fact that such strong and direct action against the church met with general approval (cf. v. 11) reveals "how little Judaism had become reconciled to the existence of the Congregation of Jesus in their midst."[7] Even when Stephen's preaching had brought down wrath on the Church, the apostles had found it feasible to remain in Jerusalem when others had to flee (8:1). No longer was this true. Agrippa knew what the people wanted, and he was ready to give it to them. Perhaps this outbreak is what Paul made reference to in 1 Thessalonians 2:14.

Providentially Peter's arrest came during the time when the "Feast of Unleavened Bread" was being observed. Since the intention was to execute Peter when the Passover was concluded, and since the festival of Unleavened Bread came during the week *after* Passover, it follows that "Passover" in this passage is used as a broad term for the whole festival season, as in Luke 22:1. Evidently scrupulous Agrippa, trying to be ceremonially correct so as to avoid criticism, would not pollute the holy season by shedding blood, so he put Peter in prison. Perhaps someone had told him about Peter's violation of Jewish exclusivism in the Cornelius episode at Caesarea. However, this is only conjectural.

The pains taken to guard Peter might give the impression that he was public enemy number one. He was chained to two soldiers, who took positions on either side of him. Two others were stationed outside the inner prison cell. Every three hours these four gave way to replacements. The explanation for such strict precautions is likely to be found in the recollection by many members of the Sanhedrin that Peter had somehow escaped from prison on a previous occasion (5:19). This must not happen again. If in addition fears were expressed to Agrippa that Peter's friends might make an effort to free him, this would help to explain the tight security. It would also be a testimony to the growth of the Jerusalem church over the years. Many from other parts of the land would be in the city for the festival, so it was thought wise to prepare for any eventuality. Agrippa eagerly awaited the time when he could bring Peter out "before the people," impressing them with his zeal for Judaism.

"So Peter was kept in the prison," and what his thoughts were we can only guess. Probably his mind turned back to the trial and death of his Lord, also at Passover time. He had failed the Master then by his denial, but by the grace of God he would not fail Him now. He knew that when one suffered as a Christian, that was the very time in which to glorify God (1 Pe 4:16).

Meanwhile, the church was bestirring itself to make urgent prayer to God on his behalf. Ordinarily the Passover season was a time of celebration, when believers recalled not only their nation's deliverance from Egypt but also their Saviour's death and resurrection. But now the usual rejoicing was muted by the need for constant prayer. The church prayed "fervently," with unusual intensity. Now was the time when the resurrection power of the Lord Jesus was desperately needed. It is to the credit of these believers that they had not fled in fear of Agrippa or sought out hiding places. One house (cf. v. 12) could not contain the whole church, so we are permitted to think of many groups, or at least of the maintenance of a "chain" of prayer, so that at no time was the voice of supplication stilled in those days of waiting.

What was the burden of the prayer? We are told only that prayer was made "for him." Petition for his release would be altogether natural in view of a previous divine intervention (5:19) and of Peter's usefulness to the Christian cause. Some may have been content to pray for his strengthening in the hour of trial, which accords with their surprise at seeing him alive and free (vv. 15-16).

12:6-11. The account passes to an explanation of how God answered prayer, defending His flock and showing that He is able to deliver His own when they are in peril. By waiting until the eleventh hour, so to speak, He tested the faith of the church and at the same time deepened the disappointment and chagrin of all who had waited with satisfaction for Peter's execution. "On the very night" preceding the day appointed for his execution, Peter was "sleeping" in his cell, surrounded as usual by guards. He had committed his soul to God, the righteous Judge (1 Pe 2:23) and was able to find rest in sleep, a remarkable testimony to the reality and effectiveness of his trust in the Lord. He had learned the secret which he was later to pass on to others, that one can cast all his anxious care on the Lord because the Lord has concern for His own (1 Pe 5:7).

When Jesus in Gethsemane had come to the point of resting in the will of God, an angel had appeared and strengthened Him (Lk 22:43). Now His disciple had committed his case to God, and an angel appeared to lead him out to freedom (cf. 5:19; Heb 1:14). If angels have a strong desire to gaze into the secrets of God's salvation (1 Pe 1:12), they are all the more eager to effect deliverance for those who proclaim that salvation. Suddenly there was a light, a voice of command rousing Peter from sleep, and a loosing of his bonds. Through it all the soldiers remained in deep sleep (cf. 1 Sa 26:12). The angel treated Peter as a parent would a child

191

in an emergency, one crisp command following another until he was ready to exit. Though his legs moved, he was in a daze, thinking that he was "seeing a vision."† Successfully passing the two guards who were stationed outside the cell, the pair stood presently before the iron gate that led to the outside. Though tightly closed, it "opened for them by itself."‡ With the opening of the gate and the departure of the angel, Peter came to himself (cf. Lk 15:17), realizing that his experience was not a dream and that he was a free man. The Lord had intervened on his behalf, leaving Herod and his followers bitterly disappointed.

It is worth observing that God ordained a different result for Peter than for James, in line with His providential ordering of events at other times (see Heb 11:35-37). It is natural to raise questions as to why some are spared and others, as fully dedicated, are called on to yield their lives; but such questions are largely futile. One can only rest in the wisdom and goodness of God, for He does all things well.

12:12-17. Peter made his report to the faithful who had been praying for him. It is impressive that he deemed this more important than taking immediately to flight. He owed it to his brethren to make contact before seeking his own safety.

The home of Mary was likely the principal meeting-place of believers in the city, perhaps the same dwelling utilized by the 120 disciples following the ascension (1:13). The mention of Mary's son, John Mark, indicates that he had some prominence in the early Church, and it prepares the reader for his share in later developments (13:5, 13; 15:37-39). Paul called him the cousin of Barnabas (Col 4:10), who must have been a frequent visitor to Mary's home. Another visitor was Peter, which accords with the close relationship between him and Mark attested in 1 Peter 5:13, where the apostle called him "my son"—presumably an indication that Peter had had much to do with his spiritual development and possibly even with his conversion. This young man had many advantages, which ultimately showed up in his character and usefulness (Col 4:10-11; 2 Ti 4:11). Mark's contacts with leading personalities of the Jerusalem church must have given him valuable help in the writing of the gospel that bears his name.

The house was filled with people engaged in prayer. Although Luke does not give information about the time (the particular watch of the night) when Peter left the prison, the impression made by the narrative is that the night was perhaps half gone. The presumption is, then, that this

---

†The same word is used of his vision on the housetop at Joppa (10:17).
‡In his *Jewish War* (6.5.3) Josephus tells of the strange phenomena occurring at Jerusalem prior to the outbreak of hostilities, which some interpreted favorably for the Jews, others as portents of doom. Included is a report that the eastern gate of the inner court of the Temple opened of its own accord (*automatōs,* the same root word as in Acts 12:10).

was an all-night prayer meeting. Believers, like their Lord, learn to value long seasons of waiting upon God.

When Peter arrived at the outer gate and knocked (the gate was locked), his knock brought Rhoda to the spot. The fact that the family could afford a servant accords with the spaciousness of the house. In true-to-life fashion Rhoda, on recognizing Peter's voice as he called to be admitted, instead of opening the door, ran back to the company to report this exciting development. Astonished, they questioned her mental balance. Perhaps the tension of the long hours had taken their toll. "You are out of your mind!" But she stood her ground. A compromise suggestion was that Peter's "angel" might have paid a visit, having so identified with him as to reflect his quality of voice.

The teaching about guardian angels is comparatively little developed in Scripture. There is no doubt about the guarding, protecting function of angels (Ps 91:11) but in such situations angels appear as a group rather than alone (note especially Lk 16:22). Even Matthew 18:10, the passage most relied on to confirm the idea of the guardian angel, is indecisive, for again the plural is used, as in Hebrews 1:14. But at least it is possible to say this much, that the passage before us testifies to a belief in Christian circles that each saint has an angel assigned to him.

What was coursing through the minds of those who proposed this explanation to Rhoda? Did they think it meant that there was a message from Peter? Or was it a more somber thought, as Johannes Munck surmises? He comments: "Probably an instance of the not uncommon belief that the moment a man dies his guardian angel appears. In this case, it would have been a sign that the Christians' prayer (cf. v. 5) had not been granted, but that Herod had had the apostle executed in prison."[8] Whether hopeful or fearful, the saints were fully alert by this time, many moving toward the entrance to determine the true state of affairs. When they opened the gate, to their amazement, Peter stood before them.

Why were they amazed? Did they lack faith? Or had they expected God to intervene at a still later hour? The questions multiply. Sometimes Christians receive such assurance from God about the answer to their prayers that they no longer feel a burden to continue their supplications, but go their way expecting the answer to follow. Apparently there had been no such assurance in this case. Perhaps we are to learn from it the lesson that we should not become so completely absorbed in our praying that we fail to listen to the voice of God meanwhile so as to learn when prayer is no longer needed.

Precious time would be lost if everyone present were given the opportunity to greet the apostle and congratulate him on his deliverance. So he motioned for silence and tried to answer their questions by relating what had happened in the prison. Then he requested them to pass on the information he had given to "James and the brethren." This was James the brother of the Lord (Gal 1:19). It would be unnatural to assume that "the brethren" were the Lord's other brothers (cf. 1:14), for the language suggests that Peter was asking James to assume the active leadership of the Jerusalem church. Luke took for granted that his readers would know which James was intended; he soon became recognized throughout the church. The brethren could have been the elders of the church (11:30) or, more generally, the believers who were not present at the prayer meeting.

From this time on, James, rather than Peter, was the acknowledged head of the Jerusalem church. Paul confirmed this by recounting a meeting he and Barnabas had with the leaders of the church and naming James ahead of Peter and John (Gal 2:9). It was James who spoke the decisive word at the Jerusalem Council (15:13-21). His leadership was made plain again when Paul went up to Jerusalem for the last time (21:18). James was in favor with the Jews because he continued faithfully to observe the Law and the customs. As a result, when he was killed (c. A.D. 62) by the highhanded action of the incumbent high priest, there was such indignation that the high priest was dismissed from his office.[9] The appearing of the risen Lord to James (1 Co 15:7) must have been regarded by the Church as in some sense prophetic of the leadership into which he was now placed.

The time had come for Peter to bid the brethren farewell. We read that he "departed and went to another place." There is no way of knowing where he went. To have informed the group of his plan (if he had one at this time) would be to endanger his safety and theirs in case Agrippa instituted interrogation of church members. Some Roman Catholic interpreters have suggested that Peter made his way to Rome, but a visit to the imperial city at such an early date is highly improbable. That he did so later, prior to the writing 1 Peter, can be reasonably established. When Agrippa was removed by death, conditions were favorable for Peter's return to the city. He was there several years later to take part in the Jerusalem Council (15:7) but after that does not appear further on the pages of Acts.

12:18-19. With the break of day Agrippa's soldiers were thrown into consternation, for they were responsible for the missing prisoner. When word of the situation reached the king, he at once ordered a thorough search, but it proved unavailing. Peter was nowhere to be found. Thinking that the circumstances pointed toward an "inside job," Agrippa grilled the guards. Though they were unable to explain Peter's escape, they were under suspicion, so the king closed the inquiry by commanding that they be executed. This was in line with rigid Roman discipline. Munck notes that similar cases are cited in Acts (16:27; 27:42) where Roman soldiers feared for their lives in case they lost custody of their prisoners.[10]

A change of scenery might help Agrippa to dismiss from his mind the unsatisfactory conclusion of his attempt to please his subjects by attacking the church, so off he went to his headquarters at Caesarea. This was the seat of government for the procurators who ruled Palestine in the name of Rome. Probably Agrippa alternated between Jerusalem and the seaside city.

> **12:20** Now he was very angry with the people of Tyre and Sidon; and with one accord they came to him, and having won over Blastus the king's chamberlain, they were asking for peace, because their country was fed by the king's country.
>
> **21** And on an appointed day Herod, having put on his royal apparel, took his seat on the rostrum and *began* delivering an address to them.
>
> **22** And the people kept crying out, "The voice of a god and not of a man!"
>
> **23** And immediately an angel of the Lord struck him because he did not give God the glory, and he was eaten by worms and died.

12:20-23. This account of the death of the king was not strictly necessary for Luke's narrative of the history of the Church (in his gospel he did not indicate what the fate of Pilate was). But we know from his writings as a whole that he had an interest in correlating the events of redemption history with secular affairs (cf. Lk 3:1-2). Beyond this, however, he may have desired to instill in his readers the spirit that Paul wished to see in his friends at Philippi—"in no way alarmed by your opponents—which is a sign of destruction for them, but of salvation for you, and that too, from God" (Phil 1:28). It is always an encouragement to the saints to realize that they do not need to fear what man can do to them, for God still occupies the throne, and He knows how to deal with those who afflict His own (2 Th 1:6).

It seems that Agrippa had a quarrel with the inhabitants of Tyre and Sidon, prominent cities on the coast of Phoenicia, although the cause is unknown. Baffled by his failure to do away with Peter, his "fighting mad" mood was worse than usual. Suing for "peace" does not in this case imply the existence of armed conflict, but only the termination of the quarrel. Necessity dictated coming to terms with Agrippa, because these cities relied on northern Palestine for much of their food supplies. The suppliants made an adroit move by establishing contact with "Blastus the king's chamberlain," since he presumably had a closer relationship with Agrippa than any others of his official household. His cooperation was doubtless gained at a price.

Herod's willingness to settle differences may be explained in part as in line with his policy of cultivating leaders and governments in his general area, a policy that made Rome look askance at him as possibly seeking to get more power into his hands. It is significant that at his death the emperor Claudius did not appoint his son to succeed him as king, but restored Roman rule through procurators.

"On the appointed day," that is, the day agreed upon when Herod would meet with the envoys from the Phoenician cities, the king made a state occasion by donning "royal apparel" and dignifying the concord by making an "address" to the visitors from the north. To the obsequious people of Caesarea, largely Gentiles, it presented an opportunity to hail their monarch as "a god" (the Jews, of course, would not take part in any such acclaim). Josephus, in describing this event, locates it during a festival in honor of Claudius.[11]§

The two accounts agree that Herod did nothing to resist or refuse the plaudits of the throng, and that from this very time he was smitten with an incurable illness that speedily brought death. Josephus credits the monarch with a speech in which he recognized that the sentence of death was on him, fate providing thereby an immediate refutation of the lying words of the multitude. Scripture does not use any such pagan terminology, but attributes death to angelic action (cf. 2 Sa 24:16) because of unwillingness to "give God the glory."

Although Luke did not tie in the death of Herod with the persecution of the Church, no doubt this connection was made by believers, and possibly by many of the Jews. Speculations as to the physical cause of death have been varied.[12] It is enough to be reminded that God knows how to bring low the proud.

> **12:24** But the word of the Lord continued to grow and to be multiplied.
> **25** And Barnabas and Saul returned from Jerusalem when they had fulfilled their mission, taking along with *them* John, who was also called Mark.

12:24. In a summary statement which surveys the situation of the Church following the incidents reported in the chapter, Luke notes that the progress of the Gospel was not really impeded by what had happened but rather was set forward (cf. 6:7; 19:20).

§His account is quite detailed. "Clad in a garment woven completely of silver so that its texture was indeed wondrous, he entered the theater at daybreak. There the silver, illumined by the touch of the first rays of the sun, was wondrously radiant and by its glitter inspired fear and awe in those who gazed intently upon it. Straightway his flatterers raised their voices from various directions—though hardly for good—addressing him as a god (*Antiquities* 19. 8. 2).

12:25. The casual reader might suppose that Barnabas and Saul had been in Jerusalem during the persecution outlined at the beginning of the chapter, but actually a period of about two years intervened between the death of Herod and the famine conditions noted in 11:28. This item about the return of the two men could have been put at the end of chapter 11, but Luke inserted it here as a transition to the events of chapter 13, which it suitably introduces.|| The trip to Jerusalem was probably not made till after the death of Herod. No data are given as to length of time spent in Jerusalem, but the contact could well have been longer than on Saul's first visit to the church (9:26-30), and probably much less turbulent.

The opportunity to become better acquainted with James, not to speak of others who had been in the church since Pentecost, would not be passed by. The mention of Mark indicates that the contact of Barnabas with Mary and her family had been renewed and this prepares the reader for the observation about her son in 13:5.

||The difficult textual situation in this closing verse of the chapter should be noted. The manuscripts which ordinarily are the most reliable have "returned to Jerusalem," which does not make sense in view of the fact that the two men went from Antioch and are said to have fulfilled their mission. Many manuscripts have the smoother reading "returned from Jerusalem," but if such were the original wording it is hard to account for the origin of the reading "returned to Jerusalem." One conjecture is that the original wording (including the terms which indicate the completion of the ministry) was "they returned having completed the ministry to (or 'intended for') Jerusalem" (B. F. Westcott and F. J. A. Hort, *The New Testament in the Original Greek*, Am. ed. [New York: Harper, 1882, Appendix, p. 94]).

PART III

THE CHURCH IN ASIA MINOR AND EUROPE–13:1–19:41

In this segment of his story Luke incorporates his report of what happened in a series of journeys undertaken by Paul and various helpers who were sent out by the church in Antioch. In this period, probably the most fruitful of the apostle's life, congregations were established in the leading cities of Galatia and in Philippi, Thessalonica, Corinth, and Ephesus (together with its hinterland in the province of Asia). It was also a period during which Paul was obliged to develop a writing ministry as a means of keeping in touch with these churches. From the letters to the Thessalonians, Galatians, and Corinthians we can learn much that reflects and illuminates Paul's experiences in founding these congregations. These experiences were characterized by a certain sameness, in that some who heard the Word rejected and others accepted it, but each situation had its own special features.

A crucially important event is reported in the midst of the record of these strenuous labors—namely, the apostolic council in Jerusalem (chap. 15). Here the question of Gentile converts was thrashed out, with far-reaching consequences for the more rapid spread of the Gospel. Paul and Barnabas, along with Peter and James the Just, played a significant role in this gathering.

A. Mission of Barnabas and Saul in Cyprus and South Galatia—13:1–14:28

As NOTED EARLIER, the Jewish Christians who evangelized Antioch do not seem to have gone any farther. But the work they started gathered strength quickly and became the base from which the Gospel went forth to the west and north.

Much less information is given about the Antioch church than about the church in Jerusalem. What stands out is its willingness to pour its life into the task of carrying the message to the regions beyond. As the Jerusalem church had fostered practically all the evangelism attempted thus far, the Antioch church was destined to have the same role in the establishing of churches (largely Gentile) in Asia Minor, Macedonia, and Achaia. But whereas the outreach of the Jerusalem church was occasioned by persecution and the dispersal of its people, no such circumstance marked the launching of the campaign from Antioch. Ernest Best quotes approvingly the observation of Johannes Weiss, "We are here concerned with a more or less fully organized mission for which a plan was made beforehand."[1] The leading of the Spirit and the responsiveness of the entire church toward the new step also stand out as characterizing this fresh advance.

1. THE COMMISSIONING—13:1-3

Having served the Antioch church as its representatives on a mission to Jerusalem, Barnabas and Saul were now designated to lead a new departure in the history of the church at Antioch and of the Church as a whole.

> **13:1** Now there were at Antioch, in the church that was *there,* prophets and teachers: Barnabas, and Simeon who was called Niger, and Lucius of Cyrene, and Manaen who had been brought up with Herod the tetrarch, and Saul.
>
> **2** And while they were ministering to the Lord and fasting, the Holy Spirit said, "Set apart for Me Barnabas and Saul for the work to which I have called them."
>
> **3** Then, when they had fasted and prayed and laid their hands on them, they sent them away.

13:1-3. Up to this time the ministry within the Antioch church had been led by Barnabas and Saul (11:23-24, 26), but now three other men are noted as sharing this leadership. Probably all five had the double gift of prophecy and teaching (cf. the combination in 1 Co 12:28). Light is thrown on the distinction between the two gifts by a passage from Paul: "But now, brethren, if I come to you speaking in tongues, what shall I profit you, unless I speak to you either by way of revelation or of knowledge or of prophecy or of teaching?" (1 Co 14:6). Since revelation is joined to prophecy in the same chapter (14:29-30), it is natural to connect the two in verse 6, which leaves knowledge to be yoked to teaching.

As a prophet, a person spoke in response to a distinct moving of the Spirit, providing edification, exhortation, and consolation (1 Co 14:3). As a teacher, one presumably had a more sustained ministry, making use of the Old Testament and the traditions of the life and teaching of the Lord Jesus as handed down in the Church (Ac 2:42; cf. Mt 28:20). The teacher provided the basic information for living the Christian life; the prophet furnished special guidance from the Lord as needed. G. B. Caird notes that the book of Revelation, written by one who calls himself a prophet, contains many hymnic passages, and there are traces of this kind of writing in Paul. He suggests, therefore, the possibility "that we owe to the inspired words of Christian prophets the beginnings of our hymnody."[2]

Of the five men, the first and last are familiar from previous chapters. Possibly during the time Barnabas and Saul were absent on their mission to Jerusalem, the other men began to take a more prominent place in the life of the church and to manifest more and more their Spirit-given gifts.

Simeon is a Semitic name for which *Simon* is the Greek equivalent.* It has been conjectured that this is the Simon who bore the cross for Jesus (Mk 15:21). If this be so, it is strange that he is not indicated as coming from Cyrene, in line with the Markan passage, especially since Lucius, who is named next, is so designated. Further, Simon was a common name, often appearing in Scripture. This Simon was known also as Niger, a Latin term meaning "black-skinned."

Lucius is not to be identified with Luke (see comments on Ac 11:28).[3] He may have been one of the company of men who first brought the Gospel to Antioch (11:20).

Manaen, which means "comforter," is of special interest because of his background, "brought up with Herod the tetrarch."† He may have been the source of information about Herod which Luke utilizes in his gospel (e.g., Lk 8:3; 13:31-33; 23:6-12). Luke records more about the tetrarch than the other synoptists (cf. Ac 4:27 also).

*In regard to Simon Peter, the manuscripts at 2 Pe 1:1 are divided, some having "Simeon," others, "Simon."
†"Foster-brother" (of Herod) is also possible.

Saul is placed last in the list, but presumably not because he was the least conspicuous in his service (cf. 11:25-26, 30).‡ If the intent is to indicate that he was the youngest in the faith, it follows that the three who are listed between Barnabas and Saul must have been believers for several years and must have come to Antioch to aid in the work.

Some interpreters are inclined to think that Luke intended to designate the first three of the five as prophets and the last two as teachers. The Greek construction makes this possible but not certain, since the particles involved are used so freely in Acts as to indicate a stylistic feature some-times employed for the sake of variety.[4]

What persons are being indicated by the phrase, "While they were min-istering to the Lord"—the prophets and teachers or the church? Since the praying and sending forth of two from this group was almost certainly undertaken by the church as a whole (v. 3) and no change of subject is indicated from verse 2, it is probable that the ministering (or worshiping) applies to the congregation. If the ministering were intended to refer to the gifted men only, it would be natural to say that they were ministering to the church rather than to the Lord. Furthermore, it is questionable that the Holy Spirit would reveal His will for the church to the leaders only rather than to the entire congregation assembled for worship.

The word "fasting" hints at an awareness of a definite need for guidance. Was the church, perchance, beginning to sense its responsibility for a missionary advance beyond Antioch? In this atmosphere of urgent desire, the Holy Spirit responded, designating Barnabas and Saul for a specific work to which He was calling them. How the Spirit conveyed this mes-sage is not stated, but it is reasonable to suppose that the human instru-ment was one of the other men mentioned in verse 1, a man with the gift of prophecy. The Antioch church, no less than the Jerusalem congregation, knew what it was to experience the reality of the Spirit presiding over the life and work of the body of Christ. Both of these chosen servants of God were gifted as preachers and teachers of the Word. The missionary task required men of the highest caliber, men who were already proven in Christian work.

There is no reason to feel that the local congregation suffered from the departure of the two brethren. Gifted men remained to provide strong leadership.

"Then" (v. 3) is not a time word, but a particle meaning "so then," and is intended to indicate the readiness with which the church acted to set apart Barnabas and Saul. It was done with fasting, prayer, and the laying

‡Noting that Barnabas is listed first and Saul last, Haenchen suggests that the sep-aration of the names is deliberate, "in order that their future association may appear founded solely on the direction of the Spirit" (*The Acts of the Apostles*, p. 395).

on of hands. The first two items appear again in connection with the designation of elders for newly created congregations (14:23). Since both men had been laboring for years in the Lord's work, the laying on of hands was not for the purpose of ordination, much less to bestow the Spirit, but rather to identify the congregation with its representatives and to signify, as it were, that the whole group was going with them in spirit, committed to faithful prayer on their behalf.

Nothing is said about financial support. The church was certainly able to provide it (cf. 11:29-30), but both men seemed committed to self-support (1 Co 9:6). Barnabas had disposed of his property for the benefit of the Jerusalem saints (4:36-37), and probably from that time on worked to support himself, a plan in which Paul was pleased to share.[5]

Apparently Saul sensed no conflict between his own call from the risen Lord to missionary service and his being set apart by men for a specific mission. Similarly, he saw no contradiction between insisting that the Gospel he preached was revealed to him by the risen Lord (Gal 1:11-12) and referring to the Gospel as something passed on to him by the Jerusalem church (1 Co 15:1-11). The Gospel was the same.

2. CYPRUS—13:4-12

Here Luke describes the first stage of the journey, the ministry on the island of Cyprus, the original home of Barnabas. This makes all the more striking the rapid emergence of Saul as the leading figure of the missionary team.

13:4 So, being sent out by the Holy Spirit, they went down to Seleucia and from there they sailed to Cyprus.

5 And when they reached Salamis, they *began* to proclaim the word of God in the synagogues of the Jews; and they also had John as their helper.

6 And when they had gone through the whole island as far as Paphos, they found a certain magician, a Jewish false prophet whose name was Bar-Jesus,

7 who was with the proconsul, Sergius Paulus, a man of intelligence. This man summoned Barnabas and Saul and sought to hear the word of God.

8 But Elymas the magician (for thus his name is translated) was opposing them, seeking to turn the proconsul away from the faith.

9 But Saul, who was also *known as* Paul, filled with the Holy Spirit, fixed his gaze upon him,

10 and said, "You who are full of all deceit and fraud, you son of the devil, you enemy of all righteousness, will you not cease to make crooked the straight ways of the Lord?

11 "And now, behold, the hand of the Lord is upon you, and you will be blind and not see the sun for a time." And immediately a mist and a darkness fell upon him, and he went about seeking those who would lead him by the hand.

12 Then the proconsul believed when he saw what had happened, being amazed at the teaching of the Lord.

13:4-5. Notable is the change in terminology denoting the relation of the missionaries to the Holy Spirit. Whereas the church had "sent them away" (v. 3), or "let them go" (indicating that the parting was not altogether easy), the two men were "sent out by the Holy Spirit." It was by His authority and designation that they went forth.

After reaching Seleucia, the seaport of Antioch, they took ship for the trip to Salamis, over one hundred miles away to the southwest, the leading city of Cyprus. Barnabas' acquaintance with the island made this a natural beginning point. Furthermore, the area had already received some Christian testimony (11:19), although nothing is indicated about its effect. Salamis offered more than one synagogue opening, and in availing themselves of these opportunities Barnabas and Saul were following the plan of proclaiming the message to the Jew first (Ro 1:16). Nothing is said here about Gentiles. Probably they were not frequenting the synagogues as much as those in the large cities on the mainland. Luke does not include any account of the results achieved at Salamis.

A third member of the party is introduced here, John Mark (cf. 12:12), a cousin of Barnabas (Col 4:10). He went along as a helper. The nature of his assistance is not indicated. It may have gone beyond ministering to the comfort and convenience of his companions, since the word for "helper" may mean also a minister in connection with Christian testimony (Lk 1:2; Ac 26:16; 1 Co 4:1). In Luke 4:20 it designates a functionary of the synagogue, which has led to the speculation that John Mark could have included catechizing of converts among his duties. Rackham suggests that he may have baptized converts (cf. 1 Co 1:13-17).

13:6-8. The journey westward to the other major center, Paphos, is noted without comment. However, "gone through" perhaps indicates more than travel. The verb occurs twenty times in Acts and nearly always connotes travel in which testimony is borne to the unsaved or believers are edified.

In this second principal city, the missionaries experienced both testing and triumph. The opposition came from a Jew, Bar-Jesus by name, who was a "magician" and a "false prophet." Some similarity is discernible between this man and Simon Magus (chap. 8). Such characters abounded in the Hellenistic period, delving into the realm of the occult and trading on popular superstition. If religion was involved, it was with the hope of finding therein a way of gain (cf. 1 Ti 6:5).

Posing as a prophet, Bar-Jesus had gained the confidence of the proconsul (the title of a ruler of a senatorial province). Quickly he perceived that the new arrivals menaced any hold he might have on the Roman official, for if Sergius Paulus began to incline toward their teaching, he could hardly do otherwise than abandon all contact with this renegade Jew. So when the proconsul expressed a desire to hear the visitors, Bar-Jesus summoned all his powers of persuasion to keep the official from becoming involved in the Christian "faith." If his superior became a believer, he could expect to be ejected from the court circle of the proconsul.

Apparently this prophet was known also by the name *Elymas*, but in what way this name relates to *Bar-Jesus* is difficult to determine. At any rate, the double name anticipates a similar situation in the case of Saul (v. 9).

13:9-12. At this point Saul took the initiative and became the actual leader of the party (vv. 13, 16, 42, 50). It is tempting to suggest that a change of name from Saul to Paul accompanied this new prominence, but Luke does not say this. He does not say that henceforth Saul was known as Paul, but that he was also known as Paul, implying that he had both names before this time. It was natural to be known as Saul in a Jewish setting, but now that he was moving out into an essentially Gentile mission, the suitability of the Roman name was obvious.

This is the last time the Jewish name is used in Acts, and it does not appear in any of Paul's letters. There is no proof that the assumption of the name Paul had any connection with Sergius Paulus. At this point the proconsul had not yet become a believer (cf. v. 12). Sherwin-White observes, "Perhaps the author was only trying to distinguish *his* Paul, the apostle, from the proconsul Sergius Paulus in the same passage."[6]

In the boldness which the Holy Spirit imparted to him, Paul faced Elymas squarely and with the utmost solemnity rebuked and unmasked him. It was a crucial moment in the history of missions.

> It was the first presentation of *the word of God* to the Roman world: and naturally it was not easy for Sergius Paulus to detect the vital distinction between the true prophets and the false. Once and for all that distinction and the separation of Christianity from all trafficking in spiritualism must be demonstrated.[7]

The indictment was severe: being allied with the devil rather than with God, and for that reason an enemy of righteousness, making use of deceit and fraud to gain control over the minds of men. As God's representative, Paul pronounced a punishment which was sufficiently drastic and obvious to make clear that his rebuke was not a matter of prejudiced opinion. The physical blindness imposed for a time would serve to symbolize the spiritual darkness in which the false prophet lived and moved (cf. Jn 3:19-20; 9:39). His helplessness was pitiable, a sharp change from his self-confidence and arrogance. God knows how to bring the wicked low before Him. When the blindness descended on the victim, Paul stood vindicated as a prophet of the Lord (cf. 2 Ki 5:27).

"Then the proconsul believed." The miracle was a strong confirmation of the teaching, as in the ministry of our Lord (cf. Mk 1:27). Nothing is said about baptism, but this in itself is hardly sufficient ground for doubting the genuineness of the conversion, especially in such a condensed narrative. Though Paul did not revisit the area, Barnabas did (15:39), probably with a view to evangelizing further and helping the church to be established in the truth.

3. PISIDIAN ANTIOCH—13:13-52

For the first time the reader is given a sample of Paul's synagogue preaching. The fullness of the narrative from this point on during the first journey is in contrast to the sketchy character of Luke's report of the Cyprus mission.

Verses 13-16. Here, however, the narrative becomes exceedingly compact, as details of travel are passed over in silence in order to bring the reader to the scene of Paul's synagogue address, which is reported with considerable fullness.

> **13:13** Now Paul and his companions put out to sea from Paphos and came to Perga in Pamphylia; and John left them and returned to Jerusalem.
>
> **14** But going on from Perga, they arrived at Pisidian Antioch, and on the Sabbath day they went into the synagogue and sat down.
>
> **15** And after the reading of the Law and the Prophets the synagogue officials sent to them, saying, "Brethren, if you have any word of exhortation for the people, say it."
>
> **16** And Paul stood up, and motioning with his hand, he said,
> "Men of Israel, and you who fear God, listen:

13:13-16. The Elymas incident had given Paul a certain prominence that is reflected in Luke's terminology, as he states that "Paul and his companions" sailed away from Paphos and landed at "Perga" in Pamphylia. This small and somewhat backward province faced the sea and was almost sealed off from the regions to the north by the Taurus mountains. It was not a promising area for evangelizing, since Greek and Roman influences had not been strong in this region and the inhabitants were not very receptive to new ideas. Some who had heard Peter preach on the Day of Pentecost were from Pamphylia (2:10). Luke does not record any ministry in connection with this visit. A suggestion has been made by Richard N. Longenecker "that the ignoring of Perga at this time was largely because of uncertainty within the missionary party itself regarding the validity of a direct approach to Gentiles."[8] Later, on the way back to Antioch, a witness was made to Perga (14:25).

An upsetting incident occurred when the trio reached this town on their way inland. John Mark decided to turn back. Significantly, he did not journey to Antioch to report to the church, but to his home in Jerusalem. No reason is given for the departure. In view of his later rehabilitation, Luke probably wished to spare him embarrassment. It is possible that Mark was not entirely in sympathy with the outlook of the older men about carrying the Gospel to the Gentiles. Mingled with this may have been a degree of displeasure over the ascendancy of Paul as the real leader of the group. Other less likely possibilities are homesickness and apprehension of dangers to be faced in penetrating the inland areas. Fortunately, Mark's withdrawal did not terminate his ministry (see comments on 12:12). But it led to a regrettable break between Paul and Barnabas at a later time (15:37-39).

The missionaries headed next for Pisidian Antioch. Sir William Ramsay, making use of Galatians 4:13, where Paul states that it was a bodily illness that led him to preach the Gospel at first to the Galatian churches, conjectured that the apostle contracted malarial fever in the lowlands of Pamphylia and sought relief in the higher altitudes of southern Galatia, where he was able to preach while recovering. He identified this ailment with Paul's thorn in the flesh (2 Co 12:7).[9] However, Paul's vision experience probably befell him prior to his association with the church in Syrian Antioch (2 Co 12:2). If the apostle contracted some illness at this time, he must have been possessed of great courage and bodily strength to make the rugged overland journey under such conditions. Luke was content to give the external facts of the journey, and in the briefest way possible.

Pisidian Antioch was part of the Roman province of Galatia. Ever since 25 B.C. it had been a Roman colony, the most important city in the southern part of the province. Its Jewish inhabitants were numerous, their settlement there going back to Seleucid days.

Paul and Barnabas made their way on the Sabbath to the synagogue, perhaps going early to meet the rulers of the synagogue and identify themselves. Paul's credentials as a former student of Gamaliel (22:3) would be sufficient to prompt an invitation to speak during the service. The invitation was tendered following "the reading of the Law and the Prophets" (cf. Lk 4:16-21). That such a homily customarily came after the reading is certified from Jewish sources.[10]

The word of exhortation could be based on the Scripture reading, but this was not a requirement. Though the invitation was addressed to both men, Paul was the one who responded (cf. Ac 14:12). His discourse may be taken as fairly representative of what he must have spoken on other occasions in the synagogues of the Dispersion. It resembled Stephen's (chap. 7) in that it contained something of a résumé of Israel's history, and also had some affinity to Peter's Pentecost sermon in its references to David and to the resurrection of Jesus. Paul's quotations from the Old Testament were less extensive than Peter's. His coverage of the life and ministry of the Lord Jesus was confined to the work of John the Baptist and to the Saviour's trial, death, and resurrection. Unlike Peter's sermon at Caesarea, Paul's included nothing about the baptism of Jesus and His deeds of mercy in Galilee.

Here and there the speaker interrupted the narration of historical events by indicating to his audience the relevance of these things to their lives (vv. 26, 32, 38, 40). He recognized that his audience was composed of two groups: "men of Israel" and those "who fear God." Paul's inclusion of the second group was not done out of mere courtesy, as is indicated by a repetition of the twofold address in verse 26.

Verses 17-21. At the beginning of his message Paul noted in passing the period of the patriarchs and then reviewed with great economy of language the Egyptian sojourn, the exodus and the wilderness wanderings, the conquest of Canaan, the period of the judges, and the beginning of the monarchy with Saul.

> **13:17** "The God of this people Israel chose our fathers, and made the people great during their stay in the land of Egypt, and with an uplifted arm He led them out from it.
>
> **18** "And for a period of about forty years He put up with them in the wilderness.
>
> **19** "And when He had destroyed seven nations in the land of Canaan, He distributed their land as an inheritance—*all of which took* about four hundred and fifty years.
>
> **20** "And after these things He gave *them* judges until Samuel the prophet.
>
> **21** "And then they asked for a king, and God gave them Saul the son of Kish, a man of the tribe of Benjamin, for forty years.

13:17-21. Important stages in Israel's history are gathered up in a very few words: "chose" refers to God's sovereign dealings with Abraham, carried forward by means of promises to Isaac and Jacob; "made great" covers the period of Joseph in Egypt; "led out" focuses on the exodus; "put up with" stresses the forbearance of God despite Israel's shortcomings in the wilderness (cf. 7:39-41). The giving of the Law is omitted (in v. 39 its inadequacy is noted). Paul did not pause to name "the seven nations" whose territory was given to Israel. They were too well known to need repetition (cf. Deu 7:1). Roughly four hundred and fifty years were required for the events listed so far (from the sojourn in Egypt to the distribution of the land to the twelve tribes under Joshua's direction). The period of the "judges" is noted, coming to a close with Samuel, a key figure in that he marked the transition to the era of the kingdom by anointing Saul as king and endeavoring to help him.

Verses 22-25. Paul completed his review of the Old Testament by moving directly from David and God's covenant with him to the inauguration of the new age, with the transitional ministry of John, the forerunner of Jesus.

> **13:22** "And after He had removed him, He raised up David to be their king, concerning whom He also testified and said, 'I have found David the son of Jesse, a man after My heart, who will do all My will.'
>
> **23** "From the offspring of this man, according to promise, God has brought to Israel a Savior, Jesus,
>
> **24** after John had proclaimed before His coming a baptism of repentance to all the people of Israel.
>
> **25** "And while John was completing his course, he kept saying, 'What do you suppose that I am? I am not *He.* But behold, one is coming after me the sandals of whose feet I am not worthy to untie.'

13:22-25. In moving on to David and his pivotal importance in redemption history, Paul dismissed Saul's failure with the simple observation that God "removed him" to make way for a man after his own heart. Having come to David, it was unnecessary to trace Old Testament developments further, for God's dealings with him pointed on to the coming of David's greater Son, even Jesus (Ps 132:11; Is 11:1-2; Ro 1:3).

Except for Peter's reference (5:31) this is the only mention in Acts of Jesus as Saviour. By referring to the Lord Jesus in this way, rather than as Messiah, Paul avoided an emphasis that might have been taken in a political sense. He was concentrating on the theme of salvation. The last and greatest of the prophets, John, by means of his "baptism of repentance," his refusal to identify himself as the coming One, and his confession of unworthiness to serve Him, sought to turn the eyes of Israel upon God's Anointed. The ministry of John was doubtless known in most places (Ac 10:36-37; 19:1-3).

Verses 26-41. The remainder of the sermon differs from the early portion in that the recital of Old Testament history was abandoned in favor of quoting Scripture relevant to the person and work of Christ. Along with this there was repeated reference to Paul's audience; they were reminded of their heritage and warned not to sacrifice it by rejecting the Saviour.

13:26 "Brethren, sons of Abraham's family, and those among you who fear God, to us the word of this salvation is sent out.

27 "For those who live in Jerusalem, and their rulers, recognizing neither Him nor the utterances of the prophets which are read every Sabbath, fulfilled *these* by condemning *Him.*

28 "And though they found no ground for *putting Him to* death, they asked Pilate that He be executed.

29 "And when they had carried out all that was written concerning Him, they took Him down from the cross and laid Him in a tomb.

30 "But God raised Him from the dead;

31 and for many days He appeared to those who came up with Him from Galilee to Jerusalem, the very ones who are now His witnesses to the people.

32 "And we preach to you the good news of the promise made to the fathers,

33 that God has fulfilled this *promise* to our children in that He raised up Jesus, as it is also written in the second Psalm, 'THOU ART MY SON; TODAY I HAVE BEGOTTEN THEE.'

34 "*And as for the fact* that He raised Him up from the dead, no more to return to decay, He has spoken in this way: 'I WILL GIVE YOU THE HOLY and SURE *blessings* OF DAVID.'

35 "Therefore He also says in another *Psalm,* 'THOU WILT NOT ALLOW THY HOLY ONE TO UNDERGO DECAY.'

36 "For David, after he had served the purpose of God in his own generation, fell asleep, and was laid among his fathers, and underwent decay;

37 but He whom God raised did not undergo decay.

38 "Therefore let it be known to you, brethren, that through Him forgiveness of sins is proclaimed to you,

39 and through Him everyone who believes is freed from all things, from which you could not be freed through the Law of Moses.

40 "Take heed therefore, so that the thing spoken of in the Prophets may not come upon *you*:

41 'BEHOLD, YOU SCOFFERS, AND MARVEL, AND PERISH;
FOR I AM ACCOMPLISHING A WORK IN YOUR DAYS,
A WORK WHICH YOU WILL NEVER BELIEVE, THOUGH
SOMEONE SHOULD DESCRIBE IT TO YOU.' "

13:26-41. Two principal lines of thought are observable here: the issue of Jesus' death and resurrection, both events fulfilling Scripture; and an appeal to accept forgiveness of sins made possible through Him. To fail to make such a response is to perish. Both Jew and Gentile are privileged to have the opportunity of responding to the message of salvation (v. 26). Both were included in Paul's commission (9:15).

The Jews of Jerusalem had had their opportunity to know and receive the Saviour, but they had not recognized Him (Jn 1:11; 8:19), nor had they seen the fulfillment of Scripture in Him (Jn 5:39). Unwittingly they had fulfilled Scripture by "condemning" Him to death (cf. Ac 3:17-18; Is 53:3). There was no (just) "ground" for putting Him to death, since the charge of blasphemy wrongly presupposed that He was not what He claimed to be. Pilate, faced with the request that Jesus be "executed," repeatedly announced that he could find no basis for such a verdict (Lk 23:4, 14, 15, 22).

After the death on the cross came the entombment (Ac 13:29), to which Paul referred also in his statement of the Gospel in 1 Corinthians 15:4. The reversal of the human verdict came dramatically in God's action of raising His Son from the dead. Witnesses encountered the Lord in the days that followed. Paul was content to limit the witnesses to those who had followed Jesus from Galilee to Jerusalem. His own experience of the risen Lord came later and under wholly different conditions, so he omitted mention of it rather than going into a detailed explanation of his early opposition and the circumstances of his conversion (a line of thought quite appropriate when defending himself, chap. 26).

"And we preach to you the good news," Paul continued (v. 32). Not only the early disciples but "we," Barnabas and Paul, proclaimed this message. It was especially important to Jews to know that the Good News concerned "the promise made to the fathers." This was hardly the promise of the Spirit, for that promise was made by the Father to the Son and was passed on to the disciples in anticipation of Pentecost (Lk 24:49), whereas this promise was made to the fathers of Israel and surely centered in the sending of the Messiah. The promise of the Spirit, so far as this appears in the Old Testament (e.g., Joel 2) is ancillary to the more central promise of the Redeemer. God has fulfilled this fundamental pledge in the person of Jesus (Lk 2:29-32).

But to whom has He fulfilled it? The manuscripts are divided between four readings: "to us the children;" "to our children;" "to their children;" and "to us their children." The second has the best manuscript support, although it is a somewhat unexpected statement. With this difficulty in mind, the RSV has "to us their children," which is the fourth reading.

The promise was fulfilled "in that he raised up Jesus." To apply this to the resurrection is dubious, for several reasons. For one thing, there are two references to the resurrection in the immediate context (vv. 30, 34), and both are explicit as pointing to resurrection from the dead. There is no mention of the dead in the passage before us. Again, it is unlikely that the promise of the Messiah would be regarded as fulfilled in the resurrection to the exclusion of the birth, life, and ministry of God's Anointed. Finally, the word "raised," although it can be used for resurrection, can also mean "raised up" in the sense of providing, bringing into the arena of history. It is used in this way by Peter in 3:22, 26 (cf. 7:37). In line with these considerations, the support given by quoting Psalm 2:7, "You are my Son; today I have begotten you," was for the purpose of referring not to the incarnation (it is not so used in the nativity accounts in the gospels) but "to the whole saving act of God through Christ."[11]

A second quotation follows immediately (v. 34), closely related to the first (v. 33) and the third (v. 35). If the first refers to the Christ-event, the second goes on to affirm that the end in view is the confirmation of the covenant made with David: "And your house and your kingdom shall endure before Me forever; your throne shall be established forever" (2 Sa 7:16). It is to this promise that "the holy and sure blessings of David" (Is 55:3) apply. The only way this promise could be realized was through the enduring, death-defying life of the Son, who is also the Messiah. Consequently the truth enunciated in Psalm 16:10—"Thou wilt not allow Thy Holy One to undergo decay"—is necessary to complete the circle of thought. His life is indestructible (Heb 7:16). Elsewhere Paul mentions together the same three ingredients of sonship, relation to David, and resurrection (Ro 1:3-4).

Judging from Peter's use of Psalm 16 in Acts 2:25-28, this must have been a leading proof text for the resurrection, doubtless stemming from Jesus' inclusion of the Psalms in His teaching about Messianic prophecy after He rose from the dead (Lk 24:44). Paul took pains, as Peter had done, to point out that Psalm 16:10 was not fulfilled in the David of history, for he died and was buried and his body suffered decay (v. 36; cf. 2:29). But the same was not true of Jesus of Nazareth (v. 37).

Having touched on the kingly aspect of Christ's work by mentioning the Davidic covenant, Paul turned in conclusion to that aspect which is of more immediate concern, the procuring of "forgiveness of sins" (v. 38). This is offered to "everyone who believes." Christ's saving efficacy is put over against the inability of the Law to free—literally, "justify"—from sin. This line of thought anticipates that more fully developed in the apostle's teaching on justification in Galatians and Romans. To say, as some do, that Paul meant to teach that the Law can free from some things, but Christ goes beyond this by freeing from all that remains, is quite foreign to the apostle's teaching. For him the Law did not justify anything, but condemned (2 Co 3:9).

There is a point of difficulty, however, in the language used here—to free (justify) "from"—since in his letters Paul does not state justification in this way. In one passage, however, he uses the word as he did here—"For he who has died is freed from sin" (Ro 6:7)—so there need be no misgivings about the passage before us. To render the verb as "free" rather than "justify" in these two passages is warranted, since in the more highly theological treatment in his letters the apostle does not identify forgiveness with justification, seeing that the latter term refers strictly to the bestowal of a righteous standing before God, for which forgiveness is a necessary preparation. Forgiveness may be granted over and over, but justification is a once-for-all pronouncement on behalf of the sinner.

The final note sounded in the sermon was a warning of judgment should God's salvation in Christ be repudiated or neglected. Such warnings are common "in the prophets," but Paul cited Habakkuk 1:5 as representative. Most of his listeners would recognize the passage and realize that it had been fulfilled in the Chaldean invasion of Judah and the ultimate destruction both of the city Jerusalem and of the Temple. The close of the Areopagus address furnishes a rough parallel in that a warning of judgment to come concluded that message (17:31) as well.

Verses 42-43. Having reported the sermon, Luke sketches briefly the effect of the message on those who attended the service.

> **13:42** And as Paul and Barnabas were going out, the people kept begging that these things might be spoken to them the next Sabbath.
> **43** Now when *the meeting of* the synagogue had broken up, many of the Jews and of the God-fearing proselytes followed Paul and Barnabas, who, speaking to them, were urging them to continue in the grace of God.

13:42-43. As the two missionaries were leaving the synagogue at the conclusion of Paul's remarks, some of the audience crowded around them with the request that a similar message be brought to them the following Sabbath. Their hungry hearts had been captivated by the realization that God had fulfilled His promises. It appears from the next verse that the service had not yet been dismissed, but with the close, which must have come very soon, many of the people, evidently greatly affected by what they had heard, rushed out of the building to overtake Paul and Barnabas. Some of these were Jews; others were "God-fearing proselytes."

It is tempting to identify these two groups in terms of the twofold description of the attendants given in verses 16 and 26, but this would require the assumption that the God-fearers were proselytes, that is, Gentiles already converted to Judaism, and would destroy the clear distinction preserved elsewhere between God-fearers and proselytes. In view of this difficulty, it is likely that in this instance "God-fearing" is to be understood simply as "worshiping," with the result that the proselytes are noted merely as having been engaged in worship during the service.

This still leaves a rather awkward situation, namely, that the God-fearers who had been so clearly noted and addressed by Paul not once but twice were not represented in the group that followed the missionaries. It is possible, of course, that they were reticent about speaking to the visitors, especially since the Jews were thronging them in considerable numbers.

The very interest being shown was indicative to the missionaries that "the grace of God" was working in many hearts. They urged them to foster it by continued inquiry and obedience to the truth as it was received.

Verses 44-52. The happenings on the following Sabbath are recounted, as well as the ultimate effects of the mission in terms of reception and rejection of the message of salvation.

> **13:44** And the next Sabbath nearly the whole city assembled to hear the word of God.
>
> **45** But when the Jews saw the crowds, they were filled with jealousy, and *began* contradicting the things spoken by Paul, and were blaspheming.
>
> **46** And Paul and Barnabas spoke out boldly and said, "It was necessary that the word of God should be spoken to you first; since you repudiate it, and judge yourselves unworthy of eternal life, behold, we are turning to the Gentiles.
>
> **47** "For thus the Lord has commanded us,
> 'I HAVE PLACED YOU AS A LIGHT FOR THE GENTILES,
> THAT YOU SHOULD BRING SALVATION TO THE END OF THE EARTH.'"
>
> **48** And when the Gentiles heard this, they *began* rejoicing and glorifying the word of the Lord; and as many as had been appointed to eternal life believed.
>
> **49** And the word of the Lord was being spread through the whole region.
>
> **50** But the Jews aroused the devout women of prominence and the leading men of the city, and instigated a persecution against Paul and Barnabas, and drove them out of their district.
>
> **51** But they shook off the dust of their feet *in protest* against them and went to Iconium.
>
> **52** And the disciples were continually filled with joy and with the Holy Spirit.

13:44-47. No information is given about the activities of the missionaries during the following week, but the great concourse of people on the next Sabbath may indicate contact with the community. Since the number of Jews in attendance at the synagogue would be approximately the same from week to week, the great increase must be credited to Gentile interest. The influence of the service held on the preceding Sabbath is evident in that the people came "to hear the word of God" (cf. v. 42).

Although the Western text does state that they came to hear Paul, it is careful to indicate that he spoke about the Lord.

That Paul was indeed the spokesman on this occasion also is clear from verse 45. It was his presentation which drew opposition from some of the Jews and turned the service into something of a debate. Luke indicates that "jealousy" was a factor, prompted by the sight of the large turnout to hear the visitors. But judging from Paul's experience in synagogues elsewhere, the opposition had other grounds as well. The Jews were not prepared en masse to receive Jesus as their Messiah, when their leaders in Jerusalem had rejected Him. What Paul had said about the law (v. 39) would not have been to their liking either. Further, since the apostle had addressed his remarks to God-fearers as well as to Jews, and had said nothing about the necessity of circumcision for such Gentiles when he offered forgiveness of sins through Jesus Christ (v. 38), it was fairly clear that he was opening the door of faith to these people. This would have been totally unacceptable to Jews, as it was to many Christian Jews (15:1).

"Blaspheming," in this context, probably indicates the derisive and reviling manner in which Paul's opponents contended with him, although the name of Jesus may have been included (cf. 1 Co 12:3).

Before long the point was reached when Paul, joined by Barnabas, had to tell the unbelieving Jews forthrightly that their attitude of rejection meant they had forfeited the right to hear the word of the Gospel further. It was their privilege to hear it "first" (cf. Ro 1:16), but their refusal of it opened the way for the missionaries to turn to the Gentiles (cf. Ro 11:11). This is the pattern that Paul's evangelism followed in city after city, even in Rome (28:25-28). Just as he had been able to support his Gospel preaching by citations from the Old Testament (vv. 33-35), so he and Barnabas could justify their intention to turn to the Gentiles by the Word of God. In Isaiah 49:6 the mission of the Servant-Messiah is seen to be larger in its scope than the confines of Israel, bringing salvation "to the end of the earth." Echoes of the same passage are discernible in the words of Simeon (Lk 2:30-32) and in the commission of the risen Lord to His disciples (Ac 1:8).

Turning to the Gentiles did not imply abandonment of ministry in synagogues as a policy for the future, but it implied a readiness to reach Gentiles, if need be, apart from any synagogue context. Indeed, this had already occurred in the case of Sergius Paulus (13:7-12) and was to be repeated in the mission to the community of Lystra (chap. 14). Such a procedure was bound to create antagonism among unbelieving Jews and to deepen their hostility toward the Church not only in the Dispersion but also in Palestine.

13:48-52. The Gentiles may not have been able to follow the synagogue discussion in all its ramifications, but they had no trouble grasping the significance of the opportunity to share in the blessings of Christ's redemption along with believing Jews. It seems that a considerable number put their faith in Christ then and there and joyfully extolled the goodness of God in sending them His word. In the expression "as many as had been appointed to eternal life" we are intended to sense not a restrictive emphasis but one of breadth. These people were "Gentiles," yet they were included, whereas members of the chosen nation Israel were excluding themselves by their unbelief (v. 46).

No doubt it was these new converts who made themselves responsible to "spread" the Good News throughout the surrounding area. Ramsay notes the suitability of Luke's observation here, since "Antioch was the governing center of a wide region which looked to it for administration."[12] Bringing the Gospel to the major cities usually resulted in a broad extension of the Church to rural sections, a deliberate element in Paul's missionary strategy (cf. 19:10; 1 Th 1:8).

Meanwhile the unbelieving Jews were busy adding to their already heavy burden of guilt by stirring up opposition to Paul and Barnabas in the city. They persuaded certain "women" of prominence that the missionaries were undesirables, and these in turn seem to have influenced the "leading men" of the community (who might not have given heed if the Jews had approached them directly), so that the missionaries were forced to leave the "district" (cf. 1 Th 2:15-16).

They responded by doing what the Lord had commanded His disciples to do under these circumstances (Mt 10:14). Shaking off the dust of one's feet was an act which symbolized repudiation. The townspeople were making themselves responsible for denying to the community further light on salvation and the opportunity to receive it from those who were capable of making the way plain.

Still, the new converts remained, and they could bear their testimony. To strengthen them for this very task, the missionaries dared to return later (14:21-23). After noting that Paul and Barnabas went on to Iconium, Luke gives a felicitous description of the believers whom they left behind: "filled with joy and with the Holy Spirit." With such equipment they could be counted on to stand fast in case persecution should be directed at them also.

4. ICONIUM—14:1-7

This city, situated about sixty miles east and somewhat south of Pisidian Antioch, belonged to the district known as Phrygia, but lay close to the border of Lycaonia. In New Testament times the area was part of the Roman province of Galatia. Iconium is today the Turkish city of Konya. The fertility of the surrounding region made it a populous place at the time the missionaries visited there.

14:1 And it came about that in Iconium they entered the synagogue of the Jews together, and spoke in such a manner that a great multitude believed, both of Jews and of Greeks.

2 But the Jews who disbelieved stirred up the minds of the Gentiles, and embittered them against the brethren.

3 Therefore they spent a long time *there* speaking boldly *with reliance* upon the Lord, who was bearing witness to the word of His grace, granting that signs and wonders be done by their hands.

4 But the multitude of the city was divided; and some sided with the Jews, and some with the apostles.

5 And when an attempt was made by both the Gentiles and the Jews with their rulers, to mistreat and to stone them,

6 they became aware of it and fled to the cities of Lycaonia, Lystra and Derbe, and the surrounding region;

7 and there they continued to preach the gospel.

14:1-2. In several respects the campaign here resembled that in Pisidian Antioch: the preaching was carried on in the synagogue, where both Jews and Gentiles were present; converts were made from both groups; and opposition developed quickly, initiated by unbelieving Jews. Probably the presentation of the Gospel followed the same lines as in the sermon reported in Acts 13, which Luke seems to have intended to serve as an example of Paul's preaching in the synagogue as he went from place to place.

In reporting the Iconium ministry the historian is content to emphasize the effectiveness of the preaching: the two men spoke "in such a manner that a great multitude believed." This translation might mislead one into thinking that the secret of success was winsomeness or the use of fine rhetoric. Any such conclusion is ruled out by Paul's own description of his spoken word (1 Co 1:17; 2:4), which doubtless characterized his proclamation from the beginning. It was powerful preaching, indeed, but the power lay in the truth of the message and in the work of the Holy Spirit as He attested that truth to the hearers. The missionaries preached for a decision, not simply to impart information.

A unique feature of this passage is that here alone among the accounts of the Galatian cities visited on this journey, the Gentiles are called Greeks. "It is . . . one of the many slight and almost accidental examples of accuracy in details, which abound in the book of the Acts, that Luke gives the name Hellenes to the population of Iconium, alone among the Galatian cities."[13] The Greek character of the community is amply attested by coins and inscriptions. Roman influence did not eradicate it but rather conserved and built upon it.

Instead of attempting a confrontation with Paul and Barnabas in open debate, the unbelieving Jews stirred up trouble by poisoning the minds of the populace against them. The tactics were similar to those employed at Antioch (13:50), except that here the opposition worked on the masses rather than on the influential people of the community.

14:3-4. By his use of "therefore" Luke seems to say that it was the persecution which caused the missionaries to stay in the city for a long time. Opposition can indeed be a challenge to God's servants to stand their ground, for this is evidence that the Gospel is making an impact (cf. 1 Co 16:8-9). But here one must reckon also with the probability that the process of sowing seeds of mistrust and hatred among the people took a long time, so that there was a period during which public ministry went on unhindered.

With the Lord's help missionaries spoke out "boldly." As they were faithful in ministering "the word of His grace" (cf. 20:32), He showed His approval by working "signs and wonders" through them. Later on, when writing to the Galatian churches, Paul recalled to the minds of his readers these miraculous manifestations (Gal 3:5). They are mentioned in Acts only in connection with the mission at Iconium and Lystra, but they must have occurred in the other two cities also. Luke majors on the preaching at Antioch; his account of the stay at Derbe gives no details about the ministry.

At Iconium matters came eventually to a head, with the city sharply "divided" in its attitude toward the visitors. The issue was no longer confined to the synagogue. It was the talk of the town, with the "multitude" ranged on the side of the Jews or on the side of the apostles. In producing division by their work, Paul and Barnabas were reproducing an important aspect of the ministry of Jesus (Lk 12:51-53).

Only here and in verse 14 does Luke use this word "apostles" for the missionaries. Probably it was intended to remind the reader that these men had been sent forth by the Holy Spirit (13:4).

14:5-7. Finally we learn the source of the agitation against the missionaries. The "rulers" of the Jews—the primary leaders of the opposition—and the leaders of the Gentile community joined forces. They were ready to resort to violence, planning to use the Jewish method of stoning the victims. Providentially the apostles learned of the plan and were able to escape. Their departure was not a sign of cowardice, but rather an act of prudence. Moreover, it was in line with the instruction given by Jesus to His disciples (Mt 10:23).

Lystra was the next stopping place, a smaller community about twenty miles to the south. Since Paul ordinarily kept to the cosmopolitan centers, the motive for going there, as Ramsay suggests,[14] may have been to find a place of refuge until it was safe to return to Iconium. As it turned out, hostility followed the missionaries to this sequestered spot, so that it was not a place of rest. Actually the apostles could not remain inactive, and were soon involved in ministry.

Before going on to describe the work in Lystra, Luke mentions that the party, always engrossed in preaching the Gospel, also touched the town of Derbe and the surrounding territory.

5. LYSTRA—14:8-18

Lystra was the home of Timothy (16:1-2). In addition to native Lycaonians there were in this city Roman colonists and officials, as well as a few Jews, though perhaps not enough to warrant a synagogue. At least Luke does not mention one. Therefore the approach of the missionaries would be different from that employed in Antioch and Iconium, where the Old Testament was central to the presentation.

Luke's account of the mission consists of three elements: the healing of a lame man; the resultant attempt of the inhabitants to worship the benefactors, leading in turn to a short message by the missionaries about the nature of God; and the stoning of Paul by determined Jews from the north.

> **14:8** And at Lystra there was sitting a certain man, without strength in his feet, lame from his mother's womb, who had never walked.
>
> **9** This man was listening to Paul as he spoke, who, when he had fixed his gaze upon him, and had seen that he had faith to be made well,
>
> **10** said with a loud voice, "Stand upright on your feet." And he leaped up and *began* to walk.
>
> **11** And when the multitudes saw what Paul had done, they raised their voice, saying in the Lycaonian language, "The gods have become like men and have come down to us."
>
> **12** And they *began* calling Barnabas, Zeus, and Paul, Hermes, because he was the chief speaker.
>
> **13** And the priest of Zeus, whose *temple* was just outside the city, brought oxen and garlands to the gates, and wanted to offer a sacrifice with the crowds.
>
> **14** But when the apostles, Barnabas and Paul, heard of it, they tore their robes and rushed out into the crowd, crying out
>
> **15** and saying, "Men, why are you doing these things? We are also men of the same nature as you, and preach the gospel to you in order that you should turn from these vain things to a living God, WHO MADE THE HEAVEN AND THE EARTH AND THE SEA, AND ALL THAT IS IN THEM.

16 "And in the generations gone by He permitted all the nations to go their own ways;

17 and yet He did not leave Himself without witness, in that He did good and gave you rains from heaven and fruitful seasons, satisfying your hearts with food and gladness."

18 And *even* saying these things, they with difficulty restrained the crowds from offering sacrifice to them.

14:8-10. What looms large here is not the preaching ministry of Paul so much as the miracle performed on the lame man. His helpless condition is indicated by a threefold description. "Lame from his mother's womb" is the identical wording used in the case of the man healed by Peter at the Temple (3:2). Other features are the same also—the intensity with which the apostle fixed his gaze on him (cf. 3:4); and the result of the miracle, leaping and walking about (cf. 3:8).

A slight variation among the manuscripts produces some uncertainty as to whether the cripple heard Paul speaking on this occasion only or whether he had been listening to him previously as well. At any rate, his bearing caught Paul's attention, who discerned in his openness and eagerness the faith necessary to be healed.§

14:11-13. The healing produced an immediate and profound effect on those who witnessed it. (Presumably they had been listening to Paul speak.) In the excitement of the moment they began talking to one another in their native Lycaonian language. In keeping with the relative unimportance of Lycaonia politically and economically, there are no literary remains of the language. The episode before us bears testimony of the fact that most of the inhabitants understood Greek, otherwise they would not have been listening to Paul, unless he spoke through an interpreter.

Despite their backwardness, the inhabitants knew something of the Greek pantheon. They quickly dubbed Barnabas Zeus, the father of the gods, perhaps because of his seniority and imposing appearance. Paul they identified as Hermes, because of his role as spokesman. In Greek mythology Hermes was the messenger of the gods and the patron of orators. The miracle had convinced these superstitious people that the gods had taken human form (a commonplace in the Homeric poems) and had come down to men (cf. 28:6). In accordance with this notion, the priest of Zeus came forth from the local temple devoted to the worship of the father of the gods and made his way into the city prepared to sacrifice to the deities who had deigned to visit the area, an honor that was in line with the mood of the crowd.

The people's excitement is made more understandable with the help of a story narrated by the Roman poet Ovid (*Metamorphoses* 8:618 ff.) relating

§The word is "saved," or "made whole," as in connection with many of the miracles of Jesus (e.g., Mk 5:28, 34, marg.).

what happened to an old couple in the Phrygian hill country. It is admirably summarized by James L. Kelso.

> Ovid tells how the Greek gods Zeus and Hermes came to this area disguised as men. They tried to find hospitality in a thousand homes, but no one offered them a place to stay except a very poor, aged couple, Philemon and Baucis, who gave them everything they had to eat. When the empty wine bowl on the table refilled itself, the peasants recognized that these men were gods! The couple were then taken up to the top of a nearby hill where they saw the gods inundate all the countryside which had denied them hospitality. They also saw their tiny hut transformed into a large marble temple with a gilded roof.[15]

14:14. The arrival of the sacrificial animals and the festal spirit of the throng must have brought inquiries from the missionaries. On learning what was afoot, they were appalled. No time should be lost. Tearing their garments, they showed their horror at the contemplated worship of men as gods (cf. Mt 26:65). The tear was from the neck down and extended about the length of one's hand. Custom dictated its appropriateness in times of distress (Jos 7:6) and especially in a season of sorrow (2 Sa 1:11).

To this demonstration of distress, the two men added their verbal protest. Luke provides a digest of their remarks.

14:15-18. To be made the recipient of divine honors was coveted recognition to the vain, pagan mind (e.g., Antiochus Epiphanes and Caligula) but it is farthest from the desire of godly men and of angels (Rev 22:8-9). Barnabas and Paul were quick to affirm that they were made of the same human "nature" as the Lycaonians. One is reminded of what Scripture says concerning Elijah being like his fellows—a challenge to imitate his titanic accomplishments in the realm of prayer (Ja 5:17).

The central purpose of the missionaries in coming to the city had been to proclaim a "gospel" which, if accepted, would wean people away from such superstitions as presently gripped them. "Vain things" means false gods, or idols (1 Ki 16:13, LXX). Paul and Barnabas had not invited worship of themselves but were pointing men to God, who is "a living God," in sharp contrast to their idols. Idolatry was common in much of the religious life of Gentiles, so the Gospel proclamation among such people called for a renunciation of this misplaced devotion (Ac 17:29-31; 1 Th 1:9). Notable is the fact that the apostles did not poke fun at the crudity of idolatry and thereby needlessly offend their audience, but were content to point out its futility and then pass at once to an exposition of the "better way."

The remainder of the address advances reasons for making a right-about-face. First, God is the Creator. Quite naturally the Old Testament is utilized here, since it has so many pronouncements on this subject. But the source is not indicated, because the Lycaonians were not familiar with the Scriptures. The quotation is from Exodus 20:11 (cf. Ps 146:6). Second, there is a brief reference to divine providence. God had permitted the nations to go their own way, neither revealing Himself as He did to Israel nor bringing severe judgment on them for their idolatrous practices. But this time of leniency had now passed (cf. 17:30-31). And during past generations God had not really been indifferent, but had borne "witness" to Himself as Benefactor of the race by making nature fruitful for the good of man. However, this is not the same thing as saying that the witness had been understood and received.

So strong was the impression made by the miracle that even this plain talk barely sufficed to divert the multitude from their purpose to honor the visitors as deities. What they had seen was so potent that the spell could scarcely be broken by words.

6. DERBE AND THE RETURN TO SYRIAN ANTIOCH—14:19-28

This paragraph covers briefly a variety of subjects, including the stoning of Paul, the move to Derbe, the return journey through the Galatian cities to the sea by way of Pamphylia, the sea trip back to Antioch, and the report given to the church in that city. It is clearly a summary account.

> **14:19** But Jews came from Antioch and Iconium, and having won over the multitudes, they stoned Paul and dragged him out of the city, supposing him to be dead.
>
> **20** But while the disciples stood around him, he arose and entered the city. And the next day he went away with Barnabas to Derbe.
>
> **21** And after they had preached the gospel to that city and had made many disciples, they returned to Lystra and to Iconium and to Antioch,
>
> **22** strengthening the souls of the disciples, encouraging them to continue in the faith, and *saying*, "Through many tribulations we must enter the kingdom of God."
>
> **23** And when they had appointed elders for them in every church, having prayed with fasting, they commended them to the Lord in whom they had believed.
>
> **24** And they passed through Pisidia and came into Pamphylia.
>
> **25** And when they had spoken the word in Perga, they went down to Attalia;
>
> **26** and from there they sailed to Antioch, from which they had been commended to the grace of God for the work that they had accomplished.
>
> **27** And when they had arrived and gathered the church together, they *began* to report all things that God had done with them and how He had opened a door of faith to the Gentiles.
>
> **28** And they spent a long time with the disciples.

14:19. Rather abruptly a new turn in the situation at Lystra is introduced. From the two cities which the apostles had already evangelized, certain Jews arrived, a testimony to their determination to oppose the Gospel and equally a testimony to the impression made by the missionaries. As the saying has it, "Nobody kicks a dead horse."

The antagonism of these men was far more deep-seated than that of the Gentiles whom they succeeded in inflaming (13:50; 14:2, 5). They could have subscribed to everything Paul included in his address to the Lystran multitude (vv. 15-17), yet they stoned him; and it was because they had heard him say that Jesus of Nazareth was the promised Messiah.

To accomplish their purpose they first had to win over the people of the place, which may have taken a few days. Possibly the chagrin of the populace at being mistaken about the identity of the two men was used by the Jews to turn them against the missionaries. Though Lystra was a Roman military colony, not many Romans lived there, and the Jews' plan proceeded without official interference.

This was the only time Paul experienced stoning (2 Co 11:25), and it must have made him reflect on what had happened to Stephen (Ac 7:58). That he was not called on to share the fate of the first martyr was due to the mercy of God, for the assailants were confident that they had permanently silenced him. When writing later to the Galatian churches, the apostle retained a vivid collection of his suffering in their midst (Gal 6:17, cf. 2 Ti 3:11).

14:20. The stoning marked the end of the ministry at Lystra for the time being. Yet that ministry had not been in vain, for a band of "disciples" gathered about Paul's form, no doubt in mourning. Imagine their joyful surprise when he stirred and rose to his feet and walked back into the city with them! The same power of God that had been efficacious through Paul to heal the cripple was potent to restore his own physical powers. God had vindicated His servant.

Yet it did not seem expedient to continue working there as long as the atmosphere was hostile, so Paul and Barnabas left for Derbe the following day. A Roman road connected the two communities. Recent surveys of the area have increased the likelihood that Derbe was about thirty miles east of the site formerly held to be the location,[16] and this raises the question whether Derbe was actually within the Roman province of Galatia. The rendering of this verse is also affected, as the journey would require more than a day. Since Luke does not say that the travelers arrived at Derbe on that same day, his wording can be understood to mean that they left Lystra with Derbe as their destination.

14:21-23. The brief statement about the work in Derbe is significant for what it says and for what it does not say. As expected, the missionaries preached the Gospel, with the result that "many" became "disciples" (literally, "they discipled many," i.e., won many converts [cf. Mt 28:19]). As a church, this believing group became in time sufficiently strong to have a representative among the number who went along with Paul on his final mission to Jerusalem (20:4).

Notable is the absence of any mention of persecution in this remote city. Years later, when Paul reminded Timothy of the sufferings he had endured on this missionary journey, Derbe was the one city in the whole region that was omitted (2 Ti 3:11). To have a peaceful mission here was a blessing after the stoning at Lystra.

It took courage to return to the very places that had resisted the Gospel and mistreated its messengers, yet the decision to return was not dictated by bravado but by the practical necessity of shepherding the converts. Doubtless many of them were encountering opposition among kinfolk and neighbors because of their commitment to Jesus Christ. They were reminded that the path they had chosen involved "many tribulations." But it led to "the kingdom of God," with its future glory and peace. The "must" of suffering that governed the Saviour's mission (Lk 9:22) applied in principle to His followers, who were taught the privilege of knowing the fellowship of His sufferings (Ac 5:41; Phil 3:8, 10). The missionaries themselves had provided an example.

Edification was not the only purpose of this return journey. Organization was needed and was effected through the selection of "elders" in each church. The apostles "appointed" them. While it is true that the word used here could indicate congregational choice (see 2 Co 8:19), such is not the case in this context.[17] Conversations with the church about the qualifications of its members for such an important post, though, are certainly not to be excluded. The solemn responsibility attached to such a function of leadership is underscored by the reference to prayer and fasting (cf. 13:3). It would fall to the lot of these men to teach the congregation and exercise authority, especially in matters of discipline (1 Ti 5:17).

It seems strange that in writing to the various churches he had founded, Paul did not refer to officers of the group (Phil 1:1 is the exception). This need not imply a conflict with Luke's account, since Paul was accustomed to use more general terms which could well be intended to denote elders (see Ro 12:8; 1 Co 12:28; 16:16; 1 Th 5:12). Such is the case also in Hebrews 13:17, 24. Luke is careful to indicate that the large church at Ephesus was governed by elders who were responsible for overseeing and shepherding the flock of God committed to their charge (Ac 20:28).

However capable and godly were the newly appointed presbyters in the Galatian congregations, they needed divine wisdom and grace, so undoubtedly they were included in the parting prayer for the congregation, which committed all the believers to the loving care and faithful protection of the Lord. What He had done for Paul and Barnabas was an indication that the churches could face the future unafraid even though the apostles were no longer available in person.

14:24-26. Reversing the route they had followed on their way to Galatia from the south, Paul and Barnabas found themselves once more in Perga of Pamphylia. Their previous visit had been marred by the defection of Mark, which may have been so upsetting as to keep them from public ministry (cf. 13:13-14). If so, this circumstance must have made them the more eager to bear their testimony here before going on. It was a wise decision, for there is no indication that either of them ever returned to this area. In later times Perga became a Christian center with several churches.

Apparently the sea journey from Attalia to Seleucia was uneventful. The missionaries returned to Antioch with a sense of satisfaction that they had "accomplished" their mission. But this was no ground for boasting, for apart from "the grace of God" it would have proved fruitless (cf. 1 Co 15:10). Actually, the word rendered "accomplished" means "fulfilled, carried out to the full limits of possibility" (cf. the use of the word in Ro 15:19; Col 4:17).

14:27-28. To judge from Luke's account, there was no appreciable interval between the arrival of Paul and Barnabas at Antioch and their report to the congregation. The people were as eager to hear it as the missionaries were to give it. In contrast to the sending out, when the church had taken the initiative (Ac 13:3), the missionaries now took charge, for it was they who "gathered the church together."

There may have been many church-in-the-house groups scattered throughout the city, but this did not demand separate congregations. The same was true of the large church at Jerusalem, with its thousands of people. They were not organized into separate entities; always they are described as constituting one church.

Another item of interest here is the tense of the verb "report," which contains a hint that more than one service was needed for the full account that the apostles were prepared to give. This impression is strengthened by Luke's "all things." Nothing of importance was omitted. This was a great occasion for the congregation and they wanted a full report. Special emphasis was laid on the fact that God had opened a door of faith to the "Gentiles," something that would strike a responsive chord among saints who were themselves mostly Gentiles (cf. comments on 11:26).

No doubt the apostles continued to minister to the people during the "long time" they were able to remain in their midst. There was no divine leading to embark at this juncture on a new missionary expedition. As the following chapter discloses, their presence was needed at a crucial meeting in Jerusalem.

B. Interlude of the Jerusalem Council—15:1-35

Further missionary work had to be postponed until a vital question affecting the whole Church had been faced and settled. For background, one needs to recall that the Jerusalem church was composed of believing Jews. Some astonishment was created there by Peter's ministry to Gentiles at Caesarea, but the situation was so surrounded by divine guidance and blessing that it was allowed to pass (11:18). It was probably viewed as exceptional rather than as normative.

The growth of the Gentile church at Antioch must have raised questions, but apparently it was the establishment of Gentile churches in Asia Minor (chaps. 13-14) that stirred into action a certain segment of the Jerusalem church. The leadership of that church throughout the world seemed threatened, and they began to doubt whether they could successfully appeal to Jews with the Gospel much longer if the Christian community was about to be dominated by Gentiles. So the meeting in the holy city was a momentous gathering for the future of the Christian cause.

Verses 1-5. Here the immediate occasion for calling the Council is set forth, together with a brief account of the journey to Jerusalem by the representatives of the Antioch church and their initial encounter with those who were to oppose them at the conference. (For a brief assessment of the problem of harmonizing this visit with those reported by Paul in Galatians, see the Introduction, under "Historical Worth.")

> **15:1** And some men came down from Judea and *began* teaching the brethren, "Unless you are circumcised according to the custom of Moses, you cannot be saved."
>
> **2** And when Paul and Barnabas had great dissension and debate with them, *the brethren* determined that Paul and Barnabas and certain others of them, should go up to Jerusalem to the apostles and elders concerning this issue.
>
> **3** Therefore, being sent on their way by the church, they were passing through both Phoenicia and Samaria, describing in detail the conversion of the Gentiles, and were bringing great joy to all the brethren.
>
> **4** And when they arrived at Jerusalem, they were received by the church and the apostles and the elders, and they reported all that God had done with them.
>
> **5** But certain ones of the sect of the Pharisees who had believed,

stood up, saying, "It is necessary to circumcise them, and to direct them to observe the Law of Moses."

15:1. Those who arrived at Antioch from Judea are given the indefinite description, "some men." Several witnesses of the Western text identify them explicitly by adding the first part of verse 5 at this point, no doubt on the ground that the platform of both groups was the same. The remarkable thing is that instead of objecting to the reception of the converts made by Paul and Barnabas on their recent trip, the new arrivals dared to direct their propaganda at the Gentile members of the Antioch church. This is evidence that the growth of this congregation during the past two or three years, unchallenged by any official inquiry from the mother church at Jerusalem, had rankled in the minds of some who belonged to that church. Now their concern was coming out into the open.

Objection was centered not in doubt about the genuineness of the faith in Jesus held by these brethren in Antioch but in concern about the incompleteness of their status. Historically, when Gentiles wished to identify with the congregation of Israel, they were required to be circumcised (Ex 12:48) and to order their lives according to the Mosaic Law, after the fashion of the Jews. Circumcision had been instituted as the seal of God's covenant with Abraham (Gen 17). Many Gentiles, however, resented this necessity as a personal indignity, so that in spite of their interest in Judaism they refused to take this step that would have made them proselytes, preferring instead the status of God-fearers (cf. 13:16).

The visitors from Jerusalem were saying that what the synagogue had done back through the years, the church must now do, namely, receive as full members only those Gentiles who met the ancient qualifications. They relegated the rest to the status of hangers-on and dared to suggest that if Gentiles chose not to submit to these requirements they could not "be saved."

It was this contention that was carried also to the Galatian churches and led to Paul's fiery epistle of protest and his affirmation of the sufficiency of faith in Christ alone for Gentile converts. If Jewish believers wished to circumcise their children and live in terms of the demands of the Mosaic Law, that was their privilege; but even so, there was no saving power in anything but the cross of Christ.

15:2. Luke is content to note that the Antioch church, through the two men who had been preaching the Gospel of the grace of God, vigorously denied the rightfulness of the Judaizers' position advocated so openly in their midst. The nature of the apostles' refutation may be gathered in a general way from the report of the Jerusalem Council which follows.

According to the Western text, the men from Judea demanded that Paul,

Barnabas, and others go up to Jerusalem, apparently because they were sure that their own position would prevail over that of the representatives of the Antioch church. However, the superior text makes it clear that the initiative was taken rather by the local church. Their existence as a Christian community as well as their plans for further missionary expansion turned on the decision. Of course it might be said that this church could have continued its present course even if the Council should support the agitators; but then the unity of the whole Christian community would have been sacrificed, and this would have had serious repercussions on evangelism as well as on Christian fellowship. The believers were haunted by the specter of two churches existing instead of one.

While there was concern, there was also confidence among the Antioch brethren. They must have known about Peter's experience at Caesarea, a precedent that had a bearing on the present controversy. Then too, Barnabas had come to Antioch with the blessing of the Jerusalem church, and there had been no official disapproval of his work. "Certain others" went along with Paul and Barnabas, among whom we may count Titus, who was a test case because he was an uncircumcised Gentile (Gal 2:1-5).

15:3. "Sent on their way" is a stock expression used not only in the Bible but in other literature, denoting far more than saying good-bye. It involved provision for the journey, including arrangement for security when necessary, and sometimes arrangement in advance for overnight stops. In Christian usage it must have included a parting prayer of committal to God and a promise of faithful intercession during the period of absence.

The existence of churches along the travel route guaranteed hospitality and the opportunity to inform the brethren of the progress of the Gospel, especially among Gentiles. This is the first mention of churches in "Phoenicia," although witness in this area has been noted earlier (11:19). Still earlier, "Samaria" had received the Gospel. They had already reported to the Antioch church (14:27) and would do so at Jerusalem as well (15:4, 12). More than anything else, Paul and Barnabas were desirous of giving a full report of their work which had resulted in "the conversion of the Gentiles." This conversion was different from their having become Christian Jews. It is emphasized that the apostles were describing what had happened "in detail," the Greek word for which is used only here and in 13:41. As Knox reminds us, "These communities derived their knowledge of the faith from the same movement which had led to the foundation of the Church of Antioch, and naturally sympathized with its teaching."[1] The reports were received with "great joy" in these Jewish and Samaritan churches, encouraging the apostles as to their possible effect on the church in Jerusalem.

15:4-5. At length the party reached its destination, and any misgivings about the reception it would have proved needless, for the apostles and elders and the church as a whole were cordial. The two men had not been to Jerusalem since the famine visit (11:30). Opportunity was given them to relate "all that God had done with them." Necessarily this included a report of their work in bringing many Gentiles into the fold.

Believers who had belonged to "the sect of the Pharisees" felt constrained to stand up and object, interposing the same contention that had been voiced at Antioch about the necessity for Gentile believers to be circumcised and to keep the Law of Moses. A legalistic bent was natural for those who had belonged to the Pharisees, but it was not inevitable—Saul himself was a Pharisee. This group in the church could not be satisfied merely to impose circumcision on Gentile converts. They also demanded full adherence to the Law, which they regarded as necessary to the promotion of morality among those who had known little of high standards of conduct in the lax environment of the Greco-Roman world.

In this initial stage the issue to be debated was made clear. Quite likely at this juncture the apostles felt the need of conferring privately with Paul and Barnabas before the matter was thrashed out in the presence of the congregation. Such a conference is reported by Paul in Galatians 2:1-10. It established unity between the leaders involved and may also have set the agenda for the open meeting which followed.

Verses 6-11. This section is devoted to Peter's testimony before the Council. It was appropriate that the one who had opened the door of faith to Gentiles at Caesarea (chap. 10) should declare the bearing of that experience on the present discussion.

> **15:6** And the apostles and the elders came together to look into this matter.
>
> **7** And after there had been much debate, Peter stood up and said to them, "Brethren, you know that in the early days God made a choice among you, that by my mouth the Gentiles should hear the word of the gospel and believe.
>
> **8** "And God, who knows the heart, bore witness to them, giving them the Holy Spirit, just as He also did to us;
>
> **9** and He made no distinction between us and them, cleansing their hearts by faith.
>
> **10** "Now therefore why do you put God to the test by placing upon the neck of the disciples a yoke which neither our fathers nor we have been able to bear?
>
> **11** "But we believe that we are saved through the grace of the Lord Jesus, in the same way as they also are."

15:6. First of all we must face the question of the composition of the meeting. Luke mentions only "the apostles and the elders." Nothing at this stage is said about Barnabas or the Judaizing group whose position is described in the previous verse, but the very fact that there was debate (v. 7) implies their presence.

Some scholars incline to identify this meeting with the one described in Galatians 2:1-10, where there is evidence of pressure put on Paul from some quarter to have Titus circumcised. Though elders are not mentioned in Galatians, it is conceivable that some of them could have been present. The apostles, on this identification of the passage, must have been James the Lord's brother, Peter, and John. One can grant the possibility of this interpretation, but it seems more natural to insert the meeting of Galatians 2 between verses 5 and 6 as a phase which Luke does not record. A reason for concluding this is the fact that the "multitude" is mentioned in such a way as to indicate that a large body of people was present during Peter's address (Ac 15:12).

Luke does not say that all the apostles were on hand. Some may have been occupied elsewhere, for it is unlikely that at this period of the development of the Church the whole group would remain in the city. On the other hand, they could have been summoned for this important gathering. As for the elders, they have been noted at an earlier point (11:30) and should be thought of as assisting James in the affairs of the Jerusalem congregation (cf. Ja 5:14).

15:7-9. Wisely, Peter did not take the floor at once, which could have given the impression of railroading. Rather, there was opportunity for "debate." Only when thoughts and emotions had been expressed and energies had spent themselves did Peter come forward. Without calling attention to his rank as apostle, his leadership of the apostles during the Lord's earthly ministry, or his great service in the early days of the Jerusalem church, and without suggesting that his testimony would settle everything, he launched out on a recital of what God had taught him on this issue. It was not something new ("you know"), and it was not something recent, but had existed "in the early days." The church ought to have grasped the lesson long ago; for Peter himself the matter had been settled quickly.

The incident at Caesarea would not have been definitive for the Church if Peter had acted on his own initiative and depended on his own wisdom. But it was God who had chosen to use him as His mouthpiece. And it was God, the one who reads human hearts as an open book, who had discerned the genuineness of the faith of Peter's Gentile audience and "bore witness" to this reality by granting them the Holy Spirit even before they had made any open confession (cf. 10:44). God had given these believers the same "cleansing" of heart bestowed on the apostles and those who had responded at Pentecost. Water baptism gave outward recognition to a work of grace already wrought. God's recognition of faith by granting the Spirit implied that nothing more—such as circumcision and shouldering the yoke of the Law—was needed for divine acceptance.

15:10-11. To impose such things as these on Gentile believers in the present situation would be to "put God to the test." It would be to question His right to receive the Caesarean Gentiles as He had done. It would be to sit in judgment on the Almighty. It would be to provoke His displeasure and even invite His chastisement (cf. 5:9). It would also have the effect of imposing a heavy and unnecessary burden on Gentile believers, which Peter characterized as a "yoke," something galling and unbearable. The word "yoke" has about the same force as *burden* or *load* (cf. Mt 23:4). Quite different is the yoke of Christ (Mt 11:30).

Was Peter talking about the Law as a way of life for the redeemed, or as a condition for salvation? He answered this question in verse 11 (cf. vv. 1, 5). One who took the Law seriously, especially as interpreted by Jesus in the Sermon on the Mount, was bound to discover how sinful he was, how greatly in need of a salvation he could not help to provide. Peter emphasized this by noting that the Law was a yoke "which neither our fathers nor we have been able to bear." Paul made a similar observation when he accused the circumcision party of failure to live up to the Law even while they were seeking to impose circumcision on Gentile converts (Gal 6:13). Salvation, said Peter, comes not by the Law at all, but by an entirely different means, "the grace of the Lord Jesus."

Quite remarkable is the way he stated the matter, indicating that the Jew has no advantage over the Gentile, for "we" (Jews) are saved "in the same way" (by grace) as "they" (Gentile believers). The thrust of the apostle's remarks is strikingly similar to the language of Paul in Galatians 2:16 (note especially the "even we"). That the two men were in accord on the nature of the Gospel is clearly indicated in Galatians 2:7-9. Peter was not contending, nor was Paul, that Christian Jews should abandon observance of the Law; this group of believers was not in view here. Even so, it is clear that such observance by believing Jews had nothing to do with their obtaining salvation. It could be helpful, however, in winning other Jews to Christ by disarming their prejudice (cf. 1 Co 9:19-20). If objection were raised that freedom from the Law was dangerous, even disastrous, from the standpoint of maintaining right conduct, the answer of Paul, and no doubt of Peter also, would resemble what is recorded in Romans 8:4.

A most important aspect of Peter's testimony was its effective refutation of the Judaizers' contention that the apostles of the Jerusalem church were favorable to their point of view in the controversy. On the contrary, Peter's position was the same as that of Barnabas and Paul.

Verses 12-21. After Peter's words, Barnabas and Paul had an opportunity to speak, giving way to James, who sought to show that the Old Testament prophetically included the salvation of Gentiles in the divine plan. With this background, the leader of the Jerusalem church was able to proceed with counsel about appropriate action to be taken in the present crisis.

> **15:12** And all the multitude kept silent, and they were listening to Barnabas and Paul as they were relating what signs and wonders God had done through them among the Gentiles.
>
> **13** And after they had stopped speaking, James answered, saying, "Brethren, listen to me.
>
> **14** "Simeon has related how God first concerned Himself about taking from among the Gentiles a people for His name.
>
> **15** "And with this the words of the Prophets agree, just as it is written,
>
> **16** 'AFTER THESE THINGS I WILL RETURN,
>   AND I WILL REBUILD THE TABERNACLE OF DAVID WHICH HAS
>   FALLEN,
>   AND I WILL REBUILD ITS RUINS,
>   AND I WILL RESTORE IT,
>
> **17** 'IN ORDER THAT THE REST OF MANKIND MAY SEEK THE LORD,
>   AND ALL THE GENTILES WHO ARE CALLED BY MY NAME,
>
> **18** 'SAYS THE LORD, WHO MAKES THESE THINGS KNOWN FROM OF
>   OLD.'
>
> **19** "Therefore it is my judgment that we do not trouble those who are turning to God from among the Gentiles,
>
> **20** but that we write to them that they abstain from things contaminated by idols and from fornication and from what is strangled and from blood.
>
> **21** "For Moses from ancient generations has in every city those who preach him, since he is read in the synagogues every Sabbath."

15:12. The company, after lively debate, was quieted by Peter's words, for no one had the temerity to challenge his experience at Caesarea or the conclusion he drew from it. This improved atmosphere was to the advantage of Barnabas and Paul as they took the floor. Luke shows sensitivity to the local situation by listing Barnabas ahead of Paul, in contrast to the order in verse 2 (cf. 4:36-37; 11:22). The historian does not quote from their remarks, since a report of their activities had already been given to the church (v. 4). It was important at this juncture, however, to emphasize how God had endorsed their work among the Gentiles by "signs and wonders," showing that He approved of their ministry as well as of Peter's at Caesarea. Circumcision had not been imposed in either case.

15:13-14. At this juncture James, exercising his authority as chairman of the gathering and head of the Jerusalem church (12:17; 21:18; cf. Gal 2:12), took charge rather than throwing the meeting open for further discussion. He sensed that the time had come for action and prepared for it by giving the gist of Peter's remarks before making his own contribution. It was expedient at this point to capitalize on the testimony of the apostle to the circumcision rather than to refer to Barnabas and Paul. Along the same line is to be understood his use of the name *Simeon,* in preference to *Simon.* "It was fitting that Peter should be addressed by a Palestinian Jew by his Jewish name and even in its most Jewish spelling."[2]

15:15-18. James was content to make his contribution consist largely in buttressing Peter's words by showing that what was happening in the experience of the Church had been anticipated "in the words of the prophets." His quotation is taken from Amos 9:11-12, as representative of other passages. There are textual problems incident to the use of the LXX rather than the Hebrew text of Amos, but these need not concern us here.[3] It is important to bear in mind that the one thing the use of Scripture was designed to support here is the fact that God was at work taking from the Gentiles a people for His name (v. 14). James seems to have been implying that the rebuilding and restoration of the tabernacle of David had occurred in the person and mission of Jesus of Nazareth, who was of the seed of David. The result was the building of His Church, a Church which at the beginning had been composed of the sons of Israel, but which now was opening itself to include also many Gentiles. Wilhelm Michaelis puts it thus:

> For Luke the rise of the Christian community is the restoration of David's *skēnē* which Amos promised and which is now being achieved. If the first part of the prophecy has been fulfilled in Jewish Christians (15:16), these should be convinced that the second part is also being fulfilled (15:17) and that the Gentile mission is thus legitimate.[4]

A different understanding of the passage is maintained by those who take "after these things" (v. 16) to refer to the taking of a people from the Gentiles (v. 14) rather than to the context in the prophecy of Amos, which deals with divine judgments on Israel by which that nation is reduced to a mere remnant. Then the remainder of the quotation is taken to refer to the restoration of Israel in the future Davidic (Messianic) Kingdom, which will also have a place for the Gentiles who will come under the rule of the Messiah. No doubt these things are predicted in Scripture at various points, but the introduction of a whole panorama of prophecy at the Jerusalem Council goes far beyond the demands of the situation. Again it should be noted that the one item James was concerned to validate from

Scripture was the inclusion of the Gentiles in the Christian fellowship (v. 14).

It may appear as a serious limitation of James' contribution that he made no reference to the central feature of the debate, the issue of circumcision. The Judaizers were quite willing to grant that Gentiles should have a place in the church, but they were not willing to receive them apart from circumcision. While James did not tackle the circumcision issue head on, he did stress the Gentiles' acceptability to God, as will be seen by the close of verses 14 and 17. That Gentiles should be called by the name of the Lord (cf. Ja 2:7) meant acceptance based on divine grace. Those whom God has received need nothing additional to fit them for membership in the household of faith.

15:19-20. James followed up his use of Scripture with a "judgment," or conclusion, that had a negative and a positive aspect. He suggested that there should be an end to the troubling of the Gentiles who were turning to God. The word "trouble," whether purposely or not, answers very closely to Peter's thought about putting a yoke on Gentile converts.[5] On the positive side, he proposed that a letter be written to the Gentile churches affected by the current dispute, asking that they abstain from certain things which were offensive to their Jewish brethren. It is clear that the items included here (v. 20) were not conceived of in legalistic fashion as conditions for salvation, since it was already the concensus of the Council that the salvation of Gentiles depended on divine grace alone, apart from human works. The purpose of the so-called decree (cf. 16:4) was to ease tension between Jews and Gentiles in the church. An additional result would be a more favorable attitude on the part of unbelieving Jews toward the Christian movement.

The decree is mentioned three times (15:20, 29; 21:25) with slight variations. "Things contaminated by idols" (15:20) is changed to "things sacrificed to idols" (v. 29) and to the singular form in the final occurrence (21:25). The expression "things contaminated" is rare, this being its only occurrence in the New Testament. However, the verb form is used twice in the LXX, each time of ritual defilement (Dan 1:8; Mal 1:7). But the term "what is sacrificed to idols" appears several times in Paul's counsel to the Corinthians (1 Co 8:1, 4, 7, 10; 10:19), where the context makes it clear that the thing sacrificed was meat. For the Old Testament background, Exodus 34:15 is relevant.

"Fornication" seems oddly inserted amid ceremonial requirements. However, Jakob Jocz may be right in his assertion, "The division between the strictly moral and the 'ceremonial' in our modern sense was entirely unknown to the Jews."[6] Some help is gleaned from the fact that among pagans the practice was rarely frowned upon and could thus be classified with ritual matters. More to the point, perhaps, is the fact that Leviticus 18:6-18 carefully excludes from lawful marriage a relationship with anyone near of kin, and strangers among the children of Israel were apparently included in this prohibition (Lev 18:26). So it may be that unlawful marriage, rather than the usual force of the word *fornication,* is intended here in Acts 15.

"What is strangled" pertains to an animal from which the blood is not drained before being used for food (Lev 17:13). "Blood," in this context, signifies the drinking of blood, a pagan practice that is expressly forbidden to Israel (Lev 17:10, 14).

In addition to the Old Testament background for the decree, there was the consideration of Jewish practice. The rabbis had long insisted that Gentiles who lived among Jews should not sacrifice to strange gods, or violate the laws of consanguinity when marrying, or labor on the Sabbath, or consume blood, or eat leavened bread during the Passover. So the apostolic decree would not come as a surprise to many Gentiles, for they would be familiar with the Mosaic requirements and also with current Jewish regulations regarding Gentiles who were in close contact with Jewish communities. Therefore they could be expected the more cheerfully to accept the restrictions involved here.

Certain witnesses for the Western text, notably Codex Bezae, have a different rendering of verse 20 and the parallel passages, omitting any reference to things strangled. This makes possible a moral rather than a ceremonial frame of reference. On this interpretation, the decree would rule out idolatry, murder, and immorality, But this is not all, for the Western text in 15:20, 29 proceeds to add a warning not to do to others what one would not care to have done to himself (invoking the golden rule in negative form). The reason for the addition is fairly clear. Three sins do not include the whole gamut of the Decalogue, so the golden rule is inserted to cover those which are not here specified. The origin of these textual phenomena is probably to be assigned to a somewhat later period of the Church, when the legalistic controversy was a thing of the past and a new moralism had crept into Christian circles.

15:21. The interpretation of James' remark is far from easy. One suggestion is that he appealed to gratitude on the part of believing Gentiles. "Since the road to the conversion of the Gentiles was by way of the Jews and their synagogues in the various cities, it was both reasonable and right to show consideration for the Jews by keeping the rules mentioned in vss 19-20—thus making co-existence possible."[7] Perhaps all James wanted to do was to underscore the fact that Gentiles who had been in the habit of attending the synagogue (available almost everywhere) were well acquainted with the Levitical regulations applicable to Gentiles (as noted above), so the request of the Council should not be regarded as arbitrary or harsh. It is just possible that he simply wanted to point out that Jews were so prevalent in the world and so attentive to what the Law requires that Gentile converts to the new faith would do well to avoid antagonizing them and making more difficult their evangelization.

Verses 22-29. Two tasks remained. One was to formulate a letter to the Gentile churches setting forth the results of the conference. Evidently James was responsible for its composition.* The other was to select two brethren to carry the communication and explain it to the various congregations in Syria and Cilicia.

> **15:22** Then it seemed good to the apostles and the elders, with the whole church, to choose men from among them to send to Antioch with Paul and Barnabas—Judas called Barsabbas, and Silas, leading men among the brethren,
>
> **23** and they sent this letter by them,
> "The apostles and the brethren who are elders, to the brethren in Antioch and Syria and Cilicia who are from the Gentiles, greetings.
>
> **24** "Since we have heard that some of our number to whom we gave no instruction have disturbed you with *their* words, unsettling your souls,
>
> **25** it seemed good to us, having become of one mind, to select men to send to you with our beloved Barnabas and Paul,
>
> **26** men who have risked their lives for the name of our Lord Jesus Christ.
>
> **27** "Therefore we have sent Judas and Silas, who themselves will also report the same things by word *of mouth.*
>
> **28** "For it seemed good to the Holy Spirit and to us to lay upon you no greater burden than these essentials:
>
> **29** that you abstain from things sacrificed to idols and from blood and from things strangled and from fornication; if you keep yourselves free from such things, you will do well. Farewell."

15:22. Luke does not record a vote on James's proposals, but agreement is clearly implied from the wording of the letter that follows (see vv. 28-29). The agreement involved "the apostles and the elders, with the whole church." From 16:4 it is apparent that the first two groups expressed their assent, followed by the congregation. If there were dissidents (15:5), they now held their peace. The decision not to require circumcision had gone against them. It was a courageous decision, for it was bound to bring the disfavor of unbelieving Jews upon the Jewish-Christian church, especially the mother church at Jerusalem. The task of that church in bearing a faithful witness to the nation would now be more difficult

*J. B. Mayor, in *The Epistle of St. James* (New York: MacMillan, 1913), pp. iii-iv, lists half a page of verbal coincidences between this letter and the epistle of James.

than ever, but it was willing to shoulder the burden for the sake of making the evangelization of the Gentiles easier. This should not be forgotten when it is pointed out that the Jerusalem church did little actively to expedite the spread of the Gospel among the Gentiles. The verdict of the Council was a tremendous contribution in itself.

Two brethren were chosen from the congregation to go to Antioch with Paul and Barnabas to provide personal assurance of the good will and spiritual unity of the saints at Jerusalem in relation to believers in Antioch, where men from Jerusalem had precipitated the controversy. Why should two be sent? Possibly they were to represent the two groups in the church, the Hebrews and the Hellenists (cf. 6:1). Judas called Barsabbas may have been a brother of the Joseph called Barsabbas (1:23). From all that is known of Silas, whether from Acts or from the writings of Paul and Peter (in 1 Pe 5:12 his name appears as Silvanus), he could very easily have been a Hellenist, able to move freely in the Greek milieu and to minister the Word of God there. These two had already achieved prominence in the Jerusalem church as "leading men among the brethren."

15:23-29. The letter was framed on behalf of the church, particularly its leaders, the apostles and the elders. A certain awkwardness surrounds the use of the word "brethren." Our translation limits it to the elders. Other possible renderings are "the apostles and elder brethren" or "the brethren, both the apostles and the elders."

The letter was directed primarily to the Gentile church at Antioch, where the agitation had begun (15:1), and secondarily to Gentile congregations in the surrounding areas (cf. 15:41; 16:4). The communication carefully dissociated the Jerusalem church from those of their number who had made the demand contained in 15:1, since there was no authorization (v. 24). The letter went so far as to indicate that in the course of the deliberations the participants had "become of one mind." So it was a united church which sent the letter and deputed the two representatives.

The letter likewise provided opportunity to commend the dedicated labor of "our beloved Barnabas and Paul." Their companions are named, and indication is given that these representatives of the Jerusalem church had something to say to the Antioch brethren, but nothing precise is said about what they were to share. We are free to suppose that the most important matter would have been Gentile freedom from the necessity of circumcision, but to state this openly in the letter would have diminished the impact of the announcement these brethren were to make to the gathered church.

Most important was the assertion that all the decisions of the Council, including the decree, had had their origin in the Holy Spirit.† The church

†W. Telfer (*The Office of a Bishop*, p. 12) affirms a connection between two things

238

had simply followed His leading (cf. 10:19-20; 13:2-3). A church with such an awareness had no reason to doubt the correctness of its decisions. An individual could experience a similar confidence (1 Co 7:40).

Noteworthy is the fact that there is no mention in the decree (v. 29) of the observance of the Sabbath. The church at Jerusalem must have found it expedient to observe the day in order not to offend the Jewish community, but it seems not to have been a great problem in the Dispersion. Where pressure was applied, Gentile Christians could stand on their freedom in Christ (Col 2:16).

To sum up the letter, it had nothing explicit to say about the Council's decision on circumcision (that being left to the spoken word of the two delegates), but it stressed the responsibility of Gentile believers to observe the requirements of the decree, which were "essentials" not for salvation but for the peace and progress of the Church. Incidentally, this is a feature of many of the letters of the New Testament—touching lightly or simply assuming the privileges of the saints, and stressing their responsibilities.

It would be difficult to overemphasize the importance of what was accomplished at Jerusalem:

1. The Gospel of divine grace was reaffirmed.
2. The unity of the Church was safeguarded.
3. The evangelization of the Gentiles could proceed without hindrance. Most of Paul's churches were founded after the Council, and they were Gentile churches.
4. The Gentile churches which had already been established were given encouragement (cf. 16:4-5).
5. The future of the Church as a whole was guaranteed. In a few years its Jewish-Christian wing was destined to fade into virtual oblivion because of persecution and the Jewish War against Rome (A.D. 66-70) or to shrivel because of heretical tendencies (Ebionitism). But before all this happened, Christianity among the Gentiles had grown strong.

One cannot fail to see the providence of God at work in the Jerusalem Council.

Verses 30-35. Attention is now directed to the reaction of the Antioch church to the decree and to the ministry of the representatives of the Jerusalem church.

here: crediting to the Holy Spirit the decision regarding Gentile freedom and the formulation of the decree, and choosing prophets (men inspired by the Spirit) to communicate the decision to the Gentile churches. He suggests that prophets were active in framing the decree. See also E. G. Selwyn, *The First Epistle of St. Peter* (New York: Macmillan, 1964), pp. 369-75.

15:30 So, when they were sent away, they went down to Antioch; and having gathered the congregation together, they delivered the letter.

31 And when they had read it, they rejoiced because of its encouragement.

32 And Judas and Silas, also being prophets themselves, encouraged and strengthened the brethren with a lengthy message.

33 And after they had spent time *there*, they were sent away from the brethren in peace to those who had sent them out.

34‡

35 But Paul and Barnabas stayed at Antioch, teaching and preaching with many others also the word of the Lord.

15:30-35. In this glimpse of the Antioch church following the Council meeting, quite naturally Judas and Silas are given special prominence as they are pictured fulfilling their appointed mission in communicating the contents of the letter to the congregation. However, they could not stop there, but went on to minister with a lengthy exhortation (v. 32). In noting that the two men were "prophets," Luke is hardly intending to suggest that their messages were predictive. Elsewhere the ministry of prophets is described in terms of exhortation or encouragement (1 Co 14:3; cf. Ac 4:36; 13:1). The spoken word brought much joy to the saints. But the blessing was not one-sided, for the pleasure of fellowship with this body of Christians was enough to make Silas ready to return to Antioch when the opportunity came (v. 40).

After the departure of Judas and Silas, the Antioch church continued to thrive under the ministry of Paul and Barnabas, aided by "many others," which is a reminder of the great wealth of gifted leadership enjoyed by this congregation (cf. 13:1).

‡A slight difficulty arises here regarding verse 34 "But it seemed good to Silas to remain there," NASB marg.), which is absent entirely from the leading manuscripts. It is undoubtedly a scribal addition designed to explain how Silas was available for service with Paul a short time later. But Luke's statement must stand that both Judas and Silas returned to Jerusalem. So we are to conclude that after the disagreement between Paul and Barnabas, Silas was summoned by Paul to return to Antioch and be ready for missionary service.

C. Mission of Paul and Silas in Macedonia and Achaia—15:36—18.17

ALTHOUGH THE MISSION began largely as a visitation of churches already founded and then moved uncertainly for a time in Asia Minor, when guidance for the next development was lacking, its decisive advance came with the crossing over into Macedonia. There Paul had new companions and faced many new situations. Several churches were established, and during this time the apostle wrote his first letters to congregations he had planted.

1. DEPARTURE—15:36-41

The unity of the Antioch church, so recently crowned with joy over the victory at Jerusalem, was disturbed by a disagreement between its two outstanding leaders, Barnabas and Paul.

> 15:36 And after some days Paul said to Barnabas, "Let us return and visit the brethren in every city in which we proclaimed the word of the Lord, *and see* how they are."
> 37 And Barnabas was desirous of taking John, called Mark, along with them also.
> 38 But Paul kept insisting that they should not take him along who had deserted them in Pamphylia and had not gone with them to the work.
> 39 And there arose such a sharp disagreement that they separated from one another, and Barnabas took Mark with him and sailed away to Cyprus.
> 40 But Paul chose Silas and departed, being committed by the brethren to the grace of the Lord.
> 41 And he was traveling through Syria and Cilicia, strengthening the churches.

15:36. "Some days" is too indefinite an interval to enable us to calculate the time involved. It was probably a relatively short time, for Paul was restless to experience more triumphs for the Gospel, especially among the Gentiles. His proposal to Barnabas was to revisit the cities they had touched on their first journey, in order to consolidate and expand the work. But due to the rupture that developed between them, neither one followed precisely this pattern.

15:37-38. The altercation centered around John Mark, their helper on

241

the first expedition (13:5). It is not likely that Barnabas, in his desire to include Mark, was motivated simply by the fact that the young man was his relative (Col 4:10). In all probability Mark had had second thoughts about his abrupt abandonment of the party (13:13) and wished to redeem himself. It is possible that the decision of the Jerusalem Council respecting Gentiles gave him a different perspective than he had had before. Understandably, Barnabas was eager to aid in his reinstatement. But Paul was adamantly against it.

We have only the surface facts here; much more may lie in the background. For example, Paul could have been aware that Mark had not only "deserted" his companions and returned to Jerusalem but had also alarmed the church there by reporting that Paul and Barnabas were prepared to receive Gentiles wholly apart from synagogue influence (note that the conversion of Sergius Paulus immediately preceded Mark's decision, 13:12). If this actually occurred, it could have stirred up exactly the kind of protest that was reported by men from Jerusalem in 15:1. At any rate, Paul felt that the stakes were too high to risk giving Mark a second chance.

One may raise the question here whether Galatians 2:13 throws any light on Paul's attitude. If we are right in identifying Paul's visit to Jerusalem in Acts 15 with his own record in Galatians 2:1-10, then it follows naturally that the incident reported in Galatians 2:11-21 must have fallen in this very period after the return of Paul and Barnabas to Antioch. Peter's temporary concession to Jewish sentiment, at the expense of his fellowship with Gentile believers, drew others, including Barnabas, to join him. Thus Paul was left alone to point out the wrong that had been done. It is unlikely, however, that Paul would have allowed this circumstance to prejudice him against Barnabas. The very fact that he had invited his colaborer to go with him on the contemplated mission (v. 36) implies a good relationship at that time.

15:39. The "disagreement" between the two men grew so sharp that they separated, bring their history of partnership in the Lord's work to a close. Our word *paroxysm* is a transliteration of the Greek word used here, which gives some idea of the violence of the disagreement (cf. Deu 29:27; Jer 39:37 LXX).

Paul owed much to Barnabas, who had given him an entrée to the apostles and the Jerusalem church early in his ministry (9:27) and had invited him to share in the ministry at Antioch (11:25-26), which opened the door for all that followed. Was Paul ungrateful? Hardly that; rather, he put principle above the closest friendship and the will of God above personal relationships, however precious (cf. Mt 12:46-50). The decision to part probably clouded Paul's standing with some in the Jerusalem church, where Barnabas was highly esteemed, and may have made his situation there on his last trip (chap. 21) much more precarious than it would have been with Barnabas at his side.

It is to Barnabas's credit that he refused to make an issue of the disagreement before the Antioch church or to seek its support on his behalf. He had led the church in its early days (11:22-24) and had brought Paul into the work. He had been the leader of the first missionary venture of the church (13:2) and had ably represented the church, along with Paul, at the Jerusalem Council. But he refused to use his prominence or his past services as leverage to enlist the congregation on his behalf or to seek from it a reprimand of Paul. This noble man accepted the situation with quiet dignity and went his way in the Lord's service. His choice of Cyprus was natural (cf. 4:36; 13:4) and quite in accord with Paul's suggestion regarding an itinerary (15:36).

The mere fact that Luke reported the contention is a sufficient refutation of the charge that he was intent in his work to present an idealized picture of the early Church. Since his purpose in the second half of Acts was to present the growth of the Church as it pertained to the work of Paul, it is not strange that at this point Barnabas's name drops out of the account. However, Luke's silence does not entitle us to think that God ceased to work through Barnabas—during this campaign Mark was being groomed for greater usefulness (2 Ti 4:11).

15:40. "But Paul chose Silas and departed." The situation was rather different from the circumstances surrounding the beginning of the first journey, when the initiative of the Holy Spirit and the prayerful, concerted action of the Church were given prominence. Yet Haenchen seems to go too far when he asserts, "Paul now set out on his missionary task independent of that congregation."[1] Surely when Luke adds that Paul was "committed by the brethren to the grace of God" he is indicating more than a detached and formal interest in the new undertaking. Paul made contact with the church as he passed through to begin his third journey (18:22), although no record is given of what transpired.

In the divine overruling, the apparent evil of the separation of these leaders yielded this measure of good, that now there were two missionary teams at work instead of one. Silas was well fitted, apparently, to be Paul's companion. As a prophet (v. 32) he could bring instruction and encouragement to God's people as well as set forth the Gospel to the unsaved. The fact that later on he was useful to Peter in the drafting of his first letter (1 Pe 5:12) demonstrates his proficiency in the Greek tongue. Like Paul, he had Roman citizenship (16:37), and he had had experience in the mother church at Jerusalem. His recent visit to Antioch naturally elicited the esteem and prayerful interest of that church on his behalf.

15:41. Yet another advantage in having Silas as a colleague appears here. The Jerusalem Council had addressed its letter not only to Antioch but to the churches of Syria and Cilicia, with Silas as one of the men deputed to communicate the message personally. This charge he was now able to fulfill. His presence with the apostle was a visible token of the victory which Paul's position had secured at the conference.

The existence of these churches is probably to be accounted for by the labors of Paul before he was called to Antioch the first time by Barnabas (cf. Gal 1:21). That some of them came into being as a result of the work of the Antioch church is a possibility, but Luke does not report such activity (in contrast to 19:10). It must have been a time of joyous reunion for Paul as he met with converts of his earlier labors and observed their progress in the Lord.

Even as Barnabas had taken a route that led to his native territory, Paul's would take him to his home city of Tarsus. But Luke, with his economy of language, does not go into details. He does not even say how Paul managed his "traveling," but it is almost certain that he went afoot, the most healthy, safe, and sure means of travel.

2. EARLY STAGES—16:1-10

Two phases of the campaign are clearly distinguishable. In the first (16:1-5), the missionaries are pictured visiting the churches of southern Galatia, to which they communicated the results of the Jerusalem conference and ministered the Word. In the second (16:6-10) we can trace the probing of new territory in the hope of finding a responsive area for testimony to the truth. The trek ended at Troas, a seaport far to the northwest, which became the point of departure for the mission in Europe.

Verses 1-5. Three things were accomplished by revisiting the churches in southern Galatia: the congregations were informed of the decision of the Jerusalem Council, believers were encouraged, and Timothy was added to the missionary team.

> **16:1** And he came also to Derbe and to Lystra. And behold, a certain disciple was there, named Timothy, the son of a Jewish woman who was a believer, but his father was a Greek,
>
> **2** and he was well spoken of by the brethren who were in Lystra and Iconium.
>
> **3** Paul wanted this man to go with him; and he took him and circumcised him because of the Jews who were in those parts, for they all knew that his father was a Greek.
>
> **4** Now while they were passing through the cities, they were delivering the decrees, which had been decided upon by the apostles and elders who were in Jerusalem, for them to observe.

5 So the churches were being strengthened in the faith, and were increasing in number daily.

16:1-3. The visit to Lystra was particularly notable, for it meant augmenting the missionary party by the addition of Timothy. As God had supplied Silas to replace Barnabas, He now supplied Timothy to replace Mark. Since this is the one incident that Luke selected for mention out of this visit to the Galatian churches, he must have seen in it great significance for the Christian cause. Indeed, this young man became one of Paul's leading helpers, so in reporting Paul's labors Luke could ill afford to neglect this background material.

Timothy is called a "disciple," indicating that he was probably converted on the first journey. Paul claimed him as his child in the faith (1 Co 4:17; 1 Ti 1:2). Paul's preaching and his miraculous deliverance from death must have made a deep impression on the lad (2 Ti 3:10-11). He had been taught the Scriptures from childhood (2 Ti 3:15) by his mother and grandmother, which was providential preparation for his conversion under Paul. "The fine fruit that has for so long been slowly ripening falls at a touch into the husbandman's basket."[2]

These women were the more driven to prayer and instruction because Timothy's father was a pagan. Whatever his intentions and promises may have been, he never identified himself with the Jewish faith. Whether the mother came to Christ at the same time Timothy did or whether she was won later, perhaps by the testimony of her son, we are not informed.

The people in the church at Lystra were able to commend Timothy for his Christian life and testimony, and the same was true of brethren as far away as Iconium. Paul was encouraged, therefore, to select him for ministry. Elders from the district met in a solemn service to consecrate young Timothy, at which time he received a spiritual gift (1 Ti 4:14), apparently that of evangelism (2 Ti 4:5). The laying on of Paul's hands probably occurred at this time (2 Ti 1:6).

A problem had to be faced, for Timothy was half Jewish, a fact that was well known to the Jews in that whole region. If he were to go forth with Paul and Silas, his uncircumcised state (a testimony to his father's resistance to Judaism) would be an offense to the Jews, and this could hinder the work of the entire team. The very fact that Paul circumcised him indicates clearly that he had no thought of giving up his ministry to his own countrymen, even though he was an apostle to the Gentiles.

Haenchen claims that in this matter of circumcising Timothy, Luke was "the victim of an unreliable tradition."[3] This verdict is based on the judgment that circumcision was so theologically conditioned, carrying with it the whole philosophy of salvation by works, that Paul could not have acted in this way, for it contradicted his teaching in Galatians.

Several things should be kept in mind here. First, Paul makes clear in Galatians that *in itself* circumcision is nothing, and the same is true of uncircumcision (Gal 5:6; 6:15; cf. 1 Co 7:19). Second, in keeping with these pronouncements, Paul could consider Timothy's circumcision as a matter of expediency, in line with his avowed principle that in spite of being a Christian he was prepared to make himself a Jew to Jews that he might the more easily win them for Christ (1 Co 9:20). Third, before long Luke had joined the missionary group, of which Timothy was by then a member (Ac 16:10), and was brought into close contact with the recent recruit. It is incredible that he would be so lacking in courtesy and interest as not to inquire into Timothy's background. The present passage is evidence that he did. He was not dependent on tradition, either reliable or unreliable.

16:4. One purpose of this trip was to acquaint the churches of Galatia with the letter from the Jerusalem Council containing "the decrees" (plural because of the several items involved). The Council had had a more limited geographical area in view, (15:23), but the letter could be of value in Galatia also. The controversy thrashed out at Jerusalem could easily arise in these more remote churches, as we know was true from the Galatian letter. Luke says nothing at all to indicate that the Judaizing activity had already invaded these congregations, which fits with the conclusion that the letter to the Galatian churches was penned at a somewhat later time.

A question arises as to which "cities" are in view here. Three have been mentioned; Pisidian Antioch has not. Judging from the information provided in verses 6-7, it was on the line of travel and probably was visited. The account is exceedingly brief here.

16:5. This is a summary such as Luke often used to close one phase of his narrative before proceeding to another. An earlier example is 9:31, but whereas there the location of a group of churches is indicated, here such information is not given. Perhaps the intention is to designate only the churches of Galatia, but since this verse rounds off the whole section dealing with the legalistic controversy and its settlement, it is more probable that the churches of Syria and Cilicia are included also. With the solution adopted by the Council, those churches, which were mainly Gentile in character, gained new confidence and new boldness in evangelism. The result was "daily" increase (cf. 2:47).

Verses 6-10. This passage is devoted entirely to travel, with no mention of ministry, for the next sphere of labor had not yet been revealed.

16:6 And they passed through the Phrygian and Galatian region, having been forbidden by the Holy Spirit to speak the word in Asia;

7 and when they had come to Mysia, they were trying to go into Bithynia, and the Spirit of Jesus did not permit them;

8 and passing by Mysia, they came down to Troas.

9 And a vision appeared to Paul in the night: a certain man of Macedonia was standing and appealing to him, and saying, "Come over to Macedonia and help us."

10 And when he had seen the vision, immediately we sought to go into Macedonia, concluding that God had called us to preach the gospel to them.

16:6-8. It seems that sometime before the missionaries arrived at Pisidian Antioch, which was on the border between Galatia (that part which was designated as Phrygia) and Asia, they received an intimation from the Spirit that they were not to evangelize Asia. ("Asia" denotes not the continent but the Roman province of that name, which occupied the western part of what we know as Asia Minor.) How this knowledge was communicated we are not told. A communication through Silas is a possibility (cf. 15:32).

Since the prohibition was confined to ministry and did not rule out travel, the party moved in a northerly direction through the eastern part of the province of Asia. Some scholars are of the opinion that their route took them back into the northern part of Galatia and that there the churches were founded which Paul addressed in his letter to the Galatians. But if that was the case, we would expect Luke to have given some account of the ministry, such as that he provided concerning the southern Galatian churches (chaps. 13-14). The narrative simply traces the route traveled until guidance was given which would permit ministry.

The northward course fits the observation that the missionaries "were trying to go into Bithynia," the province to the northeast of Asia, bordering on the Black Sea. It appears likely that when they reached Dorylaeum, which was in Asia but fairly close to the border of Bithynia, they turned west because of a warning from the Spirit of Jesus.

It must have been frustrating to have such negative guidance. But the experience was profitable inasmuch as it reminded them that the Spirit was in charge of operations. If He said no, this simply meant that when He said yes the plan would prove wiser than any which the missionaries were projecting. Their hope of reaching the cities of Asia (including Ephesus) had been dashed, followed by a similar rebuff in their effort to push into the important centers of population in western Bithynia, where both Jews and Gentiles could be reached. But this did not mean that these areas were to be deprived of Gospel testimony. Asia had its turn (chap. 19), and so did Bithynia (1 Pe 1:1).

Meanwhile the district of Mysia also had to be left untouched, since it was part of the province of Asia. But it was here, at the coastal town of Troas, a few miles south of the ancient Troy, that positive guidance finally came. Troas was an important place, a Roman colony, whose extensive city walls are still visible in part. Paul made other visits to this center (Ac 20:6; 2 Co 2:12). In addition, it seems that he was there a short time prior to his final imprisonment and death (2 Ti 4:13). The circumstances of the founding of the church there are unknown, but someone other than Paul must have started the work.

16:9-10. Here at Troas the will of God was finally made known through a "vision" which Paul had during the night. What he saw was a man of Macedonia asking for help for his country. It is unnecessary to speculate that Paul recognized him as a Macedonian by his dress or anything about his appearance. Rather, the request for Paul to come to Macedonia indicated sufficiently to what country the man belonged.

Are we to think of the Macedonian as a pagan (cf. 17:27) or as a Christian brother who had already begun a work there and was appealing for others to come to his aid? Against the latter possibility, the following should be noted: (1) he is not called a brother but "a certain man"; (2) the word rendered "help" is used nowhere else in Acts or in the rest of the New Testament to mean collaboration in the Lord's work; (3) it is doubtful, in view of Paul's preference for pioneer ministry (Ro 15:20) that he would be drawn to the idea of assisting in a work already begun, although admittedly he had done this in the case of Syrian Antioch.

Probably before the night was spent, Paul excitedly shared his vision with his companions, who were ready to agree with him that the vision was a call from God to cross over to Macedonia "to preach the gospel." This fits with the conclusion already drawn that the call for help did not come from a Christian.

For the first time, the pronoun *we* slips into the narrative (v. 10). It could easily be assumed that one of Paul's companions, either Silas or Timothy, is the narrator here; but then the question must be faced as to why this construction has not been used up to this point and ceases to be used after the campaign in Philippi is described, and why it resumes when Paul and his helpers return to Philippi for the last time on the journey to Jerusalem (20:5-6). It is fairly evident that the writer joined the party at Troas for the trip to Philippi and remained there to direct the work when Paul and the others went on to Thessalonica. He chose not to disclose how he came to join the others at Troas. Possibly he felt that Paul needed him because of his medical skill (cf. 2 Co 12:1-10), but since he included himself as one who was to preach the Gospel to the Macedonians (Ac 16:10), it is obvious that he was more than an attending physician.

Ordinarily, a move from one continent to another involves a considerable change in culture and civilization, but in the case before us this was not so. Asia and Europe, at this location, were in close proximity and were bound together by influences which went back to the days before Alexander the Great. Rome had continued to honor Alexander's aim of marrying the East to the West through Hellenization.

Alexander had moved from west to east to conquer brilliantly and infuse the Levant with everything Greek. Now a converted Jew was moving in the opposite direction, from Asia to Europe, to conquer for Christ.

3. PHILIPPI—16:11-40

THE STORY of the founding of one of Paul's most trouble-free churches is told mainly in terms of two notable conversions, together with a report of his first encounter as a missionary with Roman governmental authorities (his experience with Sergius Paulus had hardly been an encounter).

Verses 11-15. The sea journey from Troas is described, followed by information about Philippi and the first witness in this area.

> **16:11** Therefore putting out to sea from Troas, we ran a straight course to Samothrace, and on the day following to Neapolis;
> **12** and from there to Philippi, which is a leading city of the district of Macedonia, a *Roman* colony; and we were staying in this city for some days.
> **13** And on the Sabbath day we went outside the gate to a riverside, where we were supposing that there would be a place of prayer; and we sat down and began speaking to the women who had assembled.
> **14** And a certain woman named Lydia, from the city of Thyatira, a seller of purple fabrics, a worshiper of God, was listening; and the Lord opened her heart to respond to the things spoken by Paul.
> **15** And when she and her household had been baptized, she urged us, saying, "If you have judged me to be faithful to the Lord, come into my house and stay." And she prevailed upon us.

16:11-12. It is possible to gather from Luke's journals made on shipboard that he was quite at home on the sea. The first leg of the journey was from Troas to Samothrace, an island south of the coast of Thrace, which was a large territory to the east of Macedonia. The island was slightly more than halfway to Neapolis, the port of debarkation. To save time the passengers probably stayed on board overnight. The next day's run brought them to Neapolis, about 125 miles from Troas. This journey of two days is quite in contrast to a later one, which reversed this route and required five days (20:6). The missionaries must have felt that such a propitious journey was a confirmation of the vision and a token of divine prospering in the work which lay ahead of them.

Almost ten miles beyond Neapolis was the city of Philippi, which derived its name from Philip of Macedon, the father of Alexander. It had the status of a Roman colony, many of its residents being retired army veterans. The famous Egnatian Way ran right through the center of the city, furnishing access to the Adriatic Sea on the west and thence to Rome. It is tempting to suppose that Paul's thought of going to Rome, which became a fixed objective at Ephesus (19:21), had its incubation in the days at Philippi.

In one respect the wording of verse 12 is uncertain. We have a choice between rendering it "a leading city of the district of Macedonia," or "a city of the first district of Macedonia." As to the former, it is awkward to have Macedonia spoken of as a district, for it was a province. The latter fits well with the historic fact that the Romans had divided Macedonia into four districts, and Philippi was in the first district, although not the capital, a distinction which belonged to Amphipolis.

16:13-15. With the coming of the Sabbath, the visitors began to search for a place of worship. No synagogue was available in this Roman colony. Jews seem to have been few, anyway.

Since synagogues were often constructed near water to facilitate the ritual ablutions, the missionaries judged that they might find a place of worship near the Gangites River, somewhat over a mile west of the city. The word *proseuchē* can denote the place of prayer as well as the activity of prayer. Philo used it consistently in preference to the word *synagogue*. Since Luke uses the word synagogue regularly, he may be indicating here that the spot they found was merely an open place or some sort of shelter less elaborate than a synagogue building. When Luke says "We sat down," he may be indicating that some sort of seats were available. The fact that this meeting consisted of women may be adduced as an added reason for concluding that the place fell short of being a regular synagogue—Jewish law required ten men in order to warrant the building of such an edifice.

Paul and his companions did not disdain to speak to the group of women. In this informal atmosphere it was no doubt easier to get directly to the theme of the Gospel than it would have been in a characteristic synagogue service. Luke's report suggests that all four men may have spoken on this occasion, although Paul was evidently the chief speaker (v. 14). As far as the listeners are concerned, he indicates the effect on Lydia only, presumably because she was outstanding by reason of both her position and her eventual leadership in the church formed at Philippi.

Lydia was a native of Thyatira, a prosperous city of Lydia, the section of Asia Minor to the south of Mysia. Several hundred years before, in the days of Croesus, the region had gained prominence and considerable power, only to be conquered by Cyrus and the Persians. Thyatira was famous for its industry and its trade guilds. One source of income was the making of purple dye from the secretions of the mollusk or from the root of the madder plant. The woman Lydia owned a business in Philippi as "a seller of purple fabrics," which were highly prized in those days.

251

Since there was no synagogue at Philippi, her status as "a worshiper of God" is best explained as a carry-over from her days in Thyatira, a center which must have had a considerable settlement of Jews on account of its commercial importance. But Lydia had not become a proselyte to the Jewish faith, so she was the more open to the Gospel which the Old Testament anticipated. In addition, "the Lord opened her heart" (cf. Lk 24:45) so that she responded favorably to what she heard.

Luke does not say when Lydia and her household were baptized. It may have occurred somewhat later, when she was able to persuade the rest to share her faith (contrast vv. 31-32). The term "household" could indicate other members of the family (if there were any), business helpers, and servants. When Paul referred to those of Caesar's household (Phil 4:22) he was evidently designating believers drawn from the ranks of several thousand employees and slaves of the emperor rather than the emperor himself or his immediate family.

Conversions of groups were quite common in the early days of the Church, and the church in the house had a cohesive strength because it was not merely an aggregation of individuals who happened to gather periodically in a certain house; rather, it involved many who had already been associated but now found that association deepened by the transforming power of the Gospel.

The immediate result of Lydia's conversion was the lodging of the missionary party at her house in response to her insistent invitation. She had the means and the space to match her hospitable spirit. Due to her generosity, Paul found it unnecessary to pursue his trade while in Philippi. Lydia's example seems to have made the church there especially solicitous for Paul's needs, as he himself testified (Phil 4:16). He consented to set aside his rule of not taking anything from his converts, feeling that he would not be misunderstood by this congregation if he did (contrast 2 Co 11:7-9; 1 Th 2:9).

Verses 16-18. These verses provide the background for an incident that was to affect greatly the remainder of Paul's stay in the city and was to terminate his ministry so far as this visit was concerned.

> **16:16** And it happened that as we were going to the place of prayer, a certain slave-girl having a spirit of divination met us, who was bringing her masters much profit by fortune telling.
>
> **17** Following after Paul and us, she kept crying out, saying, "These men are bond-servants of the Most High God, who are proclaiming to you the way of salvation."
>
> **18** And she continued doing this for many days. But Paul was greatly annoyed, and turned and said to the spirit, "I command you in the name of Jesus Christ to come out of her!" And it came out at that very moment.

16:16. On the way to the place of prayer, the missionaries were intercepted by a demon-possessed slave girl, whose condition gave her ability at fortune-telling. "A spirit of divination" (*pythōna*) is possibly intended to relate the girl to Pythian Apollo, the Greek god so called because of the tale of his having killed a serpent (*pythōn*). The priestess of the Delphic oracle, connected with the temple of Apollo, northwest of Corinth, was often resorted to in antiquity by those who sought guidance. The term "fortunetelling" is found only here in the New Testament. Its use in the LXX, where it occurs several times, is significant in that the practice is always disapproved (see Deu 18:10 and context). In form, the term is related to the word *mantic*, and suggests a certain abnormality in the state during which the divination takes place.

This girl was a source of "profit" to those who owned her. Bengel pithily remarks, "Fraud nourishes such gain: true religion does away with it."

When did the initial confrontation occur? Some think it happened on the very Sabbath that the visitors had gone out looking for the *proseuchē*. But Luke seems to introduce it as something that developed afterward. It is hardly convincing to say that after Lydia's conversion Paul and his companions would no longer have frequented the spot outside the city, since there is no proof that others were saved on that day. The missionaries probably returned to continue their discussion with the women who habitually gathered there, in the hope of winning them to Christ.

16:17. In spite of having had no apparent contact with the missionaries, the girl was able to announce loudly and publicly that these men were in the service of "the Most High God" (cf. Mk 5:7). This title for the Deity has been found not only in Jewish and Christian literature but also in pagan.

Her second declaration concerned the message. She confessed that the missionaries were proclaiming "the way of salvation." In the ancient world at this period there was a considerable longing for salvation, although it was frequently a salvation from the vexations and burdens of life rather than from sin. In the gospels, demons were aware of the identity of Jesus but they did not speak of His saving mission.

16:18. This went on for "many days," and at length Paul had had enough. Turning around, he addressed the spirit (not the girl), commanding it in the name of Jesus Christ to come out of her. That he had not done this earlier may have been due to the fact that he recognized the peril into which an exorcism of this kind might bring him and his friends. Yet to fail to exorcise the spirit was to encourage the notion that Paul was himself affiliated with the spirit, who seemed to know him and his mission so well. Somewhat similarly, on many occasions Jesus had rebuked and exorcised the spirits that confessed Him as the Holy One of God (e.g.,

Mk 1:24-25). Testimony from such a source was not a desirable endorsement.

Verses 19-23. Beating and imprisonment came to Paul and Silas as the sequel to the exorcism. Luke did not include himself in this section (in contrast to v. 17). He would not give the impression that he and Timothy were involved.

> **16:19** But when her masters saw that their hope of profit was gone, they seized Paul and Silas and dragged them into the market place before the authorities,
>
> **20** and when they had brought them to the chief magistrates, they said, "These men are throwing our city into confusion, being Jews,
>
> **21** and are proclaiming customs which it is not lawful for us to accept or to observe, being Romans."
>
> **22** And the crowd rose up together against them, and the chief magistrates tore their robes off them, and proceeded to order them to be beaten with rods.
>
> **23** And when they had inflicted many blows upon them, they threw them into prison, commanding the jailer to guard them securely;

16:19-21. Already irritated that the girl had deviated from her normal routine by calling attention to the missionaries and their message, the owners were furious when they saw that with the exorcism their "hope of profit" had vanished. The girl was now useless to them, so they turned away from her to lay hands on Paul and Silas and drag them to the local officials. In all likelihood the terms "the authorities" and "chief magistrates" refer to the same individuals. The former is a general term for rulers or leaders, whereas the latter is *stratēgoi*, of which Sherwin-White notes, "The author is simply using the commonest Hellenistic title to render the untranslatable term *duoviri*."[1]

The complainers said nothing about the exorcism, but instead charged that the visitors were disturbing the peace, adding that the instigators were Jews trying to introduce their "customs" among those who were Romans. A deliberate appeal to local prejudice is apparent in the tension between the terms "Jews" and "Romans." Cases are on record of action by Roman authorities against foreign religions which were judged a danger to public welfare and morals, but such religions were not opposed on the ground of their being foreign. Noting the peculiarity of the accusation at Philippi, with its total lack of emphasis on "the depravity of the practices introduced by Paul" and instead its underscoring of their non-Roman character, Sherwin-White suggests that the recent expulsion of Jews from Rome by the Emperor Claudius may have been relied on here to arouse feeling against these outsiders.[2]

16:22-23. The propaganda was successful in assembling a "crowd" that was visibly incensed at the alleged introduction of foreign customs, whatever that might mean. All they knew was that their detached, Roman manner of life was being threatened, and that was enough to arouse their anger.

The spirit of the mob communicated itself to the authorities, who acted on these vague charges without examining the matter for themselves. That the mood of the crowd had swayed them is evident in the strong word Luke uses to describe their rough and unseemly tactics as they grabbed at the garments of the prisoners and literally tore them off their backs the more quickly to expose the flesh to the "rods" which were used for the flogging, a peculiarly Roman ordeal. This was one of the three occasions when Paul suffered this sort of chastisement (2 Co 11:25).

It is a strange misunderstanding of the situation that has led some to suppose that the magistrates tore their own garments to express their horror and indignation. The custom of the Jewish high priest (Mk 14:63) should not be imputed to a Gentile ruler.

Verses 24-34. The passage presents a great contrast between the ignominious imprisonment engineered by men and the mighty deliverance of God's servants which led to some dramatic conversions.

> **16:24** and he, having received such a command, threw them into the inner prison, and fastened their feet in the stocks.
>
> **25** But about midnight Paul and Silas were praying and singing hymns of praise to God, and the prisoners were listening to them;
>
> **26** and suddenly there came a great earthquake, so that the foundations of the prison house were shaken; and immediately all the doors were opened, and everyone's chains were unfastened.
>
> **27** And when the jailer had been roused out of sleep and had seen the prison doors opened, he drew his sword and was about to kill himself, supposing that the prisoners had escaped.
>
> **28** But Paul cried out with a loud voice, saying, "Do yourself no harm, for we are all here!"
>
> **29** And he called for lights and rushed in and, trembling with fear, he fell down before Paul and Silas,
>
> **30** and after he brought them out, he said, "Sirs, what must I do to be saved?"
>
> **31** And they said, "Believe in the Lord Jesus, and you shall be saved, you and your household."
>
> **32** And they spoke the word of the Lord to him together with all who were in his house.
>
> **33** And he took them that *very* hour of the night and washed their wounds, and immediately he was baptized, he and all his *household*.
>
> **34** And he brought them into his house and set food before them, and rejoiced greatly, having believed in God with his whole household.

255

16:24. Severely beaten, the two men were pushed into prison, where the jailer fastened their feet in the stocks. The intention was doubtless to pursue the case further before a higher Roman official, but in the providence of God, that did not happen. Months later, Paul reflected on the treatment he had received (1 Th 2:2).

16:25. Instead of concentrating on their sufferings or suggesting that the two men spent their time commiserating one another, the account emphasizes their good spirits, reflected in their singing. This means that Paul's emphasis on joy, in his letter to the Philippians, was not something theoretical. It had been demonstrated in their community years before, under trying conditions. To be sure, the prisoners were praying also, possibly alternating prayer with their praise. There is no indication that they waited till "midnight" to begin. Doubtless they had been so engaged for hours. These brethren could say with the psalmist, "His song will be with me in the night, a prayer to the God of my life" (Ps 42:8). "His presence turns a prison into a palace, into a paradise" (John Trapp).

Others besides God heard them. The other prisoners were listening and wondering, for they had seen the two, battered and bleeding, as they were hustled into the inner prison and fastened there with no one to minister to them.

16:26-27. It was about midnight that the answer came, in the form of an "earthquake" (cf. 4:31) intense enough to shake the foundations of the building, open the doors, and loose the prisoners' chains throughout the prison. Adjacent were the quarters of the jailer, who was jarred out of bed and roused to instant anxiety about the prisoners, fearing all had "escaped."

The opened doors* confirmed his fears. His charges must have fled. He was responsible, and since he must die for failure to keep them, it was better to die by his own hand than by order of his superiors.

16:28-29. Only the voice of Paul deterred him from self-destruction. "We are all here" (not *both*, but "all"). The chains were loosed, but the prisoners had stayed. Was it due to fear of being recaptured and punished for attempted escape, or was it due to the magnetic leadership of Paul and Silas, who had no intention of fleeing? Paul's language suggests that the whole lot had gathered together. No longer was the inner prison allowed to separate the special prisoners from the rest.

As soon as he could get lights on the scene, the jailer rushed in, all atremble with "fear." The damsel had been right. These two must be representatives of God Most High, who had now intervened on their be-

---

*The thought is not that he had seen the doors opened (in the very process) but that he saw them standing open.

half. What was it she had said about their showing the way of salvation? That was on his mind supremely just now.

16:30-32. As soon as he could secure the other prisoners, he brought out the two servants of God from the prison and demanded of them what he must do to be saved. Presumably he had not heard them preach.

Paul answered in the simplest and yet the most comprehensive of terms. "Believe in the Lord Jesus." That would bring salvation. One almost senses the atmosphere of the gospel of John here. *Believe* is pitted against *do*. Human achievement is worthless, and needless as well. The Lord Jesus has done it all. What remains is to appropriate His saving work by faith. A similar assurance was given regarding the jailer's "household" (cf. v. 15).

Shortly, the three of them were inside the house, facing people who were almost as fearful as the jailer had been. The opportunity was there for testimony, and they embraced it. Other things could wait. When the Spirit of God convicts, everything else pales into insignificance compared with the necessity of becoming right with God. Further teaching was given to enlarge on the summary word given about salvation (v. 31).

16:33-34. Only when their spiritual task had been discharged did the missionaries consent to have their physical needs met. Their wounds, left unattended the day before, now received loving ministration. As soon as this was completed, the whole group entered into a service of baptism, by which the new converts expressed their faith (cf. v. 15). Family solidarity was such that a decision on the part of the head of the household involved the rest. This could have adverse as well as good results (cf. Titus 1:11). Chrysostom notes the element of reciprocity here, remarking about the jailer, "He washed them, and he was washed; he washed them from their stripes, he himself was washed from his sins."[3] Then, at length, the physical hunger of Paul and Silas received attention. We get the picture of the jailer insisting that he serve his benefactors himself, doing it with a grateful and rejoicing heart. He and his entire household had experienced salvation.

"Having believed in God" does not refer to some prior experience that prepared him for faith in Christ, but it emphasizes his previous paganism (cf. 1 Th 1:9). He had not been, like Lydia, a God-fearer.

Verses 35-40. The final phase of the encounter with the authorities in this Roman colony reveals the two parties in roles that differed sharply from those of the previous day. Two factors likely played a part in the changed attitude of the magistrates. For one, reflection on their hasty action, taken without investigation, may have decided them not to pursue the case. Furthermore, they must have felt the earthquake, or at least learned about it, and concluded that there might be more in this situation than they had realized.† It would be safer to let the prisoners go before something worse happened. Romans could be highly superstitious at times.

> **16:35** Now when day came, the chief magistrates sent their policemen, saying, "Release those men."
>
> **36** And the jailer reported these words to Paul, *saying,* "The chief magistrates have sent to release you. Now therefore come out and go in peace."
>
> **37** But Paul said to them, "They have beaten us in public without trial, men who are Romans, and have thrown us into prison; and now are they sending us away secretly? No indeed! But let them come themselves and bring us out."
>
> **38** And the policemen reported these words to the chief magistrates. And they were afraid when they heard that they were Romans,
>
> **39** and they came and appealed to them, and when they had brought them out, they kept begging them to leave the city.
>
> **40** And they went out of the prison and entered *the house of* Lydia, and when they saw the brethren, they encouraged them and departed.

16:35-39. The "policemen" who acted as messengers for the magistrates were the same men who had inflicted the beatings the day before (the name means "those who hold the rods"). Each colony was permitted two of them.

In passing on the word that the prisoners were now free to go, the jailer must have been astonished at Paul's negative reaction. His reasoning behind refusing to leave consisted of four elements: there had been a "public" beating, without a "trial," inflicted on men who were "Romans" (possessing Roman citizenship), followed by imprisonment. A great injustice had been committed. The key item here is the claim of Roman citizenship. It could go hard with officials who had failed to honor this dignity, which accounts for the magistrates' fear when the policemen reported back to them.

The question which naturally arises, however, is why the missionaries had waited until this moment to declare their status. It has been conjectured that amid the uproar at the time of the beating the two men had tried to explain that they were Roman citizens but had not succeeded in communicating the point.

More likely, Paul had anticipated the course of events (recall that he had waited several days before exorcising the demon) and determined to withhold the information until it would count for the most on behalf of

---

†This is broadly hinted at in the reading of the Western text of v. 35, which adds, after "when day came," the following: "the praetors came together into the forum and, calling to mind the earthquake that had taken place, they were affrighted and sent the lictors."

the group of disciples he was leaving behind in Philippi. When the Roman officials realized their mistake, they would be inclined to avoid taking any illegal steps against members of the infant church. If this surmise is correct, it reveals the unselfishness of these leaders and their pastoral concern.

As for the magistrates, these men who had humiliated God's servants a few hours before were now humiliated over their own mistake and are pictured as "begging" Paul and Silas to leave the city. Their continued presence would only be a thorn in the side of those who were guilty of municipal bungling. Once more the men of God responded in the right way, refusing to put on a display of stubbornness that would take the edge off their victory.

16:40. "They went out of the prison," meaning they must have gone back to the place of confinement after the events of the early morning hours. To be found fraternizing with the jailer in his living quarters would be irregular, to say the least.

Prior to the departure from the city, the two men insisted, however, on the privilege of spending a little time with the brethren who gathered at the house of Lydia for fellowship. There is no mention of any ministry to the missionaries after their ordeal, though such may well have been proffered. Rather, they were the ones who used the opportunity to encourage the new converts, preparing them for the days ahead when they must carry on without apostolic leadership.

Luke modestly kept out of the record the fact that he stayed to shepherd this congregation. Doubtless he kept in touch with Paul and his companions, reporting from time to time on the progress of the believers. This church remained close to Paul's heart, and conversely he continued to be deeply appreciated and faithfully supported by this band of Christians (Phil 1:5, 7, 19, 26; 2:17, 25, 28, 30; 4:10-19).

4. THESSALONICA—17:1-9

Thessalonica, the most important center in Macedonia, was a populous commercial city at the head of the Thermaic Gulf and bore the name of the step-sister of Alexander the Great. In contrast to Philippi, which was a Roman colony, Thessalonica was a free city, which meant that it was not subject to the provincial administration in local affairs and could pass its own laws and have its own institutions, such as customs duties. In addition to its rulers, who were called "politarchs," it had its own popular assembly.

Our knowledge of the mission in this place which is provided by Luke can be supplemented by Paul's letters to the Thessalonians, especially 1 Thessalonians 1-2.

17:1　Now when they had traveled through Amphipolis and Apollonia, they came to Thessalonica, where there was a synagogue of the Jews.

2　And according to Paul's custom, he went to them, and for three Sabbaths reasoned with them from the Scriptures,

3　explaining and giving evidence that the Christ had to suffer and rise again from the dead, and *saying*, "This Jesus whom I am proclaiming to you is the Christ."

4　And some of them were persuaded and joined Paul and Silas, along with a great multitude of the God-fearing Greeks and a number of the leading women.

5　But the Jews, becoming jealous and taking along some wicked men from the market place, formed a mob and set the city in an uproar; and coming upon the house of Jason, they were seeking to bring them out to the people.

6　And when they did not find them, they *began* dragging Jason and some brethren before the city authorities, shouting, "These men who have upset the world have come here also;

7　and Jason has welcomed them, and they all act contrary to the decrees of Caesar, saying that there is another king, Jesus."

8　And they stirred up the crowd and the city authorities who heard these things.

9　And when they had received a pledge from Jason and the others, they released them.

17:1. The journey from Philippi to Thessalonica covered 100 miles along the Egnatian Way. If there were overnight stops at Amphipolis and Apollonia, this meant a trek of thirty miles or so per day. Some have suggested that the party may have gone by horseback.

Apparently no ministry was undertaken at these intermediate points. No description is given of the journey (cf. Gen 12:5), only of the situation at Thessalonica. Here, in contrast to Philippi, the "synagogue" provided a base of operations. Doubtless the missionaries were well aware in advance of the great opportunity presented here, not only by the city but by the territory surrounding it (1 Th 1:8).

17:2-3. It was Paul's "custom" to go to the synagogue. Identical language is used of our Lord in Luke 4:16. The ministry lasted for three Sabbaths, which does not exclude the possibility of a further ministry concentrated on reaching Gentiles, particularly since they constituted a majority of the church (1 Th 1:9). The receipt of a gift from the Philippian brethren on more than one occasion at Thessalonica (Phil 4:16) argues for a stay longer than three weeks.

In regard to this gift, a problem arises as to why Paul found it necessary to ply his trade at Thessalonica (1 Th 2:9; 2 Th 3:8). Two factors deserve consideration: the working period may have been confined to the time before the arrival of financial help; and the apostle may have felt the desirability of continuing his labors despite the aid, in order to provide an example of diligence (2 Th 3:9).

Paul "reasoned with them from the Scriptures." While "reasoned" could hint at discussion, this is not as likely here as the other meaning of the word ("to give an address"), which occurs several times in this chapter and the next. In fact, it is doubtful that any of the examples in Acts can mean anything else than delivering an address.[4]

Paul was intent on presenting the Scriptures, and his methodology involved "explaining" and "giving evidence." The former expression is literally "opening," and it is used of Jesus' instruction to the Emmaus pair (Lk 24:32), and therefore need not be thought of as necessitating the literal opening of a book. The other expression means "to bring forward by way of proof." Explanation was buttressed by marshaling the data of Scripture in support of the necessity that the promised Christ "suffer and rise again from the dead" (cf. Mk 8:31). The final stage in the presentation was the assertion that the Christ of prophecy was identical with the Jesus whom Paul was proclaiming. Here we must suppose that if we had a full account rather than a digest, there would be a setting forth of the death of Christ and His resurrection similar to what is reported in the Pisidian Antioch address (Ac 13:27-37).

Since the "I" is emphatic, it is probably intended to denote Paul in contrast to Silas and Timothy, for whereas they could expound the Scriptures respecting Christ, they could not bear witness to His resurrection as Paul could from his conversion experience (9:3-9).

17:4. The message he gave bore fruit. "Some" (Jews) were persuaded. Aristarchus was one of them (20:4; Col 4:10-11). Jason was probably another (vv. 5, 7,). The converts are said to have "joined" Paul and Silas. They attached themselves to the missionaries, casting their lot with them, come what may.

A second group of converts consisted of "God-fearing Greeks," and they were far more numerous than the Jewish brethren. This presents a difficulty, in that in his correspondence with this church Paul said that his readers had turned to God from idols (1 Th 1:9), as though they had been untouched pagans before their conversion. It does not help too much to adopt an alternate translation, "worshiping Greeks," because even that rendering implies a certain devotion to the God of Israel. Perhaps we are left to the conclusion that despite the conversion of many God-fearing Gentiles during the synagogue ministry, the number was small as compared to the vastly greater number who became believers during Paul's ministry apart from the synagogue.

Several of the leading women (cf. v. 12) constituted a third group.

17:5. The greater the response, the greater the opposition from unbelieving Jews. Jealousy is noted as the motive for stirring up trouble (cf. 13:45).

Being a minority in the city, the Jews could not mount a successful persecution without help. But it was easy to induce the rabble in the marketplace (the public square) to join them. It gave them something to do, something a bit novel. The resulting "mob" churned the city into a tumult. It was a demonstration against unwelcome outsiders, gaining momentum as it moved toward the house of Jason, where Paul and Silas were known to be guests (Timothy had not been in the public eye sufficiently to attract attention). "The rabble is apparently summoned to make the attacks upon the Christians appear like a popular movement."[5] It is difficult to be certain whether "the people" were the popular assembly or the unruly crowd itself.

17:6-7. Foiled in their attempt to locate the missionaries, who were not there at the time, the crowd decided to vent its displeasure on Jason and a few brethren who were with him, dragging them before the city authorites, the *politarchs* (cf. 16:19). Luke's accuracy in using this term has been vindicated by the discovery of several inscriptions bearing this technical word, including one on the excavated Vardar gate of the city.

It was scarcely an orderly scene, as charges were "shouted" before these dignitaries. "These men," by the position in the sentence, would seem at first to refer to Jason and the others, but the identity is clarified by what follows—Paul and Silas were meant.

Since the allegations are not likely to have been invented by the mob, we must suppose that the real initiators of the charges were the unbelieving Jews. The charge of upsetting "the world" is a hyperbole, but it reflects the closeness of communication between Jewish communities in the Dispersion. The first missionary journey had left a deep impression on Asia Minor Jews. This first allegation is somewhat vague, and the second is scarcely more precise, since "the decrees of Caesar" are not spelled out. But the third was obviously intended to be climactic, since it posed a rivalry between Jesus and Caesar. "King" is used here in a universal rather than a local sense. The unbelieving Jews would have liked nothing better than to make trouble for the Nazarenes with the Roman authorities. Despite their hatred for Rome in general and of certain worship-hungry emperors in particular, the Jews could point to the fact that sacrifices on behalf of Caesar were regularly offered in the Temple at Jerusalem. The politarchs were bound to be concerned with an accusation such as this, just as Pilate had been concerned when a similar charge was raised against Jesus Himself by the Jews (Lk 23:2).

Since it is clear from the Thessalonian letters that Paul had preached the return of Christ during this visit, the passage before us can be said to reflect that preaching, however slanted was the report of it by his adversaries.

17:8-9. The "crowd" mentioned here is apparently to be distinguished from the crowd that went to the house of Jason. It must refer to those who were in the marketplace in the vicinity of the politarchs when the mob arrived in that area of the city. The mood of alarm was being spread throughout the community.

Since Paul and Silas were not available as suspects, the only ones who could be immediately dealt with were Jason and his friends. From them the authorities exacted a "pledge." This is hardly to be thought of as bail pending a formal trial, for there was no real basis for a trial of the men who were present. More likely the pledge was assurance exacted from Jason and the others that the missionaries would leave town and would not return. That was the easiest way to dispose of the problem.

The limitation thus imposed on the apostle and his companions may be reflected in his complaint that he tried more than once to return to encourage the believers, but found no way to do it. Satan had gained an advantage in this situation (1 Th 2:18). In the same passage Paul makes the charge that the Jews had persecuted him (1 Th 2:15). He seems also to indicate that the church did not cease to be persecuted even after he and his colaborers had left the city (1 Th 2:14). Slanders on his ministry continued to be made by the Jews (1 Th 2:13-16).

5. BEREA—17:10-15

This city lay some fifty miles to the southwest of Thessalonica, on the road that led to Achaia, the province south of Macedonia. The ministry there was promising but brief, terminated by Jews who came from Thessalonica to stir up trouble (cf. 14:19).

> **17:10** And the brethren immediately sent Paul and Silas away by night to Berea; and when they arrived, they went into the synagogue of the Jews.
> **11** Now these were more noble-minded than those in Thessalonica, for they received the word with great eagerness, examining the Scriptures daily, *to see* whether these things were so.
> **12** Many of them therefore believed, along with a number of prominent Greek women and men.
> **13** But when the Jews of Thessalonica found out that the word of God had been proclaimed by Paul in Berea also, they came there likewise, agitating and stirring up the crowds.
> **14** And then immediately the brethren sent Paul out to go as far as the sea; and Silas and Timothy remained there

15 Now those who conducted Paul brought him as far as Athens; and receiving a command for Silas and Timothy to come to him as soon as possible, they departed.

17:10-12. The Thessalonian brethren located Paul and Silas, advised them of the new situation, and kept them under cover till nightfall, when they sent them on their way to Berea. Paul may have been reluctant to go, not happy at being compelled to slip out of town, but he was helpless to do anything about it, since Jason and the others had given their pledge. Timothy may have made his way to Berea independently.

The synagogue presented a fresh opportunity for testimony, especially since the Berean Jews were "more noble-minded" than those who had resisted the truth in Thessalonica. "Noble-minded" indicates a quality somewhat different from *high-minded*, referring to a generous spirit free from prejudice. The nobility consisted in this, that instead of having a suspicious attitude which was ready to reject out of hand what was set before them, they actually "received the word with great eagerness." By "the word" we are not to understand "the Scriptures," but the spoken word of the missionaries (cf. 1 Th 2:13). The point is that these people, for all their eagerness, were not gullible; they insisted on comparing what they heard with what they had—the Scriptures—considering them the final court of appeal.

Some Jews could search the Scriptures and fail to find the way of life (Jn 5:39). Paul knew from personal experience in dealing with his countrymen that their minds were veiled from an understanding of the oracles of God until they turned to the Lord Jesus Christ, who alone gives clarity of meaning to the Old Covenant (2 Co 3:14-16).

Undoubtedly the message given to these Jews in Berea was identical with that which Luke summarized in connection with his report of the mission to Thessalonica (Ac 17:2-3). The word "daily" suggests that contact was maintained with Paul and the others during the week, each message calling for fresh examination of the Scriptures to confirm what had been heard.

"Therefore" (v. 12) establishes a connection between searching the Scriptures with open mind and attaining the result, namely, that "many believed." God honors honest inquiry into His truth.

These were Jews, but there was other fruit during this mission. The synagogue here, as elsewhere, was attended by some Gentiles. Luke notes that not a few of these, both men and women, put their faith in Christ. He mentions the prominent "women" before the "men." In the accounts of all three of the Macedonian centers where the missionaries worked, women converts are given separate mention (16:14; 17:4, 12). This accords with our knowledge of Macedonian women from secular sources.

"The extant Macedonian inscriptions seem to assign to the sex a higher social influence than is common among the civilized nations of antiquity."[6]

17:13-15. Information about the campaign in Berea found its way back to the Jews of Thessalonica, suggesting that in Berea there was some opposition to the missionaries, however subdued it was. This was the signal for a determined effort to repeat in Berea what had been done in Thessalonica. Volunteers were ready to make the trip and do their utmost to stir up trouble, using the same basic method they had employed in their own city, "stirring up the crowds." Note that this was popular rather than official action. The city government of Thessalonica had not dispatched representatives to apprehend Paul. "There is no evidence that the police forces of different cities ever acted in concert."[7]

Anxious to avoid the reputation of being disturbers of the peace, the local brethren acted promptly, sending Paul alone out of town with an escort. This testifies to the position of leadership the apostle enjoyed and also to the animosity he engendered by his forthright presentation of the Gospel to his countrymen (cf. 18:12; 21:28).

Some uncertainty about the movements of Paul results from a comparison of statements in verses 14 and 15. On the one hand he was sent away "to go as far as the sea," yet we read that those who conducted him "brought him as far as Athens," a distance greater than the total he had traveled in all of Macedonia. Rackham gives a plausible account of what happened.

> A large party of Beroean Christians accompanied the apostle as far as the coast: then instead of taking ship, as might have been expected by his adversaries, he turned to the right into Thessaly with a smaller escort, while the rest of the brethren returned to Beroea.[8]

This conjecture is favored by the circumstances that Luke mentioned no port of embarkation, which was his usual custom.

For the third time Paul had been forced out of a Macedonian city. Should he give up and return to Syria? It was unthinkable. His spirit was akin to that of Livingstone, who said, "I am prepared to go anywhere, as long as it is forward." Luke does not tell us whether the apostle had planned a campaign in Achaia, the province south of Macedonia, but that is where he was being led by circumstances.

He wrote no letter to the church at Berea as far as is known, yet there is evidence that the group continued to thrive, for they took an active part in raising funds for needy believers in Jerusalem, sending a representative with Paul (20:4). As for Paul's companions in the work, it seems they rejoined him in Athens, but Timothy was sent back to Thessalonica on a mission (1 Th 3:2), whereas Silas perhaps went to Philippi. They both rejoined Paul in Corinth (Ac 18:5).

6. ATHENS—17:16-34

A situation quite different from any he had faced before confronted the apostle here. The city had been the intellectual center of Greece, especially in the sixth and fifth centuries B.C. Something of its past glory lingered on, represented in its university and its various philosophical schools, but it was living largely in the past, preferring reputation to the reality of culture.

17:16 Now while Paul was waiting for them at Athens, his spirit was being provoked within him as he was beholding the city full of idols.

17 So he was reasoning in the synagogue with the Jews and the God-fearing *Gentiles*, and in the market place every day with those who happened to be present.

18 And also some of the Epicurean and Stoic philosophers were conversing with him. And some were saying, "'What would this idle babbler wish to say?" Others, "He seems to be a proclaimer of strange deities,"—because he was preaching Jesus and the resurrection.

19 And they took him and brought him to the Areopagus, saying, "May we know what this new teaching is which you are proclaiming?

20 "For you are bringing some strange things to our ears; we want to know therefore what these things mean."

21 (Now all the Athenians and the strangers visiting there used to spend their time in nothing other than telling or hearing something new.)

22 And Paul stood in the midst of the Areopagus and said, "Men of Athens, I observe that you are very religious in all respects.

23 "For while I was passing through and examining the objects of your worship, I also found an altar with this inscription, 'TO AN UN-KNOWN GOD.' What therefore you worship in ignorance, this I proclaim to you.

24 "The God who made the world and all things in it, since He is Lord of heaven and earth, does not dwell in temples made with hands;

25 neither is He served by human hands, as though He needed anytning, since He Himself gives to all life and breath and all things;

26 and He made from one, every nation of mankind to live on all the face of the earth, having determined *their* appointed times, and the boundaries of their habitation,

27 that they should seek God, if perhaps they might grope for Him and find Him, though He is not far from each one of us;

28 for in Him we live and move and exist, as even some of your own poets have said, 'For we also are His offspring.'

29 "Being then the offspring of God, we ought not to think that the

266

Divine Nature is like gold or silver or stone, an image formed by the art and thought of man.

30 "Therefore having overlooked the times of ignorance, God is now declaring to men that all everywhere should repent,

31 because He has fixed a day in which He will judge the world in righteousness through a Man whom He has appointed, having furnished proof to all men by raising Him from the dead."

32 Now when they heard of the resurrection of the dead, some *began* to sneer, but others said, "We shall hear you again concerning this."

33 So Paul went out of their midst.

34 But some men joined him and believed, among whom also was Dionysius the Areopagite and a woman named Damaris and others with them.

17:16. It seems almost as though the apostle had no plans for a campaign here but was marking time until Silas and Timothy caught up with him. If this is a correct estimate of the situation, then the quality of his presentation before the Areopagus looms as all the more amazing, since it was not the result of long reflection and studied preparation.

But Paul was not a man to take it easy; this was not a vacation. In fact, his spirit could find no rest, "provoked" as it was by what he saw around him, a city filled with idols (in 15:39 the noun form of this verb *provoked* is rendered "disagreement"). Paul could not come to terms with the idea that idols had any place in genuine culture. Any appreciation which might have been extended to these objects as works of art was precluded by the use to which they were put. He could not be a bystander much longer. Every day he came closer to entering the arena of conflict.

17:17-18. The conclusion just stated is verified by the "so" with which verse 17 begins. For some days Paul carried on a dual ministry, presenting the Gospel in the synagogue to the Jews and God-fearing Gentiles, and carrying on daily discussion in the *agora,* or public square. Here people of all types mingled, especially those who were eager to converse.

Rather than indulge in small talk with those who had little to offer, the apostle gravitated to the "Epicurean and Stoic philosophers." The former school of thought was named after its founder, Epicurus. Deistic in point of view, the Epicureans emphasized pleasure (in the sense of tranquility and freedom from pain) as the chief end of human existence—an idea that suited the Greek temperament rather well. The Stoic system of thought, founded by Zeno of Cyprus, derived its name from the Stoa, or portico in Athens, where Zeno first taught. It was pantheistic in its outlook and emphasized duty and self-discipline, proving especially congenial to the Roman temperament. Henley's poem "Invictus" contains ingredients that are basically Stoic.

It is not at all certain that the slighting comments made about Paul and recorded here came from the philosophers themselves. More likely they came from their hangers-on who thought to show their loyalty to their teachers by heaping ridicule on the unprepossessing Jew who dared to debate with them. The term rendered "idle babbler" is picturesque, filled with local color. As the birds fluttered here and there in the square, eager to pounce on any stray scrap of food, so with this stranger. He was out to snatch up any bits of knowledge he could find, a mere seedpicker (the literal meaning) rather than a man of genuine knowledge and well digested thought.

Others had a less depreciatory estimate, emphasizing that he was a religious protagonist rather than a would-be philosopher. Yet this evaluation, for all its intended mildness, was actually far more menacing than the other, for to allege that Paul was an exponent of "strange deities" did not mean that the deities were odd but that they were foreign. Recall that Socrates lost his life on the ground that he was guilty of introducing such deities into Athens. Each city was jealous of its gods, especially those which were regarded as its patrons. To explain to his readers how such a comment could be made about Paul, Luke added that it was made because he was preaching "Jesus and the resurrection." As some have noted, in the original the two words could have been understood respectively as "healing" and "restoration." How ironic that Paul should be thought of as a polytheist!

17:19-21. A decisive moment had come. The verbs in the preceding sentences are in the imperfect tense, picturing what went on for a period of time, day after day. Now a crisis was reached—"they took him and brought him." Paul was not a prisoner, but he was under suspicion and had to be interrogated before the Areopagus. "Areopagus" could mean the hill of Ares, the god of war ("Mars," in Latin), but since the word is used also in verse 22, it doubtless has the same meaning here as there. It is very awkward to say that a person stood in the midst of a hill (cf. v. 33). The attempt to make "Areopagus" mean "an informal crowd on Mars Hill"[9] does not meet the problem. It must mean either the hill, or the court that in early times held its sessions there but later met in a location adjoining the agora.[10]

Once again the apostle found himself on the spot; but this time instead of being harried by his countrymen (there is no intimation of any involvement by the local synagogue), he was being pressed by intellectual dilettantes. But there was at least the appearance of courtesy, as they expressed the desire that he make clear "this new teaching." This probably had special reference to Jesus and the resurrection (v. 18). Actually, in his address, most of what the apostle said was not new but could have been learned in the synagogue at Athens.

The Court of Areopagus was a council which had oversight of the educational, moral, and religious welfare of the community. Bertil Gärtner is of the opinion that Paul did not meet with the entire Areopagus but only with its education commission.[11] But that this should be considered a trial is doubtful. Luke's account seems to favor the idea that a hearing of an exploratory nature was held, since no accusers were called and no verdict pronounced at the close of the session. Paul was free to go his way (v. 33).

Significant is the repetition of the word "know" in successive verses (19-20). Hereby a mild tension is established with the terms "unknown" and "ignorance" in verse 23. The supposed leaders in the realm of knowledge were sadly in need of being informed. In Athens, as Luke tells us parenthetically (v. 21), the solid quest for truth which was the glory of the ancient philosophers had largely given way to a passion for novelty, at least on the part of the population as a whole. Paul must have entered upon his assignment realizing the difficulty of handling spiritual and eternal things in such a situation, yet determining to give his best to the effort.[12]

A crucial moment in world history had come, as a Jew faced a cultivated Greek audience and discoursed on that which could bring them together. Basic to true religion is a right understanding of God, an issue which Greek philosophy had wrestled with but had failed to resolve, because it lacked specific, divine revelation. Paul's line of thought moved majestically from God to man and then to the God-man who must become the focal point of faith if a right relationship to God is to be achieved.

17:22-23. Here we have the setting for the speech proper. Paul began by noting that the Athenians were "very religious." This much-debated term could be either a criticism (cf. "ignorance" in v. 23), in which case "very superstitious" would be the preferred rendering, or it could be a compliment. The latter is more probable if Paul wished to create a friendly atmosphere for his remarks. But it is not to be construed as flattery, for this was forbidden at hearings conducted by this body,[13] and it was alien to Paul's character. Presumably the apostle was aware of the ambiguity of his language, which allowed his hearers to make their own decision on the meaning. They would then be aware from the start that they were listening to a man skillful in the handling of words and ideas.

Passing to the basis for his statement, Paul mentioned his encounter with an altar in the city which bore the inscription, "TO AN UNKNOWN GOD." Several ancient authors mention altars to unknown gods at Athens, but so far none has been noted as dedicated to a single deity. Such altars were erected "either because an unknown god was considered the author of tribulations or good fortune, or because men feared to pass over some deity, and therefore prayed and made sacrifices to an unknown god."[14] Paul was eager to grasp the opportunity to write the name of the God he knew upon that anonymous altar. This was the burden of his message.

17:24-26. God was set forth as the Creator of all things. The Christian has no difficulty in viewing the world as the handiwork of God, for he has learned to do this from the Old Testament (Ps 19; Is 40); but with the Greeks this was not the case. They regarded the physical universe as eternal, so that even if a Demiurge had shaped the things that are seen, he had done so out of preexistent materials. So the teaching about God as Creator was directly opposed to Greek ideas.[15]

The Hebrew way of designating the world was usually "heaven and earth" (Gen 1:1). Enthroned above His creation as Lord, God does not make His abode in humanly constructed temples (cf. 1 Ki 8:27). As Creator of all, God is self-sufficient. He does not need the ministrations of "human hands" (cf. Ro 11:35). He is able to care for the world He has brought into being, continuing to impart Himself by giving to all "life and breath and all things." This cancels out any thought of an absentee God.

He relates Himself not merely to individuals but to nations. "From one" (man, Adam) came in due course "every nation of mankind." This struck a blow at the Athenian pride of native origin. With increase of numbers came the need of regulation. God provided for this. The nations have their "appointed times" (not the same as the "fruitful seasons" of 14:17) for emergence and development (cf. Dan 2:36-45). Likewise the "boundaries of their habitation," the areas they are to occupy, have been determined by a wise Providence.

17:27-28. All that had been said was now focused on the purpose it is intended to serve, namely, that men may "seek God." Those who lack special revelation (Scripture) may have to "grope" for Him (suggesting that the light of nature is but semidarkness compared to the revelatory power of the Word of God). Yet the divine intent is not to tantalize those who seek, but to enable them to "find" God.

Paul did not discuss here the reason for human failure in this matter. This is developed in Romans 1:18-21. Because of sin men suppress the truth which, if followed out, would furnish just that preparation which is needed for reception of the Gospel message.

Human failure to find God cannot, as an explanation or excuse, argue for the unavailability of God, for He is "not far from each one of us." To explain and buttress this observation, Paul made another, his famous declaration, "For in Him we live and move and exist." (Compare the

270

triadic structure with the closing statement of verse 25.) Any attempt to find here a concession to Stoic doctrine is misguided, for while that system held that the divine was immanent in the human, since the human was a part of the cosmos, it did not affirm that man resided in the deity.

It is clear that Paul was speaking here of man's life as a creature, so one cannot cite as a parallel construction the Pauline teaching about the believer being in Christ. Gärtner is probably right in holding that the meaning to be conveyed by the entire expression is "man's absolute dependence on God for his existence."[16] Agreeable to this is the quotation, derived from Aratus' *Phainomena,* "for we also are His offspring." Man derives his life from God. The word "offspring" refers to creation and is no basis for the notion that all men are children of God in a spiritual sense. Such an interpretation would make the cross of Christ unnecessary and would contradict the biblical teaching that faith in Christ is needed before one can enter the family of God (Jn 1:12; Gal 3:26).

17:29. If the connection between man and God is the life derived from the Almighty, then it is folly to represent the divine by an image which originates in the thought of the creature and is bodied forth by his skill in shaping an object of "gold or silver or stone." It is an offense against the dignity of man as well as a travesty of the Deity.

Twice in the address—here ("Divine Nature) and in verse 23 ("what . . . you worship")—Paul used the neuter gender in speaking of Deity. This is understandable as an effort to find common ground with his audience, and it does not represent a lowering of his own view of God.

The apostle is probably not to be understood as charging his hearers with blatant idolatry, for these sophisticated people would doubtless have asserted that the idol had significance for them merely as a tangible aid in thinking of and worshiping the deity (cf. the Israelites' statement about the golden calf, Ex 32:4). But the commandment against making any representation of God is well founded, for such a practice only clouds the unique and spiritual nature of God. If men are God's offspring they should come to Him directly rather than by means of material objects.

17:30-31. Then the preacher moved to his conclusion by drawing a contrast between God's treatment of men in general during past ages and what He now required of them. He "overlooked" the ignorance, not in the sense of condoning it or the conduct which resulted from it, but in the sense that He did not upbraid the nations as He had the covenant nation, Israel, when idolatry marred her relationship with Him. The thought is strictly parallel to Paul's statement in 14:16 (cf. Ro 3:25).

Because of the demand that God *now* makes, that His creatures repent, it is clear that the ignorance referred to must be regarded as culpable. Men have been guilty of wrong for which they are responsible. However,

271

this aspect is not pressed in the passage before us as it is in Romans 1:18-23, where essentially the same theme is under discussion. The linking of divine forbearance with the need for repentance is clearly stated in Romans 2:4.

In the passage we are considering, the translation "declaring" is based on the support of two important manuscripts; but the other reading, which would be rendered as "commanding," is preferable here, in view of the association with repentance. God does not merely announce repentance, He demands it. The scope of the demand is universal, reaching to "all men everywhere."

The explanation for the "now" in verse 30 follows immediately. A new age had come. Paul touched first on its conclusion, which will be marked by judgment, the time for giving account, when repentance in this life will be richly rewarded, and failure to have repented will prove catastrophic.

But is this time of reckoning merely an empty threat to persuade men to straighten up their lives? By no means, for God has given "proof" (or pledge) of His firm intentions by raising the "Man" of His choice from the dead. This use of *Man* is comparable to *Son of Man* (cf. Jn 5:27). Those who have repented—and this is repentance in faith unto life—can face that judgment unafraid; for the risen Lord, the One through whom God will judge the world in righteousness, will be their Deliverer from that coming wrath (1 Th 1:10). The resurrection of Jesus Christ, which points to His future function as Judge, also points backward to confirm the efficacy of His death on the cross for the sins of men. One should compare the import of "righteousness" here with its use in John 16:8. The resurrection vindicated the claims of Jesus, including His fitness to be Judge as well as Saviour.

Paul could have furnished evidence of Christ's resurrection (cf. 1 Co 15), but his audience was in no mood to hear him out. His allusion to resurrection was too much for their prejudiced minds to receive (cf. Ac 22:21-22).

The speech is concluded. What shall we say about it? Some have questioned whether Paul could have uttered these words. Granted that much of what he says here does not appear elsewhere as credited to him, yet the address bears marked affinity to his words spoken at Lystra (chap. 14). The Areopagus address is of course longer and more philosophical in tone, but the latter feature is readily explained by the intellectual cast of his audience, whereas the Lystra message was for simple-minded folk. Those who have to defend and expound the Christian faith in a highly sophisticated atmosphere can take courage and guidance from the notable achievement of the apostle on this historic occasion.

17:32-34. The courtesy which had given Paul a hearing up to this point was wearing thin. Interruption came with the mention of resurrection, an idea repudiated by all schools of Greek thought. Two reactions are recorded. Some began to "sneer," unable to hide their disdain. Others, desiring to maintain at least the appearance of courtesy, talked about giving the apostle further opportunity to speak at another time. But he discerned their real sentiments; they were brushing him off. Had he felt that there was a genuine desire to hear more, he would doubtless have stayed longer in the city.

The session was over, so Paul left the gathering and went his way. But he was no longer a solitary figure, the one over against the many, for there were some who "believed." They were at least four in number, probably more. Two are named, one of them being an *Areopagite*, that is, a member of the council of the Areopagus. The other was a woman named Damaris. Her presence indicates that others besides council members had been present (cf. comment on 7:57). Ramsay notes a contrast with Luke's description of women in Pisidian Antioch, Thessalonica, and Berea, where their noble birth is emphasized. This woman is not given any such distinction.

No mention is made of the formation of a church in Athens, nor is there any record of a later visit by Paul to shepherd this small flock. Yet there was a church, and it is noted by patristic writers of a later time, especially by Origen.[17]

Two questions call for brief consideration. Did Paul really preach the Gospel at Athens? Those who question that he did can point to the fact that no mention was made of the death of Christ, an integral part of the kerygma (1 Co 15:3). Yet the very fact that Luke went on record as saying that some believed surely presupposes the presentation of the death of our Lord. Possibly Paul had been on the verge of developing this aspect of the truth when interrupted, and did so privately to those who gathered around him at the conclusion of the hearing. The apostle had most certainly proclaimed the death of the Saviour in his synagogue appearances in the city prior to this day.

The other question is closely related to the first. Was Paul conscious of failure at Athens, and did he attribute that failure to the philosophical orientation of the address as opposed to his usual straightforward presentation? Some have appealed to 1 Corinthians 2:2 in support of this viewpoint, as well as to his general mood of weakness and discouragement as he went on to Corinth. But the conclusion is dubious. In 1 Corinthians 2:2 there is no emphasis on the words "among you," which one would expect if the apostle were contrasting the presentation in Corinth with that in Athens. Any time four or more people respond to a message delivered to the intelligentsia, the speaker need not feel that he has failed.

What Paul learned above all at Athens is that "the world through its wisdom did not come to know God" (1 Co 1:21). The great center of learning had demonstrated its ignorance of Him. What did Corinth hold in store?

7. CORINTH—18:1-17

This city, some fifty miles almost due west of Athens, presented a challenge entirely different from the one Paul had just encountered. It was noted for its commerce rather than its culture. The church which resulted from the apostle's fairly long residence reflected the fact that the character of the city had been a factor in shaping the pre-Christian lives of its members (1 Co 1:26; 6:9-11). This congregation gave Paul more anxiety than any other. It seems that he visited it three times (2 Co 13:1) and wrote to it no less than four times, with the two letters found in the New Testament and two others (1 Co 5:9; 2 Co 2:3, 9).

It is possible to discern several stages in the work of the apostle at Corinth: (1) a period when he spoke in the synagogue on the Sabbath and labored at his trade during the week (vv. 3-4); (2) a full-time synagogue ministry dating from the arrival of Silas and Timothy (v. 5); (3) increasing opposition, resulting in a separation from the synagogue and a greatly enlarged work among the Gentiles (vv. 7-8); (4) the attempt of the Jews to have him condemned by Gallio (vv. 12-17); (5) a further ministry, about which no specific information is given (v. 18).

Verses 1-4. Luke gives prominence to Aquila and Priscilla in connection with Paul's settling in Corinth—not only because they were of great help to him there, but because they continued to aid him (18:18-19, 26; Ro 16:3; 1 Co 16:19).

> **18:1** After these things he left Athens and went to Corinth.
>
> **2** And he found a certain Jew named Aquila, a native of Pontus, having recently come from Italy with his wife Priscilla, because Claudius had commanded all the Jews to leave Rome. He came to them,
>
> **3** and because he was of the same trade, he stayed with them and they were working; for by trade they were tentmakers.
>
> **4** And he was reasoning in the synagogue every Sabbath and trying to persuade Jews and Greeks.

18:1. Once again Luke has nothing to say about the circumstances of the next journey, but simply records the change of location from Athens to Corinth. The very fact that Paul made the move in this direction shows that he was not hindered by doubt that this was a proper mission field for him. True, his original summons to Europe was to Macedonia (16:9); but there was evidently no sense of divine hindrance in moving on to Achaia such as he had experienced before going to Troas (16:6-7). If there was a shadow of a doubt, this was removed by the vision from the Lord at Corinth (18:9).

The location of the city was strategic, right on the narrow Isthmus of Corinth, which connected northern Greece with the Peloponnese. To the west, less than two miles away, was the seaport Lechaeum, on the Gulf of Corinth, which opened out onto the Ionian Sea, permitting ready shipping to Italy. To the southeast of the city, several miles away, was the port of Cenchrea, on the Saronic Gulf, which handled trade on the Aegean Sea and Asia Minor coast as well as with points farther east. Goods were transshipped across the isthmus to avoid risking the storms that frequently battered the southern tip of the peninsula.

Provoked by the recalcitrance of the leaders of the city, the Romans destroyed Corinth in 146 B.C. For a century it was allowed to lie in ruins, until Julius Caesar rebuilt it.

> The primary motive of the colonial movement was in fact to provide land for certain classes of Roman citizens, and any services which the settlements might perform in the districts where they were planted were a secondary consideration. Caesar was chiefly interested in the urban proletariat of Rome, and his eastern colonies were probably peopled from this class—Corinth, about which alone we have definite information, certainly was so.[18]

Under Nero an attempt was made to construct a canal across the isthmus, but it was abandoned, and the task remained uncompleted until late in the nineteenth century. The growth of the new Corinth was rapid. Although it was a Roman colony, its population was much larger and far more diversified than that of Philippi. But along with prosperity and luxury came an abandonment to licentious living that was notorious throughout the entire Mediterranean area. Politically it was the capital of Achaia. Religiously it was a center for the worship of Aphrodite, the goddess of love, which encouraged immorality in the service of religion.

The combination of only limited success at Athens, loneliness, and the prospect of facing this city, with its commerce and vice, accounts for the weakness and fear that gripped the apostle as he arrived to begin his work (1 Co 2:3).

18:2-3. The initial problem facing him was to find living quarters and remunerative work. He was in financial need when he came to Corinth (2 Co 11:9). Happily, his contact with Aquila and Priscilla met both requirements, for he was able to live with them and work alongside them at their common trade. They were "tentmakers," which was taken by some patristic writers to mean leatherworkers. Possibly the tents they made were sometimes of leather and sometimes of goats'-hair cloth, for which Paul's own province of Cilicia was noted.

Aquila (meaning "eagle") is called a Jew; the status of his wife Priscilla (the diminutive form of *Prisca*, "old or venerable woman") is not indicated. Opinions differ as to whether these people were already believers when Paul met them. That Aquila is called a Jew no more excludes him from being a Christian than does the same designation in the case of Apollos (vv. 24-25). It is doubtful that Paul would have taken up residence with them if they had not been believers.

If this conclusion be accepted, it follows that there were believing Jews in Rome by the middle of the first century, for Luke tells us here that this couple had been obliged to leave Rome due to the edict of Claudius banishing Jews from the city. From Suetonius we learn that the occasion for this order was a tumult among the Jews instigated by a certain Chrestus.[19] A probable conclusion, though not accepted by all, is that the Jews had become restless and agitated at the preaching of those who proclaimed Jesus as the promised Messiah (*Christus* and *Chrestus* were readily confused). The edict does not seem to have been totally or permanently effective, for the Jews were too numerous and too essential to the life of the capital to be banished for long. Certainly during Nero's reign they were back in force. Paul found many of them when he came as a prisoner to the imperial city (chap. 28).

18:4. Having sketched Paul's activity during the week, Luke now summarizes his work on the Sabbath, a ministry in the synagogue to both Jews and Greeks (for this combination see 14:1; 19:10; 20:21; cf. Ro 1:16). He was "trying to persuade" them, which suggests resistance but does not rule out some success. Doubtless Stephanas and his household became believers at this time (1 Co 1:16; 16:15).

The Western text, at this point, provides an interesting sidelight on the apostle's method of presentation in his synagogue preaching by adding the note that he inserted the name of the Lord Jesus. In other words, in dealing with the prophetic passages of the Old Testament which were Messianic in character, he identified the Lord Jesus as the One who fulfilled them.

Verses 5-11. The acceleration of the mission, aided by the arrival of his helpers from the north and his ability to devote full time to the work, is pictured as resulting in increase in converts and in intensified opposition.

> **18:5** But when Silas and Timothy came down from Macedonia, Paul *began* devoting himself completely to the word, solemnly testifying to the Jews that Jesus was the Christ.

6 And when they resisted and blasphemed, he shook out his garments and said to them, "Your blood *be* upon your own heads! I am clean; from now on I shall go to the Gentiles."

7 And he departed from there and went to the house of a certain man named Titius Justus, a worshiper of God, whose house was next to the synagogue.

8 And Crispus, the leader of the synagogue, believed in the Lord with all his household, and many of the Corinthians when they heard were believing and being baptized.

9 And the Lord said to Paul in the night by a vision, "Do not be afraid *any longer,* but go on speaking and do not be silent;

10 for I am with you, and no man will attack you in order to harm you, for I have many people in this city."

11 And he settled *there* a year and six months, teaching the word of God among them.

18:5-6. The arrival of Silas and Timothy seems to be associated with a new impetus to the testimony of the apostle. Apparently these brethren had been sent back to Macedonia by Paul when he was at Athens. Now they rejoined him and became active in preaching (2 Co 1:19).

The remainder of the verse is not wholly clear. One possibility is that these fellow workers found the apostle engrossed in the proclamation of the Gospel. But this is strange, for the preceding account indicates that up to this time he had had only a limited ministry, confined to the Sabbath. Since the imperfect tense of the verb can serve to emphasize the inception of an action, the wording of the NASB is quite feasible: "Paul began devoting himself completely to the word."

The good news about the steadfastness of the Thessalonian believers acted like a tonic, providing relief for Paul's anxiety. Perhaps an even more important factor in enabling him to give himself wholly to evangelism was the financial assistance sent by the Macedonian churches (2 Co 11:9).

The thrust of Paul's message to the Jews was, "Jesus was the Christ." A reversal of order is possible—the Christ was Jesus. In the former wording the starting point is proclamation about Jesus leading to His identification with the Messiah of prophecy. In the latter, the starting point is the Jewish expectation based on the Old Testament, concluding with a demonstration from evidence about the historical Jesus that the two are identical. This is the more natural procedure in gaining a hearing from a Jewish audience.

Resistance to the message was so strong that Paul felt it necessary to terminate his appeal to the Jews. His shaking out his garments is probably to be associated with his parting word to his countrymen, "Your blood be upon your own heads, I am clean." Paul's responsibility to reach his own people in Corinth with the Gospel had been discharged. Those who had resisted must bear the guilt of closing the door of faith for those who might otherwise have come to know the Saviour. "From now on" should not be read as committing the apostle to a lifetime of shunning the Jews. His turning to the Gentiles pertained only to the Corinthian situation. There is abundant evidence that he continued to observe the rule "to the Jew first" (Ro 1:16).

18:7-8. Paul's verbal outburst was followed by his abandonment of the synagogue. The Western text's interpretation of "from there" as a reference to his leaving Aquila's home is a misunderstanding of the situation. True, Paul went to a "house"; however, the house was not a place of residence, but a place for meeting with those interested in hearing the word of the Lord. The house belonged to Titius Justus, who, judging from his name, was a Roman. He had been a God-fearer for some time. Now, under Paul's preaching, he had become a believer.‡

Some scholars have advanced the suggestion, probably sound, that the full name of this man was Gaius Titius Justus,[20] since Paul referred to a certain Gaius as host to the whole church at Corinth (Ro 16:23), which fits the data in the passage before us. The incompleteness of the name in verse 7 is not fatal to this identification, since in no case does the New Testament list all three names when referring to a Roman.

The new location adjacent to the synagogue was convenient, so that people who had an interest in hearing Paul further had only a slight adjustment to make. Even some Jews, it seems, risked the disfavor of their fellows by identifying with Paul. One, Crispus by name, the leader of the synagogue, is singled out as a convert. Did this synagogue have only one ruler, in contrast to the situation at Pisidian Antioch (13:15), or is the definite article to be explained as indicating the prominence of this man? The latter view is perhaps preferable. This notable conversion, along with that of Gaius, led Paul to break his own rule against baptizing his converts personally (1 Co 1:14). The coming of these influential men to the Lord seems to have led "many of the Corinthians" to a similar decision.

18:9-11. The reason for the vision of the Lord granted to Paul is explained by the recent turn of events. Fed by resentment about the move next door, the defection of Crispus, and the increase in conversions among the people (many of whom had been adherents of the synagogue), Jewish antagonism seemed ready to break the bonds of restraint. Paul's apprehension is understandable. We know that he hoped to be able to return to Thessalonica to minister to his converts there (1 Th 2:17-18) and could

---

‡Some manuscripts read "Titus" instead of "Titius," but the chance that this is the Titus referred to in Paul's letters is remote.

therefore have readily interpreted increased opposition at Corinth as a signal that he should leave the work. But the vision brought not only assurance that he would be unharmed but also a command to continue his labor in the city. There were still "many" people to be won to the faith. The Lord already claimed them as His own (cf. Jn 10:16).

As a result of the vision, Paul settled down to a rather extended ministry lasting for a year and a half, second only in duration to his stay at Ephesus. He was obedient to this vision as he had been to the first (Ac 26:19).

Verses 12-17. In this transitional section Luke describes the incident that brought Paul's ministry at Corinth to a close, or nearly so. The reader is prepared for the next stage of activity, which involved a return to the mainland of Asia.

> **18:12** But while Gallio was proconsul of Achaia, the Jews with one accord rose up against Paul and brought him before the judgment seat,
>
> **13** saying, "This man persuades men to worship God contrary to the law."
>
> **14** But when Paul was about to open his mouth, Gallio said to the Jews, "If it were a matter of wrong or of vicious crime, O Jews, it would be reasonable for me to put up with you;
>
> **15** but if there are questions about words and names and your own law, look after it yourselves; I am unwilling to be a judge of these matters."
>
> **16** And he drove them away from the judgment seat.
>
> **17** And they all took hold of Sosthenes, the leader of the synagogue, and *began* beating him in front of the judgment seat. And Gallio was not concerned about any of these things.

18:12-13. The Jews, vexed by the inroads which Paul's mission had made in their former sphere of operation, determined a united action against him, choosing to appear before Gallio, who had recently become proconsul of Achaia. He was a brother of Seneca the philosopher, who praised him for his many fine traits of character. Possibly the Jews were expecting him to be a "soft touch." His handling of the case now submitted to him reveals his penetration of insight and his practical wisdom.

Archaeologists have uncovered what is almost certainly the judgment-seat to which Paul was brought. Finegan writes, "Built of white and blue marble, the bema must have presented an impressive appearance, and it served very well for the function of a public-speaking platform with the possibility of a large crowd assembled in front of it."[21]

The Jews' complaint was phrased somewhat vaguely: "This man persuades men to worship God contrary to the law." It is not clear whether Jewish or Roman law was meant. Perhaps the statement was deliberately ambiguous. Roman law forbade the proselytizing of Roman citizens, and there were some people with Roman names, as noted above, who had become believers under Paul's ministry at Corinth; but there is no certainty that they were Roman citizens. Judaism was a permitted religion, sanctioned since the days of Julius Caesar, and so far the Romans had not differentiated Christianity from Judaism. This is understandable in view of the fact that the Church began at Jerusalem and its missionary activity had thus far been carried on almost entirely by Christian Jews who worked through the synagogues wherever possible. It may be that the Jews of Corinth were hinting to Gallio that it was high time Rome distinguished between Christians and Jews and bore down on the former as operating outside Roman law.

18:14-15. At any rate, Gallio detected that he was dealing with a prejudiced group that had no case. He indicated that he was prepared to deal with a situation involving "wrong" or "crime" but refused to concern himself with Jewish religious matters, jargon, or peculiar practices. "Your own law" may have been used in deliberate contrast to the general force of *law* in verse 13. This whole sphere lay outside Gallio's proper jurisdiction.

Paul stood exonerated. Surely this deliverance must have brought to his mind the Lord's promise that no man would be able to harm him (v. 10). More important than his personal safety was the vindication of the Christian cause in the eyes of Roman authorities. The decision of Gallio was bound to be normative in similar situations elsewhere.

18:16-17. The Jews were further humiliated when they were ordered away from the judgment seat. Nor was this the end of the matter. The onlookers, for the most part Greeks, sensing Gallio's disdain for the Jewish action, saw a chance to vent their displeasure on the complainants by manhandling their spokesman, a man named Sosthenes, who had succeeded Crispus as a leader in the synagogue. It is tempting to see in this man the same individual mentioned by Paul in writing to the Corinthian church (1 Co 1:1). While this cannot be demonstrated, it is possible that Sosthenes was led to consider the Gospel more seriously as time went on and ultimately followed the course taken by Crispus. If so, the cause of Christ in Corinth must have received a fresh impetus.

"Gallio was not concerned." Many a sermon has depicted him as indifferent to religion, but this is not the meaning. Rather, he refused to be involved in a case over which he had no rightful jurisdiction. Another rendering of the statement is possible—"but Gallio paid no attention to this" (RSV)—in which case the reference is confined to the incident of the beating: Gallio did not interfere.

D. The Mission of Paul in Ephesus—18:18–19:41

1. Preliminary visit—18:18-23

The apostle had not lost sight of his objective to evangelize the Roman province of Asia. Providentially prevented from entering the area formerly (16:6), he sensed that now the time was ripe for shifting to this field of labor. But he had been away for a considerable time from Jerusalem and Antioch, the two churches which were his major contacts with the Jewish and Gentile wings of the Christian movement, so he felt it was time to return to these places. Therefore the initial visit to Ephesus was brief, but it laid the foundation for a lengthy and fruitful ministry that touched the entire province.

> **18:18** And Paul, having remained many days longer, took leave of the brethren and put out to sea for Syria, and with him were Priscilla and Aquila. In Cenchrea he had his hair cut, for he was keeping a vow.
>
> **19** And they came to Ephesus, and he left them there. Now he himself entered the synagogue and reasoned with the Jews.
>
> **20** And when they asked him to stay for a longer time, he did not consent,
>
> **21** but taking leave of them and saying, "I will return to you again if God wills," he set sail from Ephesus.
>
> **22** And when he had landed at Caesarea, he went up and greeted the church, and went down to Antioch.
>
> **23** And having spent some time *there*, he departed and passed successively through the Galatian region and Phrygia, strengthening all the disciples.

18:18. Because of his vindication before Gallio, Paul's position in Corinth was secure, and he took advantage of it by remaining "many days longer"; but his eager spirit was leading him to consider his responsibility to other areas (cf. 2 Co 10:16). He had already tarried longer here than in any other spot since the inception of his missionary travels.

Luke's account raises some problems. One is the mention of Syria as the destination of the trip now being undertaken by Paul, which would suggest Antioch as the place of intended debarkation, whereas it turned out that he landed at Caesarea, which is in Palestine (v. 22). It is possible that in the course of the journey Paul determined that he ought to visit

Jerusalem before going to Antioch. Or he may have changed ships at Ephesus, finding one which would take him to Palestine.

The other problem pertains to the "vow" made by the apostle. Paul was not a life-long Nazirite, as were Samson and John the Baptist, but he was free to assume a vow for a limited period. Why the vow was taken we do not know. It may have concerned in some way his work at Corinth. Later he assumed another vow at Jerusalem (21:23-26).

The shaving of the head normally came at the termination of the period of the vow (21:24), but here it seems to have taken place at the beginning. A passage in Josephus throws light on this. Describing the rites of purification undertaken by Queen Bernice, which occurred about a decade later than the present incident, the historian says, "She was visiting Jerusalem to discharge a vow to God; for it is customary for those suffering from illness or other affliction to make a vow to abstain from wine and to shave their heads during the thirty days preceding that on which they must offer sacrifices."[1]

Cenchrea is of interest because a church was established there, perhaps during the time of Paul's labors at Corinth (Ro 16:1). Several such churches developed in the area and were noted by Paul a short time later (2 Co 1:1).

Only Priscilla and Aquila are mentioned as Paul's traveling companions. Behind their move to Ephesus at this time was the purpose of assisting the apostle there as they had done at Corinth. Presumably Silas and Timothy remained behind to superintend the work Paul was leaving (2 Co 1:19 may apply here as well as to the period following their arrival from Macedonia).

18:19-21. The ship may have carried Jewish pilgrims bound for the Passover celebration at Jerusalem. As a glance at the map will show, Ephesus was not out-of-the-way for a ship headed for Syria or Palestine.

After seeing his associates established at Ephesus, the apostle paid a visit to the synagogue and took part in the service, meeting with an unusually cordial response. Unable to stay over, Paul did the next best thing, promising to return for further ministry if God permitted. At this point the Western text injects a comment attributed to Paul to the effect that he must observe the coming festival at Jerusalem. This sufficiently explains his inability to tarry longer (cf. 20:16).

18:22-23. This is a prime example of Luke's compressed style of narrative, due either to lack of detailed information or deliberate intent to save space for the ministry proper. Such a passage shows that Luke was not intent on glorifying Paul by recording or inventing data for effect.

At first reading it might appear that Paul greeted the church at Caesarea, but this is ruled out by two considerations. "Went up" is technical terminology for a trip to Jerusalem, which was on high ground (Lk 2:42; Ac 21:15). Also "went down to Antioch" is strange language if Paul went from Caesarea to Antioch, since both are practically at sea level, whereas the terminology is fitting for one making a journey from Jerusalem to Antioch.

The visit to Jerusalem served in a general way to maintain the ties Paul had with the leaders of the church. It may also have helped to crystallize his purpose to aid the Jewish Christian community there through donations from the Gentile churches, a plan that was consummated by a subsequent journey (24:17).

Luke says nothing about the purpose of the visit to Antioch and makes only a general statement as to the time spent there. But there must have been opportunity for reporting on the mission in Greece as well as for a renewal of fellowship with a highly motivated missionary church. As it turned out, this was Paul's final visit to this place, at least so far as the record goes.

His departure is commonly represented as the beginning of the third missionary journey, but this is somewhat artificial in view of the lack of resemblance between this event and the commencement of the earlier journeys.[2] To begin with, the trip involved a revisiting of the churches in southern Galatia (cf. 15:36), but the very brevity of the account, in contrast to the fullness of the description in the following chapter, makes it clear that a return to Ephesus was the main objective.

2. EMERGENCE OF APOLLOS—18:24-28

Before narrating the Ephesian ministry, Luke inserts information about what happened there during Paul's absence. His source for this account may well have been the apostle himself, who must have learned from Priscilla and Aquila about the visit of Apollos to Ephesus. In the composition of his work, Luke probably felt the desirability of including something on the ministry of Apollos as a background for the right understanding of the incident, reported at the beginning of the next chapter, involving the disciples who knew only the baptism of John.

18:24 Now a certain Jew named Apollos, an Alexandrian by birth, an eloquent man, came to Ephesus; and he was mighty in the Scriptures.

25 This man had been instructed in the way of the Lord; and being fervent in spirit, he was speaking and teaching accurately the things concerning Jesus, being acquainted only with the baptism of John;

26 and he began to speak out boldly in the synagogue. But when Priscilla and Aquila heard him, they took him aside and explained to him the way of God more accurately.

27 And when he wanted to go across to Achaia, the brethren en-

couraged him and wrote to the disciples to welcome him; and when he
had arrived, he helped greatly those who had believed through grace;

28 for he powerfully refuted the Jews in public, demonstrating by
the Scriptures that Jesus was the Christ.

18:24-25. The description of Apollos is unexpectedly full, indicating
the importance to be attached to him and his work, and demonstrating
that Luke was not so taken up with Paul as to ignore other men who made
a contribution to the spread of the Gospel. This Jew was a native of
Alexandria, the great Egyptian metropolis, which had a large segment
of Jews in its population. It is tempting to conjure up a picture of Apollos
as being acquainted with Philo, the famous contemporary philosopher and
prolific author of Hellenistic Judaism, and as having familiarity with Greek
as well as Hebrew learning. The word "eloquent" actually connotes not
so much oratorical skill as sophistication. Apollos was a cultured man.

"Mighty in the Scriptures" refers to his adeptness in handling the Old
Testament, of which he had been a keen student from his early days. This
is a generous appraisal in view of the deficiency which Aquila and Priscilla detected (v. 26). But considering his limited opportunties, he had
attained to a notable grasp of the Word. More than this, he had been
"instructed in the way of the Lord." This seems to be parallel to "the way
of God" (v. 26) and denotes God's way of salvation, His plan as set forth
in the Scriptures. Apollos understood this from the prophetic standpoint
but was not yet informed as to the richness of its fulfillment in Jesus of
Nazareth.

What he did know about Jesus he was proclaiming "accurately" as he
discoursed in the synagogue. Presumably "the things concerning Jesus"
included the high points of His life and work as well as something about
His teachings. It is well to note the confirmation hereby provided of the
existence of a reliable tradition concerning Jesus and His work. If the
Western text as attested by Codex Bezae is trustworthy here, Apollos received this instruction in his native place, i.e., Alexandria.

But now, after this recital of assets, comes the liability. For all his
knowledge, and despite being "fervent in spirit" (cf. Ro 12:11), he was
"acquainted only with the baptism of John." His gospel, then, was one of
anticipation and preparation rather than of absolute fulfillment. He knew
nothing of the baptism with the Holy Spirit based on the finished work of
Jesus Christ.

To explain the status of Apollos is indeed difficult. How could a man
be so limited in his understanding of Christianity after more than two
decades had passed since the death and resurrection of Christ and the
outpouring of the Spirit? Nothing is known of earliest Christianity in
Egypt. Some of John the Baptist's followers may have left Palestine for

Egypt while the ministry of Jesus was still in progress, when they had no knowledge of Pentecost. This much is clear, that Apollos had not been instructed by those who still followed John in preference to Jesus. What he knew and proclaimed was the prophetic ministry of our Lord. What he lacked was information on His Messiahship as demonstrated by His exaltation and the pouring out of the Spirit. John the Baptist had not proclaimed publicly that Jesus was the Messiah.

18:26. The boldness displayed in the preaching of Apollos is to be traced to his knowledge of the way of the Lord, his assurance that God's plan would be consummated for the welfare of mankind, plus his own fervency of spirit. But these admirable features could not hide from two of his hearers the glaring omission in his preaching. Aquila and Priscilla ventured on the delicate and difficult task of instructing the preacher.

"They took him aside." The Greek hints at privacy, no doubt the privacy of their home. They indulged in no open criticism of this man, for indeed it was not what he said but what he left unsaid that troubled them. They were able to point out that John himself had predicted the baptism with the Holy Spirit through the coming One (Mk 1:8). No statement is given about the reaction of Apollos, but the sequel supplies all that is needed. Evidently he received with humility and gratitude the help extended to him, leading to a greatly enlarged understanding and ministry.

Students of early Christianity are intrigued as they reflect on the implications of such a conference. Here were representatives of Roman Christianity meeting with a representative of Alexandrian Christianity. True to the situation here, Rome had something to teach Alexandria, although later Alexandrian Christianity made a larger contribution along doctrinal and philosophical lines than Rome could offer.

Did Apollos receive Christian baptism? Nothing is said about it (in contrast to the men described in 19:5). Perhaps it was judged unnecessary in view of the fact that the disciples of Jesus, having received John's baptism, were not rebaptized as believers in Jesus. G. W. H. Lampe ventures the opinion, "Possibly a direct commission from the Lord was deemed to have conferred upon him the Spirit, for he ranked very high among the apostles, being regarded by the Corinthians as standing approximately upon the same level as St. Peter or St. Paul."[3]

18:27-28. In the course of their conversations Aquila and Priscilla must have mentioned the work of Paul at Corinth. When Apollos expressed a desire to visit the church there, the believers at Ephesus smoothed the way for him by writing to the church at Corinth, urging them to receive the brother. The identity of the "brethren" who performed this service is not stated. Possibly Aquila and Priscilla had won certain persons to the faith prior to the arrival of Apollos.

Luke is content to summarize the ministry of this man in Achaia by noting that he "helped greatly" the saints in that area. For more complete information we need to consult 1 Corinthians 1-4. Not only did he help the saints by his teaching, but he brought pagans into the fold (1 Co 3:5). Luke emphasizes his ministry to the Jews, in which he confronted them with the teaching of their Scriptures which led irresistibly to the conclusion, "Jesus was the Christ" (or, "the Christ was Jesus"). No mention is made of a ministry in the synagogue, which had been closed to Christian testimony (Ac 18:6).

Through Aquila and Priscilla, Paul made a distinct contribution to the growth and usefulness of Apollos that greatly affected the Corinthian congregation. Understandably the Alexandrian, trained in rhetoric and captivating in speech, appealed to many of the Corinthians, some of whom developed such an adulation for him that they tended to depreciate Paul (1 Co 1:12; 4:6). Yet Apollos cannot be held responsible for this factionalism, and seems to have refused to return to Corinth lest he strengthen this tendency (1 Co 16:12).

A good case can be made for the position that he is the one who wrote the Epistle to the Hebrews, while Pauline elements in that book can be readily accounted for by the contact which he had with Paul both directly and indirectly (through Aquila and Priscilla as well as through the apostle's converts in Corinth).

3. TRIUMPHS OF THE GOSPEL—19:1-20

The setting for Paul's next campaign was the city of Ephesus, which he had long desired to evangelize, because he recognized its strategic position for reaching all the province of Asia with the Gospel (19:10).

Several distinctives characterize the time spent in this city.

1. It was more prolonged than any other, extending to approximately three years (vv. 8, 10, 22; cf. 20:31).
2. It included a ministry to certain men who were imperfect in their knowledge of the faith and therefore in their personal experience (vv. 1-7).
3. Much of the time Paul's public ministry was conducted in the hall of Tyrannus rather than in the synagogue (v. 9).
4. Some unusual miracles were wrought by Paul, confirming the truth of the message he preached (vv. 11-12).
5. The power of occultism, which lingered even among some who had become believers, was broken (v. 19).

6. In the midst of success, Paul envisioned an enlarged ministry which would take him to the West (v. 21).
7. The mission in Ephesus was broken off, as far as Paul was concerned, by a mammoth riot staged on behalf of the goddess Artemis and her worship (vv. 23-41).
8. Additional information supplied by Paul himself pictures vividly his pastoral care of the converts (20:20, 31) and the extreme danger to which he was exposed in connection with his labors in the city (1 Co 15:32; 2 Co 1:8-10).

Verses 1-7. This paragraph deals with Paul's arrival at Ephesus and his encounter with a group of men who had an incomplete faith.

Luke has nothing to say about the city as such, but considerable information is available from ancient historians and geographers and augmented by the work of modern archaeologists. Today its great port is silted in and the site is virtually uninhabited, but in Paul's time the place was approaching the zenith of its glory. It was the leading city of the province of Asia, enriched by extensive commerce from both east and west. The population of the city approached a third of a million. In view of all this, it is not at all surprising that of the seven churches of Asia addressed in Revelation 2 and 3, the church at Ephesus should be mentioned first. Writing to the Ephesian church a few years after Revelation was written, Ignatius of Antioch called it "famous to eternity."

The two edifices mentioned in Acts 19, the temple of Artemis and the theater, have been unearthed. The temple was found some twenty feet below the surface of the ground. It was one of the seven wonders of the ancient world and certainly one of the largest buildings of antiquity, while the theater was discovered to have been large enough to seat around twenty-five thousand people.

The opening section of this chapter is clearly intended to be viewed in connection with the close of chapter 18, not only because Apollos is mentioned in both portions but because there is a reference to the baptism of John in both. Still, the connection should not be pressed to the point of insisting that the men Paul dealt with were converts of Apollos before he had been enlightened by Aquila and Priscilla. If Apollos knew these men, it is unthinkable that he would have gone off to Corinth without sharing with them his new understanding of the faith. We do well to assume that this group was independent of Apollos and probably detached from the brethren mentioned in 18:27.

> **19:1** And it came about that while Apollos was at Corinth, Paul having passed through the upper country came to Ephesus, and found some disciples,

287

2 and he said to them, "Did you receive the Holy Spirit when you believed?" And they *said* to him, "No, we have not even heard whether there is a Holy Spirit."

3 And he said, "Into what then were you baptized?" And they said, "Into John's baptism."

4 And Paul said, "John baptized with the baptism of repentance, telling the people to believe in Him who was coming after him, that is, in Jesus."

5 And when they heard this, they were baptized in the name of the Lord Jesus.

6 And when Paul had laid his hands upon them, the Holy Spirit came on them, and they *began* speaking with tongues and prophesying.

7 And there were in all about twelve men.

19:1. In describing Paul's arrival at Ephesus, Luke is content to picture him as having traveled through "the upper country." This must be the territory lying between Pisidian Antioch and Ephesus (cf. 18:23). It could suggest traversing the Lycus valley or a route somewhat to the north, on a more direct line between Antioch and Ephesus.[4] There is no solid basis for assuming, as Deissmann did, that the apostle visited the towns in northern Galatia on this occasion.

Rather strangely, Luke has nothing to say here about Paul's reunion with Aquila and Priscilla or his fellowship with the brethren mentioned in 18:27. Instead, he abruptly introduces an encounter between the apostle and a group of "disciples." In what sense they warranted the term *disciples* is much debated. One needs the remainder of the narrative to make the picture at all clear.[5]

19:2-7. Something about these "disciples" moved Paul to inquire about their spiritual history. They may have appeared to lack the fruit of the Spirit, such as joy and peace, or they may have failed to manifest the gifts of the Spirit, or both. Such a lack would have aroused his suspicions—hence the question, "Did you receive the Holy Spirit when you believed?" The question serves as a reminder that faith in the Lord Jesus and the reception of the Holy Spirit go hand in hand; the one leads to the other. Paul was probing to find out if they really believed, in the evangelical sense.

Quite astonishing is the answer, "No, we have not even heard whether there is a Holy Spirit." The problem here is to understand how anyone connected either with John the Baptist or with Jesus in the days of His flesh could be entirely ignorant of the Holy Spirit. If these men were Jews, which is probable, they should have known of the Spirit from the Old Testament. Perhaps the language is intended to be construed somewhat as in John 7:39, "For the Spirit was not yet *given*."

These men must have understood that John's baptism signified repentance when they submitted to be baptized with that baptism. Now Paul indicated to them that John's ministry, including his baptizing activity, had pointed to One who was coming after him, namely, Jesus. From the Christian standpoint, John's baptism is incomplete because it is only preparatory.

This handful of disciples, now better informed, confessed their readiness to put faith in the Lord Jesus and accept baptism in His name. This willingness to accept baptism "in the name of the Lord Jesus" is clear evidence that they were not adherents of a Baptist sect arrayed against the Christian movement. That such competition existed is well attested. In fact there are several hints of it in the gospel according to John (1:6-9, 20; 3:30; 10:41).

Notable is the way Paul handled the deficiency about the Holy Spirit. Instead of offering instruction on this subject, he referred the needy ones to Jesus Christ. F. D. Bruner puts it well by saying,

> The remedy for those who know little or nothing of the Holy Spirit is not special instruction or knowledge on access to the Spirit, or a new set of conditions, a new regimen of emptying, added obediences, deeper commitment, or ardent prayer, but instead simply the great fact: the gospel of faith in the Lord Jesus Christ and baptism in his name.[6]

The problem confronting the Ephesian "disciples" was not ignorance of how to experience baptism with the Spirit, as some have surmised, but failure to have put their faith in Jesus Christ for salvation and receive baptism in His name. When this was done, the Holy Spirit was granted to them. The fact that they were able to speak with tongues (presumably ecstatic utterance, as in 1 Co 12-14) and to prophesy (the manward aspect of their testimony) left no doubt about the presence of the Holy Spirit in their lives (cf. Ac 10:46). If the original followers of the Lord needed the outward tokens of the Spirit's coming at Pentecost to assure them of the reality of His presence and power, and of the unique character of the period thus introduced, how much more did these men, with less preparation, need such tokens!

The laying-on of hands by Paul was not an indispensable condition for the reception of the Spirit (recall the case of the company in the house of Cornelius, 10:44). The situation resembled that of the believers in Samaria (8:17) and of Paul himself (9:17). Imposition of the hands seems to have been a regular feature of Christian baptism, and baptism marked the occasion for the reception of the Spirit (2:38). This in itself was sufficient reason for the practice of the early Church not to defer baptism in favor of a long period of prerequisite instruction and probation.

In regard to the development of Christianity in these early days, the overall importance of the passage should be sought in the uniting of men still closely attached in some sense to John the Baptist with the mainstream of the Church's faith and life, thus making the formula "One Lord, one faith, one baptism" (Eph 4:5) a reality.

It is doubtful that any special significance is to be attached to the figure "twelve" in this passage, since it is only an approximation rather than a precise number. As Meyer notes, we have here "a simple historical statement, not in order to represent the men 'as a new Israel.' "[7]

Verses 8-10. Here Luke describes the second phase of Paul's ministry, or more accurately, the next two, since the initial period of activity in the synagogue was followed by a longer period of testimony elsewhere. A. Schlatter remarks, regarding the remaining narratives of the chapter, that they "are all intended to show the shattering effect Paul had on the whole religious life of Ephesus."[8]

> **19:8** And he entered the synagogue and continued speaking out boldly for three months, reasoning and persuading *them* about the kingdom of God.
>
> **9** But when some were becoming hardened and disobedient, speaking evil of the Way before the multitude, he withdrew from them and took away the disciples, reasoning daily in the school of Tyrannus.
>
> **10** And this took place for two years, so that all who lived in Asia heard the word of the Lord, both Jews and Greeks.

19:8-9. In view of the difficulties Paul had encountered on his missionary travels in staying very long in the synagogue, "three months" seems an extended time indeed. It can be explained by two factors: (1) the initial cordial reception given him on his arrival from Corinth (18:19-20) and (2) the cosmopolitan character of Ephesus, which promoted toleration and made it rather difficult for the Jews to display their feelings too violently. The situation was much the same as that in Syrian Antioch.

Paul's message is summarized as "the kingdom of God." While the eschatological aspect of the Kingdom may have been included, the terms "reasoning" and "persuading" favor the interpretation that the Gospel, centering in Jesus Christ as the fulfillment of Old Testament hopes, was the main thrust.

A great number of Jews remained unconvinced. With the passage of time they grew more restless under such preaching and more combative. The increasing hostility was a testimony to the impact Paul was making. Ultimately, rather than face a barrage of criticism and debate from week to week (not very fertile ground for the Spirit's work), the apostle "withdrew," taking with him those who had received the Lord Jesus.

In this passage "the multitude" refers to the congregation of the synagogue. Earlier, Luke has used it of the assembled church (6:2; 15:12).

Paul's new location was "the school of Tyrannus." The Greek word is *scholē*, which denotes first of all leisure; then discussion, or lecture (a favorite way to employ leisure among the Greeks); then a group attending such lectures; and finally, the place in which such instruction was given (cf. our use of the word *church* for both congregation and building).

An illuminating addition in the Western text at this point states that Paul's daily activity in this place went on from the fifth to the tenth hour, i.e., from 11:00 A.M. to 4:00 P.M. This was siesta time for the inhabitants. It has been conjectured that Paul was able to rent the hall at a nominal figure because it was not used at this time of day. To draw people, the apostle had to give them something sufficiently attractive and potent to cause them to pass up their rest period.

By combining various Scripture references it is possible to piece together in a rough way a picture of his schedule in those days. It seems that he worked at his trade during the early morning hours to support himself (20:34), then gave public instruction in the middle of the day at the school of Tyrannus, and during the remainder of the day turned to visitation of Christians in their homes (20:20) and individually (20:31). It is possible that toward the end of the day he sometimes had to return to his trade in order to make enough to sustain himself and those dependent on him. It was a busy life, indeed.

19:10. This heavy schedule was maintained for "two years," with the result that not only the city but also the province became familiar with Paul's teaching. One would tell another, whose curiosity was piqued to attend, and so the outreach of the Gospel was great. Luke's wording here—"all Asia"—may sound highly exaggerated, yet it is corroborated by the admission of a detractor (v. 26). There is other testimony along the same line, such as the winning to Christ of Epaphras, Philemon, and Archippus—all of them from Colossae—during this time. Through the witness of these and others, churches sprang up throughout Asia, not only at Colossae but at Hierapolis and Laodicea (Col 4:13), in addition to the other locations mentioned in Revelation 2 and 3. Paul's own testimony is to the same effect (1 Co 16:19). His strategy was to evangelize the hinterland through people he had brought to Christ and trained for service. This latter activity must have included instruction on how to reach "both Jews and Greeks." It is clear that Paul did not go out into the province, but remained in the city.

Verses 11-20. A specific instance of divine intervention on behalf of Paul and his work came in connection with the attempt of Jewish exorcists to imitate the apostle. Their attempt is pictured against the background of some unusual manifestations of divine healing.

19:11 And God was performing extraordinary miracles by the hands of Paul,

12 so that handkerchiefs or aprons were even carried from his body to the sick, and the diseases left them and the evil spirits went out.

13 But also some of the Jewish exorcists, who went from place to place, attempted to name over those who had the evil spirits the name of the Lord Jesus, saying, "I adjure you by Jesus whom Paul preaches."

14 And seven sons of one Sceva, a Jewish chief priest, were doing this.

15 And the evil spirit answered and said to them, "I recognize Jesus, and I know about Paul, but who are you?"

16 And the man, in whom was the evil spirit, leaped on them and subdued both of them and overpowered them, so that they fled out of that house naked and wounded.

17 And this became known to all, both Jews and Greeks, who lived in Ephesus; and fear fell upon them all and the name of the Lord Jesus was being magnified.

18 Many also of those who had believed kept coming, confessing and disclosing their practices.

19 And many of those who practiced magic brought their books together and *began* burning them in the sight of all; and they counted up the price of them and found it fifty thousand pieces of silver.

20 So the word of the Lord was growing mightily and prevailing.

19:11-12. The ministry in word was accompanied by a ministry of miraculous works. Such things may have occurred in other places (Ro 15:18-19), but Luke has noted them only occasionally (13:11; 14:3; 14:10; 16:18). No miracles are reported at Thessalonica, Berea, Athens, or Corinth (though Paul himself cited them in connection with the latter city, 2 Co 12:12). The miracles at Ephesus were indeed "extraordinary," recalling the healing of the woman who touched the hem of the garment of Jesus (Mt 9:20-22) and the cure provided for those upon whom the shadow of Peter fell (Ac 5:15). In addition, there were exorcisms. The extraordinary miracles were so unusual as to appear incredible to some moderns. Yet Luke, a man with medical training and experience, does not discount them. In the wisdom of God they may have been deemed necessary to appeal to such a superstitious city as Ephesus (cf. 19:18-19).

19:13-16. Certain wandering Jewish exorcists, noting the power seemingly possessed by Paul, determined to capitalize on his success by using his formula for casting out demons, "the name of the Lord Jesus."

That there were Jewish exorcists in the time of our Lord is demonstrated by Matthew 12:27 (cf. Tobit 8:1-3 for an earlier period). "Magic and exorcism, and that above all for curative purposes, were uncommonly popular and prevalent throughout the entire Roman Empire. Nor did the Jewish people form an exception."[9] Bruce M. Metzger notes, "Of all ancient Graeco-Roman cities, Ephesus, the third largest city in the Empire, was by far the most hospitable to magicians, sorcerers, and charlatans of all sorts."[10]

In this superstitious sphere, syncretism was common. The magical papyri of Egypt reveal the use of the names of Israel's God—*Yahweh, Sabaoth*, and others—along with those of other deities. It is startling to read in the Paris Magical Papyrus the following: "I adjure thee by the god of the Hebrews Jesus." Commenting on the use of the name *Jesus* in this setting, Deissmann observes, "It was probably inserted by some pagan: no Christian, still less a Jew, would have called Jesus 'the god of the Hebrews.' "[11]

Behind the use of magic was the idea that if one possessed the proper formula he could compel the unseen powers to do his bidding. Sceva had not actually been a high priest in Israel, but he claimed to belong to a high priestly family. F. F. Bruce remarks,

> It was well known throughout the Near East that Jewish high priests had access to the secret name of the God of Israel and its true pronunciation, and by all magical canons the command of such a secret carried with it enormous power over the spirit-world.[12]

These exorcists looked on Paul as a competitor whom they expected to outflank by their maneuver. They were in this business for profit, whereas Paul was performing a service.

Their plans were ruined when an evil spirit refused to recognize them as having any control over him. Their use of the name *Jesus* was second-hand and therefore spurious. The reward for their misdeed was a severe trouncing, as the man they were dealing with, galvanized by the super-human strength of the demon that possessed him, stripped and wounded them. This recalls the case of the Gerasene demoniac (Mk 5:2-4).

It is awkward to read that "both of them" were overcome, since seven individuals were involved. There is evidence that the Greek word rendered "both" can mean "all" in certain cases,[13] and it should be so translated here.

19:17-20. The effect of this incident on the general populace is indicated first—"Fear fell on them all" (cf. 5:5). No longer could the name of the Lord be taken lightly. Men stood in awe of the power He had exhibited in their midst.

The effect on the Ephesian church was even greater, in that it stirred the saints to confess the hold that the occult had retained on them even after they became believers. They gathered up the "books" of magic lore and put them to the torch in a great, public display of housecleaning. The work of grace, despite the strong preaching of Paul, had been incomplete, for the hold of former practices had not been broken. Now they freely disclosed their "practices." This is a literal translation and makes good sense, but this word occurs in the magical papyri with the meaning of magical spells or formulas, and is so treated here by the New English Bible.

It is not entirely clear whether the "many" of verse 19 were Christians also, or whether they were pagans who were shaken by what had transpired and were so gripped by fear that they joined others who were ridding themselves of the paraphernalia of magic. The latter seems probable.

The value of what was consumed was reckoned at "fifty thousand pieces of silver." Since no specific coin is mentioned, it is impossible to estimate the amount involved. The intention is to give the impression of a very large figure.

Luke concludes his account of the episode with a summary statement about the growth of "the word of the Lord." Although the wording is the same as in verse 10, the sense is somewhat different; there the message of the Gospel is in view, whereas here the Christian faith, or cause, better conveys the meaning. A cleansed and revived church was the key to continuing increase. By this time the foundation had been laid for a large and strong church upon which others could build (cf. Jn 4:38), especially the apostle John toward the end of the century.

With the growth of the church in Ephesus, a practical problem must have arisen. Could all these believers have met together in one place? We know there was a church in the house of Aquila and Priscilla (1 Co 16:19), which suggests that the school of Tyrannus was not used for fellowship purposes but for evangelism and instruction. It is possible that several house churches came into being, as in the city of Rome (Ro 16:5, 14).

4. PLANS FOR FUTURE WORK—19:21-22

In this passage Luke shows that far from making the apostle complacent, the success enjoyed at Ephesus spurred him to seek new areas of ministry.

> **19:21** Now after these things were finished, Paul purposed in the spirit to go to Jerusalem after he had passed through Macedonia and Achaia, saying, "After I have been there, I must also see Rome."
> **22** And having sent into Macedonia two of those who ministered to him, Timothy and Erastus, he himself stayed in Asia for a while.

19:21-22. The ministry at Ephesus proved to be a watershed for Paul's career. He felt that from the standpoint of a pioneer missionary, sufficient groundwork had been laid for the future expansion of the Gospel in the eastern Mediterranean area. The Jerusalem church had taken over responsibility for the evangelization of Palestine. He himself had worked for years in Syria and Cilicia, where the Antioch church could be counted on to do its part in the future. More recently he and his helpers had laid the foundations for the church in Asia Minor and Greece. It was time to look elsewhere.

The choice lay between Egypt and the West, notably Rome. Possibly his contact with Apollos at Ephesus had something to do with the decision not to go to Egypt (1 Co 16:12). For all we know, Paul may have been aware that others had gone or were going to Egypt, in which case his principles would take him elsewhere (2 Co 10:15-16).

But if he avoided Egypt because it already had Christian testimony, ought not the same consideration have applied to Rome? Two things need to be said on this. As W. L. Knox notes, Rome was so large that Paul could find many to whom the Gospel had not yet been made known.[14] Even more relevant is the apostle's intention to make Rome a springboard for sending the message of Christ out into the whole western Mediterranean area. He had no idea of settling down in Rome (Ro 15:24).

The fact that Paul was seriously considering a change of field for his work shows that in his own estimation, his success at Ephesus had reached a high plateau. Others could carry it on. The apostle's pioneer spirit was eager to push forward to other frontiers of testimony. Therefore we can understand that in the providence of God, it was just at this juncture, rather than at some earlier time, that the disturbance led by Demetrius occurred, thrusting Paul out.

Although he had twice returned to Antioch after missionary travels, his present plan to visit Jerusalem and then go on to Rome shows that Paul did not regard Antioch as a permanent home base. His plan and his corresponding movement was directed inward to Jerusalem and outward into the Roman world.* There is evidence that the decision had been gradually forming over a long period of time (Ro 1:13; 15:23) and actually envisioned a penetration of the West which would take Paul beyond Rome to Spain (Ro 15:24).

But why should he begin the realization of this plan by going in another direction—to Jerusalem? The basic reason was to consummate an important aspect of his work, the taking of a fund to Jerusalem which would

---

*W. L. Knox, in The Acts of the Apostles, pp. 54ff. has pointed out that Luke adopted the travel story as the framework for his writing. In his gospel he pictured Jesus moving toward Jerusalem, His goal, to accomplish redemption in fulfillment of Scripture. In the Acts he pictured Paul "beginning from Jerusalem" and leading a campaign of evangelization with Rome as his objective. This is the overall pattern of Luke's dual composition, Luke-Acts.

help to meet the need of the poor saints there and hopefully would cement good relations between the church in Judea and the congregations (largely Gentile) which Paul had founded in Asia Minor and Greece (Ro 15:25-26).

Some attention should be given to the words "Paul purposed in the spirit." Was this his own spirit or the Holy Spirit? In favor of the former alternative is the verb "purposed" (rather than *was moved* or *was led*) and the prominence given to his own person in the statement, "I must also see Rome." It is often difficult to distinguish between the Holy Spirit and the human spirit where a believer is concerned, because of the close relation between the two (cf. Ro 8:16; 9:1).

With his future movements in mind, Paul dispatched two of his trusted helpers to prepare the way, no doubt to advise the churches of Macedonia and Achaia of his forthcoming pastoral visit en route to Jerusalem. As it turned out, he stayed in Corinth for three months, then returned via Macedonia to Jerusalem (Ac 20:3).

Apparently Timothy did not accompany Paul from Corinth to Ephesus (18:18) but must have come later, perhaps with Apollos. He then fulfilled a mission to Corinth on Paul's behalf (1 Co 4:17), not to be confused with the visit now being considered.

As for Erastus, the name occurs in three references. The other two are Romans 16:23, where he is described as being the city treasurer of Corinth; and 2 Timothy 4:20, where Paul seems to say that when he himself was made a prisoner for the second time and was taken to Rome, Erastus stayed in Corinth rather than accompanying him. The reference in Romans has taken on added interest since the excavations at Corinth a few years ago. "A re-used paving block preserves an inscription, stating that the pavement was laid at the expense of Erastus, who was *aedile* (Commissioner of Public Works). He was probably the same Erastus who became a co-worker of St. Paul."[15] Looking further at the references to Erastus, 2 Timothy almost certainly refers to the same individual as Acts 19:22, since Timothy was involved in both instances. But uncertainty clouds the reference in Romans 16:23, since it is difficult to suppose that a city official would have the leisure to be in Paul's company at Ephesus. But the possibility should be granted.

Paul himself remained in Asia for a time (Ac 19:22). It was during this period that an event occurred which confirmed him in the realization that there were many adversaries (1 Co 16:9) and which persuaded him to expedite his plan to leave the city and begin to take the steps that would facilitate his move to the West. To this event we turn.

5. ARTEMIS EPISODE—19:23-41

The incident of the silversmiths has been called "the most instructive picture of society in an Asian city at this period that has come down to us."[16] Ramsay also concludes from the numerous accurate details that the author must have based his account on eyewitness reports.[17] The fact that the story is narrated at some length seems to indicate that it had special relevance for the overall purpose of the book.

The effort to bring Paul into disrepute and to curtail or arrest his work is shown to have failed, for neither the civil nor religious authorities were influenced by it. When the apostle left Ephesus he did so voluntarily.

19:23 And about that time there arose no small disturbance concerning the Way.

24 For a certain man named Demetrius, a silversmith, who made silver shrines of Artemis, was bringing no little business to the craftsmen;

25 these he gathered together with the workmen of similar *trades*, and said, "Men, you know that our prosperity depends upon this business.

26 "And you see and hear that not only in Ephesus, but in almost all of Asia, this Paul has persuaded and turned away a considerable number of people, saying that gods made with hands are no gods *at all.*

27 "And not only is there danger that this trade of ours fall into disrepute, but also that the temple of the great goddess Artemis be regarded as worthless and that she whom all of Asia and the world worship should even be dethroned from her magnificence."

28 And when they heard *this* and were filled with rage, they *began* crying out, saying, "Great is Artemis of the Ephesians!"

29 And the city was filled with the confusion, and they rushed with one accord into the theater, dragging along Gaius and Aristarchus, Paul's traveling companions from Macedonia.

30 And when Paul wanted to go into the assembly, the disciples would not let him.

31 And also some of the Asiarchs who were friends of his sent to him and repeatedly urged him not to venture into the theater.

32 So then, some were shouting one thing and some another, for the assembly was in confusion, and the majority did not know for what cause they had come together.

33 And some of the crowd concluded *it was* Alexander, since the Jews had put him forward; and having motioned with his hand, Alexander was intending to make a defense to the assembly.

34 But when they recognized that he was a Jew, a single outcry arose from them all as they shouted for about two hours, "Great is Artemis of the Ephesians!"

35 And after quieting the multitude, the town clerk said, "Men of Ephesus, what man is there after all who does not know that the city of the Ephesians is guardian of the temple of the great Artemis, and of the *image* which fell down from heaven?

36 "Since then these are undeniable facts, you ought to keep calm and to do nothing rash.

37 "For you have brought these men *here* who are neither robbers of temples nor blasphemers of our goddess.

38 "So then, if Demetrius and the craftsmen who are with him have a complaint against any man, the courts are in session and proconsuls are *available;* let them bring charges against one another.

39 "But if you want anything beyond this, it shall be settled in the lawful assembly.

40 "For indeed we are in danger of being accused of a riot in connection with today's affair, since there is no *real* cause *for it;* and in this connection we shall be unable to account for this disorderly gathering."

41 And after saying this he dismissed the assembly.

19:23. Luke begins by noting the magnitude of the incident—"no small disturbance" (cf. 12:18 for the identical expression). It concerned "the Way." While from the Christian standpoint "the Way" suggested the absoluteness of the claim of Jesus Christ (Jn 14:6) and the efficacy of the salvation He achieved, in this context, as in verse 9, we are intended to see "the Way" through the eyes of those who opposed it. This is especially characteristic of the references in the book of Acts (9:2; 22:4; 24:14).

19:24. The ringleader of the disturbance was Demetrius, who apparently was an artisan who had advanced to the point where he headed a business making "silver shrines of Artemis." He was able to furnish employment for many "craftsmen" and can be thought of as the head of their guild of silversmiths. Business had been good—until recently. The word rendered "business" can also mean "gain," or "profit," and this sense is appropriate here; but the fact that the same word means "business" in the following verse has no doubt influenced the translators.

The shrines were probably not statuettes of the goddess but small representations of her seated in her temple.[18] Devotees purchased these and presented them at the temple as an act of worship.

Though shrines of terracotta or marble have been found, none made of silver has been located, for which a logical explanation is that they were too valuable to keep and so were melted down by the priests.[19]

Artemis is rendered "Diana" in the KJV, due to the influence of the Latin Vulgate at the time the KJV was made (cf. the comment on 17:19). Diana was indeed the Latin equivalent of the Greek Artemis, the virgin goddess of the hunt. But Artemis of Ephesus, while retaining association with wild animals, had really become the embodiment of the fertility of nature, and in keeping with this her representation was multibreasted.

19:25-27. Demetrius's speech to the men of his own and related crafts consisted first of all in an appeal to their self-interest. The "prosperity" of all of them was being endangered by Paul's success in turning people away from the worship of gods made with hands (see comment on v. 35).

Demetrius gave grudging acknowledgment of the success of the apostle's preaching.

Something of the same sort occurred a few decades later in Bithynia, for acording to the letter of the governor Pliny to the emperor Trajan, the temples until recently had become almost deserted, with little demand for sacrificial victims.

Warming to his subject, Demetrius cleverly moved from the economic to the religious sphere, from the appeal to the pocketbook to an appeal to local pride in Artemis, the great goddess whose worship was in danger of being neglected. For effect, he permitted himself the exaggeration that not only all of Asia but also "the world" worshipped her. It is tempting to give "Asia" the wider meaning of the continent rather than the province in this case, on the ground that it fits well with the larger category of "the world." But against this is the word's uniform use in the New Testament, plus the fact that *world* must not be confused with "the globe," but refers simply to the inhabited earth known to the ancients.

It would have been unseemly to press the issue of economic loss before the public, and little sympathy could be expected, but to stress the blot on the good name of the goddess was strategic. Intelligent people might say, "Let Artemis defend herself" (cf. Judg 6:28-32), but not the masses. Demetrius had planned his approach carefully, expecting the complaint against Paul to catch on with the populace.

19:28-29. His expectation was realized, for the enraged craftsmen concertedly began to chant, "Great is Artemis of the Ephesians!" Ramsay is probably right in contending that no verb should be introduced here (there is none in the original). He understands the expression not as a statement of fact but as an apostrophe, a cry of adoration—"Great Artemis of the Ephesians!"[20] The Williams translation adopts this suggestion.

The noise attracted attention throughout much of the city, and people were drawn almost involuntarily to the theater, the only place where a large crowd could assemble. It was also the place where questions of public interest were discussed. Word must have spread quickly that the demonstration was against Paul and not simply in behalf of Artemis, which would account for the seizure of Paul's associates, Gaius and Aristarchus.†

19:30-31. Believers as well as others were drawn to the general area of the theater, and when they learned that the agitation had Paul as its primary target, they were insistent that he should not go into "the assembly"

†For the possibility that only Aristarchus was originally designated as a Macedonian in the text, leaving Gaius to be identified with the Gaius of Derbe (20:4), see *BC* on this passage. Yet *Gaius* was a common name, so a Macedonian Gaius cannot be ruled out.

(not the technical word for assembly as in v. 41, but rather a term for the crowd, as in 12:22, where it is rendered "people"). Paul was brave, but there was no reason to risk his life at the hands of men who had been turned into fanatics.

It has been suggested that this was the occasion when Priscilla and Aquila endangered their own lives to save Paul (Ro 16:3-4). This is possible, but there may have been other situations involving greater peril for Paul (20:19; 2 Co 1:8-9).

The present crisis was unquestionably perilous, causing "some of the Asiarchs" to exert pressure on Paul to stay away from the scene. The word "Asiarchs" means literally, "rulers of Asia," which is too general to give much help in identifying them.

> The title either designates the annual presidents, and perhaps the ex-presidents, of the provincial council of Asia, or it also covers the administrators of the various temples of the imperial cult, which were under the charge of high-priests appointed by the provincial council, or it may merely designate the city deputies to that council.[21]

Such men, by virtue of their office, had to be concerned with the political and religious welfare of the community. The very fact that such men of prominence and wealth were Paul's friends reveals with utmost clearness that they did not regard him as dangerous or as carrying on an unlawful activity. Here is positive proof that the imperial cult (the worship of the Roman emperor) had not yet come to the point of opposing the Christian cause. The action of Gallio (18:14-15) may have been influential in making the Asiarchs‡ favorable to Paul.

19:32-33. Meanwhile the situation in the theater continued to be one of "confusion" (cf. v. 29 and 2:6), with no one taking charge and with widespread uncertainty as to what the tumult was all about.

The opening statement of verse 33 is quite obscure. One possibility is the wording of the NASB: "And some of the crowd concluded it was Alexander." This seems to mean that when the Jews put him forward, some of the people were disposed to think that he was the central figure around whom the disturbance had taken its rise. Or, the subject of the verb may be thought of as an indefinite "they," yielding the following: "And they brought Alexander out of the multitude," followed by an explanation that the Jews were the ones who called on him to step out and make clear to the throng that they, in contrast to Paul and his Christian friends, were not the occasion for the trouble.

‡Sherwin-White notes Luke's accuracy in using the plural. "If the author of Acts had not known the peculiarities of the organization of Asia, he might well have made an error. In some other eastern provinces the corresponding title went only with the office of President of the Council. There was only one Lyciarch, and only one Pontarch or Bithyniarch" (*Roman Society and Roman Law in the New Testament,* p. 90).

19:34. This move failed to quiet the multitude. Alexander was not given a chance to speak. In their state of mind the crowd would be scarcely less upset at the appearance of a non-Christian Jew than at the appearance of Paul himself, for both were monotheists unsympathetic to their pagan cult. Granted, however, is the certainty that Paul would have been in the more precarious position as a possible victim of violence.

The only effect of this move by the Jews was to set off a fresh wave of chanting, lasting for two hours, in honor of Artemis. Something of a parallel is the Muslim frenzy sometimes seen after the Ramadan fasting, when celebrants become like men intoxicated as they repeat, "There is no God but Allah, and Muhammed is his prophet."

19:35-41. At this point a new figure appeared, and his role was decisive in restoring order. He is called "the townclerk," which hardly suggests the importance of his office. A. H. M. Jones provides some historical perspective on this.

> The post was not . . . one of great political importance during the Hellenistic age. But as the vitality of politics ebbed and the magistrates tended to become lay figures, the clerk of the city, who was bound from the nature of his office to know the ropes of the ship of state, became a more and more dominant figure, and in the Roman period he, either alone or supported by the principal magistrates, very frequently moves decrees and takes the lead in council and assembly.[22]

F. D. Gealy observes that *chancellor* or *secretary of state*, although not ideal renderings, would better convey a proper appreciation of his function.[23] His duties were many, in connection with both the senate and the assembly. He was the chief executive officer of the municipality and acted as liaison between the city government and the Roman authorities. The Greek word is *grammateus*, which in a Jewish context would mean "scribe," as in "chief priests and scribes," but here has a totally different connotation.

This officer showed his wisdom by letting the demonstration spend its energies before intervening. To be howled down might tarnish his standing.

He began his speech by voicing matters of common knowledge concerning the city's relation to the goddess Artemis and her worship, emphasizing her greatness (and thus expressing his agreement with the crowd before going on to find fault with their conduct) and two other items which have not come to the fore previously in the narrative. One was the fact that Ephesus was "guardian" of the temple of the goddess. This honor and responsibility did not exclude a similar relationship to the imperial cult. Ramsay pictures an Ephesian coin, from a somewhat later period, exhibiting the goddess and three emperors to whom temples had been built in the city.[24] The other item was the observation that the image of the goddess had fallen from heaven (a meteorite?). This was the tradition which helped to give sanctity to her worship. The *grammateus* showed himself more astute than Demetrius, who had failed to introduce this point as a counterpoise in his remarks about Paul and his doctrine (v. 26).

Shifting to a consideration of the men who had been dragged into the theater (and by inference including Paul), the official exonerated them of misconduct since they were not "robbers of temples" (no doubt used here in the general sense of those who commit sacrilege in any form) or "blasphemers" of the goddess. This may be taken as evidence that Paul and his helpers had been circumspect in their approach to the question of idolatry at Ephesus. Presumably they had avoided poking fun at the tradition about the image which had fallen from heaven. Now their restraint was standing them in good stead. Herein lies a lesson in missionary strategy: to attack idolatry among people who cherish their gods and know nothing better, since they have not yet received the Gospel, is to leave them in a vacuum.

The town clerk could not fault Paul and his friends, but suggested that if there were a "complaint," Demetrius and the craftsmen must use legal means rather than mob action (v. 38). The text can mean either that "the courts are in session" (now) or that they are held from time to time as needed. The proconsuls or governors presided at such sessions.

In connection with his final word to the instigators of the riot, the official referred to "anything beyond this," which sounds quite vague. Sherwin-White's interpretation is helpful:

> According to the clerk, no specific charges of impiety had been made, but Demetrius was alleging that in some way the prestige of the city was being attacked. This is the "further matter" which might be brought up at what the clerk calls a "regular assembly."[25]

It is clear that this official did not take lightly the commotion of the day (v. 40). He was in touch with the Roman authorities and knew their attitudes.

> The reference to the 'regular assembly' ... is valuable. The city assemblies were on their way out. Roman policy aimed over a long period at the elimination of the democratic element ... No such fate has yet overtaken the civic assembly at Ephesus, but the town clerk has his fears.[26]

His words about the city's inability to give a legitimate explanation for the "disorderly gathering" sent the crowd away in a mood of solemnity that contrasted sharply with the mad uproar that had prevailed. No one challenged his order to disperse.

Luke makes his point without calling attention to it, namely, that Paul had been cleared of the charge of responsibility for economic depression among the silversmiths and (what was more important) of crime against the religious establishment.

PART IV

THE WITNESS OF PAUL THE PRISONER–
20:1–28:31

In this entire section the central human figure continues to be Paul, but the account shows that his situation became radically altered. No longer was he establishing churches or even visiting them, except as they were located on his line of travel to Jerusalem. A journey that was designed to improve relations between his congregations and the mother church, thereby freeing him to go on his way to Rome, created new problems for the Jerusalem church and left him a prisoner in the hands of the Roman authorities. Yet, in the providence of God, this detention gave the apostle opportunities for witness he could not otherwise have had, including the appeal before Caesar at Rome.

The apostle's speeches are given prominence, with three features predominating: considerable autobiography, with the risen Lord's intervention in his life marking the critical turning point; witness to the resurrection of Jesus, a major issue separating believing and unbelieving Jews; and Paul's mission to the Gentiles, portrayed as not demanding a forsaking of his Jewish heritage or a sacrificing of his concern for the salvation of his people, Israel.

In this portion of the book we see that Paul's contact with Rome finally became personal and direct. It was a contact destined to be meaningful for the future of Christianity and the history of the world.

A. JOURNEY TO JERUSALEM—20:1–21:16

THIS SECTION FOLLOWS naturally and logically from the intimation of Paul's plans sketched in 19:21. It was advisable to revisit the churches of Macedonia and Achaia before making what might be a final departure from this region. Paul's main objectives were to confirm believers in their faith, to supervise the concluding phases of the gathering of the fund for the poor in the Jerusalem church (1 Co 16:1-5), and to mend relations with the Corinthian congregation. As it turned out, the apostle may also have undertaken some further evangelization in new territory.

Verses 1-6. Here we follow Paul as he journeyed from Ephesus to Corinth and back again as far as Philippi. It is likely that the time required was the greater part of a year.

> **20:1** And after the uproar had ceased, Paul sent for the disciples and when he had exhorted them and taken his leave of them, he departed to go to Macedonia.
>
> **2** And when he had gone through those districts and had given them much exhortation, he came to Greece.
>
> **3** And *there* he spent three months, and when a plot was formed against him by the Jews as he was about to sail for Syria, he determined to return through Macedonia.
>
> **4** And he was accompanied by Sopater of Berea, *the son* of Pyrrhus; and by Aristarchus and Secundus of the Thessalonians; and Gaius of Derbe, and Timothy; and Tychicus and Trophimus of Asia.
>
> **5** But these had gone on ahead and were waiting for us at Troas.
>
> **6** And we sailed from Philippi after the days of Unleavened Bread, and came to them at Troas within five days; and there we stayed seven days.

20:1-3. Farewells were said shortly after the uproar in the theater. To continue longer might have been harmful to the church's relationship to the community. Aquila and Priscilla may have left with the apostle or about the same time. They were headed for Rome, it seems (Ro 16:3), to prepare the way for Paul's forthcoming visit to that city (Ac 19:21) with which they were so familiar (18:2).

Luke's account of Paul's movements can be supplemented by a comparison with 2 Corinthians 1-2, where we learn that although a door of testimony was open for him at Troas, where he would board ship for

307

Macedonia, he did not remain there to minister because of anxiety over the situation at Corinth and particularly over the failure to make contact with Titus at this point (2 Co 2:12-13). It is likely that the meeting between the two occurred at Philippi. Having received Titus's report, Paul remained there long enough to write 2 Corinthians, with its recital of his trials in Asia and his exposition of the ministry; his counsel on the completion of the fund for Jerusalem; and his warnings in view of lingering opposition to him in the Corinthian church, fomented largely by outsiders. Titus was sent once more to Corinth, this time to try to complete the fund already referred to (2 Co 8:6, 17).

Some think Paul wrote from Thessalonica rather than from Philippi, because Timothy was with him when he wrote (2 Co 1:1), and this young man had especially close ties with the Thessalonian congregation (1 Th 3:2, 6). Luke is content to say that Paul passed through the districts of Macedonia.

He would naturally visit the churches already established there. Moreover, it is probable that this was the time when he preached the Gospel in western Macedonia, going as far as the border of Illyricum. This trip was fresh in his mind as he wrote about it a short time later from Corinth (Ro 15:19). On this journey he would have been able to take the Egnatian Way, which terminated at Dyrrhachium on the Adriatic Sea. It is possible that on the way to Corinth from this northwest area he ministered at Nicopolis on the west coast of Achaia. At a later time he planned to winter there (Titus 3:12). On this entire journey Paul was making good his announced purpose to preach the Gospel in the regions beyond, as he had so recently declared (2 Co 10:16). The trip was possible only because of the easing of the Corinthian situation as reported by Titus. Paul did not have to hurry to Corinth.

His stay in the city lasted for "three months" (cf. 1 Co 16:6). Plans were well under way to take ship for the Holy Land as soon as navigation was safe after the winter storms. Hostile Jews learned of this and plotted to murder him, no doubt after he was on board. Jostled by his countrymen on a crowded ship filled with people headed for the Passover celebration, he would be an easy mark for an assassin's knife.

Learning of the plot, the apostle quickly changed his plan, deciding to go overland through Macedonia, where he could get shipping for the journey. This delay forced him to abandon the hope of reaching Jerusalem by Passover. The best he could do was to aim for Pentecost (v. 16). Discovery of the plot was a reminder to Paul of what the Lord had promised him in Corinth several years before (18:10). Not only was his life spared, the contribution of the churches remained intact.

20:4-5. Troas was the point of rendezvous with his traveling companions. The list includes men from churches which were planted on all three of Paul's journeys. Their function was to carry the gifts of their people to the needy at Jerusalem.

Notable is the lack of representatives from Philippi and Corinth. However, in view of "us" (v. 5), it is likely that Luke took that role for the Philippian church and that he made the journey to Troas with Paul and went on to Jerusalem with him. With respect to Corinth, there are two possibilities. Bruce suggests that the absence of a Corinthian representative could hint at trouble there, presumably the church's stubborn refusal, out of a spirit of defiance toward the apostle, to complete its share.[1] But the fact that Paul had spent the whole winter in Corinth, plus the fact that the letter to the Romans, written in this period, does not reveal any rift in his relationship with the Corinthian church, makes this improbable. One would think that pride alone would have been sufficient to move the congregation to take its place alongside the others. The alternate solution is the more credible, namely, that the breach with the church was so fully healed that they celebrated it by asking the apostle to be their representative. This would mean a shift from Paul's earlier recommendation (1 Co 16:3), but the following verse shows that he was prepared to go. The church may have acted on this basis.

20:6. By the time Paul and Luke left Philippi, Passover had already come and gone. Now less than seven weeks remained till Pentecost.

The journey to Troas was made in the face of adverse winds and required "five days" (contrast 16:11). Why Paul stayed "seven days" at Troas is not stated, but a ship for the journey southward may not have been available any sooner. The interval gave opportunity for a ministry that the apostle had not been able to offer at other times (16:8-11; 2 Co 2:12-13). From the latter passage it is evident that some believers were there on Paul's second visit. Meanwhile the church had doubtless grown in size.

Verses 7-12. Luke describes the apostle's activity on the final day of his stay in Troas, giving special prominence to these elements: the breaking of bread by the congregation, Paul's discourse, and the Eutychus incident. The course of events seems to have been as follows: believers came together for a meeting, which was to include the observance of the Lord's Supper. Paul prepared the way for this by extended teaching, which was interrupted by the fall of Eutychus. After this the apostle led the congregation in table fellowship which included the Lord's Supper, and then talked further before parting from these friends.

> **20:7** And on the first day of the week, when we were gathered together to break bread, Paul *began* talking to them, intending to depart the next day, and he prolonged his message until midnight.

309

8 And there were many lamps in the upper room where we were gathered together.

9 And there was a certain young man named Eutychus sitting on the window sill, sinking into a deep sleep; and as Paul kept on talking, he was overcome by sleep and fell down from the third floor, and was picked up dead.

10 But Paul went down and fell upon him and after embracing him, he said, "Do not be troubled, for his life is in him."

11 And when he had gone *back* up, and had broken the bread and eaten, he talked with them a long while, until daybreak, and so departed.

12 And they took away the boy alive, and were greatly comforted.

20:7. From this passage it may be assumed that Christians gathered together "on the first day of the week," the Lord's Day, our Sunday (cf. 1 Co 16:2). The influence of the Saviour's resurrection on the observance of that day is clear, as well as the effect of His example in breaking bread with His own on the evening of that day (Lk 24:29-30). If Luke were following the Jewish reckoning of time here, the Supper would have actually been eaten in the early morning of the following day. But it is clear that the day is being reckoned from sunrise to the following sunrise, not from sunset to sunset, for the meeting was at night, preparatory to Paul's departure "the next day," a journey made in daylight.[2] Bruce points out that many of the believers were employed by pagans, which would make assembling during the day difficult, if not impossible; hence the night meeting.[3]

From a comparison of verses 7 and 11 it is evident that the observance of the Lord's Supper was deferred until Paul had spoken at some length, in fact, until midnight. It might be his last opportunity to minister the Word to them.

20:8-10. Mention of the "lamps" (torches) is probably intended to have a bearing on what befell Eutychus. The air was close (it was springtime), and the room full of people (Eutychus was sitting on the windowsill) added to the stuffiness. After several hours the combination of weariness after a day's work and the bad air, not to mention the rhythm of Paul's voice, took its toll. Unable to stay awake, the lad slipped from his place and fell through the window to the ground. Luke says that he was picked up "dead." The physician does not say that he was mistakenly thought to be dead. Paul's falling upon the lad and embracing him should be understood in the light of an Old Testament incident (2 Ki 4:32-35). While it might seem that the words of the apostle, "his life is in him," were intended to indicate that he had not expired, the probable meaning is that (now) the life that had ceased was present as a result of the ministration given. The lad was indeed "fortunate," in line with the meaning of his name.

310

20:11-12. The meeting was resumed, and at this juncture the company observed the Lord's Supper (broke bread) and then enjoyed a fellowship meal. The procedure here was the reverse of what is indicated in 1 Corinthians 11:20-21. Afterward Paul "talked with them a long while." The word "talked" is not the same as the one used in verse 7; it points to more informal conversation. After all, the Lord's Supper was the climax of the gathering. What followed until daybreak was a time of sharing the precious reality of knowing Him.

Lest readers wonder still about Eutychus, Luke concludes this section by noting that the people took the boy away (presumably to his home) "alive." In his restoration they were comforted. They had been remembering the Lord's death. They had also been reminded through Eutychus of His return to life through resurrection. The "daybreak" that morning must have cheered them with its promise of eternal day in the presence of the living Lord, when there would be no more parting such as was necessary from Paul.

Verses 13-16. These verses describe the journey from Troas to Miletus. The presence of several place names in the narrative, as well as observations about Paul's method of travel, indicates that Luke kept notes on this trip to Jerusalem.

> **20:13** But we, going ahead to the ship, set sail for Assos, intending from there to take Paul on board; for thus he had arranged it, intending himself to go by land.
>
> **14** And when he met us at Assos, we took him on board and came to Mitylene.
>
> **15** And sailing from there, we arrived the following day opposite Chios; and the next day we crossed over to Samos; and the day following we came to Miletus.
>
> **16** For Paul had decided to sail past Ephesus in order that he might not have to spend time in Asia; for he was hurrying to be in Jerusalem, if possible, on the day of Pentecost.

20:13-16. Paul chose to go on foot from Troas to Assos, about twenty miles away, a much shorter route than the ship had to take. He even delayed his departure after the vessel had cleared the port of Troas. Possibly he made a pastoral call at the home of Eutychus before leaving. He would have felt somewhat responsible for the lad's fall and the anxiety created among family and friends. The overland trek allowed the apostle to be alone with his thoughts. What were they? Musings on what lay before him (v. 23; cf. v. 3)? Or reflections on what God had wrought in Macedonia and Achaia, from which he had recently departed?

Making connection with the ship as previously arranged, he sailed with his companions to Mitylene on the island of Lesbos, the ship taking the inland passage between the island and the mainland. After overnight stops at Chios and Samos, cities bearing the same names as the islands on which they were situated, the party had only one more day aboard until they were able to go ashore at Miletus. Luke gives the reason for bypassing Ephesus. Much as Paul would have welcomed the opportunity to renew fellowship with the church there, he felt it necessary to safeguard his time so as to reach Jerusalem by Pentecost.

Verses 17-35. Here Luke (who was present, v. 15) sets down Paul's message to the Ephesian elders, after noting that the apostle summoned them to meet him. Even this arrangement meant an outlay of several days (Miletus was some thirty miles from Ephesus), which, in view of Paul's eagerness to arrive at Jerusalem, shows the strategic importance which he attached to the Ephesian church and the desirability of encouraging its leaders.

Some introductory observations about the address may be useful:

1. It belongs to a type known as the farewell discourse, which is fairly common both in the Bible and in related literature.[4] Examples from the Old Testament are the speeches of Jacob (Gen 49) and of Moses (various parts of Deuteronomy), and from the New Testament the discourse of Jesus in the upper room (Jn 13-16).
2. The parallels between the farewell address of Paul and the upper room discourse of Jesus are especially close: (a) separation was imminent (v. 25; Jn 13:33; 16:28), producing sorrow in those who would be left behind (vv. 37-38; Jn 16:6, 22); (b) those who were addressed had to carry on, and they had the benefit of the speaker's example (vv. 18-21, 27, 31, 33-35; Jn 13:34; 15:12, 18, 20, 24); (c) they also had the help of God's Word (v. 32; Jn 15:7) and the Spirit (v. 28; Jn 14:16, 26; 15:26-27); (d) they would need these encouragements—the example and the supernatural enablement—because of problems and dangers which would face them both from without (v. 29; Jn 16:2, 33) and from within (v. 30; Jn 13:18, 21); (e) a word of blessing was pronounced upon them (v. 32; Jn 14:27). Along with these resemblances there is a striking element of difference. The elders listened to Paul without breaking in, whereas the disciples interrupted the Master repeatedly during His discourse.
3. It was the privilege of an apostle to leave such a message, but others who ministered in Christ's name shrank from any such function.[5] The Miletus address is a testimony to the apostolic consciousness of Paul.
4. The impression of authenticity created by this speech is confirmed by the parallels in thought and expression between it and statements in Paul's letters. Luke did not compose it by putting down what Paul

might have said on such an occasion.⁶ Indeed, he had no need to do so, since he was present at the time.

20:17 And from Miletus he sent to Ephesus and called to him the elders of the church.

18 And when they had come to him, he said to them, "You yourselves know, from the first day that I set foot in Asia, how I was with you the whole time,

19 serving the Lord with all humility and with tears and with trials which came upon me through the plots of the Jews;

20 how I did not shrink from declaring to you anything that was profitable, and teaching you publicly and from house to house,

21 solemnly testifying to both Jews and Greeks of repentance toward God and faith in our Lord Jesus Christ.

22 "And now, behold, bound in spirit, I am on my way to Jerusalem, not knowing what will happen to me there,

23 except that the Holy Spirit solemnly testifies to me in every city, saying that bonds and afflictions await me.

24 "But I do not consider my life of any account as dear to myself, in order that I may finish my course, and the ministry which I received from the Lord Jesus, to testify solemnly of the gospel of the grace of God.

25 "And now, behold, I know that you all, among whom I went about preaching the kingdom, will see my face no more.

26 "Therefore I testify to you this day, that I am innocent of the blood of all men.

27 "For I did not shrink from declaring to you the whole purpose of God.

28 "Be on guard for yourselves and for all the flock, among which the Holy Spirit has made you overseers, to shepherd the church of God which He purchased with His own blood.

29 "I know that after my departure savage wolves will come in among you, not sparing the flock;

30 and from among your own selves men will arise, speaking perverse things, to draw away the disciples after them.

31 "Therefore be on the alert, remembering that night and day for a period of three years I did not cease to admonish each one with tears.

32 "And now I commend you to God and to the word of His grace, which is able to build *you* up and to give *you* the inheritance among all those who are sanctified.

33 "I have coveted no one's silver or gold or clothes.

34 "You yourselves know that these hands ministered to my *own* needs and to the men who were with me.

35 "In every thing I showed you that by working hard in this manner you must help the weak and remember the words of the Lord Jesus, that He Himself said, 'It is more blessed to give than to receive.'"

20:18-21. The apostle seems to have presupposed his audience's knowledge of his work at Ephesus from the very beginning ("from the first day"). It is natural that those who were appointed elders would have been among the first converts. What they did not know firsthand they had no doubt acquired from others.

"I was with you the whole time" confirms the impression given by 19:10 and the entire narrative of the Ephesian ministry that Paul had remained in the city instead of evangelizing the surrounding territory personally.

In his letter to the Ephesians, the apostle urged "humility" on his readers (Eph 4:2); this address to the elders was the only time he referred to it as an element of his own character (v. 19). As for his "tears" (cf. Phil 3:18), these were the kind that are shed by men "who seldom if ever weep for things in the ordinary course of nature" (Bengel). His lot was made harder by "the plots of the Jews" (cf. 9:23; 20:3; 23:12; 25:3; 2 Co 11:26). These things were not permitted to affect his ministry of the Word. Nothing profitable was omitted. "Shrink" is not too helpful a rendering here, although it fits well in verse 27, where the same verb occurs. The idea conveyed is to hold back, suppress, or keep silence.[7]

Matching the completeness of the message was the twofold sphere of proclamation—"publicly" (the school of Tyrannus) and "from house to house." This may be intended to suggest not merely contact with individual families but also with groups of people (the church in the house). The same breadth of activity characterized his outreach to the unsaved, which embraced "both Jews and Greeks." Despite the great differences between these two, he treated them basically alike, for they were all sinners. They needed "repentance toward God" because of their sin (central to the preaching of John the Baptist and Jesus) in order to be candidates for salvation; and they needed "faith in our Lord Jesus Christ" in order to receive forgiveness, righteousness, and life. Recall that in writing the epistle to the Ephesians Paul underscored this same truth, that both groups needed the same message (Eph 2:1-3) and when they received it they became one rather than two in Christ (Eph 2:12-22).

20:22-24. A major problem is encountered immediately in the phrase "bound in spirit." A reference to 19:21 is not very helpful, due to the difference in construction. Dupont argues quite convincingly in favor of "spirit" meaning the Holy Spirit,[8] making three points: the other interpretation would call for the word "spirit" to be in the accusative case rather than in the dative (cf. 21:11); Lucan usage elsewhere, involving the dative and expressing constraint or control, clearly refers to the Holy Spirit rather than to the human spirit (e.g., Lk 2:27; 4:1); and the heavy emphasis in Acts on human accommodation to the Spirit (8:29; 10:19; 11:12; 16:6-7) needs to be brought to bear on the interpretation of the verse before us. The word "bound," then, serves the purpose of expressing Paul's sense of obligation to be obedient to the dictates of the Holy Spirit.

This compulsion did not provide any great light on what was to befall the apostle, beyond the disclosure that there would be outward "bonds," humanly imposed (note the correlation with "bound" in v. 22) and attendant "afflictions," or tribulations. These intimations had come to him "in every city." Luke did not mention them, but Paul threw out a hint in writing to the Romans from Corinth (Ro 15:30-31). As we know from later developments, Paul's spirit remained unfettered, because he was obedient to the will of the Lord. He was ready and willing to lay down his "life" if need be.* But he could not come to terms with the idea that he should stop short of fulfilling "the course" God had given him. He was able to recognize the termination when it was finally upon him (2 Ti 4:7), but that time was not yet. The ministry he had received from the Lord Jesus was a sacred trust, so He alone must determine how it should be conducted and when it should be concluded.

In preaching the Gospel entrusted to him, Paul was careful to make clear that it was a gospel of "grace" (cf. Gal 1:6).

20:25-27. Another term containing the concept of the Gospel is "the kingdom" of God (cf. 19:8; 28:31). Paul moved in the succession of Christ (Lk 8:1) and of others who were apostles before him (Lk 9:2). *Grace* and *Kingdom* are not in opposition.

But there is a somber side to Christian proclamation. As Paul departed, with no expectation of seeing these people again, he could the more freely speak of the manner in which he had discharged his responsibility as a custodian of the Gospel. He had resisted the temptation to withhold the reminder that rejection of the Gospel of God's grace can only bring judgment. This explains his reference to being "innocent of the blood of all men" (cf. Ac 18:6; Eze 3:17-21). His next statement bore on the same subject. "The whole purpose of God" had been told forth in his preaching rather than its sterner aspects being kept secret (cf. Eph 1:11).

20:28-31. Having reviewed his own ministry, the apostle bade the elders face their responsibility to carry on his work. They were not only elders, charged with the duty of ruling the house of God, but "overseers," which from the context is not thought of so much from the standpoint of administration as of shepherd oversight and care (note the reference to the congregation as the flock of God). There was no place for tyranny or pride (cf. 1 Pe 5:2-3). Elders must stand ready not only to teach as pastors (shepherds), as in Ephesians 4:11, but also to "be on guard" for the flock in view of the dangers about to be noted.

*A possible rendering of verse 24 is, "I do not regard for myself my life as a thing even worth mentioning" (F. J. Foakes Jackson and Kirsopp Lake, in *BC* 4:260, n.; see also Walter Bauer, *Greek-English Lexicon of the New Testament and Other Early Christian Literature* [Chicago: U. of Chicago, 1957], S. V. *logos*).

But before pointing out these threats, Paul sought to impress on his hearers the preciousness of the flock in the sight of God. The Church of God was purchased "with His own blood." A textual problem calls for attention here. Many manuscripts have "the church of the Lord," but the most important ones have "the church of God." The explanation for the former reading is quite simple. Some scribes revolted at the thought of the blood of God being shed for the church, so took the liberty of changing *God* to *Lord*.

A difficulty remains, namely, the unexpectedness of the wording in saying that God purchased the Church "with His own blood." An easing of the problem can be achieved by the rendering, "with the blood of His own," which remains true to the Greek and at the same time points to the Son as the One who shed His blood. With this change the verse includes a reference to all three persons of the Trinity in their several relationships to the Church. The early chapters of Acts contain allusions to the crucifixion, but here the cross is not viewed as an event involving man's rebellion and guilt but rather in its theological aspect, as a divine provision for human sin, a truth hinted at in 2:23a.

The idea of God's people as a flock is familiar from the Old Testament (Ps 95:7), and the same is true of their description as an assembly (Deu 9:10; cf. Ac 7:38). Something of this background lingers in a passage like Galatians 1:13, "I used to persecute the church of God." Paul could not get over the fact that he had been guilty of moving against the congregation of the God of his fathers, even though he had done it in blind ignorance.

He foresaw the congregation at Ephesus being in danger from two quarters. Some would arise to attack it from without. They are called "wolves," which is natural after designating believers as the flock (cf. Jn 10:12). The apostle's experience in Ephesus, as related in the previous chapter, hints at what persecution may be expected when the Word is fearlessly proclaimed.† The danger from within, however, can best be stated in terms of schism, breaking the church apart in order to have "disciples" who would idolize a human leader and share his quirks of doctrine. This threat was real, as reflected in 2 John and 3 John (cf. Rev 2.4).

Once again (v. 31) the apostle reverted to his own example, this time in terms of being alert to present and potential dangers, citing his ministry of warning believers throughout his stay in the city, which he conducted with such earnestness as to shed "tears."

20:32-35. After committing the elders to the word of God's grace, which

†The figure of the wolf is sometimes used also with reference to the intrusion of heretical teaching, as in Ignatius *Phila.* 2.2.

was doubtless customary when parting from the saints (14:23, 26; 15:40), the apostle returned to the subject of his own example during his ministry at Ephesus (vv. 33-35).

As there is a correspondence between this address and the upper room discourse of Jesus, so likewise there is a certain similarity between this committal and the great prayer of our Lord, basically a prayer for the disciples, which followed his discourse (Jn 17). The grace which was needed throughout the pilgrim journey and even beyond (1 Pe 1:13) was to be regarded as mediated through the Word.

Some commentators would refer the phrase, "which is able to build you up," to God, in which case *who* should replace "which." But the Greek construction will not permit this. To "build up" the people of God is a primary function of the Word and of the ministry of the Word. Paul is very fond of using the term *edification* (seven times in the Corinthian letters alone).

"Inheritance" is an Old Testament concept. Israel had inherited Canaan as the land promised to the fathers; but above and beyond this, the God of the fathers was Israel's inheritance (Ps 16:5). The Christian's inheritance is a leading theme of Paul's letter to the Ephesians (1:14, 18; 5:5). Grace is the basis for it, and the Word of God communicates the promise of it to the saints who await it and have been set apart ("sanctified") for this glorious future.

The words spoken here would seem to be entirely fitting as a close for the discourse. It is somewhat surprising to find Paul continuing, and on a more distinctly mundane level. But it is rather characteristic of him. Compare, for example, his counsel to the Corinthians about the contribution they had agreed to raise (1 Co 16:1-4), coming immediately after his lofty words of exhortation at the close of the resurrection chapter (1 Co 15:58). Form must not stand in the way of fulfilling practical needs. So it is here. He wanted the elders to be hard-working men of integrity and could think of no better way to impress his desire upon them than to cite his own disinterested labor in their midst.

His words about coveting no man's money or possessions recall the testimony of Samuel as he recounted his public service for Israel (1 Sa 12:3). Instead of seeking or desiring the goods of another, Paul was content to work with his hands to support himself and those who labored in the Gospel with him. Later, in writing Ephesians, he touched on this again. "Let him who steals [and what is stealing but putting into action covetous thoughts?] steal no longer; but rather let him labor, performing with his own hands what is good, in order that he may have *something* to share with him who has need" (Eph 4:28). B. F. Westcott comments as follows on this passage:

317

Our faith constrains us to serve one another. Stealing is the typical form of using the labour of another to supply our wishes, while it is our duty to make our own labour minister to the needs of others. The inspiration of labour is not personal gain but fulness of service.[9]

In support of his teaching and his practice, the apostle proceeded to quote a saying attributed to Jesus, "It is more blessed to give than to receive." Although the saying is not to be found anywhere in our gospels, it evidently came down through the medium of oral tradition. The use of it here suggests that the sayings of our Lord which do appear in our gospels and yet fail to be expressed in Acts or the epistles were nevertheless known, and many of them were used in the teaching of converts.[10] The saying before us gives insight into the character of God and goes far toward explaining the Gospel.

Verses 36-38. Luke describes the painful parting between Paul and the Ephesian elders, made all the more difficult by the prospect that they would probably never see each other again.

> **20:36** And when he had said these things, he knelt down and prayed with them all.
>
> **37** And they *began* to weep aloud and embraced Paul, and repeatedly kissed him,
>
> **38** grieving especially over the word which he had spoken, that they should see his face no more. And they were accompanying him to the ship.

20:36-38. There is nothing like prayer to bring hearts together in the high emotion of brotherly love. That love for Paul which the elders felt deep down but was ordinarily restrained now broke all barriers. Grown men embraced and kissed him, revealing the intensity of their devotion to this stalwart servant of Christ, their gratitude for his unselfish manner of life in their midst, and their sorrow that he would so soon be whisked out of their sight, not to be seen by them again, according to his own forecast. It was a moving scene, and did not terminate until Paul was once more on board his ship, ready to sail on but leaving a portion of his heart behind with these dear people. He could not tarry, for he was pastor-at-large to all the Gentile churches. Like his Lord, he must go to Jerusalem, if need be to die, that he might fulfill his course.

Chapter 21, verses 1-6. The story of Paul's trip to Jerusalem continues, concentrating on the visit to Tyre, a Phoenician city which originally was an island community famous for its commerce. David had had friendly relations with Hiram, one of its kings. Nebuchadnezzar and Alexander the Great had each had a part in its destruction, the former destroying the mainland part of Tyre and the latter destroying the island part of the city by building a causeway out from the mainland. Although its heyday was past in Paul's time, Tyre was still a prosperous place.

> **21:1** And when it came about that we had parted from them and had set sail, we ran a straight course to Cos and the next day to Rhodes and from there to Patara;
>
> **2** and having found a ship crossing over to Phoenicia, we went aboard and set sail.
>
> **3** And when we had come in sight of Cyprus, leaving it on the left, we kept sailing to Syria and landed at Tyre; for there the ship was to unload its cargo.
>
> **4** And after looking up the disciples, we stayed there seven days; and they kept telling Paul through the Spirit not to set foot in Jerusalem.
>
> **5** And when it came about that our days were ended, we departed and started on our journey, while they all, with wives and children, escorted us until *we were* out of the city. And after kneeling down on the beach and praying, we said farewell to one another.
>
> **6** Then we went on board the ship, and they returned home again.

21:1-3. Luke provides here a brief account of the itinerary between Miletus and Tyre. The word "parted" does not indicate any final farewells but rather the actual, physical separation incident to going on board (cf. Lk 22:41). Three places are mentioned in verse 1, and it is evident from the map that the distance between them was approximately the same, a normal day's run in each case. It is probable that "Cos" and "Rhodes" refer to the cities rather than to the islands on which they were situated.

Ramsay has an interesting observation regarding the daily progress of the ship.

> The ship evidently stopped every evening. The reason lies in the wind, which in the Aegean during the summer generally blows from the north, beginning at a very early hour in the morning; in the late afternoon it dies away; at sunset there is a dead calm, and thereafter a gentle south wind arises and blows during the night. The start would be made before sunrise; and it would be necessary for all passengers to go on board soon after midnight in order to be ready to sail with the first breath from the north.[11]

Patara was on the coast of Lycia. At this seaport town the travelers found a ship that was due to sail directly to Phoenicia rather than follow the coastline. To change ships, therefore, meant saving time, even though there would be a delay of several days at Tyre for the unloading of cargo. It was evidently a considerably larger vessel than the one they had taken down the coast, and it was able to brave the open sea. Approximately four hundred miles separated Patara from Tyre.‡

‡The Western text includes Myra, another Lycian port, after the mention of Patara, but it is questionable that so great a distance (Rhodes to Myra) could have been covered in one day. The addition, if it is such, may have been made under the influence of 27:5.

319

No stop was made at Cyprus, which was passed on the port side. Luke uses what may be a technical nautical term when he says that those on board "sighted" Cyprus and kept it in view for a long time, the only land to break the monotony of the open water.

There was nothing to report until the ship docked at Tyre and proceeded to discharge its cargo. Tyre was geographically in Phoenicia but administratively was part of "Syria," as was Palestine.

21:4-6. Paul and his group now had "seven days" of waiting, but it was not wasted, for they made a point of "looking up the disciples." As we use it, *looking up* suggests previous acquaintance, which is doubtful in this instance. The word here means "to look for by searching" (cf. Lk 2:16). Both fellowship and hospitality would naturally follow. Tyre had probably been evangelized some years before (Ac 11:19), when the nucleus of the church had been formed.

Luke's account concentrates on one item, the effort of the saints to dissuade Paul from going on to Jerusalem. This message came, we are told, from the Tyrian disciples "through the Spirit." Paul had already been made aware directly and repeatedly of what was in store for him (20:23). It may well be that the disciples at Tyre interpreted the information about the dangers to be faced as sufficient warrant for concluding that Paul should not go. The matter is discussed more fully at verse 11.

The farewell scene on the beach recalls somewhat Paul's departure from Miletus. There was prayer and kneeling down on both occasions (cf. Eph 3:14), but no tears are recorded here. The time of association had been brief (seven days, as compared with up to three years in the case of the Ephesian elders). Yet "they all," including wives and children, turned out for the farewell, a tribute to the hold Paul had established on them in a brief time. The chances are that the group was small and closely knit.

Verses 7-14. With the arrival at Caesarea, Palestinian soil was now under the feet of the sojourners. The principal event at this coastal city was the coming of Agabus the prophet, with his poignant announcement of what would befall the apostle at Jerusalem.

> **21:7** And when we had finished the voyage from Tyre, we arrived at Ptolemais; and after greeting the brethren, we stayed with them for a day.
>
> **8** And on the next day we departed and came to Caesarea; and entering the house of Philip the evangelist, who was one of the seven, we stayed with him.
>
> **9** Now this man had four virgin daughters who were prophetesses.
>
> **10** And as we were staying there for some days, a certain prophet named Agabus came down from Judea.
>
> **11** And coming to us, he took Paul's belt and bound his own feet and hands, and said, "This is what the Holy Spirit says: 'In this way the Jews

at Jerusalem will bind the man who owns this belt and deliver him into the hands of the Gentiles.'"

12 And when we had heard this, we as well as the local residents *began* begging him not to go up to Jerusalem.

13 Then Paul answered, "What are you doing, weeping and breaking my heart? For I am ready not only to be bound, but even to die at Jerusalem for the name of the Lord Jesus."

14 And since he would not be persuaded, we fell silent, remarking, "The will of the Lord be done!"

21:7. The one stop between Tyre and Caesarea was at Ptolemais: In Crusader times it was known as Acre, and today it is called Akka. Here, too, Paul found some brethren. Luke's earlier narrative has not recounted the establishing of a church here any more than at Tyre. The voyage to this spot did not take long, and the visitors tarried for only a day. "Finished" is an uncertain translation in this verse. Field gives several examples in a nautical context and concludes by saying, "In all these cases there is no question of *finishing* the voyage but only of *continuing* or *performing* it."[12]

21:8-9. Although Luke does not say how the party made the trip from Ptolemais to Caesarea, forty miles away, the one-day stop at the former place suggests that the ship continued to Caesarea, which had a good harbor. The overland route in this area was rugged, something to be avoided if possible.

Here at Caesarea Paul was destined to be detained for two years after making several appearances before Roman governors and other officials (23:33–26:32).

Lodging was available at the home of Philip "the evangelist," who is thus distinguished from Philip the apostle. Probably the primary intention is to remind the reader that this man had been active in preaching the Word following his appointment to the Seven (see chap. 8). His four daughters were also gifted by the Spirit. They are called "prophetesses," though apparently they did not prophesy on this occasion, since a visitor by the name of Agabus, prominent in more than one place in the Church (11:28), assumed this role. The daughters were also "virgins." Two or three years before, Paul had given counsel to the Corinthians on both subjects (1 Co 7:25-40; 11:5). The phenomenon of women prophesying was not regarded as strange in the early church (Ac 2:17).

It may be that Agabus, more than any other, was designated to foretell events that were important for the Church in general (cf. 11:27-28). He seems to have moved freely from Jerusalem (indicating the continuance of spiritual gifts in that congregation) to various places where believers congregated.

21:10-11. Agabus came down "from Judea." It is just possible that in this instance "Judea" stands for Jerusalem (cf. Jn 7:3), although admittedly it is often used in distinction from the city.

Dramatically the prophet reached for Paul's "belt" (not made of leather but of folded cloth) and proceeded to bind his own feet and hands with it. This recalls occasional symbolic acts by prophets of old (e.g., Is 20:24; Jer 13:11). When Jesus announced what would befall Him at Jerusalem, He was His own prophet and did not supplement His words by anything acted out (Mt 16:21).

The prophet added an interpretation of his action, indicating it pointed to what the Jews would do to Paul, binding him and turning him over to the Gentiles. A slight difficulty inheres in this statement, since the Jews did not actually bind him nor turn him over to the Romans; but Paul ended up in this condition because of the action of the Jews in seizing him (v. 27). No doubt the wording is influenced by the desire to draw a parallel between Paul and the Lord Jesus (Lk 18:32).

As indicated above, this is a convenient place to discuss the rightness or wrongness of Paul's going up to Jerusalem in the face of explicit indications from the Holy Spirit that to do so would mean a loss of freedom. Several things should be pointed out.

1. The prophecy of Agabus was not accompanied by a prohibition against going. Verse 4 contains a prohibition, without any details, and may have been due to the human transmitters rather than to the Spirit, as already noted.

2. Paul was fully aware of the sort of reception he would have (20:23; cf. Ro 15:31) but did not understand that this information constituted an order to change his plans. To picture Paul as willfully disobedient through this drawn-out experience is a serious charge, for which there is no justification. In fact, 20:23 must be given precedence over 21:4. "Now the Spirit could never instruct men to give advice to one which, if followed, would be an attempt to escape the very pathway of suffering that the Spirit indicated was lying ahead of him."[13] It was due to direct, divine revelation that Paul left Jerusalem at the end of his first visit (22:17-21), and it was by similar revelation that he went up from Antioch to Jerusalem to meet with the apostles in the circumcision controversy (Gal 2:2). There is no indication of human mediation in either case. These two experiences of direct guidance would naturally make him suspicious of a claim of divine guidance by others on his behalf, as in 21:4. There are hazards in acting on secondhand guidance (see 1 Ki 13).

3. Too much hung on this visit to turn back now, with the goal almost in sight. Paul saw the tremendous possibilities in bringing to Jerusalem

the fund given by the Gentile churches as a means of developing a greater sense of understanding and brotherhood between his converts and the mother church. He saw also the necessity of being there in person to answer the damaging rumors that had been floating around concerning his attitude toward the Law and the customs of the Jews. It was imperative that he remove misunderstanding. The unity of the whole Church depended on it.

4. We read of no divine rebuke for Paul's going. Instead, the Lord encouraged him by a vision (after his capture), in which his testimony in Jerusalem was gratefully acknowledged and a like testimony in Rome promised (23:11).

5. We may think that Paul accomplished less as a prisoner than he would have accomplished had he refrained from going to Jerusalem. But who is in position to assert without contradiction that this would have been so? Actually, Paul would not have been able to get the attention of a Jerusalem mob, the Sanhedrin, two Roman governors, king Agrippa, and the court of the emperor if he had remained a free man. His experience demonstrated the truth of the saying, "Man's extremity is God's opportunity."

Those who think that Paul made a mistake in going to Jerusalem despite the warnings of what would happen to him argue that the trip resulted in the assumption of a vow that required his presence and purification in the Temple, and this in turn led to his seizure and later to his imprisonment. The implication is plain—all this could so easily have been avoided if Paul had only been willing to stay away from Jerusalem.

But one should realize that it was not simply Paul's going to Jerusalem that lay at the root of the problem (he had been there several times before), but his readiness to take a vow upon himself. The exegete must come to terms with this; the journey to Jerusalem is merely auxiliary to the real issue. This will require discussion at a later point in the chapter.

21:12-14. The Agabus incident created a deep impression, especially since it came on the heels of the disclosure made at Tyre (v. 4). Apparently even Luke (note the "we") joined in the effort to change the apostle's mind, together with the other traveling companions.

One can only marvel at the strength of Paul's resolve. Some may label it stubbornness; but before doing that, it is well to reflect that he was not doing it in his own strength, but was bound in the Spirit (20:22). He knew full well the love that his friends had for him and their fear of losing his valuable leadership in the church, but he knew that he must follow the course allotted to him in the plan of God. Deeply ingrained in his redeemed nature was a determination not to please men but God (Gal 1:10). In this scene one can almost sense the influence of Another who had had to withstand the vigorous opposition of His followers on the issue of going up to Jerusalem (Mt 16:22). Paul, like his Master, refused to be moved. He stood on "the will of the Lord" so doggedly that his friends came to recognize in his very determination, based on commitment, that the trip to Jerusalem was in the divine plan, unlikely as this seemed to human reason.

Verses 15-16. These verses are devoted to the trip from Caesarea to Jerusalem and the arrangements for lodging on arrival in the holy city.

> **21:15** And after these days we got ready and started on our way up to Jerusalem.
>
> **16** And *some* of the disciples from Caesarea also came with us, taking us to Mnason of Cyprus, a disciple of long standing with whom we were to lodge.

21:15-16. Luke does not give a precise indication of the length of time spent in Caesarea, but it was several days. The reader is left to wonder whether this indicates that Pentecost had already passed or whether it was still in the offing, so that no haste was required for the remainder of the journey. Luke says nothing about Pentecost in this narrative.

"We got ready" suggests substantial preparations. Since the distance to be covered was at least sixty miles and much of it uphill travel, several days would be required if the party went on foot. Ramsay, emphasizing the warmth of the season and the need of freshness on arrival, thinks that the verb used here suggests the use of horses and possibly of vehicles also.[14]

The distance to be covered required a two-day journey at least, which is the basis for the addition in the Western text to the effect that the brethren from Caesarea who went along did so for the purpose of taking the group to Mnason, who lived in a certain village where they were to spend the night. But this is quite clearly an addition to the original text. The chances are that Mnason had a home in Jerusalem. At festival time the city would be crowded and accommodations difficult to find. Rather than put a burden on the church there, the believers at Caesarea made the arrangements involving Mnason. He was a convert to the faith from the early days of the Church (a good reason in itself for holding that his home was in Jerusalem rather than thirty miles away). In view of his being from Cyprus, he may have had association with Barnabas (4:36). Luke could well have sought him out for information about the Church in the days following Pentecost. That Mnason was a Hellenist is almost certain from his willingness to entertain uncircumcised brethren.

B. CONFERENCE WITH LEADERS OF THE JERUSALEM CHURCH—21:17-26

The narrative includes two facets: the meeting between the new arrivals and James, including the elders of the church; then the incident of the vow, which took Paul into the Temple and led to his seizure by the mob.

21:17 And when he had come to Jerusalem, the brethren received us gladly.

18 And now the following day Paul went in with us to James, and all the elders were present.

19 And after he had greeted them, he *began* to relate one by one the things which God had done among the Gentiles through his ministry.

20 And when they heard it they *began* glorifying God; and they said to him, "You see, brother, how many thousands there are among the Jews of those who have believed, and they are all zealous for the Law;

21 and they have been told about you, that you are teaching all the Jews who are among the Gentiles to forsake Moses, telling them not to circumcise their children nor to walk according to the customs.

22 "What, then, is *to be done?* They will certainly hear that you have come.

23 "Therefore do this that we tell you. We have four men who are under a vow;

24 take them and purify yourself along with them, and pay their expenses in order that they may shave their heads; and all will know that there is nothing to the things which they have been told about you, but that you yourself also walk orderly, keeping the Law.

25 "But concerning the Gentiles who have believed, we wrote, having decided that they should abstain from meat sacrificed to idols and from blood and from what is strangled and from fornication."

26 Then Paul took the men, and the next day, purifying himself along with them, went into the temple, giving notice of the completion of the days of purification, until the sacrifice was offered for each one of them.

21:17-19. Their destination reached, the travelers were cordially received by "the brethren" (cf. Ro 15:31). The official meeting with James and the elders took place on the following day. "All" the elders came, indicative of the importance of the meeting. This is the last time Luke indicates his presence ("us") until 27:1. The representatives of the Gentile churches who had come with Paul were included in the conference. Apparently there was no general convocation of the church such as took place when the circumcision issue was discussed (chap. 15). No mention is made of Peter.

Paul's report of his work "among the Gentiles" followed the introductions and greetings. Strangely, nothing is stated here about the fund that had been raised among these same Gentile churches on behalf of the poor at Jerusalem. Undoubtedly the church knew about it in advance because of Paul's earlier visits to the city, when the plan was being formulated. Bruce suggests the possibility that the brethren in Jerusalem may have come to look on this fund as something due them, somewhat on the analogy of the yearly Temple tax brought by Dispersion Jews and paid into the treasury, in which proselytes to Judaism participated along with native sons of Israel.[15]

The difficulty may lie, however, not in the attitude of the Jerusalem church but with Luke himself, since he has avoided mentioning the reason for Paul's entourage from the time it gathered around him at the beginning of the trip to the holy city (20:4). He does allow this aspect of the mission to appear at one point (24:17) but only as Paul's statement. It can be granted, of course, that the item which Luke makes room for in the present narrative, to which he turns immediately, is of greater import than the collection.

21:20-21. The reader cannot help feeling the suddenness of the swing from Paul's emphasis on "Gentiles" to the elders' insistence that "Jews" were their major problem. This does not mean that they intended any depreciation of Paul's work. On the contrary, they were relieved, and began glorifying God for what they had heard. But they could not help bringing into the open what had long bothered them, namely, the misrepresentation of his attitude toward the Mosaic Law and the customs of the nation that had been reported to the mother church from the Dispersion where Paul was laboring.

Who were "the thousands" of believing Jews who had been misinformed? Their identity is made clear from verse 22. They were members of the Jerusalem church, and they were zealots (the very same word that is used for the Zealot party) for the Law. If a general meeting had been called to present Paul to the church, one can imagine that a great deal of animosity would have been shown. We can see the wisdom of James in restricting the meeting to the elders. They could help to clear up the misrepresentation as they later mingled with the rank and file of the church. And one can be sure that there were misrepresentations.

We have no evidence whatsoever that Paul taught "all the Jews" to forsake Moses, to cease circumcising their children, and in general to abandon the customs which distinguished the Jews from other people. These were false reports, but they made the task of the Jerusalem church in reaching the Jews with the Gospel very difficult, since everyone knew that Paul was a Christian Jew. His battle was for Gentile freedom from the Law and had nothing directly to do with the Jew.

While the apostle's stand may have satisfied James and the elders, they felt that actions would speak louder than words and that the fears of the Jerusalem church could be relieved once for all if Paul would be willing to demonstrate his loyalty to the law and "the customs." This latter term

refers to the cultic requirements of the Law in distinction from the moral
and ethical legislation (6:14; cf. Lk 1:9).

21:22-26. A proposal was made to Paul that he identify himself with
four men who were under a (Nazirite) "vow," assuming the expenses incident to the fulfillment of the vow, which included the offering of sacrifices. The hair, probably intended to symbolize the life of the individual,
was shaved off and burned as an offering (Num 6:18). It is probably correct to think of the four men as poor, unable to pay their own expenses.

Josephus calls attention to the action of King Herod Agrippa I when he
began his reign over Judea in A.D. 41. "On entering Jerusalem, he offered
sacrifices of thanksgiving, omitting none of the ritual enjoined by our law.
Accordingly he also arranged for a very considerable number of Nazirites
to be shorn."[16]

Haenchen explains the situation as follows:

> At that time there were four poor Nazirites in the Jerusalem Christian
> community. The period of their Nazirate had already elapsed. The ex-
> pense, which they could not afford, was to be assumed by Paul (the as-
> sumption of such expense counted as a pious deed); he had only to report
> this to the priest concerned and agree upon the time of absolution. Since
> Paul had come from abroad, he was however considered to be levitically
> unclean. He had therefore first to regain levitical purity by a purification
> ritual. This consisted of being sprinkled with the water of atonement on
> the third and seventh day after reporting to the priest. Only when he was
> levitically clean could Paul be present at the absolution ceremony of the
> four, which took place in the 'holy place.'[17]

It was evidently on the seventh day, when Paul reported for the final ceremony, that the riot occurred (cf. v. 27).

The purpose in citing the Jerusalem Council decree (v. 25) is fairly
clear. James and his friends, many of whom had taken part in that meeting, wished to assure Paul that they were not interested now, any more
than when the Council met, in imposing the Law on Gentiles (did they
glance in the direction of his companions as they spoke?).

Two questions emerge here. One is somewhat inconsequential—where
did the money come from to pay the expenses of the Temple ceremony?
It would have been questionable to deduct it from the fund for the poor
saints, although the four men qualified for this description, unless the suggestion were made by the elders. Did Paul's companions come to his help?
Did he have a reserve from his labors in past days? Who can tell?

The other question is far more significant. Did Paul violate his convictions in agreeing to the proposal presented to him?

1. The assumption of a Nazirite vow on his own initiative (18:18) indicates that Paul would have seen no harm or wrong in this situation.

Actually there is no reference to a vow in connection with Paul in verse 24 unless it is implied in the words "purify yourself along with them." Hort remarks,

> Yet the time spoken of appears too short for him to begin and complete a vow in. It is therefore more probable, though not mentioned in Acts, that he was already proposing to offer sacrifice in the Temple on his own account, possibly in connexion with a previous vow, possibly also, I cannot but suspect, in connexion with the Gentile contribution to the Jewish Christians, not mentioned in chapter 21 but clearly mentioned in 24:17.[18]

2. Paul was not ashamed to refer to this incident when defending himself before Felix (24:17-18).
3. We should not lose sight of Paul's purpose in making the trip to Jerusalem. He could not have rested content with handing over the fund that his churches had raised if the real objective of the trip—a unifying of the Jewish and Gentile wings of the church—was not achieved. Evidently he felt it could not be achieved without this demonstration of his personal loyalty to the Law and the customs.
4. Earlier the apostle had declared that he became as a Jew to the Jew (though he was no longer strictly a Jew but a Christian) in order to win Jews, and under the Law (though he was no longer under it himself) in order to win such people to Christ (1 Co 9:20-21). It would help the Christian Jews of Jerusalem to win non-Christian Jews if the suspicions concerning Paul could be laid to rest. This consideration alone should be sufficient to clear him of the charge of compromise.
5. There remains the problem of the animal sacrifices which the Law required in connection with the fulfillment of the Nazirite vow (Num 6:13-17). Was Paul denying the finished work of Christ in paying for these? If so, the four Christian Jews involved were doing the same; and the elders, along with James, were likewise guilty, for they knew what the Temple ceremonies required. Knowing Paul as we do from Galatians and Romans on the theological side and from Acts on the personal side, it is simply beyond credence that he would permit himself to do anything which would suggest a contradiction of the redemption for sin acomplished once and for all at the cross. His action may raise questions for us, but apparently did not for him. There is no suggestion of regret or any stirring of conscience over his participation.

C. ARREST—21:27-40

IT WAS NOT ARREST in a legal sense, at the beginning, but seizure by a mob. What the Jews in the Dispersion had been unable to do because of the protection afforded Paul by the authorities, they were able to accomplish in Jerusalem, where they were in a majority and where the Roman presence was muted by apprehension that the populace might become offended and raise a tumult difficult to control. Tension usually characterized Jewish-Roman relations, especially in Palestine. Behind the crowd in the Temple were thousands more who were like-minded about Paul, and behind them was the Sanhedrin, grieved and alienated because of his defection to Christianity years before (chap. 9). So the apostle was indeed in a perilous position.

It is significant that the Jerusalem church, despite the sympathy which James and the elders felt for Paul, made no protest either to Jewish or Roman authorities on his behalf, so far as the record indicates. Humanly speaking, he had to stand alone.

> **21:27** And when the seven days were almost over, the Jews from Asia, upon seeing him in the temple, began to stir up all the multitude and laid hands on him,
>
> **28** crying out, "Men of Israel, come to our aid! This is the man who preaches to all men everywhere against our people, and the Law, and this place; and besides he has even brought Greeks into the temple and has defiled this holy place."
>
> **29** For they had previously seen Trophimus the Ephesian in the city with him, and they supposed that Paul had brought him into the temple.
>
> **30** And all the city was aroused, and the people rushed together; and taking hold of Paul, they dragged him out of the temple; and immediately the doors were shut.
>
> **31** And while they were seeking to kill him, a report came up to the commander of the *Roman* cohort that all Jerusalem was in confusion.
>
> **32** And at once he took along *some* soldiers and centurions, and ran down to them; and when they saw the commander and the soldiers, they stopped beating Paul.
>
> **33** Then the commander came up and took hold of him, and ordered him to be bound with two chains; and he *began* asking who he was and what he had done.

34 But among the crowd some were shouting one thing *and* some another, and when he could not find out the facts on account of the uproar, he ordered him to be brought into the barracks.

35 And when he got to the stairs, it so happened that he was carried by the soldiers because of the violence of the mob;

36 for the multitude of the people kept following behind, crying out, "Away with him!"

37 And as Paul was about to be brought into the barracks, he said to the commander, "May I say something to you?" And he said, "Do you know Greek?

38 "Then you are not the Egyptian who some time ago stirred up a revolt and led the four thousand men of the Assassins out into the wilderness?"

39 But Paul said, "I am a Jew of Tarsus in Cilicia, a citizen of no insignificant city; and I beg you, allow me to speak to the people."

40 And when he had given him permission, Paul, standing on the stairs, motioned to the people with his hand; and when there was a great hush, he spoke to them in the Hebrew dialect, saying,

21:27-29. Certain Jews from Asia started the trouble. It is quite possible that they had been in the theater at Ephesus during the disturbance instigated against Paul (chap. 19) and had chafed over the fact that he had eluded the mischief that had been planned for him. Having come to Jerusalem, probably for the celebration of Pentecost, they saw their opportunity and seized it. No longer were they a minority. Paul was soon in their grasp.

Even so, they sought help from their fellow Jews, inciting them on the ground that Paul had turned against his own people, the Law, and the Temple (cf. 6:13). As though this were not enough, he deserved death for having "brought Greeks into the temple." Gentiles were permitted in the outer court (Mk 11:17), but a barrier separating this court from the inner Temple areas bore an inscription at intervals, stating that no stranger was allowed within the limit and enclosure of the sanctuary. Any Gentile caught would be put to death. Two museums house this inscription, excavated from the soil of Palestine by archaeologists. According to Josephus, when the Roman general Titus addressed a message to the Jewish rebels in the city during the siege, he made reference to the barrier with its inscription and added, "Did we not permit you to put to death any who passed it, even were he a Roman?"[1] As the Jews construed the matter, this warning did not necessitate a legal trial when one violated it. He could be dealt with on the spot.[2] The mob intended to do just that.

Luke informs us that the assumption about violation of the Temple in this case was false, based merely on observation that one of Paul's companions, whom they had seen with him in the city, was a Gentile. Evidently they recognized Trophimus (20:4) from having seen him in Ephesus. But Paul had not taken him into the Temple.

Later on, in writing Ephesians, the apostle expressed a great truth which the unsaved Jew could not understand or accept—that in Christ the barrier between Jew and Gentile had been broken down (Eph 2:14). Jewry was blind to this reality and persisted in maintaining the exclusivism of Israel's place in the economy of God.

The parallel between Jesus and His servant Paul is obvious as the gospels are studied along with Acts: (1) both made a journey to Jerusalem which proved epochal in their lives; (2) both were apprehended there; (3) both were falsely accused. But whereas our Lord was soon led away to die, Paul was permitted in the providence of God to have several more years of labor, though under the restriction of imprisonment most of the time.

21:30-36. This passage describes the tumult that ensued when Paul was seized. Riot conditions developed as "all the city was aroused" (cf. Mt 21:10). People ran toward the Temple from every quarter, jamming the court of the Gentiles. The mob took hold of Paul and dragged him "out of the temple." This refers to the Temple proper, the elevated inner portion (cf. Ac 3:2-3).

> The men who dragged Paul out of the 'sanctuary' (i.e., the Court of Women) and closed the gates leading to the Court of the Gentiles (Acts 21:30), during the riot leading to his arrest, were obviously members of the Temple police, more precisely the post mounted at the "rampart" during the day-time.[3]

If the outer gates leading to the city had been closed, people would not have been able to enter the area to participate in the riot. The Temple police either were unable to hold off the crowd or made no effort to do so.

The beating of Paul was of course not a judicial process. If he were a guilty man, as declared in the outcry against him, the proper method of punishment was stoning, to be administered outside the city (7:58). But so great was the hatred for Paul that the crowd sought to beat him to death on the spot, willing to violate the sanctity of the Temple court by murder.

Meanwhile, a report of the violence was brought to the commander of the Roman garrison, which was stationed in the castle of Antonia immediately adjacent to the Temple area at the northwest corner. Learning that the city was in "confusion" (cf. 2:6, a nonviolent episode involving the multitudes), the commandant quickly ordered troops to charge down the steps into the court and take control of the situation. The presence of "centurions" suggests a complement of at least 200 men out of a garrison of

1,000. Since he was responsible for order in the city, the commander went in person at the head of the troops.

Fearing retaliation for the beating they were administering to Paul, the crowd desisted, whereupon the apostle was taken into custody and bound with chains (as predicted in v. 11) while the commander tried to learn from the crowd what he had done. But the confusion of many voices was too much, so he ordered the prisoner removed to "the barracks," where the noise of the tumult would not penetrate to disturb his examining Paul directly. The removal proved to be anything but easy, as the crowd, resentful at seeing their prey snatched from their grasp, surged about the soldiers, who finally lifted Paul and carried him up the stairs. Closing in behind the soldiers the crowd pressed hard, crying all the while, "Away with him!"—the cry that the mob had voiced regarding Jesus in the presence of Pilate (Lk 23:18). It was a demand not for removal but for death.

21:37-40. Despite the beating, Paul was still able to speak and sought a word with the commander (Greek *chiliarch*, or military tribune). His name was Claudius Lysias (Ac 23:26). The request was spoken in Greek, which caused the commander to realize that he did not have in custody the Egyptian who had caused the authorities trouble by leading a revolt at the head of four thousand men who took to the desert under his leadership (21:38). Ideas about the Messiah being a second Moses were current in Israel. "The Messianic pretenders mentioned by Josephus evidently saw themselves in the light of this second Moses tradition. They led their followers into the desert, or attempted to divide the waters in the manner of Moses."[4]

In identifying himself for the benefit of the Roman officer Paul was content to say that he was "a Jew of Tarsus in Cilicia, a citizen of no insignificant city.[5] He was content at this point to state his municipal citizenship.

> It is not surprising . . . that there is a certain ambiguity in Paul's references to his personal status as represented in Acts. He thinks of himself first and foremost as a citizen of Tarsus, and only refers to his latent Roman status when it is expedient to do so.[6]

One cannot withhold admiration for the apostle in this situation. There he stood, in chains, bruised and exhausted, half beaten to death, yet anxious to bear a testimony to the milling crowd in the court below. When permission was given to speak, he took his place on the stairs. The whole scene, including the speech that follows, belies the accusation of his detractors at Corinth that his personal presence was unimpressive and his speech contemptible (2 Co 10:10). As he motioned to the crowd with his hand, the hubbub gradually died down until there was "a great hush," quite in contrast to the uproar of a few minutes earlier.

Paul made ready to speak to them "in the Hebrew dialect." It is generally assumed, and probably correctly, that this refers to Aramaic. While it is true that Hebrew had been kept alive and was used by the rabbis and by those who read the Scriptures in the Palestinian synagogues, the composition of Paul's audience was hardly such as to warrant an address in Hebrew. He spoke in the everyday language of the Palestinian Jew.

D. Defense Before the People—22:1-21

The continuity with Acts 21 is evident. Paul endeavored to explain to his countrymen how it was that despite his original opposition to the followers of Jesus he had become one himself. This is the second of three accounts of his conversion in Acts: Luke gives a description of it in chapter 9, which seems to depend considerably on Paul's as recorded here (Luke may have been in the crowd as he spoke); then the apostle went over the same ground but with different emphases when speaking before Agrippa (chap. 26). The presence of three accounts of the same event signals the importance to be attached to the apostle's conversion, whereas the varying emphasis in the three narratives justifies what might otherwise be regarded as unnecessary repetition.

Aside from the introductory statements (vv. 1-2) the speech falls naturally into three segments: Paul's preconversion life in Judaism (vv. 3-5); his conversion by divine intervention (vv. 6-16); and his commission to serve Christ (vv. 17-21).

Verses 1-5. In this initial phase of his defense, Paul was careful to make it clear that his Jewish background was beyond criticism—in fact, outstanding. Any shift could not be laid to defection but only to divine intervention in his life.

> 22:1 "Brethren and fathers, hear my defense which I now *offer* to you."
> 2 And when they heard that he was addressing them in the Hebrew dialect, they became even more quiet; and he said,
> 3 "I am a Jew, born in Tarsus of Cilicia, but brought up in this city, educated under Gamaliel, strictly according to the law of our fathers, being zealous for God, just as you all are today.
> 4 "And I persecuted this Way to the death, binding and putting both men and women into prisons,
> 5 as also the high priest and all the Council of the elders can testify. From them I also received letters to the brethren, and started off for Damascus in order to bring even those who were there to Jerusalem as prisoners to be punished.

22:1-2. Paul prepared his hearers for the nature of his message by call-

333

ing it a "defense" (*apologia*). This yields our word *apology*, which is commonly used in the sense of excuse, but is not suitable here, where the technical force of *defense* is required (cf. 25:16; 1 Co 9:3; Phil 1:7, 16; 2 Ti 4:16; 1 Pe 3:15). The verb is used several times in Acts 24-26.

Paul was far from apologetic in his speech. Neither was he retaliatory, despite the roughing up he had had. By addressing his audience as "brethren and fathers," he emphasized that he had much in common with them. His choice of Aramaic underscored the desire to establish rapport. Known as a Jew of the Dispersion (v. 3), he could have been expected to speak in Greek. The crowd was immediately impressed and became the "more quiet," permitting him to be heard despite the tenseness of the situation.

22:3-5. Paul began by emphasizing his Jewish antecedents. He was not a proselyte to Judaism, but a Jew by birth (cf. Phil 3:5). Although his birth had occurred in Tarsus (cf. 21:39), making him technically a Dispersion Jew, yet he was brought up in Jerusalem and was therefore at home in the life and customs and religion of his nation. Moreover, he had the advantage of education under the famous rabbi Gamaliel (cf. 5:34).

"Strictly" suggests a certain severity and narrowness of viewpoint which is not necessarily conveyed by the original. As a matter of fact, Gamaliel belonged to the school of Hillel, which was the more liberal of the two predominant schools of thought (the other being that of Shammai). The idea here is rather that of care, of exactness, and of thoroughness in the training.

In describing his hearers along with himself as "zealous for God," Paul expressed a generous verdict identical to that which he had recently stated in his letter to the Romans (Ro 10:2). His own zeal as a young man had been not only for God and for the Law but also for the traditions of the fathers (Gal 1:14).

An important book by W. C. van Unnik[7] shows that the three verbs used in verse 3—"born," "brought up," and "educated"—are found frequently in ancient writers and in this same order. The second indicates home rearing. It appears, then, that Paul was brought to Jerusalem at an early age, years before he took his rabbinical training under Gamaliel, and this seems to be affirmed also in 26:4.

There has been considerable hesitancy on the part of some New Testament scholars to accept Luke's statement about Paul's training under Gamaliel. Among the objections brought forward, three will be noted here.

First, if Paul had studied under Gamaliel, is it not strange that he should turn out to be such a violent persecutor of the Church, when Gamaliel was so mild in his attitude? However, experience shows that pupils do not always agree with their teachers. Paul saw more clearly than Gamaliel the danger to Judaism presented by the Christian faith (Phil 3:6).

Second, some have expressed doubt that Paul could have written so negatively about the Law if he had studied under this man. But what the apostle was concerned to correct was the misunderstanding that the Law was intended to be a means of justification of the sinner. That he had a high regard for the Law is apparent (Ro 7:12; 8:4; Gal 3:24).

Third, it has been objected that Paul's use of the Old Testament shows he was at home in the narrative and edificatory tradition of Judaism but not in the legislative tradition, which is the heart of the Talmud. Yet this allegation seems to be contradicted by Paul's evident awareness and use of Hillel's principle of analogy, as in Romans 4:1-8.[8] It is significant that Joseph Klausner, with his unquestioned knowledge of Jewish tradition and scholarship, did not question Paul's study under Gamaliel.[9] For Luke to report Paul saying in public, in the city of Jerusalem, that this was his training without being sure of the facts would indeed be a blunder that would put his credibility in serious jeopardy with his readers.

The speaker insisted that he showed his zeal for God by persecuting the Church, but since he was speaking to unbelievers he was careful to refer to it as "this Way" (cf. 9:2), which would sufficiently identify the movement and at the same time indicate his former abhorrence of it. His relentlessness was revealed by including "women" in his persecution, with "death" as the penalty for conviction of belonging to this heresy and refusing to give it up. Regarding the ability of the "high priest" and the "Council" to substantiate all this, Rackham is probably correct in supposing that, in view of the more than two decades which had elapsed since that period in Paul's life, he "is really appealing to their records."[10] They were bound to have had familiarity with his activities, since from them he received letters of introduction and authorization to brethren in the Damascus area as he started out on this crusade to foreign cities. The purpose of alluding to the persecuting zeal was to demonstrate that in those early days he had had no personal interest in the Way, much less identification with it.

It may not be out of order to raise a question here. Why was it necessary to indulge in so many autobiographical details if Paul was such a well-known figure in Palestinian Judaism? For this reason, that more than twenty years had gone by since he had waged war against the Church. A new generation had arisen that knew not Saul of Tarsus. Besides, many in the audience were from areas in the Dispersion and would not have been likely to know of his background. Certainly the Sanhedrin would have been anxious to do all in their power to efface his memory.

Verses 6-16. This passage describes Saul's confrontation with the heavenly Lord resulting in a complete revolution in his life and activity.

> **22:6** "And it came about that as I was on my way, approaching Damascus about noontime, a very bright light suddenly flashed from heaven all around me,
>
> 7 and I fell to the ground and heard a voice saying to me, 'Saul, Saul, why are you persecuting Me?'
>
> 8 "And I answered, 'Who art Thou, Lord?' And He said to me, 'I am Jesus the Nazarene, whom you are persecuting.'
>
> 9 "And those who were with me beheld the light, to be sure, but did not understand the voice of the One who was speaking to me.
>
> 10 "And I said, 'What shall I do, Lord?' And the Lord said to me, 'Arise and go on into Damascus; and there you will be told of all that has been appointed for you to do.'
>
> 11 "But since I could not see because of the brightness of that light, I was led by the hand by those who were with me, and came into Damascus.
>
> 12 "And a certain Ananias, a man who was devout by the standard of the Law, *and* well spoken of by all the Jews who lived there,
>
> 13 came to me, and standing near said to me, 'Brother Saul, receive your sight!' And at that very time I looked up at him.
>
> 14 "And he said, 'The God of our fathers has appointed you to know His will, and to see the Righteous One, and to hear an utterance from His mouth.
>
> 15 'For you will be a witness for Him to all men of what you have seen and heard.
>
> 16 'And now why do you delay? Arise, and be baptized, and wash away your sins, calling on His name.'

22:6-16. By delving into his background in Judaism, the groundwork had been laid to show that it was only supernatural intrusion into his life that had effected Paul's change of attitude and set him on an entirely different course. The intervention came when he had almost reached his destination, each mile firing his zeal as he pictured to himself how he would go about stamping out the new faith in this Syrian community. The hour was important too, for at "noontime" the sun is blazing in its intensity. It was just then that the brilliant light flashed "from heaven" (cf. 26:13). It was more than an atmospheric phenomenon, for it recalled the various self-disclosures of God in Old Testament days through the glory-light (e.g., Eze 1:4, 28).

For verses 8-9, see the discussion on 9:4-5. It should be noted in passing that Paul called Jesus "the Nazarene," another touch designed to establish rapport with the audience, since this was the usual Jewish way of identification (Jn 18:5; Ac 6:14). Jewish believers in Jesus were known as the sect of the Nazarenes (24:5).

A casual reading of verse 10 might easily suggest to the reader that Paul's question and the risen Lord's answer had to do with the events of the next few days, but this is almost certainly wrong. The information Paul sought and which the Lord promised to provide had to do with his future work[11] (cf. v. 15).

Blinded by the light, Paul had to be led into the city, where he was sought out and ministered to by a certain Ananias. The description of this man as "devout" in terms of "the law" and as enjoying a good reputation in the eyes of "the Jews" is another deliberate attempt to underscore the entire incident as "kosher." The blindness testified to the reality of the confrontation with the Lord whom he had been unconsciously persecuting. The sending of Ananias testified to the divine purpose that Paul, now humbled by his experience, was to have the privilege of being a "witness" of what he had "seen and heard" during his confrontation. This put Paul on a par with the original apostles and actually gave him an experience they had not enjoyed (except by anticipation at the transfiguration), namely, seeing the Lord in His resplendent glory. Note that Paul avoided describing the sphere of his witnessing as twofold, to Jews and Gentiles, deferring reference to Gentiles as long as possible lest he be interrupted before completing his story (cf. v. 21).

With sight restored, Paul "looked up" at Ananias, the first follower of the Nazarene he viewed with respect and admiration. He was now a changed man.

The message through Ananias was phrased in such a way as to underscore the fact that the Damascus road experience had been regular, in the sense that "the God of our fathers" had intervened that Paul might "know" the divine "will" (he thought he had been doing God service all the time he had been persecuting). It was a part of God's purpose that Paul should see the "Righteous One," an evident reference to Jesus the Christ (cf. 3:14; 7:52).

It is possible that verse 14 should not be ended with a period, since the first word of verse 15 can be rendered "that" as well as "for," and in this instance may be intended to introduce the content of the "utterance from His mouth," namely, that Paul should be a witness for Him to all men.

As the servant of the Lord (Ro 1:1), Paul had to learn to obey the Lord's will, which called for his baptism as an initial step. Although the Jewish leaders for the most port spurned the baptism which John had preached because it demanded repentance and confession of sins, the masses flocked to his baptism. It is possible that some in Paul's audience had submitted to John's rite. But Paul's baptism was not identical, for he was to call on the "name" of the Lord Jesus. Yet even this did not cause his audience to break its silence, though the tension must have been mounting in some of his hearers.

Verses 17-21. This statement of Paul's commission has a somewhat later context than the conversion, placed in the setting of Jerusalem and the Temple, the very area where the speech was being given.

> **22:17** "And it came about that when I returned to Jerusalem and was praying in the temple, I fell into a trance,
>
> **18** and I saw Him saying to me, 'Make haste, and get out of Jerusalem quickly, because they will not accept your testimony about Me.'
>
> **19** "And I said, 'Lord, they themselves understand that in one synagogue after another I used to imprison and beat those who believed in Thee.
>
> **20** 'And when the blood of Thy witness Stephen was being shed, I also was standing by approving, and watching out for the cloaks of those who were slaying him.'
>
> **21** "And He said to me, 'Go! For I will send you far away to the Gentiles.' "

22:17-21. The apostle needed a little more time, for he had another point to establish. He wanted to make clear that his distinctive work among the Gentiles was definitely in the plan of God and had been authorized by Him. After his conversion he came back to "Jerusalem," the holy city of his people, and entered the "temple," the place where Israel's God was worshipped (cf. 3:1), the place which Paul had wrongfully been accused of defiling. He had not broken with his nation. There in the Temple he had fallen into a "trance" and in that state realized that the risen Lord was communicating a command that he leave Jerusalem at once because of the unwillingness of the people to accept his "testimony" about Him (cf. 9:28-29). The Saviour had come to His own and had been rejected (Mt 23:37; Jn 1:11). His servant should not expect any better treatment (Jn 15:20).

Yet Paul would have his hearers realize that even then, despite the command to leave, he was reluctant to go, so confident was he that his own people would be impressed by the fact that the leading persecutor had become an advocate for the cause he had once opposed so bitterly. He had approved the death of Stephen and had vowed inwardly to bring about the death of many more. But even as he spoke these words to the throng he had to face the reality that Jerusalem had not changed. His former zeal for Judaism against the followers of Jesus was no asset to him now, for his countrymen regarded him as a renegade.

Paul hoped to make it clear that his life's work among the Gentiles was not of his choosing. He had returned to Jerusalem after his conversion intent on remaining there, only to hear the Lord commanding him to "go" where he was being sent—"to the Gentiles." It is likely that Paul intended to go on and show that in responding to this command he was not obliged to spend all his energies on the Gentile mission, and in fact had used every opportunity to witness first to his own people. However, the word "Gentiles" was the last he could utter, for it was the signal for an outbreak of protest from hundreds and thousands of throats. Here ended a brave witness given under most difficult circumstances.

Why was the word *Gentiles* so offensive to the crowd? Was it an expression of their disdain for those they regarded as their inferiors? Hardly, for the synagogues throughout the Dispersion were doing their best to make converts to Judaism among these very people. No, they were protesting against Paul, and in some measure against the Jerusalem church for supporting him in his stand, as he sought to convert Gentiles to the Lord Jesus without imposing circumcision and the keeping of the Law. This was regarded as treason against the faith of the fathers. The unique position of the Jew was being undermined. Of course, the word *Gentiles* had been a key to the disturbance which had occasioned the speech, and it now brought to the minds of his hearers the assertion that he had brought Gentiles into the Temple. This was sufficient cue to stir up the crowd all over again.

E. The Aftermath—Paul and the Commander—22:22-30

The apostle had not sought to clear himself from charges. Like Stephen he had used his defense as an opportunity for witness. The result was a renewal of the demand for his life and a renewed intervention of the Romans to save it. Yet the Romans were prepared to use torture to extract the truth from the prisoner, an ordeal from which Paul was spared by declaring his Roman citizenship.

22:22 And they listened to him up to this statement, and *then* they raised their voices and said, "Away with such a fellow from the earth, for he should not be allowed to live!"

23 And as they were crying out and throwing off their cloaks and tossing dust into the air,

24 the commander ordered him to be brought into the barracks, stating that he should be examined by scourging so that he might find out the reason why they were shouting against him that way.

25 And when they had stretched him out with thongs, Paul said to the centurion who was standing by, "Is it lawful for you to scourge a man who is a Roman and uncondemned?"

26 And when the centurion heard *this*, he went to the commander and told him, saying, "What are you about to do? For this man is a Roman."

27 And the commander came and said to him, "Tell me, are you a Roman?" And he said, "Yes."

28 And the commander answered, "I acquired this citizenship with a large sum of money." And Paul said, "But I was actually born *a citizen*."

29 Therefore those who were about to examine him immediately let go of him; and the commander also was afraid when he found out that he was a Roman, and because he had put him in chains.

30 But on the next day, wishing to know for certain why he had been accused by the Jews, he released him and ordered the chief priests and all the Council to assemble, and brought Paul down and set him before them.

22:22-23. The word *Gentiles*, as we have seen, was all that was needed to spark another outbreak of rioting, with insistent demands that Paul's life be forfeited. The crowd showed its contempt by referring to him as "this fellow" (cf. Mt 26:61 RSV). It was a scene of Oriental excitement marked by outcries, the throwing off of garments, and the casting of dust into the air. Instead of being palliated by the address, the people were outraged.

22:24. This was enough to alarm the commander of the Roman garrison, who must have been standing nearby (cf. 21:39-40). The Romans had learned by experience how volatile a Jewish crowd could be, and the commander knew he would be held responsible if trouble on a large scale developed from this incident. Unable to understand Aramaic, he was no further along in getting at the reason for the uproar than he had been before Paul's speech, so he decided to resort to "scourging" the prisoner as soon as they had him safely inside the barracks again. He hoped that this procedure would compel Paul to reveal the whole story that so far was an enigma.

22:25-26. A "centurion" was in charge of the scourging, which was to be carried out by a band of soldiers. They had taken Paul and had "stretched him out with thongs" before he objected. The thongs were used to tie the prisoner in a fixed position (presumably to a post which was somewhat inclined) so that the back, stripped of all clothing, would be in position to receive the lash. This was administered not by a long whip, such as a slave driver might use, but by a fairly short but deadly instrument consisting of a stout handle to which was attached a leather thong or several of them, knotted or weighted with bits of bone or metal which could cut deeply into the flesh. Paul was faced with a frightful ordeal which might incapacitate him for a long time. It was far worse than the Jewish floggings in the synagogue which he had endured and worse than the beating with wooden rods at the hands of the Roman lictors in Philippi. This scourging was the same kind of punishment Jesus had received at the close of His trial (Mt 27:26), rendering Him unable to carry the cross all the way to Golgotha.

Paul had a recourse unavailable to his Master, for he was a Roman citizen and knew that such scourging was illegal for a person who had this standing. So he simply raised the question as to whether the proceedings were "lawful" in the case of one who was "a Roman" and "uncondemned." He had not objected when he was bound, for this had been predicted (Ac 20:23; 21:11). But there had been nothing to indicate that he must submit to this further indignity. His question effectively halted preparations for the scourging while the centurion made haste to report to his superior. It was a serious offense to treat a Roman citizen in this fashion.

22:27-28. The commander came in person to investigate this new turn of events, quizzing the prisoner to get at the truth regarding his status. When Paul affirmed his Roman citizenship, the commander volunteered the information that in his own case it had cost him a large sum of money to acquire it. To this Paul rejoined that he had this rank by reason of birth, indicating by this that his parents had been citizens before him.

It is apparent that Paul had a double citizenship, for he had already told the commander that he had citizenship with reference to Tarsus (21:39), so the question now raised must apply simply to Roman citizenship. Such double citizenship was not possible at every period. Sherwin-White comments, "Not until the imperial period did it become normal for a man of peregrine [alien] origin to make a real use of his citizen status without surrendering his connexion with his original home."[12]

On the great sum paid by Claudius Lysias the same writer notes, "It was the bribe given to the intermediaries in the imperial secretariat or the provincial administration who put his name on the list of candidates for enfranchisement."[13] How Paul's parents had gained this coveted rank is not known. It may have been on the basis of some service rendered to the state.

In passing, one should observe in this connection the name of the commander. As Sherwin-White notes, "It is not in dispute that this man secured the citizenship from the emperor Claudius."[14] Since Claudius had reigned only a few years before, this fits in well with the Lucan narrative (Nero, the Caesar to whom Paul appealed, succeeded Claudius).

Notable is the fact that Paul's statement about his Roman citizenship went unchallenged. The reason is simple. It would cost a man his life if he advanced the claim without having the rank. If the census archives failed him, one who claimed Roman citizenship by birth "could produce a copy of the original *professio* or registration of his birth recording his Roman status and made before a magistrate."[15] Some scholars have conjectured that Paul, because of being away from home most of the time, may have carried a certificate with him for just such emergencies as he had now encountered. At Jerusalem he had relatives who could vouch for him on the citizenship issue (23:16).

Worth observing is the readiness of the commander to chat with Paul about this matter of citizenship, hardly concealing a bit of envy for the man who had come into this high standing by birth. The sharp eye of Sherwin-White has discerned how neatly this sort of a situation fit the era of Claudius, when a man might come up through the ranks and acquire citizenship at quite a price. It was not long until this status could be secured with much less difficulty. "The historical atmosphere of the Lysias incident is exactly right for the time of Claudius."[16]

22:29. Without further questioning Paul was untied and removed from the place of torture. The fear of the centurion and the commander is understandable (cf. 16:38). A man could lose his position and be severely punished for subjecting a Roman citizen to scourging. Paul was detained, but not again was he made to suffer indignities. "Luke shows triumphantly how much better it is for Paul to be a Roman among the heathen than to be a Jew among his fellow-countrymen."[17]

22:30. Still baffled by the incident in the Temple court, the commander determined to bring Paul before the Sanhedrin the following day, issuing orders for it to convene, a highly unusual procedure on his part. In his frustration he could think of no better way to solve this puzzling case. The apostle was "released" from confinement for this occasion but remained a prisoner.

It seems that the commander made no further effort to extract information from Paul directly, unless there is a hint in the words "wishing to know for certain" that Paul had told him some things which he hoped would now be confirmed or denied by means of the Council session. Although the members of the Sanhedrin had not been in the mob, they were presumably better informed about the church and about Paul's activities than the people in general.

A difficulty naturally arises here, already alluded to. Was the commander in a position to *order* the Council to meet? Probably not under normal circumstances; but if Paul was suspected of conduct which threatened the security of the country, the Roman official presumably would not hesitate to act. Also, as Hanson points out, this was not a regular meeting of the Council, so protocol was not binding.[18]

F. Defense Before the Sanhedrin—23:1-11

One can only speculate whether Luke was present on this occasion. The likelihood of such a thing is admittedly remote, but with the discovery that the prisoner was a Roman, the commander may have been ready, even eager, to grant Paul the privilege of an attending physician, especially after the mauling in the Temple court. The scene at the Council meeting was of such a nature that one could not expect Luke's presence to be indicated.

No one can read this section without being impressed with Paul's resourcefulness in a tight situation. Some scholars find here a resort to such outright expediency as to reflect on the apostle's character. But they must concede that this very reflection, if allowed, means that the narrator has not held back something uncomplimentary, which supports his credibility as a historian. We may rest assured that Luke did not include this passage merely to underscore the cleverness of the man whose career he had dedicated himself to delineate. Rather, he was concerned to show how much Pharisaism at its best had in common with Christian faith and how readily it could be a stepping-stone to that faith, or at the very least that "the bridges between Jews and Christians have not been broken."[19]

23:1 And Paul, looking intently at the Council, said, "Brethren, I have lived my life with a perfectly good conscience before God up to this day."

2 And the high priest Ananias commanded those standing beside him to strike him on the mouth.

3 Then Paul said to him, "God is going to strike you, you whitewashed wall! And do you sit to try me according to the Law, and in violation of the Law order me to be struck?"

4 But the bystanders said, "Do you revile God's high priest?"

5 And Paul said, "I was not aware, brethren, that he was high priest; for it is written, 'YOU SHALL NOT SPEAK EVIL OF A RULER OF YOUR PEOPLE.'"

6 But perceiving that one part were Sadducees and the other Pharisees, Paul *began* crying out in the Council, "Brethren, I am a Pharisee, a son of Pharisees; I am on trial for the hope and resurrection of the dead!"

7 And as he said this, there arose a dissension between the Pharisees and Sadducees; and the assembly was divided.

8 For the Sadducees say that there is no resurrection, nor an angel, nor a spirit; but the Pharisees acknowledge them all.

9 And there arose a great uproar; and some of the scribes of the Pharisaic party stood up and *began* to argue heatedly, saying, "We find nothing wrong with this man; suppose a spirit or an angel has spoken to him?"

10 And as a great dissension was developing, the commander was afraid Paul would be torn to pieces by them and ordered the troops to go down and take him away from them by force, and bring him into the barracks.

11 But on the night *immediately* following, the Lord stood at his side and said, "Take courage; for as you have solemnly witnessed to My cause at Jerusalem, so you must witness at Rome also."

23:1-5. A major difficulty must be faced here. Why is there no reference

343

to the alleged offense of the prisoner that led to the uproar in the Temple area (21:38), especially since the purpose of this session was to supply information on this very point for the commander (22:30)?

In all probability Paul was leading up to the Temple incident by his opening remarks, but was interrupted by the summary order of the high priest (v. 2). What favors this interpretation is the apostle's claim of a "good conscience." He was not aware of wrongdoing in this matter any more than in others. C. A. Pierce suggests that the word "good" in this passage means "free from the guilt of profanation of the Jewish Religion."[20] So when Paul consented to take part in the purification rites he saw no conflict with his Christian convictions; otherwise he could not claim a good conscience. It is one of the most remarkable things about this man that he could on various occasions affirm in the most positive way his sense of freedom from conscious transgression (1 Co 4:4; Phil 3:6; 2 Ti 1:3). The Philippian passage would seem to cover his part in the death of Stephen; this is confirmed by Timothy 1:13.

Paul's reference to conscience comes in connection with his statement, "I have lived my life." Since "lived" is not the usual word but one which could mean "lived as a citizen," some would limit the thought to the apostle's public life,[21] but "before God" makes this conclusion somewhat doubtful. Prior to Paul's time the word had been used in the sense of *walk*[22] (i.e., live), with no necessary reference to the state or to public life. Here, however, there may be a glance at Paul's relationship to the Jewish nation (cf. his opening word, "Brethren").

No sooner had Paul made his opening statement than he was cut short by a crisp order, delivered by the high priest to those near the prisoner, to strike him "on the mouth" (cf. Jn 18:21-22). This was an obvious indication that the apostle had offended him by what he had said. Ananias the high priest held office for a decade or more and wielded considerable influence not merely by reason of his office but because of his great wealth. He was not averse to the use of violence when it served his purpose, so his command regarding Paul was in character.

Stung by the injustice of what Ananias had ordered, the apostle responded at once with the warning, "God is going to strike you." He may have had no particular event in mind, but some feel that he was prophesying the death of the high priest, which proved to be a violent one at the hands of Jewish rebels soon after the war with Rome began (Ananias was pro-Roman in his sympathies). The apostle's indignation can be measured by the epithet he hurled at the high priest—"You whitewashed wall!" The language recalls somewhat the words of Jesus addressed to the scribes and Pharisees (Mt 23:27). This was supposed to be a hearing "according to the law," but the order given was contrary to the Law. Leviticus 19:15

344

may have been in Paul's mind. There was a saying which ran, "He who strikes the cheek of an Israelite strikes, as it were, the glory of God."

Over against the prophecy that God would strike Ananias, the by-standers posed a question which was also a complaint, "Do you revile God's high priest?" The mention of God was deliberate, as though to contest the idea that God would move against His own servant.

This cooled off the aroused apostle, who apparently shifted abruptly to an apology for his sharp thrust, citing Scripture (Ex 22:28) which forbade speaking evil of the ruler of the nation. Though Paul had no respect for Ananias the man (and there were many who agreed with him), he was bound to respect his office. In the same way David had refused to touch Saul the king, though he had ample ground for finding fault with him as a man (1 Sa 24:6; 26:9-11). Since Israel no longer had a king in Paul's day, the high priest was the ruler of the people.

A difficulty remains, lodged in Paul's statement that he was not aware that the one who had given the order was the high priest. Was it poor eyesight that accounts for his failure to identify Ananias? This is unlikely in view of the wording at the opening of the chapter—"looking intently." It is tempting to take Paul's language as ironical (i.e., he could not bring himself to recognize such a man as high priest), but this is rendered doubt-ful by the past tense, "I *was* not aware." Likewise, it is awkward to find the word "brethren" put forward here, singularly out of place if the apostle was being caustic. Furthermore, can we really suppose that he would create prejudice needlessly and to his own detriment in such a delicate situation?

Perhaps the best that can be done is to fall back on the fact that Paul did not know Ananias personally. He had not had contact with the San-hedrin for more than twenty years. The high priest may not have been wearing his official robes on this occasion, since he was not ministering in the Temple and, in view of the fact that the meeting had been called by Claudius Lysias, may not have been presiding.

23:6-8. It may seem strange that Paul broke off his defense, which was scarcely begun, and sought rather to divide the Council by raising the issue of resurrection. But he evidently sensed that the interference of the high priest meant that no ordered defense would be tolerated and would be useless anyway, under the circumstances.

As to the propriety of driving a wedge between the Pharisees and the Sadducees, it must be realized that if this session should provide agree-ment by the Council that Paul was guilty of a religious offense, the com-mander might well conclude that his own responsibility was to turn him over to this body for formal trial. Paul's life and the possibility of any future ministry were at stake.

But was the apostle justified in crying, "I am a Pharisee?" There would be no ground for objection had he said, "I *was* a Pharisee" (cf. Phil 3:5). However, on this occasion he was not saying that he was a Pharisee and therefore no longer a Christian, but that on the issues which divide Pharisees from Sadducees he stood firmly with the former group. Pharisaic theology, now crowned by his discovery of the Messiah in the person of Jesus, was still his possession (cf. 15:5). This was his spiritual heritage. "A son of Pharisees" is probably intended to look beyond immediate parentage to a line of Pharisaic ancestors.

Now comes the bombshell: "I am on trial for the hope and resurrection of the dead!" Was this equivalent to the hope of resurrection such as Pharisaism maintained (cf. Jn 11:24)? It might appear so from Paul's reference to this very outcry when his case was being heard by Felix (24:21). One could point also to 24:15, and possibly to 26:6-8. But the latter passage seems to have latent in it the idea of the salvation to be brought to Israel by the Messiah. And certainly 28:20, in view of what follows in 28:23, does not permit us to think merely of the event of resurrection as being Israel's hope. The hope centered rather in the Messianic salvation, which will indeed be crowned by resurrection, of which the resurrection of Jesus of Nazareth is the guarantee. So Paul was saying that the real issue in his case was not an alleged infringement of the sanctity of the Temple but rather the theological issue of the nature of the hope of his people.

The announcement had the desired effect. Instantly the rift between the two parties became evident, the Pharisees rallying to Paul's support and the Sadducees opposing. It was on the same issue that the Sadducees had sought to trap Jesus (Mt 22:23-33).

Because the word "all" at the end of verse 8 is literally "both," some interpreters conclude that "resurrection" is one item, and that the other is "angel" or "spirit," the latter two not being sharply distinguished. But the Greek word for *both* is sometimes used in the sense of "all" (see comment on 19:16). If "angel" and "spirit" are differentiated, what is the meaning of "spirit"? "Evil spirit," or "demon," is a possibility (cf. Mt 8:16), but this sense will not fit in verse 9 of our passage; so it is best to take "spirit" in the sense of disembodied human spirit, as in Hebrews 12:23.

23:9-10. "We find nothing wrong with this man." The Pharisees were ready to exonerate Paul on the spot, granting the possibility that he had been spoken to by an angel or spirit on this matter of resurrection. Perhaps the reference was to the vision that Paul had mentioned in addressing the crowd in the Temple court (22:17-18). The tenor of the Pharisees' plea had much in common with the point made by one of their most prominent members, Gamaliel, that the danger of opposing God must be avoided at all costs (5:39). Proclamation of the resurrection was the background in both cases.

The commander, noting the ferocity of the dissension between the two parties, was afraid that the prisoner would be "torn in pieces" and consequently sent his troops into the fracas to whisk him away. It could be said that Paul was no safer in the presence of the highest court of his people than he had been in the midst of the mob in the Temple area. In both cases he owed his preservation, humanly speaking, to the interference of the Romans.

23:11. Something better than the security provided by Rome became the experience of the prisoner that night. "The Lord stood at his side," with a message that commended him for his testimony (which must include his word before the Council) up to this time and promised that his hope of bearing witness at Rome (19:21) would be realized. He could sleep in peace the rest of the night.

G. PLOT AGAINST PAUL'S LIFE—23:12-22

The apostle needed this assurance from a heavenly source, for his enemies lost no time in concocting a plot designed to end his life.

> **23:12** And when it was day, the Jews formed a conspiracy and bound themselves under an oath, saying that they would neither eat nor drink until they had killed Paul.
>
> **13** And there were more than forty who formed this plot.
>
> **14** And they came to the chief priests and the elders, and said, "We have bound ourselves under a solemn oath to taste nothing until we have killed Paul.
>
> **15** "Now, therefore, you and the Council notify the commander to bring him down to you, as though you were going to determine his case by a more thorough investigation; and we for our part are ready to slay him before he comes near *the place.*"
>
> **16** But the son of Paul's sister heard of their ambush, and he came and entered the barracks and told Paul.
>
> **17** And Paul called one of the centurions to him and said, "Lead this young man to the commander, for he has something to report to him."
>
> **18** So he took him and led him to the commander and said, "Paul the prisoner called me to him and asked me to lead this young man to you since he has something to tell you."
>
> **19** And the commander took him by the hand and stepping aside, *began* to inquire of him privately, "What is it that you have to report to me?"
>
> **20** And he said, "The Jews have agreed to ask you to bring Paul down tomorrow to the Council, as though you were going to inquire somewhat more thoroughly about him.

21 "So do not listen to them, for more than forty of them are lying in wait for him who have bound themselves under a curse not to eat or drink until they slay him; and now they are ready and waiting for the promise from you."

22 Therefore the commander let the young man go, instructing him, "Tell no one that you have notified me of these things."

23:12-15. It is tantalizing that Luke does not identify the plotters beyond calling them "Jews." Perhaps the word is used here as in John, where rather often it carries the connotation of those who actively oppose Jesus. If so, there were Jews who saw in Paul the gravest danger to the continuance of Judaism in its pure and exclusivist form. Since the Sanhedrin had let him slip through their fingers by their disunity, these men were prepared to offer themselves as a cohesive force pledged to kill Paul or be killed themselves in the attempt. They showed their seriousness by putting themselves under an oath, really a curse (anathema), committing themselves to abstain from food and drink until they accomplished their mission. In other words, they were inviting God to destroy them if they failed to fulfill their pledge.

Some writers (e.g., Schlatter and Jeremias) have identified them as Zealots, and S. G. F. Brandon is inclined to agree.[23] Schlatter concedes that there is difficulty involved in this identification when he writes, "The high priest consented, although there was an inexorable, bloody feud between the Sadducees and Zealots, and Ananias was especially obnoxious to them."[24] Apparently the Pharisees, due to the defense of Paul, were not approached, but it was felt that they would attend the gathering if the high priest summoned the Council, and by the time they learned of the plot it would be too late to interfere on behalf of Paul as they had done before. As for the Zealots and the Sadducees, they would forget their differences for the sake of eliminating a common enemy, just as the Pharisees had joined with the Sadducees to seek the death of Jesus, becoming a party to treachery in the betrayal by Judas. They would justify their resort to violence by affirming that they were acting for the faith of their fathers and were doing God service (Jn 16:2). Paul had similarly justified his stern measures as a persecutor of the Church (Ac 26:9).

The plan was to lie in wait for Paul and murder him before he reached the meeting place of the Council. If need be, the conspirators were prepared to die when they attacked the escort of soldiers, in order that some of their number might reach Paul to destroy him. It was a bold plot, quite in keeping with the fanatical spirit of the Zealot party. One need not picture these forty men as starving to death after the failure of their scheme, for Jewish lawyers skilled in the art of casuistry could readily be persuaded to find a way of relieving them from their oath.

The willingness of the leaders of the Sanhedrin to cooperate with the plotters rather than hold a bona fide trial reveals how conscious they were of the weakness of their case against Paul. The all-wise God permitted the plot to germinate that the evil intents of sinful men might be disclosed; yet He overruled in such a way that Paul was moved one stage nearer Rome, in accordance with His promise (23:11). How this was achieved is disclosed by what follows immediately.

23:16-22. An amazing story unfolds here, one which illustrates the sovereignty of God. At a time when the Jerusalem church was either too petrified by fear to lift a finger in Paul's behalf, or too concerned with its own future relation to Judaism to risk any attempt at intervention, from within the apostle's own kindred God raised up a helper for him in his time of need.

The problem is to do justice to two factors. On the one hand, if Paul's sister and her son were Christians, how would the son have learned of the plot? On the other hand, if they were not believers, would not the typical Jewish prejudice against the Nazarenes be so powerful as to smother the yearning desire to be of help to Paul? Luke has left us to our speculations, for he supplies no details. Perhaps the sister had become a believer through the testimony of Paul following his conversion (9:28).

It was the son who had the courage to enter the castle, once he had learned of the plot, and to seek out Paul to share the information about it. A centurion fell in with Paul's request that the young man be conducted to the commander. To the centurion, the apostle was "Paul the prisoner." This was the label that identified him from this time on for years to come. In fact, he used the label several times when writing from prison (Eph 3:1; 4:1; Phile 1, 9). Paul made sure that people realized that this incarceration was not due to some criminal act but solely to his loyalty to Christ and His cause (Phil 1:13).

The story of what went on in the Castle of Antonia is so vivid and circumstantial that it suggests Luke's presence with Paul on this occasion. It closes with a warning from the commander to the informant not to be loose of tongue, as someone had been in providing him with the information he bore. Secrecy was all-important, and so was time.

H. TRANSFER TO CAESAREA—23:23-35

Immediately the commander set to work to remove the prisoner beyond the reach of the conspirators and to do it in such a way as not to attract notice. Even as the previous section has shown to what great lengths the Jews would go to be rid of Paul, the present passage shows the lengths to which the Romans would go to protect a citizen of the Empire, even if he were a Jew.

23:23 And he called to him two of the centurions, and said, "Get two hundred soldiers ready by the third hour of the night to proceed to Caesarea, with seventy horsemen and two hundred spearmen."

24 *They were* also to provide mounts to put Paul on and bring him safely to Felix the governor.

25 And he wrote a letter having this form:

26 "Claudius Lysias, to the most excellent governor Felix, greetings.

27 "When this man was arrested by the Jews and was about to be slain by them, I came upon them with the troops and rescued him, having learned that he was a Roman.

28 "And wanting to ascertain the charge for which they were accusing him, I brought him down to their Council;

29 and I found him to be accused over questions about their Law, but under no accusation deserving death or imprisonment.

30 "And when I was informed that there would be a plot against the man, I sent him to you at once, also instructing his accusers to bring charges against him before you."

31 So the soldiers, in accordance with their orders, took Paul and brought him by night to Antipatris.

32 But the next day, leaving the horsemen to go on with him, they returned to the barracks.

33 And when these had come to Caesarea and delivered the letter to the governor, they also presented Paul to him.

34 And when he had read it, he asked from what province he was; and when he learned that he was from Cilicia,

35 he said, "I will give you a hearing after your accusers arrive also," giving orders for him to be kept in Herod's Praetorium.

23:23-24. The apostle was conducted out of the city under cover of darkness at the hour of nine o'clock, surrounded by 470 men. In the event of an attack on Paul resulting in his death, the commander would be held responsible. He might even be accused of working hand in glove with the conspiring Jews. So he supplied ample protection during this trip to Caesarea, the city where the Roman governor Felix had his headquarters.

23:25-30. Along with the troops went a letter from the commander to the governor. "The Roman law required that a subordinate officer, in sending a prisoner to his superior, should send along with him a written statement of the case."[25]

The term "most excellent" was reserved for important personages (cf. Lk 1:3). It is roughly equivalent to *honorable* used in reference to the mayor of a city.

The letter gave a summary account of the events surrounding Paul's arrest and detention in Jerusalem. There was an understandable desire to magnify somewhat the conduct of the writer in all of this, leading him to a misstatement or two, especially the claim that the rescue of Paul was due to the commander's knowledge that the threatened man was a Roman. This knowledge had not come until later. Again, no mention was made of the order for a scourging of the prisoner. The final statement about Paul's accusers is technically incorrect, for at the time of writing the commander had not yet informed the accusers of Paul's departure from the city and of their rights in the next development of the case; but by the time the letter reached the governor this contact had been made and the information imparted.

On the positive side, Claudius Lysias exonerated Paul of anything criminal (v. 29), which was doubtless the main value of the letter as far as the historian was concerned. The verdict expressed concurs with that of Gallio at an earlier time (18:14-15) and of Festus and Agrippa later on (26:31-32).

23:31-32. Slipping out of Jerusalem when the city had become quiet, the force of foot soldiers and mounted men would attract little attention. Ahead of them lay Antipatris, forty miles away by a descending and somewhat winding road, where an ambush could be disastrous. The town, built by Herod the Great and named in honor of his father Antipater, was used by the Romans as a relay station for troop movements. Since the remainder of the journey to Caesarea, covering some twenty-five miles, was over the plain where the cavalry could make good time, the foot soldiers were no longer needed and could return to Jerusalem at a more leisurely pace.

23:33-35. At Caesarea the responsibility of the cavalry detachment was to present the letter and the prisoner to the governor, Antonius Felix, who governed from A.D. 52-60. He had been a slave, but like several others had gained the status of freedman under the emperor Claudius and was one of his favorites. This accounts for his elevation to the high post he now held, an honor that went to his head. At any rate, Tacitus in *Historiae*, describes him as "exercising the powers of a king with the disposition of a slave." His repressive measures only increased the restlessness of the masses in Judea, and his unscrupulous self-enrichment aroused their anger. According to Josephus, his use of brigands to assassinate objects of his dislike brought on a period of lawlessness which led up to the war with Rome.[26]

On reading the letter from the commander in Jerusalem, Felix inquired of Paul concerning his home province and was informed that it was Cilicia. Acting on that knowledge, he agreed to hear the case. Sherwin-White points out the unexpectedness of this, since Felix might well have preferred to avoid taking responsibility by returning Paul to his native area for trial, especially since Paul was a Roman citizen. The suggestion he makes is that Cilicia, like Judea, was an administrative district of the province of Syria, and "the Legate of Syria was not to be bothered with

351

minor cases from Judea . . . and the status of Cilicia did not require that its natives should be sent back to it for trial."[27]

Ancient rulers could be temperamental when it came to listening to the complaints of their subjects. There is a story of Philip, the father of Alexander the Great, to the effect that when an old woman presented herself and begged him to hear her cause, she was repulsed by his impatient word, "I haven't time." Nothing daunted, she quickly replied, "Then stop being king." The story concludes with the observation that he not only listened to her but also to all the others—at once.[28]

There would naturally have been a slight delay until Paul's accusers could arrange to be present (cf. v. 30). Meanwhile the prisoner was detained in the governor's residence, which was evidently equipped with rooms suitable for such a purpose. This helps to explain Luke's comment in 24:26.

I. Defense Before Felix—24:1-27

WHILE MOST OF THE CHAPTER is properly described as a defense in the light of charges brought against Paul, it concludes with an account of further personal contacts between him and the governor.

Verses 1-9. This section deals with the charges brought against Paul by Tertullus on behalf of the Sanhedrin.

> **24:1** And after five days the high priest Ananias came down with some elders, with a certain attorney *named* Tertullus; and they brought charges to the governor against Paul.
>
> **2** And after *Paul* had been summoned, Tertullus began to accuse him, saying *to the governor,*
> "Since we have through you attained much peace, and since by your providence reforms are being carried out for this nation,
>
> **3** we acknowledge *this* in every way and everywhere, most excellent Felix, with all thankfulness.
>
> **4** "But, that I may not weary you any further, I beg you to grant us, by your kindness, a brief hearing.
>
> **5** "For we have found this man a real pest and a fellow who stirs up dissension among all the Jews throughout the world, and a ringleader of the sect of the Nazarenes.
>
> **6** "And he even tried to desecrate the temple; and then we arrested him.*
>
> **8** "And by examining him yourself concerning all these matters, you will be able to ascertain the things of which we accuse him."
>
> **9** And the Jews also joined in the attack, asserting that these things were so.

24:1-9. Before there could be a defense, the case against Paul had to be presented. For this purpose, some "five days" after the arrival of the prisoner a group appeared, representing the Sanhedrin, with Ananias at their head. Along with them came a certain Tertullus, who is called an "attorney." This term, which occurs only here in the New Testament, basically denotes a public speaker, one with a good flow of words. But in this passage it has a more specialized meaning, attested by the papyri, namely, "attorney," or "advocate."

Tertullus was evidently engaged by the Sanhedrin to present their case

---

*Some manuscripts have a longer text, including verse 7 and additions to verses 6 and 8. See discussion in the commentary.

against Paul. His name is Latin. "It is probable that Tertullus made his plea against Paul before Felix . . . in Latin, though Greek was allowed in such provincial courts by grace of the judge."[1] He could have been a Greek or even a Jew (cf. *Paulus,* the name of the prisoner). Several times he identified himself with the Jewish people ("we"), but this is not decisive since he could have adopted this stance for the sake of those who had asked for his services. More significant is the statement, "We wanted to judge him according to our law," but this is found in a portion of the text that is of doubtful authenticity (see Bruce). Verse 9 seems to distinguish between Tertullus and the Jews. Munck suggests that he was the regular legal consultant of the Sanhedrin. Favorable to this conclusion is the brief time available for securing and briefing a stranger.

About one thing there is no doubt—his command of the rhetoric requisite to such an occasion. While we probably have only a summary of his speech, it is evident that he gave almost as much attention to complimenting the governor as to the exposition of the case for the plaintiffs.

It is true that he spoke only in broad generalities of "peace" and "reforms," tracing these to the governor's "providence" (forethought, or foresight), for specific instances of benefit to the nation would have been hard to find. Even the reference to peace was a dubious compliment, for the ruthless way in which risings had been put down only made others inevitable as a protest. The meaning of "reforms" is doubtful, but the reference may have been to those very measures which were used to secure peace. Order was purchased at the expense of more strife in the future.

The advocate was careful to observe all the necessary expressions of respect, addressing the judge as "most excellent" Felix (cf. 23:26)

In voicing "thankfulness" for the governor's alleged benefactions, Tertullus was certainly not speaking the mind of most Jews, for at the end of the two-year period mentioned in verse 27 Nero summoned Felix to Rome to give account for serious disturbances between Jews and Gentiles in Caesarea. When the investigation was broadened to include his administration as a whole, the evidence against him was so overwhelming that he was recalled. He would have been severely punished had it not been for the intercession of his brother Pallas on his behalf.[2]

The word "kindness" must have been spoken with tongue in cheek, but this was conventional rhetoric not intended to be taken too literally and yet demanded by the occasion.

After asking for a hearing and promising to make it brief, Tertullus got down to the business at hand.

First, Paul was a "pest" (v. 5). The full import of the term appears when one discovers that literally it means "pestilence" or "plague" (cf. Lk 21:11, the only other occurrence in the New Testament). What he had been to the Church as its persecutor (Gal 1:13), he had become in turn to the very body that had encouraged him in his persecuting role. But the argument was made more concrete by adding, "a fellow who stirs up dissension," and not here and there but "throughout the world" (cf. Ac 17:6; 21:28), an obvious exaggeration.

"Dissension" is a rather weak rendering here, since it could suggest squabbles among the Jews that were of no consequence to the Roman authorities, whereas Tertullus was putting in a prominent place a charge that he hoped would impress the governor as weighty. The term was intended to have political overtones, as in Luke 23:19, where it denotes a riot that in reality was an insurrection. Possibly the word was intended to be somewhat ambiguous, able to cover an overt revolt against the government but also capable of being used in the more restricted sense of upheavals (in this case, among the Jews) which were violent enough to create alarm for the state (see comments on 18:2). Sherwin-White points out (following Cumont) that the letter from the Emperor Claudius to the people of Alexandria contains a close parallel to this charge. In this letter the monarch objects to certain politically objectionable activities of the Jews as "stirring up a universal plague throughout the world."[3] With reference to 24:5 the same author notes that the Jews "knew that the governors were unwilling to convict on purely religious charges and therefore tried to give a political twist to the religious charge."[4] In Paul's case the charge was untrue, as Roman officials had already ruled (18:12-16; 19:37-40).

In the second charge Paul was made out to be a "ringleader of the sect of the Nazarenes." Of some interest is the fact that this is the only place where the plural is used; in all other instances *Nazarene* is a reference to Jesus. It is not known to what extent Felix was informed about this group, but he could at least gather from the tone of voice and facial expression of Tertullus that it was thoroughly despised by the Jews as a whole. At a later time the word *sect* took on the meaning of "heresy." What was implied in this case was that the Nazarenes were a divisive force in Judaism which the Romans ought not to look on with favor, since it was so dissimilar as to lie outside the scope of being a permitted religion, the status enjoyed by Judaism. Paul was singled out as a "ringleader" of this sect. Rackham comments, "We also note that the preeminence of Paul in the church is no exaggeration of S. Luke's: his enemies, taking a figure from the army, acknowledge him to be a *front rank man* or head of the file."[5]

As a third item, Tertullus charged Paul with violating the sanctity of the Temple (v. 6). The allegation was considerably modified from the original assertion (21:28), since here only an attempt at the desecration of the sacred place was claimed. Even in this softened form the charge was

355

important, for two reasons. First, it was more specific than the other two items mentioned by Tertullus and should have been capable of proof or disproof. Second, it concerned the Romans almost as much as the first charge, since they were agreed that even if one of their own number violated the Temple by seeking to go in, they would permit the Jews to put him to death (see comment on 21:27).

"We arrested him" suggests that from the first the Jews had contemplated a trial. This is contrary to the narrative in chapter 21, where the mob is pictured as trying to kill Paul on the spot. "But it was essential to the case of Tertullus to maintain that Paul was legally a Jewish 'temple-prisoner' with whom Lysias had no right to interfere."[6]

At this point the listing of complaints against Paul ends, and the termination seems rather abrupt. Some manuscripts, particularly those of the Western type, supply a longer text, as follows: "And we wanted to judge him according to our law. But Lysias the commander came along, and with much violence took him out of our hands, ordering his accusers to come before you," (NASB marg.). If this addition were to be accepted, the words which follow about "examining him" would refer to Lysias rather than Paul. In other words, Felix was being challenged to corroborate the testimony of Tertullus by checking with Lysias. This is awkward, if not impossible, since the "him" at the beginning of verse 8 must be the same individual denoted by the "him" at the close of the verse, where the reference can be only to Paul. A further difficulty lies in the phrase, "concerning all these matters," for Lysias would not have been competent to bear witness on the first two charges. So the added material is rightly rejected and consigned to a marginal reading.

Looking back over the allegations against Paul—a troublemaker among the Jews who would bear watching by the Romans, a follower of the Nazarene (who had entertained Messianic pretensions, only to be rejected by His own nation), and one who thought so little of the place his countrymen honored as most holy that he could try to bring a Gentile in and defile it—one can sense the cord of unity that runs through them all. It is neatly expressed by Munck as "an attempt to separate Paul and the Jewish Christians from the Jewish religion."[7] It is well to bear this in mind as one scrutinizes the apostle's reply in its various facets. Possibly T. W. Manson is right in saying, "It is probable that the strong desire of a large section of the Early Church to hold on to their Jewish affiliation was not unconnected with the wish to have the status of a *religio licita*,"[8] but this should be understood not from the standpoint of expediency but of conviction. In the case of Paul one need only point to Romans 11.

Verses 10-21. This section gives a report of Paul's defense, which was given after members of the Jewish delegation affirmed the correctness of the statements made by their spokesman.

24:10 And when the governor had nodded for him to speak, Paul responded:

"Knowing that for many years you have been a judge to this nation, I cheerfully make my defense,

11 since you can take note of the fact that no more than twelve days ago I went up to Jerusalem to worship.

12 "And neither in the temple, nor in the synagogues, nor in the city *itself* did they find me carrying on a discussion with anyone or causing a riot.

13 "Nor can they prove to you the charges of which they now accuse me.

14 "But this I admit to you, that according to the Way which they call a sect I do serve the God of our fathers, believing everything that is in accordance with the Law, and that is written in the Prophets;

15 having a hope in God, which these men cherish themselves, that there shall certainly be a resurrection of both the righteous and the wicked.

16 "In view of this, I also do my best to maintain always a blameless conscience *both* before God and before men.

17 "Now after several years I came to bring alms to my nation and to present offerings;

18 in which they found me *occupied* in the temple, having been purified, without *any* crowd or uproar. But *there were* certain Jews from Asia—

19 who ought to have been present before you, and to make accusation, if they should have anything against me.

20 "Or else let these men themselves tell what misdeed they found when I stood before the Council,

21 other than for this one statement which I shouted out while standing among them, 'For the resurrection of the dead I am on trial before you today.'"

24:10-21. Receiving a nod from the governor indicating that it was now his turn to speak, the apostle responded by taking up the charges in order. His opening statements, like those of Tertullus, were intended to take account of the dignity and capacity of Felix, but in Paul's case there was a brevity and restraint that were in marked contrast to the fulsomeness and flattery of the previous speaker. It was his earnest desire to remain within the bounds of truth (2 Co 13:8).

"Many years" needs not suggest that Paul was ignorant of the length of time Felix had been in office. He was not intending to be precise, but was indicating merely that the governor had had sufficient opportunity (over a period of five or six years) to become acquainted with the Jewish people

357

and their situation (cf. v. 22). The same purpose underlies the choice of the word "judge" rather than *governor.* Felix had tried enough cases to have a store of information about the history, customs, and outlook of the nation, and Paul was counting on this understanding as he opened his defense.

Speaking to the first charge, the apostle intimated that his time in Jerusalem had been too limited to have organized a riot even if he wanted to. It is not easy to accommodate what happened to "twelve days." Meyer seeks to do it by supposing that the five days of verse 1 are to be reckoned from the organizing of the conspiracy and the departure of Paul from Jerusalem.[9] But this is hardly natural. Since Luke has not given a day-by-day account, one can only surmise how the time period was reckoned. In addition to the question of time, Paul brought in the matter of purpose. The reason he went to Jerusalem was "to worship." Probably this can be connected with his desire to arrive at the city for the celebration of Pentecost (20:16). Finally, he did not engage in public disputation or proclamation, much less stir up "a riot" (v. 12). His last visit, then, was in marked contrast to his first as a believer, when he had preached and debated at every opportunity (9:28-29; 22:18).

To meet the second charge, that he was a leader of the discredited sect of the Nazarenes, Paul conceded that he had such a connection, but his own preference was to speak of it as "the Way" (v. 14). *Sect* sounds negative and divisive; *way* sounds positive and purposeful. Further, he countered the sectarian allegation by asserting that his worship was directed to "the God of our fathers." He had not alienated himself from Israel's God any more than from her devoted saints. Also, he had not forsaken the sacred writings of his people. His faith was fully in line with what is found in the Law and the prophets.

Despite the comprehensive nature of the language, it is likely that Paul had in mind more than anything else the promise of a Messiah (cf. Lk 24:44-46); for the hope of resurrection, to which he adverted immediately, was decidedly vivified and strengthened by the resurrection of Jesus Christ. But in this delicate situation Paul declined to turn aside and discuss the Messiah question directly, preferring rather to proclaim resurrection in terms familiar from the Old Testament, where a resurrection of "the righteous and the wicked" is set forth (Dan 12:2). Proclamation of the resurrection as an item of faith had won him support from the Pharisees in the Council (Ac 23:6-9). Also it is probable that Felix, by virtue of his acquaintance with Judaism, would know that apart from the Sadducees, belief in resurrection was generally held among the Jewish people. In referring to "these men" (v. 15), Paul may have motioned with his hand to the Pharisees in the group from Jerusalem, especially if they were seated together. He must have ignored Ananias and the other Sadducees who were with him.

"In view of this," (i.e. the hope of resurrection), Paul sought to maintain a blameless conscience both Godward and manward (cf. 23:1). At the resurrection he would have to give account to God, meanwhile he must live uprightly before his fellows. He was fully aware of the extent to which spiritual convictions motivate conduct.

At length, Paul injected the real reason for being in Jerusalem. It was "to bring alms" to his nation and "to present offerings" (v. 17). This is the only time in Acts that the collection for the poor saints at Jerusalem is mentioned, though it is often referred to in Paul's letters to churches. Here again the language was carefully chosen—the "nation" was stated as the beneficiary rather than the Church. This was a deliberate stroke to emphasize that the church in Jerusalem had not sundered itself from the people of God who made up the nation of Israel. But admittedly the Church was the recipient.

J. E. H. Hull presents a plausible reason for the apostle's great concern over this fund.

> It was the fact of persecution (Acts 8:1) that initially led to the poverty of the Christian community in Jerusalem. It is possible that Paul was so concerned to relieve the destitution there (e.g. I Cor. 16:1ff.) partly because he realized that he had contributed to it through his persecuting zeal.[10]

Somewhat uncertain is the meaning of the second statement of purpose, "to present offerings." He did present offerings in connection with the rites of purification (21:26), but apparently he had not had this in view when he went to Jerusalem. It may be, as some suppose, that the sentence is elliptical, Paul's meaning being on this order: "I came to Jerusalem to bring alms to my nation, and I entered into the Temple to make offerings"[11] (so Walker). Luke may have been compressing to save space. There is a possibility also that Paul had intended to present thank offerings at Jerusalem for the successful completion of the trip and other blessings.

By this statement Paul indicated that he was moving into a discussion of the third charge, his alleged violation of the Temple. He admitted to having been there and suggested the reason for it, namely, his purification after living so long among the unclean Gentiles. But there had been "no crowd or uproar," none, that is, of his making. What had developed along these lines was strictly due to "certain Jews from Asia" (cf. 21:27).

Here the apostle broke off without finishing the sentence. The technical word for this phenomenon of grammatical irregularity is *anacoluthon* (a Greek term meaning "lack of sequence"). Such constructions are fairly common in Paul's writings, so Luke may well have been reproducing his exact words here. The abruptness of the construction makes for suspense, which creates an atmosphere of expectancy that something weighty will follow. In this case it did, for the apostle was able to make the telling point that it was the duty of these Asian Jews, the ones who were responsible for the fracas in the Temple, to be present for this trial. Their failure to appear could readily be interpreted as a demonstration that they could not substantiate their wild claim that Paul had brought a Gentile beyond the barrier into the inner confines of the Temple area (21:28). Paul scored heavily on this item.

To round off his presentation he turned to the representatives of the Sanhedrin ("these men") to challenge them to make an accusation against him based on what he had said when he stood before them. The only thing he could suggest himself was his assertion that "the resurrection of the dead" was at issue (v. 21; cf. 23:6). No member of the Council was likely to challenge his statement of what had happened, for it was factual. Any challenge could only lead to the disclosure of a cleavage on this point between Pharisees and Sadducees, which would have been an embarrassment to them in the present situation. So they remained silent. R. P. C. Hanson is of the opinion that this speech is substantially what Paul would have given before the Council had he not been interrupted.[12]

Verses 22-23. These verses give the governor Felix's twofold reaction to what he heard. He delayed a decision on the case, meanwhile keeping Paul in custody.

> **24:22** But Felix, having a more exact knowledge about the Way, put them off, saying, "When Lysias the commander comes down, I will decide your case."
>
> **23** And he gave orders to the centurion for him to be kept in custody and *yet* have *some* freedom, and not to prevent any one of his friends from ministering to him.

24:22-23. Now all eyes were on Felix. What would the governor decide? His decision was to "put off" both parties. The trial was suspended, at least until he could confer with Lysias, the commander.

Rather strangely another factor is introduced here, the knowledge which Felix possessed of "the Way." Several questions need to be asked, the first of them being of a grammatical nature. How should the comparative adjective, used adverbially, be rendered? In our translation "a more exact knowledge" is the wording, which may be taken to mean a more exact knowledge than people might suppose.[13] However, since the Koine period of the Greek language brought considerable flexibility into the use of the comparative, with fairly numerous examples of its use in a so-called elative or heightened sense best expressed by *very*, some grammarians prefer the rendering, "a very accurate knowledge" (Nigel Turner; Blass-Debrunner). An even stronger wording is "perfect knowledge" (*BC*). A decision between these is difficult. They all emphasize in some measure the knowledge Felix possessed of Christianity, and that was important to Luke. If a ruler was well acquainted with the faith and found himself unable to convict a leading representative of it, though he himself was not a believer, he became another Gallio (18:14-15).

A second question relates to the source of this knowledge. How was it acquired? To find the answer simply in the information provided by Paul in his speech is inadequate, for it was a defense against certain allegations rather than an exposition of the Christian faith. The answer may lie in the fact that the governor's wife was a Jewess (v. 24), but doubtless there were other contacts also. Felix had been in the country for several years and could hardly have failed to learn a great deal if he was at all receptive to information on the religious situation among the people he was expected to govern.

A third question relates to the bearing of this knowledge, however obtained, upon the decision to suspend the trial. Probably Felix was convinced of the innocence of Paul (cf. Pilate's attitude toward Jesus), so could not pronounce against him, yet felt a reluctance to incur the displeasure of the high court of Judaism. Already a course was being taken which continued to be followed as long as he had jurisdiction (cf. v. 27). So far so good. But then, how is the reference to Lysias to be explained? Clearly the governor gave the impression that no decision could be reached until his testimony was heard. After all, he had been an eyewitness of the turmoil at the Temple, something which could not be said for the Sanhedrin. Yet the odd thing is that no further session of the court was held after the arrival of Lysias. For that matter, there is no record that he arrived at Caesarea at all.

What had started out ostensibly as a temporary thing—namely, that Paul was "kept in custody," with freedom to have visitors—became a drawn-out arrangement. We can only conclude that the Sanhedrin grew weary of waiting and withdrew to Jerusalem, where it had other business to attend to. For Paul the long detention was alleviated somewhat by the ministration of friends in Caesarea who loved him dearly (cf. 21:8-14). Yet all the while the presence of a military guard reminded him that he was a prisoner. But he was a prisoner for the sake of Christ and for this reason was certain to see Rome in the Lord's good time. In this he was comforted. Human companions, including Luke, did their best to minister to his needs.

Verses 24-27. This passage describes the governor's changing attitude toward Paul. After his initial fear in response to Paul's presentation of the

Gospel, Felix's spiritual concern became a monetary one. In the end, self-interest prompted him to leave Paul in prison, although he was aware of the apostle's innocence.

> **24:24** But some days later, Felix arrived with Drusilla, his wife who was a Jewess, and sent for Paul, and heard him *speak* about faith in Christ Jesus.
>
> **25** And as he was discussing righteousness, self-control and the judgment to come, Felix became frightened and said, "Go away for the present, and when I find time, I will summon you."
>
> **26** At the same time too, he was hoping that money would be given him by Paul; therefore he also used to send for him quite often and converse with him.
>
> **27** But after two years had passed, Felix was succeeded by Porcius Festus; and wishing to do the Jews a favor, Felix left Paul imprisoned.

24:24-27. The next contact between the governor and the prisoner occurred a few days later, when Felix "arrived" with Drusilla his wife. To speak of arrival is a bit strange, seeming to imply the governor had been away in the meantime. This may well have been the case, and it would have served as a broad hint to the Sanhedrin representatives that they might as well go home. The meaning could be, however, that the couple arrived from their sumptuous quarters and came into the humble surroundings of the apostle (cf. 25:7).

Drusilla was the daughter of Herod Agrippa I, mentioned in chapter 12, and the sister of Herod Agrippa II, about to be mentioned in chapter 25. According to Josephus,[14] Drusilla was given in marriage by her brother to the king of Emesa, a small domain on the Orontes River, but was lured from her husband and persuaded to marry Felix, who was attracted by her great beauty. This alliance, made when she was still in her middle teens, was contrary to Jewish law, seeing that Felix had not agreed to become a Jew.

Since this visit to Paul was not a part of the trial but only a private meeting, the apostle was free to discuss what was closest to his heart, "faith in Christ Jesus." According to the Western text it was Drusilla, rather than Felix, who expressed a desire to see and hear Paul. However, the remainder of the passage has nothing to say of her reaction, but concentrates on that of Felix.

The chances are good that in speaking of faith in Christ, Paul gave his personal testimony, including an account of his conversion. But Felix was not ready for faith, and Paul sought to make him aware of his sinful condition by speaking of those things that peculiarly fitted his character and conduct. What he needed was "righteousness," in contrast to the injustice which had characterized his regime thus far, and "self-control," especially in the area of passion (Felix was thrice married). And unless there was repentance, he would have to face the "judgment to come," which was inevitable for one whose life evidenced a lack of these qualities (Ro 1:18; Eph 5:3-6).

Such preaching, man to man, made Felix uncomfortable and fearful, if only for a short time, as the following verse indicates. But Paul had fulfilled his obligation as a witness for Christ. To speak thus frankly would not help his case in the eyes of the governor, but for that very reason it is an example of holy boldness, which those should consider who tend to berate him for dividing the Council to save himself (23:1-10) and for failing to preach Christ when the Council came to Caesarea for the trial before Felix (24:1).

Further meetings were held from time to time, probably by Felix alone in conference with Paul, but inspired by cupidity rather than by concern for his spiritual condition. Paul himself may have excited cupidity in the governor by his statement about bringing alms to his nation (24:17). Furthermore, the prominence of the apostle as a Christian leader and the loving esteem in which he was held (21:12-13) opened to Felix the possibility that a ransom might be forthcoming for his release. But as time passed and Paul showed no signs of cooperation (if indeed Felix disclosed his intentions), this hope faded from the mind of the governor.

At the end of "two years," when Felix was recalled, he felt that it was to his advantage to keep Paul imprisoned in order to gain favor with the Jews. This is testimony to the fact that he considered Paul innocent of the charges laid against him. A partial parallel with Pilate can be seen here, for the latter actually affirmed the innocence of Jesus yet capitulated when the threat of having his misrule exposed at Rome put fear into him. Felix was no better off if his future was to be decided on his record as governor.

J. Defense Before Festus and Appeal to Caesar—25:1-12

This narrative is briefer than the account of the trial before Felix which precedes and of the hearing before Agrippa which follows. The appeal to Caesar at the end of this section is the logical conclusion to the developments after the seizure of Paul in the Temple, as well as the key to all that follows in the remainder of the book.

> **25:1** Festus therefore, having arrived in the province, three days later went up to Jerusalem from Caesarea.
> **2** And the chief priests and the leading men of the Jews brought charges against Paul; and they were urging him,
> **3** requesting a concession against Paul, that he might have him brought to Jerusalem, (*at the same time,* setting an ambush to kill him on the way).

4 Festus then answered that Paul was being kept in custody at Caesarea and that he himself was about to leave shortly.

5 "Therefore," he said, "let the influential men among you go there with me, and if there is anything wrong about the man, let them prosecute him."

6 And after he had spent not more than eight or ten days among them, he went down to Caesarea; and on the next day he took his seat on the tribunal and ordered Paul to be brought.

7 And after he had arrived, the Jews who had come down from Jerusalem stood around him, bringing many and serious charges against him which they could not prove;

8 while Paul said in his own defense, "I have committed no offense either against the Law of the Jews or against the temple or against Caesar."

9 But Festus, wishing to do the Jews a favor, answered Paul and said, "Are you willing to go up to Jerusalem and stand trial before me on these charges?"

10 But Paul said, "I am standing before Caesar's tribunal, where I ought to be tried. I have done no wrong to *the* Jews, as you also very well know.

11 "If then I am a wrongdoer, and have committed anything worthy of death, I do not refuse to die; but if none of those things is *true* of which these men accuse me, no one can hand me over to them. I appeal to Caesar."

12 Then when Festus had conferred with his council, he answered, "You have appealed to Caesar, to Caesar you shall go."

25:1-5. It was probably in the year A.D. 60 that Festus succeeded Felix, although some place it a little earlier. Only three days were spent in Caesarea before the new governor departed for Jerusalem, the real center of the nation's life. This time note is valuable as an indication of the determination of Festus to fulfill his official duties without delay (cf. vv. 6, 17).

Not a great deal is known about Festus. Josephus relates an incident in which he allowed an appeal to Caesar, to this extent providing a parallel with Paul's situation.[15] Agrippa had built an addition to his palace from which he could view what went on in the Temple, which vexed the Jews and led to the erection of a barrier which shut off his view. Festus supported Agrippa and ordered the barrier removed, whereupon the Jews secured his consent to send a deputation to Nero, who sustained their complaint.

The leaders of the nation lost no time in getting the ear of Festus, pressing him to bring Paul to Jerusalem for trial, alleging certain charges against him. But, as Luke adds, their real purpose was to intercept Paul on the way and kill him. Observe the changed situation as compared with that noted in 23:13-15. Now the plot was no longer inspired by a few men but was the official plan of the leaders of the Jews. This seems to indicate that they had abandoned hope of getting a conviction against Paul under Roman justice. Judging from verse 24, there was pressure on Festus also from the populace of Jerusalem, which could usually be counted on to respond in the form of a demonstration when the Council requested it (cf. the manipulating of the crowd at the trial of Jesus before Pilate as reported in Lk 23:13-23).

However, Festus refused to be badgered, and indicated that he was about to return to Casarea. There he would reopen the case, receiving testimony from the leading men of the Jews, and would try to determine the merits of their charges (v. 5). He did not relish having incompetent and unrepresentative persons pressing charges out of personal bias. Probably the group was roughly the same as the leading men referred to in verse 2.

25:6-12. True to his promise, Festus acted with promptness, taking up the case the very next day after his arrival. "The tribunal" refers to the official judgment seat used during court proceedings (cf. 18:12). By this time the accusers were ready also, having made the trip from Jerusalem about the same time as the governor. So Paul was summoned to confront them, one against the many, but confident that the truth was on his side and that the Lord was with him. "After he had arrived" is a reference to Paul rather than to Festus. So, when we read that the Jews "stood around him," Paul is the one in view. By their numbers and the vigor of their allegations they would browbeat and confuse him if they could. Paul was like a man doing battle for his life in a ring surrounded by ferocious animals.

One charge after another was voiced against him, and they were "serious." However, they had a fatal limitation—they could not be established. Proof was lacking. Luke does not bother to detail the accusations, for in the main they were what had been set forth in the presence of Felix, judging from what is reported of Paul's defense (v. 8). The mention of Caesar was new, but Paul sought to expose the underhandedness of the attack, namely, that it put forward the charge of creating disturbances (24:5) far and wide and was thereby calculated to give the impression of rebellion and of disloyalty to Caesar. Paul brought the motive of his accusers out into the open.

Festus was astute enough to realize that from the Roman standpoint there was no case against Paul, but he was prepared "to do the Jews a favor" in order to get his regime off on the right foot. The Jews were notoriously difficult for a foreigner to govern. His proposal was that the apostle be returned to Jerusalem for a continuance of the trial there. This does not mean that the governor had in mind to turn the case over to the Sanhedrin (the words "before me" exclude any such notion), but rather that he would have the Jews on hand as consultants. He contemplated no new developments, however. Paul was to stand trial "on these charges."

It was a strange request, unfair on the face of it. Paul's first experience before the Sanhedrin, plus the trial before Felix, had convinced him that he could not expect an impartial hearing. A hostile atmosphere would make a proper verdict more difficult to render in Jerusalem than in Caesarea. The very fact that the Jewish leaders had been willing to wink at a plot against his life and to cooperate in its execution was enough in itself to warn him about the folly of acceding to the proposal of Festus, which after all was but an echo of the request of the Jews themselves (v. 3).

It would help our understanding if we had some clue to Festus's thoughts at this time. C. F. D. Moule makes the following suggestion. He interprets the "favor" of verse 9 in these terms, that the governor

> wanted to give them a chance to assassinate Paul, yet without Festus appearing to play into their hands (for that might have endangered his reputation at Rome). He can prove no charge against Paul; neither can he hand him back to the Sanhedrin, from whom he has already been rescued by the Romans. All he can do is to see whether he can make it appear that Paul himself has asked for a transfer to Jerusalem: that will give the Jews a chance to get at him on the journey without Festus being responsible. It will be "just too bad" that the prisoner got assassinated on the way (after all, it was his own choice to be moved!)—and there will be an end of the Governor's "headache"![16]

This not improbable suggestion would become all the more plausible if Festus knew of the original plot of the Jews against Paul. On this Luke provides no information.

Paul's reply was a firm refusal. It was his right to be tried "before Caesar's tribunal." To retry the case in Jerusalem would be to take it out of a strictly Roman setting and would give the Jewish leaders excessive influence in the court of Festus, as Sherwin-White notes.[17] Paul affirmed his right to be tried where he stood, in a truly Roman court. He was aware that he had done no wrong to the Jews and appealed to the fact that the governor realized this also (v. 10). One senses in these words, "as you also very well know," a tone of reproach. Festus was not acting as a proper judge, but was resorting to expediency.

Going on, Paul affirmed that he would readily accept "death" if his deeds deserved it (cf. 20:24). By linking this statement with "the things of which these men accuse me," he made it very clear that the Jews were insisting that his crimes were so great only the death penalty would suffice. It is recorded that this had been their thrust from the beginning of the trouble in Jerusalem (21:31; 23:12; 25:3), and it is implied in places where it is not stated (23:29; 25:15).

The situation was similar to that which had involved Jesus, as the Jews needed Roman consent in order to carry out the death penalty they so much desired. But Paul had a recourse not open to Jesus. As a Roman citizen he could make his appeal to Caesar, which was the very thing he proceeded to do (v. 11). The way for this had been prepared by the circumstances noted in verse 10, where the governor's court is viewed as representative of the emperor's jurisdiction. Since the lesser court had failed to give justice, Paul exercised his right to appeal to the higher court.

It may seem strange that he said nothing about his Roman citizenship in this connection, nor does Luke mention it here; but this was scarcely necessary since the status had been sufficiently set forth earlier (22:25-29; 23:27). Paul must have realized that such an appeal as he was making, which would remove his case from Palestine and from contact with the mainstream of Jewry, would result in further alienation of his nation from him. This would be a heavy price to pay, yet his willingness to pay it shows that in his estimation his situation was desperate. He knew the unbounded animosity cherished toward him by unbelieving Jews who would go to any length to kill him if he returned to Jerusalem for trial.

The appeal did not mean that Festus was obliged to send Paul to Rome, but it was necessary that he do this if he were not willing to carry on the case himself.[18] This option probably was taken into consideration when he "conferred with his council," a group of legal experts available to him. Since Festus was unwilling to take the case himself, as it would mean offending the Jews, and since Paul was unwilling to go to Jerusalem, the only course left was to send him to Caesar (Nero). And so the human factors in this intense drama had finally brought about the result which the risen Lord had predicted and promised—that Paul would bear witness to Him at Rome (23:11).

This realization must have given the apostle great comfort and cheer in an otherwise uncomfortable situation. There was no guarantee that he would be set free, but Nero at this time was not the monster he turned out to be in later years. He had made no move yet against the Church as he did in his later effort to make Christians responsible for the burning of Rome in the year 64.

It was fortunate for Paul that Festus did not decide to continue his own jurisdiction and come to a verdict, for if he had acted on the evidence, he could only have cleared the apostle. In that case Paul would have been in constant jeopardy, and without protection, because of the determination of his enemies to put him out of the way.

K. Defense Before Agrippa—25:13—26:32

Though the legal assistants of the governor had counseled him about sending Paul to Caesar, they apparently provided no help in formulating a statement of explanation suitable to submit to the emperor. So Festus must have regarded the coming of King Agrippa as a highly fortunate circumstance, since this man had insight into Jewish matters that the governor lacked, and could presumably help him in his dilemma.

Verses 13-22. This passage relates the conversation between governor Festus and Agrippa concerning Paul. Agrippa's willingness to hear the prisoner opened the way for the hearing on the following day.

25:13 Now when several days had elapsed, King Agrippa and Bernice arrived at Caesarea, and paid their respects to Festus.

14 And while they were spending many days there, Festus laid Paul's case before the king, saying, "There is a certain man left a prisoner by Felix;

15 and when I was at Jerusalem, the chief priests and the elders of the Jews brought charges against him, asking for a sentence of condemnation upon him.

16 "And I answered them that it is not the custom of the Romans to hand over any man before the accused meets his accusers face to face, and has an opportunity to make his defense against the charges.

17 "And so after they had assembled here, I made no delay, but on the next day took my seat on the tribunal, and ordered the man to be brought.

18 "And when the accusers stood up, they *began* bringing charges against him not of such crimes as I was expecting;

19 but they *simply* had some points of disagreement with him about their own religion and about a certain dead man, Jesus, whom Paul asserted to be alive.

20 "And being at a loss how to investigate such matters, I asked whether he was willing to go to Jerusalem and there stand trial on these matters.

21 "But when Paul appealed to be held in custody for the Emperor's decision, I ordered him to be kept in custody until I send him to Caesar."

22 And Agrippa *said* to Festus, "I also would like to hear the man myself." "Tomorrow," he said, "you shall hear him."

25:13-22. King Agrippa, a descendant of Herod the Great, was the son of that Agrippa who had imprisoned Peter (chap. 12). But he did not become king of the Jews as his father had been. His domain at this time included the territories to the north and east of the Sea of Galilee, formerly ruled by Philip and Lysanias (Lk 3:1), plus some cities in Galilee and Perea. He kept his hand in Jewish politics as much as discretion allowed, and made trips to Jerusalem from time to time.

Accompanying him to Caesarea was his sister Bernice, who was also sister to Drusilla. Her relationship with Agrippa was morally suspect, as was much of her life—so much so that she shocked even the Romans by her conduct. The royal pair came to greet Festus, since he had recently arrived to take over the procuratorship of Judea. Their stay was long enough to prompt the governor to seek Agrippa's help on Paul's case.

In explanation of his predicament, the governor reviewed the course of events since his arrival in the country insofar as they had a bearing on Paul's case. For our purpose this section (vv. 13-22) can be passed over, except for noting the parallels between the statements of Festus and what has already been related by Luke. Verse 15 will be seen to reflect verses 1-2; verse 16 covers the ground of verses 4-5; verse 17 practically repeats verse 6; verse 18 recapitulates verse 7; verse 19a recalls verse 8 (19b has not been anticipated in the immediate context, but it goes back to the trial before Felix as reported in 24:21, indicating that the same issue must have come up before Festus); verse 20 goes back to verse 9; and verse 21 covers the material of verses 11-12.

One new feature is introduced in verse 20, namely, the governor's confession that he did not know how to go about investigating such matters as the Jews had brought up against Paul. Particularly was he baffled by the discussion of resurrection (v. 19). Religion was not the long suit of Roman officials, and lay quite outside their province (cf. 18:15). Festus cited his incompetence as sufficient reason for wanting the case transferred to Jerusalem. It remains very doubtful, however, that he would have suggested the move apart from Jewish pressure (cf. 25:2-3).

The restrained eagerness of Agrippa to hear Paul (v. 22) was exactly what Festus had hoped for. It relieved him of the necessity of making a request to the same effect. Agrippa, being a Herodian, knew much more about things Jewish than did the average Roman official. The Herods had always been valuable to the Romans for this reason and because they remained fundamentally loyal to Rome, even if it meant turning against their Jewish subjects in a crisis. Emperor Claudius eulogized Agrippa in a letter to the Jewish nation and its rulers, calling him "a man of the greatest piety." So Festus was understandably hopeful that with the assistance of such a man he might find the conflict between Paul and his countrymen more intelligible.

Verses 23-27. Here we have the setting for the defense of Paul in the presence of Festus, Agrippa, and others, which occupies Acts 26. There is no indication that Festus consulted Paul as to his willingness to speak. In all probability the apostle had no advance notice and therefore no opportunity to marshal his thoughts. But the help of the Holy Spirit had been promised for just such situations as this (Lk 12:11-12).

25:23 And so, on the next day when Agrippa had come together with Bernice, amid great pomp, and had entered the auditorium accompanied by the commanders and the prominent men of the city, at the command of Festus, Paul was brought in.

24 And Festus said, "King Agrippa, and all you gentlemen here present with us, you behold this man about whom all the people of the Jews appealed to me, both at Jerusalem and here, loudly declaring that he ought not to live any longer.

25 "But I found that he had committed nothing worthy of death; and since he himself appealed to the Emperor, I decided to send him.

26 "Yet I have nothing definite about him to write to my lord. Therefore I have brought him before you *all* and especially before you, King Agrippa, so that after the investigation has taken place, I may have something to write.

27 "For it seems absurd to me in sending a prisoner, not to indicate also the charges against him."

25:23-27. Luke calls attention to two special features of the occasion, and this may point to his personal presence there. First, he notes the personnel, consisting of the governor, Agrippa and Bernice, the commanders (five in number, answering to the five cohorts stationed in Caesarea), and the dignitaries of the city. These last were outstanding citizens with whom Festus counted it expedient to maintain good relations. Second, by a single expression, "with great pomp," Luke suggests the glitter and glamour of the entrance of the whole company into the hall where the hearing was to be held.

> Festus decided to make Paul's "hearing" an occasion for a compliment to the king. In compensation for their loss of liberty and real power, the dependent princes and wealthy provincials found scope for their ambition in the outward show of dress and ceremonial, of decorations and grand titles.[19]

The word rendered "pomp" is phantasia (cf. *fantasy*), suggesting the transitory character and vanity of all this outward show. In sharp contrast was the entrance of the man Paul, chained and in humble garb. What a pity that the Church which he did so much to establish gradually came to adopt so much of the pageantry of the world!

Addressing the company surrounding him, and especially king Agrippa, who was singled out twice for mention by the governor, Festus provided an explanation for this gathering. Pointing to Paul, he indicated that this was the man whom the Jews, both at Jerusalem and at Caesarea, had besought him with strident voices to execute. His own inquiry into the case had not disclosed any criminal acts that would warrant the death penalty. He went on to cite the appeal of the prisoner to Caesar, who is called here

"Sebastos," the Greek equivalent of the Latin *Augustus*, the title taken by Octavian after he came to power. The term means "the revered one," and is closely parallel to the modern expression "His Majesty." What Festus omitted was any mention of what had precipitated Paul's appeal—the governor's request that he go to Jerusalem for trial.

It was Festus's expressed hope that something would come out of the present session to illuminate the problem presented by an insistent nation demanding the death of an apparently innocent man. His perplexity was obvious.

> The complication and prolongation of the trial of Paul arose from the fact that the charge was political—hence the procurators were reluctant to dismiss it out of hand—and yet the evidence was theological, hence the procurators were quite unable to understand it.[20]

Since the governor had not found Paul guilty of the charges brought against him, he was not bringing Agrippa into the situation to have him pass on this very matter, but only to have his help in penetrating the mystery of a baffling case. He was looking for advice on how to inform Caesar of the basis for sending the prisoner to Rome. To send him without a clear statement of the charges would be unreasonable.

Of considerable interest is the way in which the governor referred to the emperor, calling him "my lord." There was a time when men felt they could question Luke's accuracy at this point. The doubt was based on the well-known fact that both Augustus and Tiberius had refused the use of this title for themselves, because it exalted them unduly and hinted that those whom they ruled were virtually their slaves. However, there is ample evidence today, especially from the papyri, that in Nero's time this title was freely used. A. Deissmann observes that this change in the Roman attitude is to be traced to the influence of the East, with its tradition of despotism, to which the West gradually capitulated. He goes on to say,

> The fact that a New Testament writer well acquainted with this period makes Festus the Procurator speak of Nero simply as 'the lord' now acquires its full significance in this connexion. The insignificant detail, questioned by various commentators, who, seated at their writing-tables in Tübingen or Berlin, vainly imagined that they knew the period better than St. Luke, now appears thoroughly credible.[21]

Chapter 26, verses 1-3. This chapter is almost entirely given over to Paul's defense before Agrippa. It is the most important of the apostle's statements on his own behalf.

Before following the remarks of Paul in his address to Agrippa, attention should be given to a few preliminary considerations. As noted above Luke was probably present on this occasion. This impression is deepened by the description of Paul stretching out his hand (26:1). The movement registered in the memory of his friend.

The apostle's accusers were not there, so it was not necessary for him to speak to specific charges. This gave him greater freedom concerning the content of his address, allowing him to say something about his own spiritual pilgrimage and the nature of the message he had been commanded to communicate. Paul was very conscious, however, of the people who were before him, especially Agrippa. The words of Festus (25:26) prepare the reader for the prominence the Herodian had from start to finish. He, rather than Festus, invited Paul to speak, who in turn acknowledged him as the one to whom he particularly directed his words (26:2). Toward the end the speaker gave repeated attention to his chief auditor (26:19, 26-28). When the address was finished, it was the king who rose first to declare the session terminated, and his was the final word on the case (26:32).

This occasion, including the speech itself and the verdict of the two rulers at its conclusion, was obviously of great importance to the historian. He has recorded the vindication of Paul given by Festus (25:25) and follows it now with the still stronger verdict of Agrippa, who, unlike Festus, was an acknowledged expert on Jewish matters (26:32).

The content of Acts 26 can be summarized as follows: Paul's introductory words (vv. 1-3); his early life in Judaism (vv. 4-11); his conversion and commission (vv. 12-18); his Christian witness (vv. 19-23); his verbal exchanges with Festus and Agrippa (vv. 24-29); and the conference between the two officials (vv. 30-32).

Observe that the Ananias episode, which has such a prominent place in the first account of the conversion (chap. 9) and is mentioned in the second (chap. 22), is not included here. It would have had only minor interest for a Gentile audience.

> **26:1** And Agrippa said to Paul, "You are permitted to speak for yourself." Then Paul stretched out his hand and *proceeded* to make his defense:
>
> **2** "In regard to all the things of which I am accused by the Jews, I consider myself fortunate, King Agrippa, that I am about to make my defense before you today;
>
> **3** especially because you are an expert in all customs and questions among *the* Jews; therefore I beg you to listen to me patiently.

26:1-3. The word *defense* occurs twice here, which raises a question as to the propriety of the language, seeing that this was not a trial and indeed could not be after the case had been appealed to Caesar. No witnesses were called against Paul or in his favor. Yet he spoke of making his defense, and Luke uses the same terminology (v. 24). The apostle maintained he was being judged (v. 6). One need only recognize that terms of this kind are not confined to a strictly legal situation but can be used more generally (cf. 19:33; 2 Co 12:19). Paul did indeed speak to clear himself; but more than that, he was intent on creating understanding in his hearers. He was not unmindful of the things about which he had been "accused by the Jews," but he was not speaking directly to these accusations.

He had a word of commendation for Agrippa's knowledge of Jewish matters. That the king should have such knowledge is not surprising, for he had spent several years in the land, in addition to his upbringing in Rome where he undoubtedly had studied Jewish history and customs in preparation for his government service. Some years later Josephus claimed that Agrippa wrote sixty-two letters "testifying to the truth of the record" of events which the historian had put down in his *Jewish War*.[22] The same author noted also that Agrippa was "thoroughly conversant with Hellenic culture."[23] He would have been able to grasp much that eluded the comprehension of Festus.

Verses 4-11. Following his introduction, the apostle plunged at once into a recital of his life in Judaism. This was designed to lead to the conclusion that he had not been guilty of apostasy from the faith of his fathers but rather had seen the input of his early training fulfilled and expanded as the result of a crisis in his life.

> **26:4** "So then, all Jews know my manner of life from my youth up, which from the beginning was spent among my *own* nation and at Jerusalem;
>
> **5** since they have known about me for a long time previously, if they are willing to testify, that I lived *as* a Pharisee according to the strictest sect of our religion.
>
> **6** "And now I am standing trial for the hope of the promise made by God to our fathers;
>
> **7** *the promise* to which our twelve tribes hope to attain, as they earnestly serve *God* night and day. And for this hope, O King, I am being accused by Jews.
>
> **8** "Why is it considered incredible among you *people* if God does raise the dead?
>
> **9** "So then, I thought to myself that I had to do many things hostile to the name of Jesus of Nazareth.
>
> **10** "And this is just what I did in Jerusalem; not only did I lock up many of the saints in prisons, having received authority from the chief priests, but also when they were being put to death I cast my vote against them.

11 "And as I punished them often in all the synagogues, I tried to force them to blaspheme; and being furiously enraged at them, I kept pursuing them even to foreign cities.

26:4-5. An obscurity needs to be cleared up, if possible, concerning the description Paul gave of his life during his youth. Was a contrast intended between "among my own nation" and "at Jerusalem"? If so, Paul was indicating that part of his youth had been spent in the Jewish community at Tarsus and the rest of it in Jerusalem. This would conflict with his testimony in 22:3. But "from the beginning" is quite meaningless if it applies to separate times and places. Furthermore, "all Jews" could hardly have known of his life in Tarsus, when he had as yet not achieved prominence. But Jews as a whole, especially those who were now trying to ruin him, were fully aware of his promise and progress as a student (cf. Gal 1:14) and of his later activity as persecutor of the Church, for all this had occurred in the Jerusalem area. As for the word "and," in this case it is a translation of *te*, which is used of "something additional, but in intimate relation with the preceding."[24] The nation was spread out, yet it had its focal point at Jerusalem. Here the contrast between "nation" and "Jerusalem" is slight, whereas in 22:3, where "born in Tarsus" and "brought up in the city of Jerusalem" are separated by a *but*, the contrast is pointed.

It was well known that in his youth Paul lived "as a Pharisee" (cf. Phil 3:5, where this affiliation is linked with observance of the Law), "according to the strictest sect" of the Jewish religion. Josephus pictures the Pharisees as "a body of Jews with the reputation of excelling the rest of the nation in the observances of religion, and as exact exponents of the laws."[25] Clearly the word *religion*, both in Acts and in Josephus, refers to the sphere of religious observance (cf. Ja 1:27).

26:6-8. Being a Pharisee and abiding by the distinctives of the party did not separate Paul from the great mass of his countrymen, with whom he shared "the hope of the promise made by God" to the fathers of Israel. There is an observable shift here from man to God, from obligation to promise, from practice to doctrine.

It would be unfair to single out the word "attain" as indicating that the realization of the hope was thought of in terms of earning it by works. Paul the Christian used the same word to express his anticipation of the experience of the resurrection (Phil 3:11). This term is used in the sense of arrival, of reaching a goal. In the passage before us, the apostle avoided defining the hope in terms of the coming of the Messiah, being content at this stage to link the hope with resurrection. He wanted to point up the anomalous situation in which he found himself—a prisoner charged by his own people (see RSV here) regarding a hope shared by the "twelve tribes." The latter expression not only rebukes the erroneous judgment that the ten northern tribes were permanently lost, but emphasizes the ideal unity of the nation under God (cf. Mt 19:28; Ja 1:1). "The regeneration of Israel is bound up with the resurrection of Jesus, which the Jews denied. This is the link in the argument which leads to the abrupt question which follows."[26] It seems that at this point (v. 8) the apostle shifted from direct address to Agrippa to a sweeping inclusion of his audience as a whole ("you" is plural). If among the Gentiles there was unbelief about resurrection, it was basically because their conception of God was deficient. *God* can do what otherwise might well be considered impossible.

26:9-11. Before he was a believer in Jesus, Paul had shared with the vast majority of his people the conviction that the dead would be raised. But just as firmly, he had refused to believe that Jesus of Nazareth had been raised. How could God honor in this fashion One who was a false Messiah, One whom He allowed to languish and die on a cross in ignominy and shame? Paul had considered it his duty as a loyal son of Israel to show himself "hostile" to such a pretender by persecuting His followers. So he had launched a campaign in Jerusalem, seeing to it that "many of the saints" were imprisoned. That he should speak thus of believers in the Lord Jesus, calling them "saints," indicates the change of attitude that dated from his conversion. It also reflects his sense of guilt.[27]

He confessed here that he had voted the death penalty against them, which goes beyond the statement in 8:3. Based on the words, "I cast my vote," some have concluded that Paul must have been a member of the Sanhedrin at that time. However, the expression may have been metaphorical (Josephus used it in this sense). At that stage in his life he had been too young (7:58) to belong to this august body of elders. It is likely that we are to picture him as chief prosecutor giving his verdict on the guilt of those whom he had ferreted out in the course of his persecuting activity.

Much of his detective work had taken place in the "synagogues" (the incidental reference shows that at this period Jewish believers continued to frequent the synagogues, which fits into the speaker's effort to show that the Nazarenes were not guilty of revolt from the faith of their fathers). Here the persecutor had "punished" those who were pointed out to him by informers. (Recall that Paul himself suffered thus at the hands of synagogue officials in the course of his missionary work [14:19; cf. 2 Co 11:24]).

"I tried to force them to blaspheme" is an improvement over the wording of the KJV, for it does not carry the implication that he was successful (cf. Gal 1:13). Years later, in the early part of the second century, Pliny the Younger, then governor of Bithynia, made a report to the emperor

Trajan in which he indicated that if people who were suspected of being Christians consented to blaspheme Christ, he let them go, since he had been informed that this was one thing "people who are really Christians cannot possibly be made to do."[28]

The misplaced zeal of the persecutor had carried him even to "foreign cities," an allusion which prepares the way for the account of the risen Lord's intervention in his life.

Verses 12-18. The apostle recounted his journey to Damascus with authority from the chief priests (for this, see comment on 9:2) and the event which became the great turning point in his life.

> **26:12** "While thus engaged as I was journeying to Damascus with the authority and commission of the chief priests,
>
> **13** at midday, O King, I saw on the way a light from heaven, brighter than the sun, shining all around me and those who were journeying with me.
>
> **14** "And when we had all fallen to the ground, I heard a voice saying to me in the Hebrew dialect, 'Saul, Saul, why are you persecuting me? It is hard for you to kick against the goads.'
>
> **15** "And I said, 'Who art Thou, Lord?' And the Lord said, 'I am Jesus whom you are persecuting.
>
> **16** 'But arise, and stand on your feet; for this purpose I have appeared to you, to appoint you a minister and a witness not only to the things which you have seen, but also to the things in which I will appear to you;
>
> **17** delivering you from the *Jewish* people and from the Gentiles, to whom I am sending you,
>
> **18** to open their eyes so that they may turn from darkness to light and from the dominion of Satan to God, in order that they may receive forgiveness of sins and an inheritance among those who have been sanctified by faith in Me.'

26:12. Rather than "chief priests," Paul could have said "high priest" (9:1), but the plural is used in 9:14, 21. There may be a special reason for the choice of terminology here. The chief priests were active in pressing charges against Paul (25:15), so it seems he was pointing out that at that earlier time he had been in the service of the very company which was now seeking his life. Only an extraordinary influence could have put a gulf between him and his confederates. Paul went on to explain what that influence was—an "arrest" by a higher authority than that which had sanctioned his mission to Damascus.

26:13-15. The "light from heaven" is mentioned in all three accounts of the conversion, whereas the time of day is referred to only here and in 22:6. What is especially significant is the fact that the words of the risen Lord to Paul appear in all three accounts in almost identical language.

The self-revelation of the Lord Jesus Christ is the central item in all the narratives.

However, there is one important addition in verse 14 of chapter 26: "it is hard for you to kick against the goads." Dubious is the effort to find in this proverbial expression an indication that the very fury of Paul's persecution was but a reaction to the working of an accusing conscience set in motion by the witness of Stephen and others. The explanation of W. J. Sparrow-Simpson is much to be preferred:

> The saying, "It is hard for thee to kick against the goad," does not imply that S. Paul had suffered from misgivings, still less that he consciously opposed the will of God. The ox which resents the goad has no misgivings as to the superiority of the course which it desires to pursue. S. Paul, like the ox, did not know it to be the better way. That this interpretation is correct is confirmed by the whole drift of the Lucan narratives and by S. Paul's distinct assertions in his letters. His self-judgment was he 'did it ignorantly in unbelief.' "[29]

Also worthy of consultation is the discussion by Johannes Munck.[30]

Now that Paul had seen the Lord in His glory, like the prophet of old (Is 6) he was under divine constraint to go and tell. This is the burden of what follows immediately.

26:16-18. Apart from the opening command, the remainder of this passage is not found in the other two accounts. It concerns the purpose behind the self-disclosure of the risen Lord to this erstwhile foe of the Church. The first aspect of that purpose was to set Paul aside to the two-fold office of "minister" and "witness." As minister he was to have a servant's role (cf. 1 Co 4:1). The word *minister* denotes one who takes directions from above. As witness he was authorized to declare what he had seen and heard on this occasion and on others which would follow. The function of a witness is closely related to that of an apostle, covering much the same ground (cf. Ac 1:21-26). Of course not every witness is an apostle, but every apostle is a witness.

It was anticipated that fidelity to this appointment would bring Paul into disfavor with his countrymen. They would oppose him, as his present situation fully demonstrated. But the promise was that he would be delivered from the Jews as well as from the Gentiles who made common cause with them. Paul had to stay alive if he was to minister. This had a bearing on his innocence. Despite all efforts to destroy him, he had been preserved. God had been with him.

The second aspect of the purpose behind the revelation of the Lord on the Damascus road had to do with the task itself—the work to be performed and the result to be achieved (v. 18). There is some similarity to the language of Isaiah 42:6-7, where the Servant (Messiah) is pictured as given for a covenant to the people (Israel) and a light to the nations, to open the blind eyes and deliver those who sit in darkness. Paul's ministry was to be an extension of his Lord's. There is an implication here that Jews as well as Gentiles are in this benighted condition, needing spiritual illumination. It is in these very terms that the gospel according to John pictures the situation (e.g., Jn 3:19-21; 9:39-41). Paul's blindness had this significance (Ac 9:9). Satan's effort is to keep the unsaved in the darkness where sin has plunged them.

The linking of darkness with Satan and light with God is typically Pauline (13:10-11; 2 Co 4:4-6). The same apostle yoked light with inheritance (Col 1:12-13) as he did here, and inheritance with sanctification, as in 20:32. The Colossians passage teaches that the inheritance consists of a place in the Kingdom of God's Son. Such is the glorious future of those who even now enjoy "forgiveness of sins." That blessing, in turn, depends on the exercising of *faith* in the Lord Jesus. Here we have an epitome of the Pauline Gospel.[31]

Verses 19-23. In logical sequence, Paul turned to consider the response which he had made to the call and commission of the Lord Jesus.

> **26:19** "Consequently, King Agrippa, I did not prove disobedient to the heavenly vision,
>
> **20** but *kept* declaring both to those of Damascus first, and *also* at Jerusalem and *then* throughout all the region of Judea, and *even* to the Gentiles, that they should repent and turn to God, performing deeds appropriate to repentance.
>
> **21** "For this reason *some* Jews seized me in the temple and tried to put me to death.
>
> **22** "And so, having obtained help from God, I stand to this day testifying both to small and great, stating nothing but what the Prophets and Moses said was going to take place;
>
> **23** that the Christ was to suffer, *and* that by reason of *His* resurrection from the dead He should be the first to proclaim light both to the *Jewish* people and to the Gentiles."

26:19-23. The vision (and the accompanying revelation) was so real and so authoritative that Paul could never think of disobeying it (cf. 1 Co 9:1, 16). He pictured the ever widening circle of witness that was his—Damascus, Jerusalem, Judea, then the Gentiles—a series which recalls somewhat the ingredients of our Lord's commission to the eleven (1:8). Nothing was said about a ministry in Arabia, which came soon after the conversion (Gal 1:17). This may indicate that Paul's reason for going into Arabia was not primarily to minister but to meditate and to become properly oriented to his mission.

The emphasis here falls on a witness to Damascus, the very place he had planned to ravage so far as the Church was concerned (vv. 11-12). How startled the inhabitants of that city must have been to see such a transformed man. For Paul's witness in Jerusalem, see 9:28. The reference to Judea is very awkward in the Greek, for there is an abrupt change in construction. Furthermore, the present text conflicts with Galatians 1:22, where Paul denies contact with the churches of Judea at this period of his life. Also, Luke's account in 9:28 confines itself to Jerusalem. Rackham makes the suggestion that what Paul may be expected to have said is, "both at Damascus first and at Jerusalem and then in every country, both to Jews and Gentiles."[32] The text may have suffered corruption at an early period.

So much for the geography. But what did Paul proclaim? He answered, that men should "repent and turn to God" and show their repentance by appropriate "deeds." Thus Paul put himself in line with John the Baptist (Mt 3:2, 8), Jesus (Mt 4:17), and Peter (Ac 2:38) in teaching the indispensability of repentance and the proof of it in terms of a changed life. Since Gentiles were included in Paul's sphere of testimony, it is clearly wrong to hold that repentance is the demand made on Israel and faith the demand made on the Gentiles. Both groups needed both elements (20:21), since repentance for sin prepares the way for faith in Christ.

Paul's preaching activity got him into trouble with the unbelieving Jews who seized him in the Temple. It was while he was being obedient to the divine call (26:19) that they stopped his work. This left them in the position of opposing God (cf. 5:39). Paul did not pursue the subject of his arrest, seeing that this whole matter had been covered already in his trials before the governors, but was content to say that he was apprehended "for this reason" (literally, "on account of these things"). What he apparently had in mind was his conversion and subsequent efforts to win both Jews and Gentiles to Christ. Antagonism was strong because the man Paul had been the darling of the Pharisees as a youth and the hope of the Sanhedrin as the chief persecutor of the sect of the Nazarenes. He was hated as a turncoat. But God had been with him to supply all needed "help."

What Paul insisted on here, as on previous occasions, was that the proclamation from his lips which offended the Jews, far from being alien to their spiritual inheritance, was actually nothing different from what the Law and the prophets had predicted (v. 22; cf. 24:14). Jesus of Nazareth had experienced the same resistance and had pointed out its inconsistency (Jn 5:45-47). For Paul the great thrust of the Old Testament was not its ethical teaching, important as that was, but its Messianic prophecy, which pointed to the coming of the Christ, His suffering (death), His resurrection, and His subsequent proclamation (through His servants) of the

Good News of salvation to Israel and the Gentiles (cf. Eph 2:14-18, noting that here the meaning is that the Lord came and preached *after* His redemptive mission had been completed. See also Luke 24:46-47). By yoking his own proclamation with the prophetic content of the Old Testament, the apostle was strongly affirming the unity of the biblical message. What the Old predicts the New presents in terms of fulfillment.

Verses 24-29. The reactions of Festus and Agrippa to Paul's presentation, revealing much about the two men, had the effect of bringing the speech to a close.

> **26:24** And while *Paul* was saying this in his defense, Festus said in a loud voice, "Paul, you are out of your mind! *Your* great learning is driving you mad."
>
> **25** But Paul said, "I am not out of my mind, most excellent Festus, but I utter words of sober truth.
>
> **26** "For the king knows about these matters, and I speak to him also with confidence, since I am persuaded that none of these things escape his notice; for this has not been done in a corner.
>
> **27** "King Agrippa, do you believe the Prophets? I know that you do."
>
> **28** And Agrippa *replied* to Paul, "In a short time you will persuade me to become a Christian."
>
> **29** And Paul *said*, "I would to God, that whether in a short or long time, not only you, but also all who hear me this day, might become such as I am, except for these chains."

26:24-25. Suddenly the address was interrupted by an outburst from Festus, which actually served to terminate the discourse, although it is likely that Paul had said most of what he had in mind. At any rate there was no resumption of the speech. The outburst was unexpected in that Paul had been addressing Agrippa rather than Festus. Clearly the governor was lost by the discussion of things beyond his ken, particularly resurrection.

"Paul, you are out of your mind!" was not meant to be derogatory, as though the apostle was no more than a raving maniac who deserved to be excluded from society. In explanation for his comment, Festus continued, "Your great learning is driving you mad." The reference to learning may have been induced by the mention of the Law and the prophets, which seemed to imply that Paul had mastered their contents; this was an area doubtless quite unfamiliar to this Roman. Along with the evidence of learning went a fearlessness and an enthusiasm that made the governor restless. Was he listening to a man possessed? Paul himself did not approve of a display of charismatic enthusiasm which would draw the accusation of madness (1 Co 14:23), and in the present situation he was able to assure the governor that what he had been speaking was "sober truth."

It is noteworthy that neither here nor elsewhere did Festus address Paul as a criminal. Even here he did not seek to silence him, for he was impressed as well as confused by the apostle's fervor.

26:26-29. Having dealt with Festus, Paul resumed his contact with Agrippa, first by referring to him (v. 26), then by speaking to him directly (v. 27). The apostle was reminding Festus as politely as possible that the one whom he was primarily addressing was familiar with "these matters." But Festus was not dismissed from his concern, for Paul hoped to elicit from Agrippa an admission of the truth of what he had been saying so that Festus also would not treat Christianity cavalierly.

"I am persuaded that none of these things escape his notice," Paul continued. Agrippa presumably had a reasonably good familiarity with the Scriptures and also with the events of the life of Christ and the beginnings of the Church. Probably the last two items are gathered up together in the expression, "this has not been done in a corner." The proverbial language serves well to underscore the fact that although Christianity took its rise in a small land, it nevertheless happened at the crossroads of the world. So the things Paul had been talking about were not to be construed as esoteric, nor were they available only to those with special learning, but were matters of public knowledge (cf. Jn 19:20; Ac 4:25-28).

There followed immediately Paul's challenge to Agrippa, "Do you believe the Prophets?" It was an embarrassing moment for the king. If he were to agree with Paul, how would he appear in the eyes of Festus, who had just asserted Paul's madness? Yet he could not renounce the prophets or the Law and remain in any kind of favor with the Jews.

In his reply (v. 28) he sought to get himself off the hook by calling attention to the fact that this occasion had not been set up as an evangelistic service. If Paul was resorting to evangelism, thinking he could win over a ruler with the same ease whereby he gathered converts among the rank and file of men, he was mistaken. "In a short time you will persuade me to become a Christian."

This is a much discussed statement and translations vary greatly. The NASB rendering interprets the verb *persuade* as having future reference here, and it adopts the variant reading "become" (rather than "make") despite its limited support among the manuscripts. Better is the rendering of Bruce: "In brief you are persuading me [i.e., "trying to persuade me"] to act the Christian" (so also Haenchen, Williams). The key here is the specialized meaning of *make*, namely, "to act or play the part," as when Jezebel said to Ahab, "Is this the way you act the king over Israel?" (3 Kings 20:7, LXX). Another rendering is suggested by Nigel Turner, as follows: "You are trying to persuade me that you have made me a Christian in a short time."[33]

In other words, Agrippa was not at all prepared to acknowledge that he was near the Kingdom. He remained aloof, standing on his royal dignity. He could no more think of putting his trust in Jesus than had the bulk of his subjects. The cross was a stumbling block to him, as it had been to Paul, and he had not received any revelation to convince him of the resurrection of the Nazarene.

Paul ignored the sarcasm and with impassioned utterance expressed his longing that whether it required little or much persuasion, not only the king but all present might become as he was, a believer. Then, suddenly recollecting that he was wearing the tokens of a prisoner, he added as an afterthought, "except for these chains." What a revelation of the true nobility of spirit possessed by the apostle! He would share the best he had and refuse even to wish on others what had been unjustly imposed on him.

Verses 30-32. The governor and his guest conferred. Luke may have established connections with subordinates in the employ of Festus through whom he was able to secure information about this conversation.

> **26:30** And the king arose and the governor and Bernice, and those who were sitting with them,
>
> **31** and when they had drawn aside, they *began* talking to one another, saying, "This man is not doing anything worthy of death or imprisonment."
>
> **32** And Agrippa said to Festus, "This man might have been set free if he had not appealed to Caesar."

26:30-32. Agrippa had heard enough. Perhaps his conscience was beginning to give him trouble. His act of rising from his seat served to end the hearing. But Festus needed a brief conference with the king in order to be able to draft a report to Nero, for which Agrippa unhesitatingly gave his opinion that Paul merited neither death nor imprisonment. This had been the impression of all the Romans involved in the case up to this time, but Agrippa was a man well informed on Judaism, so his judgment was on that account the more weighty. Paul's address had been so free of political or revolutionary overtones, and his passion to proclaim Jesus as the Christ had been so much in the forefront, that any suggestion of an offense against the empire appeared ridiculous. In later years, when Rome had become a persecutor of Christians, Luke's record would be a standing reminder to all who read it that "from the beginning it was not so."

After Agrippa's declaration of Paul's innocence, it may seem strange to the reader that he was not released. Agrippa seems to indicate that the prisoner's appeal had ruled this out. Sherwin-White's explanation is as follows:

This does not mean that in strict law the governor could not pronounce an acquittal after the act of appeal. It is not a question of law, but of the relations between the emperor and his subordinates, and of that element of non-constitutional power which the Romans called *auctoritas*, "prestige," on which the supremacy of the Princeps so largely depended. No sensible man with hopes of promotion would dream of short-circuiting the appeal to Caesar unless he had specific authority to do so.[34]

L. Voyage and Shipwreck—27:1-44

This vivid chapter (Ac 27), filled with high adventure, is without parallel in the New Testament. Its closest counterpart in the Old Testament is the story of Jonah (Jon 1), but there Jonah's relationship to God is quite different from Paul's in the account before us.

Why should we be treated to such a detailed narrative? The answer is to be found partly in the presence of Luke, upon whose mind the incidents of this journey were indelibly impressed. He has portrayed "the best-known voyage of antiquity."

But beyond the fulfillment of the historian's obligation to present the facts is the spiritual value of the story. It provides ample evidence of the providence of God and His faithfulness. When the promise was given to Paul that he would see Rome and bear witness there (23:11), no assurance was given of a calm and uneventful trip. But the God who had spoken through the prophet, saying, "When you pass through the waters, I will be with you" (Is 43:2) is seen in this chapter as fulfilling His word. In keeping with this, one cannot fail to note also that in the midst of the utmost danger and distress Paul, with the Lord's help, rose to the occasion by being a source of strength and direction to all on board, despite his status as a prisoner.

A landlubber who endeavors to comment on Luke's description is greatly indebted to those who are seamen or travelers in that part of the world where the sea journey was taken. (A map of the region is also of great help.) One such traveler is James Smith, whose valuable work has been widely acclaimed, and justly so. A quotation or two will serve to communicate the impressions and conclusions of this investigator.

> A searching comparison of the narrative, with the localities where the events so circumstantially related are said to have taken place, with the aid which recent advances in our knowledge of the geography and the navigation of the eastern part of the Mediterranean supply, accounts for every transaction, clears up every difficulty, and exhibits an agreement so perfect in all its parts as to admit of but one explanation, namely that it is a narrative of real events, written by one personally engaged in them, and that the tradition respecting the locality is true.[1]

Regarding the actual language employed in writing this chapter, the same author comments,

No sailor would have written in a style so little like that of a sailor; no man not a sailor could have written a narrative of a sea voyage so consistent in all its parts, unless from actual observation.[2]

Verses 1-8. In the first unit of his narrative Luke traces the stages of the journey from Caesarea to Crete.

> **27:1** And when it was decided that we should sail for Italy, they proceeded to deliver Paul and some other prisoners to a centurion of the Augustan cohort named Julius.
>
> **2** And embarking in an Adramyttian ship, which was about to sail to the regions along the coast of Asia, we put out to sea, accompanied by Aristarchus, a Macedonian of Thessalonica.
>
> **3** And the next day we put in at Sidon; and Julius treated Paul with consideration and allowed him to go to his friends and receive care.
>
> **4** And from there we put out to sea and sailed under the shelter of Cyprus because the winds were contrary.
>
> **5** And when we had sailed through the sea along the coast of Cilicia and Pamphylia, we landed at Myra in Lycia.
>
> **6** And there the centurion found an Alexandrian ship sailing for Italy, and he put us aboard it.
>
> **7** And when we had sailed slowly for a good many days, and with difficulty had arrived off Cnidus, since the wind did not permit us *to go* farther, we sailed under the shelter of Crete, off Salmone;
>
> **8** and with difficulty sailing past it we came to a certain place called Fair Havens, near which was the city of Lasea.

27:1-8. Luke makes his presence known as a companion of Paul by the recurring use of "we," especially in recounting the early stages of the trip to Italy. "They" is an indefinite subject, presumably referring to those who were charged by Festus with making the necessary arrangements for the journey. "Other prisoners" are noted as being sent at the same time, the whole group being in the charge of a "centurion" named Julius. (Another centurion, who had figured in Paul's situation at Jerusalem [22:25], was left unnamed.) Perhaps the man now indicated is named not only because his responsibility was greater but also because his name was notable (Julius recalls the first Caesar) and because his command (the Augustan Cohort) bore a prestigious title, that given to the first ruler of the empire. There is evidence for such a cohort in Syria during this period.[3]

The journey was begun aboard a ship that claimed for its home port Adramyttium, a city in the southern part of Mysia in northwest Asia Minor. It was due to sail along the coast of Asia. Simply because the ship put in at Sidon for a stop, the reader is not to assume that "Asia" means the continent. The reference is to the coast of Asia Minor. Presumably no ship to Italy was available at that time, so the present arrangement was made.

385

It provided these options: to continue on the same vessel to its destination and then proceed to Macedonia; to go overland to the west coast and take ship for the Adriatic crossing to Italy; or to look forward to transshipping at one of the ports of Lycia on the southern coast of Asia Minor, then sail west across the Mediterranean. It developed that the latter course was taken.

In addition to Luke, Paul was accompanied by Aristarchus. This man had been with him at Ephesus (19:29) and again on the trip to Jerusalem as a representative of the church at Thessalonica (20:4). Since he was with Paul when the apostle wrote two of his captivity letters (Col 4:10; Phile 24), it is likely that he experienced the storm and shipwreck with the others. There is just a possibility, however, that he continued on the Adramyttian ship in order to bring news of Paul's affairs to the churches of Macedonia and that he later crossed over to Rome to be with him. He became Paul's fellow prisoner there, but whether this means he was detained or that he simply chose to share Paul's confinement, is uncertain. Ramsay judges that he made the voyage to Rome as Paul's slave.

A day's run brought the ship to Sidon, where a stop was made. Permission was given by the centurion for Paul to visit his "friends" in the city, still under guard, of course (much as Ignatius, several decades later, was allowed similar courtesies by his Roman guards as he made the trip to Rome, where he faced martyrdom). Sidon may have received the Gospel many years before, when the coast of Phoenicia was evangelized (11:19). Paul had had no contact with the place on his way to Jerusalem, when he had stopped at Tyre (21:3) and Ptolemais (21:7) and had fellowship with believers; but at an earlier time he had probably visited the city and the church (15:3).

The expression, "his friends," is literally "the friends," and because of this some are inclined to understand it as a technical designation for Christians. But two things need to be said. The definite article in Greek is used rather often in a possessive sense, which is natural here. Also, the term *friends* is not certified as a regular way of designating believers in the history of the early Church. It did not have the same flavor of spiritual kinship which was conveyed by *brethren*.

Heading north once more, the ship sailed "under the shelter of Cyprus." This in itself does not tell us whether the course taken was to the west of the island or to the east, but the explanation given here provides the answer—"the winds were contrary." This does not mean contrary to their regular pattern, but contrary to the progress and safety of the ship. Since the winds were from the west at this time of year (late summer), there was danger of being driven ashore if the western passage were taken. No such hazard would be encountered by skirting the island on the east side. The narrative confirms this picture by going on to state that the ship then moved along "the coast of Cilicia and Pamphylia." If the western course had been taken, these locations would have been distinctly off line to the east, and contact would have been made directly with the coast of Lycia. As it was, the latter area was reached only by pursuing a course for some time along the coast.

"At Myra in Lycia," more precisely, no doubt, at Andriake, its port city, an Alexandrian ship bound for Italy was located. Later information (v. 38) indicates that it was a grain ship. "It is an interesting evidence of the difficulty of sailing directly or indirectly westward that Myra is due north of Alexandria."[4] While such ships could sail directly from Rome to Egypt, the return to the west could not be made directly. Once the transfer had been made to this large ship (in addition to cargo it carried nearly three hundred people, as we learn from v. 37) and the journey was continued, progress was painfully slow between Myra and Cnidus on the coast of Caria.

The segment from Myra to a point off Cnidus was negotiated "with difficulty," requiring "many days," presumably because of contrary winds (v. 7). That the ship could make progress at all was due to "the advantage of a weather shore, under the lee of which she would have smooth water ... and a westerly current."[5] Here it was necessary to face the open sea. But to avoid being exposed to northwest winds that battered the ship,[6] a course was established not straight to the west, as was sometimes possible, but almost due south to gain the shelter of the island of Crete. The first town to be sighted and passed on the starboard side was Salmone. Still experiencing much difficulty due to the wind, the ship finally made Fair Havens near the southern tip of the island (v. 8).

Verses 9-12. This section relates the circumstances that led to an attempt to go farther, a move that invited disaster.

27:9 And when considerable time had passed and the voyage was now dangerous, since even the fast was already over, Paul *began* to admonish them,

10 and said to them, "Men, I perceive that the voyage will certainly be *attended* with damage and great loss, not only of the cargo and the ship, but also of our lives."

11 But the centurion was more persuaded by the pilot and the captain of the ship, than by what was being said by Paul.

12 And because the harbor was not suitable for wintering, the majority reached a decision to put out to sea from there, if somehow they could reach Phoenix, a harbor of Crete, facing northeast and southeast, and spend the winter *there.*

27:9-12. Autumn had come by this time. Ramsay estimates that the arrival at Fair Havens occurred on September 25, which meant that good sailing weather would now be problematical due to the likelihood of storms. Apparently "considerable time" was spent at Fair Havens while the strong wind continued to blow. As Luke states presently, Fair Havens, despite its name, was not a suitable place for wintering. But Paul, with his eye on the calendar (it was now early in October, with the Fast, or Day of Atonement, already past), and knowing that in a few days the coming of impossible conditions could be expected, was prepared to advocate that the ship remain where it was, despite the inadequacy of the harbor. He had a foreboding of disaster. To be sure, apart from revelation Paul could have been mistaken, as he was in predicting loss of life (v. 10). God corrected him on this point (vv. 22-24).

It seems that there was a conference between the pilot and the captain (not owner, as KJV reads), the centurion, and Paul, with others listening in and ready to offer advice (v. 12). It may seem strange that the two former, being used to the sea, would advocate going on in an effort to reach Phoenix on the south coast of Crete and winter there. But as Ramsay explains the matter, they were in the imperial service and anxious to get their cargo to Rome as soon as possible. A few miles saved now would mean earlier arrival in the spring.

The centurion respected their opinion more than that of Paul. After all, Phoenix was a safer harbor than Fair Havens, and what did Paul know about nautical matters? He may well have underrated the apostle, a man who had experienced more than once the perils of the deep (2 Co 11:25). At any rate, he was to regret his decision before many hours had passed.

The identification of Phoenix with the modern Lutro was suggested by Smith, but he has not been generally followed.[7] Lake and Cadbury look somewhat favorably on Phineka, about a mile west of Lutro, as answering to the site, and of course this name is almost identical with *Phoenix*.[8]

Verses 13-20. Here is depicted in dramatic fashion the encounter with the gale that rendered the ship helpless.

> **27:13** And when a moderate south wind came up, supposing that they had gained their purpose, they weighed anchor and *began* sailing along Crete, close *inshore.*
>
> **14** But before very long there rushed down from the land a violent wind, called Euraquilo;
>
> **15** and when the ship was caught *in it,* and could not face the wind, we gave way *to it,* and let ourselves be driven along.
>
> **16** And running under the shelter of a small island called Clauda, we were scarcely able to get the *ship's* boat under control.
>
> **17** And after they had hoisted it up, they used supporting cables in

undergirding the ship; and fearing that they might run aground on *the shallows* of Syrtis, they let down the sea anchor, and so let themselves be driven along.

18 The next day as we were being violently storm-tossed, they began to jettison the cargo;

19 and on the third day they threw the ship's tackle overboard with their own hands.

20 And since neither sun nor stars appeared for many days, and no small storm was assailing *us*, from then on all hope of our being saved was gradually abandoned.

27:13-20. A change in the weather seemed to confirm the wisdom of the decision to sail on. The warm breeze from the south was too tempting to resist, so they weighed anchor and headed for Cape Matala, three to four miles to the west. Rounding it, they took a northwesterly direction across the Gulf of Messara toward their desired haven.

But before long there was a sudden shift in the direction and velocity of the wind, putting the ship at the mercy of Euraquilo, the northeaster. It was violent (the Greek word, when transliterated, is *typhonic*). Smith quotes a captain of the Royal Navy as testifying that in this area "southerly winds . . . almost invariably shift to a violent northerly wind."[9] Had the wind been from the south or the west, the ship would have been carried onto the shore of the island.

The suddenness and severity of the blow have something of a parallel in the storm which had struck the Sea of Galilee and terrified the disciples (Mk 4:37). Indeed, the terrain on the north and east sides of the Sea of Galilee bears a similarity to that of Crete, except that the mountains on the island are higher, producing more drastic atmospheric changes. However, this was no sudden squall that would subside quickly, but the opening wedge of a storm that was to continue for days.

In the face of such a stiff wind it was impossible to tack and gradually make progress toward Phoenix. All that could be done was to allow the ship to be driven before the gale, since there was no time to reef the mainsail (v. 15). Some respite was provided, however, when the sailors were able to steer the vessel into quieter water in the shelter of an island called Clauda (sometimes spelled Cauda).

Here three steps were taken. First, the dinghy, which must have been partly submerged, was with difficulty hoisted onto the ship. Some have concluded from the "we" that Luke himself lent a hand in this operation. Possibly so, but the same pronoun in the preceding verse suggests that the working personnel rather than the passengers on the ship are meant in both places. A second action was taken, namely, to pass ropes under the vessel, probably crosswise[10] rather than lengthwise, to ease the stress on the timbers, which by this time may have begun to spring leaks. A third measure is somewhat obscure, although "lowered the gear" is a reasonable translation. The NASB takes this to mean that they "let down the sea anchor." More probable is the conclusion of Smith that "the yard with the sail attached to it"[11] was lowered. Otherwise there would be no mention of something which simply had to be attended to if the ship was to be kept from foundering. The foresail was left in place to give stability of motion.

From then on the plan was to allow the wind to strike the ship on the starboard side and keep it pointed toward the northwest by means of the rudders and foresail, so as to achieve a generally westward direction. As Luke notes, if the ship were allowed to run without restraint before the gale, it would head in a southwesterly direction and ultimately go aground on the coast of North Africa, the dreaded shallows and sandbanks of Syrtis.

Once these measures were taken, those aboard ship "let themselves be driven along" (v. 17). The verb is in the imperfect tense, suggesting that this continued to be the case unless something is noted to the contrary. Smith goes on record as considering that no change took place in the direction of the wind during the rest of the voyage.[12] After consulting navigators familiar with these waters, he found that their observations on the drifting rate of a large ship in a sustained strong wind made it possible to test Luke's account that thirteen days and a fraction were consumed in the journey from Clauda to the point of shipwreck.[13] His lengthy discussion is summarized by Ramsay.

> Accordingly, the ship drifted, with her head to the north, steadied by a low sail, making lee-way proportionate to the power of the wind and waves on her broadside. As Smith shows in detail, the resultant rate of motion would vary, according to the size of the ship and the force of the wind, between ¾ and 2 miles per hour; and the probable mean rate in this case would be about 1½ miles per hour; while the direction would approximate to 8° north of west. The ship would continue to drift in the same way as long as the wind blew the same, and the timbers and sails held; and at the calculated rates, if it was under Cauda towards evening, it would on the fourteenth night be near Malta.[14]

In this connection it should be noted from verses 18 and 19 that the time is reckoned from Clauda rather than from Fair Havens.

The next day, to decrease the danger of the ship's offering too much resistance to the storm, they began to jettison "the cargo" (cf. Jon 1:5), but apparently this was discontinued (the remainder of the cargo was cast out later and for a different purpose, according to v. 38). A day later still another expedient was followed, the tossing overboard of all "the ship's tackle" that could be spared.

After these measures were taken, those on board faced the monotony of days without sun and nights without stars. Likely there was heavy rain, for the word "storm" is formed from the root *to pour*. Gradually hope of being delivered faded away, since the heavens could not be consulted to determine direction, and the ship could not be expected to hold together indefinitely.

Verses 21-26. This passage recounts God's encouragement given to Paul and through him to all who were on board.

> **27:21** And when they had gone a long time without food, then Paul stood up in their midst and said, "Men, you ought to have followed my advice and not to have set sail from Crete, and incurred this damage and loss.
>
> **22** "And *yet* now I urge you to keep up your courage, for there shall be no loss of life among you, but *only* of the ship.
>
> **23** "For this very night an angel of the God to whom I belong and whom I serve stood before me,
>
> **24** saying, 'Do not be afraid, Paul; you must stand before Caesar; and behold, God has granted you all those who are sailing with you.'
>
> **25** "Therefore, keep up your courage, men, for I believe God, that it it will turn out exactly as I have been told.
>
> **26** "But we must run aground on a certain island."

27:21-26. It was at this juncture that Paul began to assert himself and to restore hope. His counsel had been ignored, hence the desperate straits on board ship. But he was content to bide his time until spirits were low before offering the gentle reminder that his suggestion at Fair Havens should have been taken. In other words, if he had been right then, it could be assumed that he would be worth listening to now, even at this late hour. He saw that people around him were downcast and miserable. Loss of hope was matched by loss of appetite. Even if food stocks were not affected by the storm (an unlikely assumption), seasickness must have taken its toll.

"Keep up your courage" was Paul's appeal (vv. 22, 25). This could have been treated as whistling in the dark except for his assurance that there would be no loss of life. God had enlightened him on this point. The ship would go, but they would survive. Cynical faces must have looked at him with astonishment as he went on to explain that in the purpose of God he must appear in Caesar's court, so his life had to be spared, and God had graciously included his fellows on board in the reprieve. What a man! Yes, and what a God! Paul could readily suppose, in the face of this divine intervention, that God was not only guaranteeing his arrival in

Rome but was encouraging him to expect that the trial would not result in death (cf. Phil 1:19, 25).

But the even more obvious lesson here, one to which the unsaved are virtually oblivious, is how much unbelievers owe to the presence and intercession of the godly. Joseph had been the means of preserving Egypt. Paul was the saviour of the mariners. That day on shipboard, pagans had a glimpse of a great marvel—a man so in touch with God that not only his life but the lives of those who traveled with him were spared. His firm belief in God's fidelity must have revived their hope. The footnote about being cast on "a certain island" made little difference in view of the promised deliverance.

Verses 27-32. The approach to the island is recounted in this section.

> **27:27** But when the fourteenth night had come, as we were being driven about in the Adriatic Sea, about midnight the sailors *began* to surmise that they were approaching some land.
>
> **28** And they took soundings, and found *it to be* twenty fathoms; and a little farther on they took another sounding and found *it to be* fifteen fathoms.
>
> **29** And fearing that we might run aground somewhere on the rocks, they cast four anchors from the stern and wished for daybreak.
>
> **30** And as the sailors were trying to escape from the ship, and had let down the *ship's* boat into the sea, on the pretense of intending to lay out anchors from the bow,
>
> **31** Paul said to the centurion and to the soldiers, "Unless these men remain in the ship, you yourselves cannot be saved."
>
> **32** Then the soldiers cut away the ropes of the *ship's* boat, and let it fall away.

27:27-32. After days without a change, on "the fourteenth night" the sailors sensed that the ship was approaching land. Perhaps they detected in the distance the faint sound of waves breaking on the shore.

Two problems emerge here (v. 27). If the translation "as we were being driven about" is accepted, the impression is created that the ship was zigzagging in the water instead of maintaining a steady course. A better rendering would be "still drifting" (NEB), for the *dia* which is compounded with the root *pherō* may have the force of continuity or completeness. Another possibility is "drifting across" (Lake and Cadbury).

The second problem concerns the place in which the drifting occurred—"the Adriatic Sea." To most readers this calls up a picture of the body of water between the Grecian and Italian peninsulas, as distinct from the Mediterranean. But to the ancients, the Adriatic included the waters between Crete and Malta and at times even the sea to the coast of North Africa.[15] Deissmann seems to have erred on two counts, placing the course too far to the north (perhaps under too limited a concept of the meaning of Adria) and representing the course as involving much zigzagging, presumably under the impression that *diapheromenōn* required the idea of being driven up and down.[16]

Soundings were taken by the crew, the first revealing a depth of 120 feet,* and the next, a short time later, of 90 feet. This created concern lest the ship be driven on the rocks, so the motion was slowed during the rest of the night by the dropping of four anchors from the stern. To drop anchor from the bow under present conditions would result in swinging the vessel around so that the waves would strike it broadside, something to be avoided at all cost.

During the period of tense waiting for "daybreak" a strange thing happened. Luke reports an attempt by some of the sailors to lower the dinghy in order to escape from the ship (v. 30). They had received Paul's word about being cast on an island but had difficulty in accepting his assurance that all would be saved. It was a foolhardy venture, indicative of panic. To prevent their escape, the soldiers acted almost as foolishly as the sailors, cutting the ropes of the ship's boat and letting it fall into the sea. Now anyone who reached land would have to swim.

Verses 33-38. The paragraph dwells on the personal preparation for going ashore once the island was reached.

> **27:33** And until the day was about to dawn, Paul was encouraging them all to take some food, saying, "Today is the fourteenth day that you have been constantly watching and going without eating, having taken nothing.
>
> **34** "Therefore I encourage you to take some food, for this is for your preservation; for not a hair from the head of any of you shall perish."
>
> **35** And having said this, he took bread and gave thanks to God in the presence of all; and he broke it and began to eat.
>
> **36** And all of them were encouraged, and they themselves also took food.
>
> **37** And all of us in the ship were two hundred and seventy-six persons.
>
> **38** And when they had eaten enough, they *began* to lighten the ship by throwing out the wheat into the sea.

27:33-38. Because of nausea and anxiety, people had not been eating during the storm. Paul, by now the real leader on board though still a prisoner, spoke kindly but firmly. Food was necessary for their "preservation"—more vividly put by NEB, "your lives depend on it." To get them started, the apostle "took bread and gave thanks to God" in the sight of all the people. He had developed a rapport with those around him so that

*The Greek word for *fathom* denotes a stretching out—it was the distance between finger tips when the arms are extended, approximating six feet.

he could do this openly. As the saying goes, he had "earned the right to be heard."

It is odd that anyone would suppose that Paul was observing communion, especially in the presence of many who were not believers. Though the language fits the communion, clearly the situation does not. It was an ordinary meal, with all two hundred and seventy-six partaking. There is some manuscript authority for the reading "seventy-six," but the grain ships were often large and needed a good-sized crew. Josephus reports that a ship on which he was traversing the Adriatic, only to founder in the sea, had six hundred people aboard.[17] Once they had eaten, Paul's companions had strength enough to toss overboard the remaining wheat, "to lighten the ship" so that it could readily be run aground. There is no implication that the people had been partaking of the wheat for their meal.

Verses 39-44. This portion of the story is given over to an account of the shipwreck.

> **27:39** And when day came, they could not recognize the land; but they did observe a certain bay with a beach, and they resolved to drive the ship onto it if they could.
>
> **40** And casting off the anchors, they left them in the sea while at the same time they were loosening the ropes of the rudders, and hoisting the foresail to the wind, they were heading for the beach.
>
> **41** But striking a reef where two seas met, they ran the vessel aground; and the prow stuck fast and remained immovable, but the stern *began* to be broken up by the force *of the waves.*
>
> **42** And the soldiers' plan was to kill the prisoners, that none *of them* should swim away and escape;
>
> **43** but the centurion, wanting to bring Paul safely through, kept them from their intention, and commanded that those who could swim should jump overboard first and get to land,
>
> **44** and the rest *should follow,* some on planks, and others on various things from the ship. And thus it happened that they all were brought safely to land.

27:39-44. "They [the crew] could not recognize the land," for Malta was not near the shipping lanes. But they sighted a certain "bay" (not "creek," as in the KJV) "with a beach" (in contrast to rocks at other points). The Greek word for *bay* translates ultimately into our word *gulf.* Indentation is the gist of the term.

Since the beach looked promising, it was resolved to cast away the anchors that had been dragging and head for the shore after loosing the ropes which had been used to strap the rudders in place to make them useful again. Further, they hoisted the foresail to the wind to pick up speed. What they could not see as they started for the shore was a hidden reef "where two seas met." That is, there was deeper water on either side of it. On the reef the prow of the vessel stuck fast, exposing the stern to the still surging waves that began to batter it to pieces.

It was expedient to leave the ship as soon as possible. But the soldiers feared that their prisoners would swim off and escape, so they advocated killing them lest they themselves would have to answer for failure to keep them in custody. In this situation, once again Paul proved to be the saviour of others, for the centurion's decision to spare him brought the same treatment for the others (v. 43).

Soon the water was dotted with swimmers bobbing up and down and then with those who could not swim, clinging to anything that would keep them afloat. It has been conjectured that "various things" should be rendered "certain ones," giving a picture of the swimmers taking the non-swimmers on their backs into the water. But the usual understanding of the phrase appears the more likely. Luke was able to close the narrative with the triumphant assertion, "They were all brought safely to land," verifying Paul's prediction based on God's disclosure to him (vv. 22, 24).

Some students (e.g., Haenchen) complain that the prominence given to Paul in this chapter is artificial—Luke was contriving to find the hero role for him in one way or another. This prominence would indeed stand out like a sore thumb if the apostle had not displayed extraordinary qualities elsewhere. But his personal magnetism and sterling character, his outstanding leadership, and his Spirit-filled life, affecting enemies and friends alike, are so clearly etched on the history as a whole that there is no good reason for distrusting this portion of the narrative. He was no less dynamic as a prisoner than as a free man; and for this information we are not dependent simply on Luke, for after reaching Rome Paul made a profound impression both on the praetorian guard and on others in the imperial service (Phil 1:13).

M. STAY AT MALTA—28:1-10

IN THIS NARRATIVE Luke continues to highlight the role of Paul, whereas virtually no notice is taken of what befell the non-Christians who were stranded on the island after the shipwreck. Paul is pictured mainly as a worker of miracles.

28:1 And when they had been brought safely through, then we found out that the island was called Malta.

2 And the natives showed us extraordinary kindness; for because of the rain that had set in and because of the cold, they kindled a fire and received us all.

3 But when Paul had gathered a bundle of sticks and laid them on the fire, a viper came out because of the heat, and fastened on his hand.

4 And when the natives saw the creature hanging from his hand, they *began* saying to one another, "Undoubtedly this man is a murderer, and though he has been saved from the sea, justice has not allowed him to live."

5 However he shook the creature off into the fire and suffered no harm.

6 But they were expecting that he was about to swell up or suddenly fall down dead. But after they had waited a long time and had seen nothing unusual happen to him, they changed their minds and *began* to say that he was a god.

7 Now in the neighborhood of that place were lands belonging to the leading man of the island, named Publius, who welcomed us and entertained us courteously three days.

8 And it came about that the father of Publius was lying *in bed* afflicted with *recurrent* fever and dysentery; and Paul went in *to see* him and after he had prayed, he laid his hands on him and healed him.

9 And after this had happened, the rest of the people on the island who had diseases were coming to him and getting cured.

10 And they also honored us with many marks of respect; and when we were setting sail, they supplied *us* with all we needed.

28:1. For the first time the island is designated by name. Malta is the modern name; *Melita* (more properly *Meli'ē*) is the form used by the ancients. There is no land between it and Crete.

28:2. The term "natives," which Luke uses for the inhabitants of the island (cf. v. 4), is literally "barbarians." All the remaining examples of the word are in Paul's writings (Ro 1:14; 1 Co 14:11; Col 3:11). After observing that the word denotes non-Greek birth, Ramsay draws the inference that this confirms the generally received view that Luke was a Greek, for no Jew would have applied the term to the people of the island.[1] Luke was conscious that these people had a different language from his own (the natives probably spoke a Phoenician dialect, since Malta had long ago been colonized by the Phoenicians). There is a suggestion also of limited culture ("rough islanders" is the NEB rendering). Paul felt an obligation to preach the Gospel to barbarians (Ro 1:14), and he may have done so here in connection with the miracles, but there is no record of it.

Luke's use of the term *barbaroi* as indicative of the backward state of the people prepares the reader for their display of superstition (vv. 4-6). At the same time, it creates a tension with the "extraordinary kindness" shown to the victims of the shipwreck by these very people. Kindness is not dependent on degree of culture; it can crop up anywhere. The refugees' immediate need, which these people supplied, was warmth, for rain was intensifying the discomfort begun by the plunge into St. Paul's Bay (as it is known today).

The islanders received "all" in the party. This is the only clear indication in the entire narrative of the presence of others besides Paul and his companions, although the "us" of verse 7 may be inclusive (less likely in v. 10).

28:3-6. Soon Paul began to busy himself keeping up the large "fire" which the natives had started to help the visitors. Because of the rain, he may have had to search for brush that was sufficiently dry to burn. This raises a question as to his freedom of movement. Perhaps the centurion, knowing that the possibility of escape from the island was slight, relaxed surveillance, ordering him to be unhandcuffed.

As Paul put his "sticks" on the fire, a viper, aroused by the heat, came out of the bundle and bit him. Seeing the creature hanging from his hand, the natives began to comment to one another about the phenomenon. Likely they had observed him under guard when he had first appeared, and had concluded that he was "a murderer." Now "Justice" was recompensing him for his crime, not waiting for a human court to act.*

When Paul, without any show of fear or anxiety, calmly shook off the viper into the fire, they continued to rivet their eyes on him, looking for the telltale swelling and the collapse that betokened the stroke of death.

*Hesiod, one of the early Greek poets, in his *Works and Days*, uses this word *dikē* in the sense of punishment (line 239), then goes on to picture *dikē* as a virgin daughter of Zeus, who sits beside him and keeps him posted on acts of human injustice, that he may take appropriate action (line 256). This usage of *dikē* illumines the passage under consideration.

But when nothing happened, an entirely different verdict seemed in order. This man could not be a murderer; he must be "a god." Apparently it did not occur to them to wonder how a god would permit himself to fall into human custody.

28:7-8. The second episode has something in common with the first, in that hospitality was the setting for a miracle. Now, however, it was extended by "the leading man" on the island, one named Publius. A better rendering is "chief magistrate" (NEB), which takes account of his official position rather than of his personal influence. This was the proper title for the highest official of the Roman administration on Malta. Possibly news of what had happened to Paul at the fire was conveyed to him, leading to the invitation to him and his party to spend a few days. The magistrate may have been thinking of his father's condition and hoping that something could be done for him.

Judging by 27:3, no objection would have been raised by Julius, who felt he owed to Paul the preservation of all who had been aboard the ship. Paul was glad to respond, ministering by prayer and the laying on of his hands (the one passage in Acts where this act occurs in connection with healing). Luke the physician was there and available, but the man with the gift of healing took over. As far as one can tell, Luke was completely free of envy. There must have been other situations as well in which he stood aside that Paul might minister in the name of the Lord.

28:9-10. This one healing, occurring as it did within the circle of the administrative family, was soon heralded abroad with the result that many presented themselves and were cured of their various diseases. In view of the language employed here ("honored us"), it is a reasonable conclusion that Luke took a hand in the care of the patients and received the gratitude of the people along with Paul. Whatever their precise nature, these "marks of respect" should be thought of as tokens of gratitude rather than as professional fees. When the party left the island, many of the inhabitants who had reason to be grateful were on hand to make sure that the travelers had ample supplies for the remainder of their trip.

N. At Rome—28:11-31

Notices of time and place are prominent in this closing segment of Luke's account. It reads as though it were composed from a series of entries in a diary.

Verses 11-16. This section constitutes a log of the journey from the island of Malta to Rome, which was brightened by encouragement from brethren along the way.

28:11 And at the end of three months we set sail on an Alexandrian ship which had wintered at the island, and which had the Twin Brothers for its figurehead.

12 And after we put in at Syracuse, we stayed there for three days.

13 And from there we sailed around and arrived at Rhegium, and a day later a south wind sprang up, and on the second day we came to Puteoli.

14 There we found *some* brethren, and were invited to stay with them for seven days; and thus we came to Rome.

15 And the brethren, when they heard about us, came from there as far as the Market of Appius and Three Inns to meet us; and when Paul saw them, he thanked God and took courage.

16 And when we entered Rome, Paul was allowed to stay by himself, with the soldier who was guarding him.

28:11-16. After a stay of "three months" at Malta it was possible to make a fresh start, since navigation was reopened in the early spring or, as in this case, in the late winter. Fortunately an Alexandrian ship was available, probably a grain ship which had spent the winter at the island because of stormy weather. It had for its figurehead the Twin Brothers Castor and Pollux, the Dioscuri, who were legendary sons of Zeus and Leda. Noted for their athletic prowess, they became chiefly famous as the guardian gods of mariners and were especially popular in Egypt and at Rome, where there were several temples in their honor. By "figurehead" we are probably to understand that the ship had images of the deities affixed to its prow.

The first stop was at Syracuse, a city on the east coast of Sicily, which had been colonized by Greeks several centuries before and had grown wealthy through commerce. Now it belonged to the Romans, who made it the seat of government for the island. "Three days" were spent here, a delay which may have been occasioned by inclement weather or lack of breeze.

From this point on the journey was made by heading almost due north. The first stop was at Rhegium on the toe of Italy, reached after "we sailed around," an expression of uncertain meaning. It may denote tacking. Aided by a south wind, the rest of the journey to Puteoli was completed without difficulty. Located near Naples, this city had the most commodious harbor in all of Italy (at this time Ostia at the mouth of the Tiber had not been fully developed) and was the terminal port for many of the grain ships.

How to account for a stay of "seven days" here is a puzzle. Possibly, as Hanson suggests, the centurion went on to Rome to make arrangements for his prisoners and then returned to take them the rest of the way.[2] At any rate, the delay was welcome, since Paul and his little company were with "brethren," a note which attests some evangelization of Italy before Paul's arrival. Of course the presence of Christians at Rome is attested by Paul's writing a letter to them before he left Greece the last time.

The historian records the arrival at the capital of the empire in laconic fashion—"and thus we came to Rome." It had long been in Paul's thinking and planning (19:21; 23:11). The journey from Puetoli to Rome was made overland and was the more pleasant because the final stages, from the Market of Appius (forty-three miles from Rome) and from Three Inns (thirty-three miles from the city), were made in company with groups of believers who had come out from Rome to meet the party. We are not told how information about the impending arrival had reached them, but the church at Puteoli may have sent messengers ahead.

The amazing thing is that nothing further is reported about Paul's contact with the church at Rome. Rather, the remainder of the chapter is taken up with the apostle's testimony to unsaved Jews. This silence is probably not intended to suggest tension between Paul and some in the church, such as he reported later on (Phil 1:15, 17), for then it would be strange that Luke would have anything to say about brethren coming from Rome to greet the apostle. In keeping with the evangelistic thrust of the book as a whole, in that the accent does not fall heavily on fellowship with believers (though this is noted from time to time), the close of Luke's narrative emphasizes contact with unbelievers. Paul was grateful for the two delegations, for he had long cherished the hope of reaching Rome (Ro 1:13), of meeting old friends and making new ones. He was encouraged.

Lest the reader gain the impression that the relative freedom Paul had enjoyed since the shipwreck was to continue, Luke mentions that he was guarded by a soldier and lived by himself. No notice is taken of Paul being formally delivered to the Roman authorities except in the Western text, which states that the centurion delivered the prisoners as a group to the *stratopedarch*.

There is a problem in identifying this figure, for the word itself is quite rare. One view, favored by Ramsay and some others, is to identify the term with the *princeps peregrinorum*, the officer who commanded soldiers charged with special missions outside of Rome. Sherwin-White, however, inclines to another view, identifying this term

> with the officer known as *princeps castrorum*, the head administrator of the *officium* of the Pretorian Guard. This post happens to be known only from the Trajanic period onward, but it corresponded in duties and standing to the like-named officer in the legionary army, the *princeps praetorii legionis*, the head of the organizational command of a legion. This necessary post is testified, in the legions, from the time of Claudius onwards, and there is no reason to suppose that the *princeps castrorum* of

the Pretorian Guard was a later creation. The official is the personage most likely to be in executive control of prisoners awaiting trial at Rome in the Julio-Claudian period.[3]

Verses 17-22. The remainder of the chapter is devoted to Paul's contacts with the Jews at Rome. Designedly he first sought out the key figures for a conference (as reported in this section) prior to inviting a more general audience to hear his presentation of the Gospel (vv. 23-28).

> **28:17** And it happened that after three days he called together those who were the leading men of the Jews, and when they had come together, he *began* saying to them, "Brethren, though I had done nothing against our people, or the customs of our fathers, yet I was delivered prisoner from Jerusalem into the hands of the Romans.
> **18** "And when they had examined me, they were willing to release me because there was no ground for putting me to death.
> **19** "But when the Jews objected, I was forced to appeal to Caesar; not that I had any accusation against my nation.
> **20** "For this reason therefore, I requested to see you and to speak with you, for I am wearing this chain for the sake of the hope of Israel."
> **21** And they said to him, "We have neither received letters from Judea concerning you, nor have any of the brethren come here and reported or spoken anything bad about you.
> **22** "But we desire to hear from you what your views are; for concerning this sect, it is known to us that it is spoken against everywhere."

28:17-20. The apostle waited "three days," during which time he doubtless made inquiries through Luke and others regarding the Jewish community. He received information from Jewish Christians about "the leading men," to whom he issued an invitation to come to his quarters. He could be reasonably sure of a favorable response (cf. 13:15). It was natural that he should give an explanation for his presence in Rome as a prisoner and that in doing so he should seek rapport with his hearers as he had done in his addresses to his own people in Jerusalem (chaps. 22, 23).

He did not deal with the grounds on which the Jews sought a verdict against him, but put forward these three things: (1) he was not guilty of any offense against the Jewish people or their customs; (2) the Roman authorities in Palestine had been ready to release him, but the Jews had objected, so he was forced to appeal to Caesar; (3) he had not advanced any counter charges against his nation (see 28:19). In other words, while normally he would have been happy to submit to Jewish justice, under the circumstances it was not available, so he had been compelled to fall back on his Roman citizenship and "appeal to Caesar."

In addition to these items, the apostle put his finger on what he felt was the real issue—"the hope of Israel," which according to his proclamation (cf. 26:22-23) centered in the person of Jesus of Nazareth as validated by His resurrection from the dead. That Paul went on to speak more specifically of Jesus and His mission is likely, since in their reply the Jewish leaders asked him his opinion of the Nazarenes, which implies that Paul must have made a reference to Jewish believers in Jesus.

28:21-22. Since the visiting group had been invited by Paul to confer with him, they felt that they must respond with courtesy rather than with debate. Their attitude, however, was cautious and noncommittal. Whether their alleged lack of information about Paul from Judean sources is true or not, we are hardly in position to judge. This much is evident, that the Jews in Rome were aware of the existence of the sect of the Nazarenes and knew that it had encountered opposition "everywhere." They made it appear as though all this opposition belonged to other places and that they themselves were relatively unfamiliar with the teachings of this sect. Against this background they sought Paul's opinion of it.

As a matter of fact, Christian Jews were numerous in Rome (vv. 14-15; cf. Ro 16) and had been witnessing for years (see comment on 18:2; cf. Ro 1:8). It is probable that the Roman church was founded by believing Jews, and it is certain that this element was still strongly represented there. But growing resistance to the Gospel in Palestine and the East may well have stiffened the attitude of Jewry at Rome. Paul's teaching in the epistle to the Romans about the futility of works to establish one's righteousness before God and his observation about the failure of the Jewish nation to attain righteousness, plus his treatment of the Law and circumcision, could have contributed to opposition right there in Rome, even among some Christian Jews. The apostle was to feel this alienation more and more as time went on (Phil 1:12-17; Col 4:11).

Verses 23-29. This second session with the Jews differed from the first in that Paul faced a larger group and one that was prepared to argue with him on the issue of the hope of Israel.

> **28:23** And when they had set a day for him, they came to him at his lodging in large numbers; and he was explaining to them by solemnly testifying about the kingdom of God, and trying to persuade them concerning Jesus, from both the Law of Moses and from the Prophets, from morning until evening.
>
> **24** And some were being persuaded by the things spoken, but others would not believe.
>
> **25** And when they did not agree with one another, they *began* leaving after Paul had spoken one parting word, "The Holy Spirit rightly spoke through Isaiah the prophet to your fathers,
>
> **26** saying,

'GO TO THIS PEOPLE AND SAY,
"YOU WILL KEEP ON HEARING, BUT WILL NOT UNDERSTAND;
AND YOU WILL KEEP ON SEEING, BUT WILL NOT PERCEIVE;

27 FOR THE HEART OF THIS PEOPLE HAS BECOME DULL,
AND WITH THEIR EARS THEY SCARCELY HEAR,
AND THEY HAVE CLOSED THEIR EYES;
LEST THEY SHOULD SEE WITH THEIR EYES,
AND HEAR WITH THEIR EARS,
AND UNDERSTAND WITH THEIR HEART AND TURN AGAIN,
AND I SHOULD HEAL THEM." '

28 "Let it be known to you therefore, that this salvation of God has been sent to the Gentiles; they will also listen."

29†

28:23. The visitors agreed to come back to hear Paul at a future time and showed that they were in earnest by setting a day for their return. This arrangement gave Paul opportunity to pray and reflect on what he would say. It also permitted the Jews to busy themselves in spreading the word among their associates, so that "large numbers" came at the appointed time. Probably some of the sharpest minds in the Jewish community were recruited for the anticipated discussion. Paul's lodging must have been commodious to accommodate such a large group. Haenchen thinks of an "inn in which Paul has rented a room."[4] The group showed perseverance by staying through the day, a testimony also to Paul's ability to hold an audience.

He talked about "the kingdom of God." Here, as elsewhere in Acts, this is a comprehensive term for the Gospel. To this Gospel Jesus was central, and in speaking to the Jews it was expedient to include a careful exposition of the Old Testament in its prophetic portions. There is no reason to doubt that the death and resurrection of the promised Messiah were included in the presentation (cf. 26:22-23; Lk 24:44-47).

28:24. Results were similar to those which Paul had experienced elsewhere in dealing with his countrymen. Some were persuaded, whereas others refused to believe and by their attitude confirmed the truth of what Paul had already written the Roman church about the nation Israel (Ro 10:3). Like the God of Israel Himself (Ro 10:21), all day long the apostle had been stretching out his hands to a disobedient and obstinate people.

28:25-29. When these two groups, the believers and the unbelievers, began to argue back and forth "with one another," it was time to bring the session to a close. In fact, people began to leave as soon as Paul spoke a "parting word," which was a rebuke to those who had resisted

†Verse 29, which reads, "And when he had spoken these words, the Jews departed, having a great dispute among themselves," has insufficient manuscript authority to warrant its inclusion in the text. It is a virtual repetition of verse 25a.

his message. It was the more telling in that it was not his own but the word of Isaiah the prophet, whose authority was unquestioned by the Jewish nation. As surely as their fathers had needed the rebuke of the evangelical prophet, they themselves merited the same (Is 6:9-10). No doubt Paul had been quoting Isaiah as he expounded the prophets that day in relation to God's plan of salvation. That he should appeal to the same source for the stern warning against rejecting the message gave the admonition special weight. The Holy Spirit had spoken through Isaiah. That same Spirit was sent to convict the world of sin, righteousness, and judgment (Jn 16:8). Though they belonged to the covenant people, the audience had sin. By means of the resurrection of Jesus, which Paul had proclaimed, they were pointed to the basis of true righteousness in the sight of God—the finished work of Jesus the Christ on the cross. If they persisted in the obstinacy of unbelief, the judgment already resting on them for their sin would be sealed (Jn 3:18, 36). God stood ready to "heal," but He would not heal apart from true repentance and faith.

It should be observed that in reporting Paul's positive presentation of the Gospel, Luke was content to give a skeleton outline, a mere summary; and while the Law and the prophets are mentioned, no proof text from them is cited, whereas it was the apostle's rebuke to the unbelievers in his audience that was clothed in the language of a quotation from Isaiah.

To the Scripture the apostle added a reminder that a gracious God was not to be defeated by Israel's apostasy. His salvation was for the Gentiles too, and they were ready to "listen" (v. 28). Paul was speaking from experience, for he had seen time after time how readily Gentiles responded when the sons of Israel, who should have been prepared by their Scriptures for the reception of the Gospel, closed their minds and hearts against it. This observation fittingly summarizes the thrust of the entire book. One may profitably compare the situation at the end with that in the early chapters. As Leonhard Goppelt expresses it, the redeemed community which at first stood "distinct from Israel" while it sought to present salvation to the covenant nation now stood "opposite the Jews as they rejected God's salvation."[5] The breach was widening.

Verses 30-31. Here Luke appends a kind of postscript, one which leaves the reader in suspense as to what ultimately happened to Paul.

> **28:30** And he stayed two full years in his own rented quarters, and was welcoming all who came to him,
> **31** preaching the kingdom of God, and teaching concerning the Lord Jesus Christ with all openness, unhindered.

28:30-31. For two full years Paul lived "in his own rented quarters." As Lightfoot points out,[6] the language seems definitely intended to distinguish a fixed abode from the temporary arrangement suggested by verse 23. Some doubt that there is any reference here to living quarters, on the ground that *misthōma* means wages, or earnings, which would warrant the rendering, "at his own expense." Yet the idea of expense is somewhat removed from the word's usual meaning of recompense for work, so it is well to retain the translation of the NASB even though no parallel for this rendering has yet been discovered. It seems demanded by the context.

During this time Paul "was welcoming all who came to see him." While Jews were certainly not turned away, the likelihood is that the visitors were mainly Gentiles. The apostle had preached the Gospel in Rome to the Jew first. Now he was fulfilling his obligation to others (Ro 1:16). As to the manner of his presentation, it was "with all openness." He held nothing back, as one can gather from verses 23-28. This was his response to the God-given opportunity which is expressed in the word "unhindered." Though he was a prisoner, the Word of God was not imprisoned. Paul was free to declare it. This clearly indicates that the Roman government at this time was in agreement with its governors in Judea, who looked on Christianity as a permitted religion, as one of the sects of Judaism. The time would soon come when a change of judgment took place, and doubtless Jewish official opposition to Paul had something to do with this shift in attitude.

We come back to the mention of the "two full years." It is probable that the writer knew what happened at the conclusion of this period. Why did he not include it as part of his account—that is the mystery. The matter has been discussed somewhat in the Introduction (under "Date"). But as to the period itself, some would explain it as the time required by law within which a plaintiff was obliged to present his case. There is no evidence that release was mandatory after two years if the prosecution failed to appear, but there was pressure to see to it that cases actually came to trial. "The protection of the accused person lay not in any provision for automatic release if his accuser were absent, but in the severity of the sanctions against defaulting prosecutors."[7]

An early attempt to explain Luke's silence regarding Paul's affairs beyond the two-year period is hinted at in the Canon of Muratori, a late second-century document dealing with the origin of the books of the New Testament. The author implies that the reason for the omission of any account of Paul's journey to Spain is that Luke was not personally present.

Whether Paul ever reached Spain or not (the matter should be kept open), there is fairly strong evidence that he was released and continued his work. He was later arrested, brought back to Rome, and suffered martyrdom under Nero. In his captivity letters he expressed not merely a hope (Phile 22) but a confident expectation (Phil 1:25) of release. Furthermore, the pastoral epistles contain items which cannot be fitted into the book of Acts, suggesting that they reflect later events. Paul left Trophimus sick at Miletus (2 Ti 4:20; cf. Ac 21:29) and deposited certain articles at Troas which he now needed in his final incarceration (2 Ti 4:13). Evidently Paul had a ministry in Crete after his release; it is unreported in Acts (Titus 1:5).

It would be interesting to know to what extent the focus on Rome in the closing chapters of Acts was influential in the early centuries toward securing the Roman's church's eventual eminence in Christendom. Perhaps Luke realized that such influence was a possibility and for this very reason avoided any specific reference to the local congregation, choosing rather to let future developments unfold in the providence of God.

Looking back over chapters 27-28, one concludes that Luke was trying to leave with the reader a powerful impression that this segment of the apostle's life and work conformed to the pattern of his ministry as a whole. He was beset by danger and opposition, as was the Lord Jesus Christ, but maintained a steady, consistent witness to the truth. Paul was still alive and bearing his testimony despite the limitations imposed on him, a pattern for Christian service in the world. His example is intended to encourage the Church to count on the faithfulness of God, who delivered His servant from the peril of death and will yet deliver others. He is the God of resurrection, whose cause must triumph.

NOTES

INTRODUCTION

1. Jacques Dupont, *The Sources of the Acts*, p. 166.
2. Max Wilcox, *The Semitisms of Acts*, p. 181.
3. Interested readers will find a profitable discussion by D. F. Payne in *Apostolic History and the Gospel*, ed. Ward Gasque and Ralph Martin, pp. 134-50.
4. Johannes Munck, *The Acts of the Apostles*, p. liii.
5. Josephus *Antiquities* 20.5.1-2.
6. A. T. Robertson, *Word Pictures in the New Testament* (Nashville: Broadman, 1943), 4:245; W. M. Ramsay, *St. Paul the Traveler and the Roman Citizen*, pp. 389-90.
7. For further information on this general subject see William M. Ramsay, *The Bearing of Recent Discovery on the Trustworthiness of the New Testament* (Grand Rapids: Baker, 1953), especially chap. 3; R. P. C. Hanson, ed., *The Acts*, pp. 2-11; and A. N. Sherwin-White, *Roman Society and Roman Law in the New Testament*, especially pp. 172-93.
8. A. N. Sherwin-White, p. 189.
9. Thucydides *History of the Peloponnesian War* 1.22.
10. Bertil Gärtner, *The Areopagus Speech and Natural Revelation*, pp. 8-11, 27-30.
11. Bo Reicke, "A Synopsis of Early Christian Preaching," in *The Root of the Vine: Essays in Biblical Theology*, pp. 128-29.
12. J. H. Ropes, ed., *BC* 3.
13. Eldon J. Epp, *The Theological Tendency of Codex Bezae Cantabrigiensis in Acts*.
14. C. K. Barrett, *New Testament Essays* (Naperville, Ill.: Allenson, 1972), p. 104.
15. 1 Clement 5-6.
16. Tacitus *Annals* 15.44.

1:1-26

1. F. C. Burkitt, *Christian Beginnings*, p. 96.
2. Bo Reicke, *Glaube und Leben der Urgemeinde*, p. 14.
3. B. F. Westcott and F. J. A. Hort, *The New Testament in the Original Greek* (New York: Harper, 1882), Appendix, p. 73.
4. A. Schlatter, *The Church in the New Testament Period*, p. 13.

2:1-47

1. Bent Noack, "The Day of Pentecost in Jubilees, Qumran, and Acts," in *Annual of the Swedish Theological Institute* 1(1962): 73-95.
2. H. N. Ridderbos, *The Speeches of Peter in the Acts of the Apostles*, p. 16.
3. For additional information see Philip Carrington, *The Primitive Christian Catechism* (Cambridge: U. Press, 1951); C. H. Dodd, *Gospel and Law* (New York: Columbia U., 1951); E. F. Harrison, "Some Patterns of the New Testament Didache," in *BS* 119:118-28; E. G. Selwyn, "Essay II"; "Appended Note", in *The First Epistle of St. Peter* (New York: Macmillan, 1964), pp. 363-488.

3:1-26

1. C. F. D. Moule, "The Christology of Acts" in *Studies in Luke-Acts*, p. 166.
2. Ibid., pp. 180-81.
3. Anton Fridrichson, *The Apostle and His Message* (Uppsala: Uppsala Universitets Arsskrift, 1947), p. 9.

4:1-37

1. Joachim Jeremias, in *TDNT* 1:793.
2. Jeremias, *Jerusalem in the Time of Jesus*, p. 180.
3. Ibid., p. 179.
4. Emil Schürer, *A History of the Jewish People in the Time of Jesus Christ* (Edinburgh: T. & T. Clark, 1890), 2:1:204-5.
5. *TDNT* 3:271.
6. Richard Longenecker, *The Christology of Early Jewish Christianity*, p. 107.
7. *Manual of Discipline* 1:11-13.

5:1–6:7

1. *Manual of Discipline* (trans. Gaster) 6:24-25.
2. J. Jeremias, *Jerusalem in the Time of Jesus*, pp. 160-63, 180.
3. Josephus *Antiquities* 20.5.1.
4. Leonhard Goppelt, *Apostolic and Post-apostolic Times*, p. 53.
5. Reginald H. Fuller, *The New Testament in Current Study* (New York: Scribner, 1971), pp. 127-28; J. A. Fitzmyer, "Jewish Christianity in Acts in Light of the Qumran Scrolls," in *Studies in Luke-Acts*, ed. Keck and Martyn, p. 238.
6. See a good discussion of the problem in R. P. C. Hanson, *The Acts*, pp. 91-92.
7. Jeremias, p. 252.

6:8–8:3

1. Joachim Jeremias, *Jerusalem in the Time of Jesus*, p. 66.
2. A. N. Sherwin-White, *Roman Society and Roman Law in the New Testament*, p. 152.
3. Martin H. Scharlemann, *Stephen: a Singular Saint*, p. 91.
4. See Johannes Munck, *The Acts of the Apostles*, p. 285.
5. Cf. Philo *On Abraham* 70-72; Josephus *Antiquities* 1.7.1.
6. W. Tarn, *Hellenistic Civilization*, 3d rev. ed. (London: Arnold, 1953), p. 102; Tacitus *Histories* 5.5.
7. See J. Juster, *Les Juifs* (Paris: Librairie Paul Geuthner, 1914), pp. 209-10.
8. Josephus *Antiquities* 2.9.7.
9. Philo *Moses* 1.21-24.
10. Scharlemann, pp. 44-47.
11. Ibid., p. 46.
12. F. Godet, *Commentary on St. Paul's Epistle to the Romans* (Edinburgh: T. & T. Clark, 1883), 1:181.
13. *IDB* 3:422b.
14. Franz Delitzsch, *Commentary on Isaiah* (Edinburgh: T. & T. Clark, 1873).
15. C. K. Barrett, "Stephen and the Son of Man," in *Apophoreta*, p. 36.
16. C. F. D. Moule, "From Defendant to Judge—and Deliverer: An Enquiry into the Use and Limitations of the Theme of Vindication in the New Testament," *Bulletin of the Studiorum Novi Testamenti Societas* 3:47.
17. Bo Reicke, *The New Testament Era*, p. 145.
18. Ibid., p. 91.
19. Sherwin-White, p. 40.

8:4-40

1. See "The Acts of Peter" in Edgar Hennecke, *New Testament Apocrypha*, ed. Wilhelm Schneemelcher, trans. and ed. R. McL. Wilson (Philadelphia: Westminster, 1964), 2:282-86. Reports of encounters in other places are found in "The Pseudo-Clementines," pp. 549-52.
2. G. W. H. Lampe, *The Seal of the Spirit*, p. 72.

9:1-31

1. For a fuller discussion of this matter see Jacques Dupont, "The Conversion of Paul," in *Apostolic History and the Gospel*, pp. 176-94.
2. Josephus *Antiquities* 15.8.2.
3. F. F. Bruce, *New Testament History*, p. 238, n. 14.

4. Horst R. Moehring, "The verb *akouein* in Acts 9:7 and 22:9," *NovTest* 3:80-99. C. F. D. Moule takes the same position in his *Idiom Book of New Testament Greek* (New York: Cambridge U., 1959), p. 36. But see Nigel Turner, *Grammatical Insights into the New Testament*, pp. 86-90.

5. F. F. Bruce, *Commentary on the Book of the Acts*, p. 197.
6. *Martyrdom of Polycarp* 9.1.
7. R. B. Rackham, *The Acts of the Apostles*, p. 133.
8. H. V. Morton, *In the Steps of St. Paul*, p. 44.
9. William M. Ramsay, *The Cities of St. Paul*, p. 88.
10. Josephus *Antiquities* 18.5.1-3.
11. Bo Reicke, *The New Testament Era*, p. 193.

9:32—11:18

1. R. B. Rackham, *The Acts of the Apostles*, p. 145.
2. M. D. Goulder, *Type and History in Acts*, p. 18.
3. A. N. Sherwin-White, *Roman Society and Roman Law in the New Testament*, p. 160.
4. I. Howard Marshall, "The Resurrection in the Acts of the Apostles," in *Apostolic History and the Gospel*, p. 104.

11:19—12:25

1. C. H. Dodd, *More New Testament Studies*, (Grand Rapids: Eerdmans, 1968), p. 16.
2. Tacitus *Annals* 15.44.
3. H. B. Mattingly, "The Origin of the Name *Christiani*," *JTS* (NS) 9:26-37.
4. Suetonius *The Lives of the Caesars* 5.18.2.
5. F. F. Bruce, *The Book of Acts*, p. 243.
6. Joachim Jeremias, *Jerusalem in the Time of Jesus*, pp. 332-33.
7. L. Goppelt, *Apostolic and Post-apostolic Times*, p. 59.
8. Johannes Munck, *The Acts of the Apostles*, p. 114.
9. Josephus *Antiquities* 20.9.1.
10. Munck, p. 114.
11. Josephus, 19.8.2.
12. Bruce, *New Testament History*, p. 263.

13:1—14:28

1. Ernest Best, "Acts XIII. 1-3," *JTS* (NS) 11:346.
2. G. B. Caird, *The Apostolic Age*, p. 64.
3. One should consult, however, William M. Ramsay, *The Bearing of Recent Discovery on the Trustworthiness of the New Testament* (Grand Rapids: Baker, 1953), pp. 370-84; H. J. Cadbury, "Lucius of Cyrene," in *BC* 5:489-95.
4. Kirsopp Lake and Henry J. Cadbury, *BC* 4:141; Robert W. Funk, ed., *A Greek Grammar of the New Testament* (Chicago: U. of Chicago, 1961), p. 230b.
5. A. Schlatter, *The Church in the New Testament Period*, p. 113.
6. Sherwin-White, *Roman Society and Roman Law in the New Testament*, p. 153.
7. R. B. Rackham, *The Acts of the Apostles*, p. 201.
8. Richard N. Longenecker, *The Ministry and Message of Paul*, p. 43.
9. William M. Ramsay, *St. Paul the Traveler and the Roman Citizen*, pp. 92-97.
10. Israel Abrahams, "Rabbinic Aids to Exegesis," in *Cambridge Biblical Essays*, p. 166.
11. C. S. C. Williams, *The Acts of the Apostles*, p. 164. He notes the varied application of this text elsewhere in the New Testament—to the baptism of Jesus in the Western text of Lk 3:22 and to the ascension in Heb 1:5; 5:5.
12. Ramsay, p. 109.
13. Ramsay, *The Cities of St. Paul*, p. 359.
14. Ibid., p. 408.
15. James L. Kelso, *An Archaeologist Follows the Apostle Paul*, p. 48.
16. Bastian Van Elderen, "Some Archaeological Observations on Paul's First Missionary Journey," in *Apostolic History and the Gospel*, pp. 151-61.
17. See the discussion in W. Telfer, *The Office of a Bishop*, p. 192.

15:1-35

1. W. L. Knox, *St. Paul and the Church of Jerusalem*, pp. 223-24.
2. Kirsopp Lake and H. J. Cadbury, *BC* 4:175.
3. See F. F. Bruce, *The Book of Acts*, p. 310, for a discussion of the textual phenomena.
4. *TDNT* 7:374-75.
5. See Ernst Haenchen, *The Acts of the Apostles*, pp. 448-49.
6. Jacob Jocz, *The Jewish People and Jesus Christ* (London: SPCK, 1954), p. 68.
7. Johannes Munck, *The Acts of the Apostles*, p. 140.

15:36—16:10

1. Ernst Haenchen, "The Book of Acts as Source Material for the History of Early Christianity," in *Studies in Luke-Acts*, p. 271.
2. Alexander Whyte, *Bible Characters: Stephen to Timothy* (New York: Revell, n.d.), p. 289.
3. Haenchen, *The Acts of the Apostles*, p. 482.

16:11—18:17

1. A. N. Sherwin-White, *Roman Society and Roman Law in the New Testament*, p. 93.
2. Ibid., pp. 80-81.
3. Chrysostom *Homer* 36.2.
4. G. Schrenk, *TDNT* 2:94.
5. Ernst Haenchen, *The Acts of the Apostles*.
6. J. B. Lightfoot, *Saint Paul's Epistle to the Philippians* (London: Macmillan, 1910), p. 56.
7. Sherwin-White, p. 98.
8. R. B. Rackham, *The Acts of the Apostles*.
9. W. G. Morrice, "Where Did Paul Speak in Athens—on Mars' Hill or Before the Court of the Areopagus?," in *ExpT* 83:378.
10. J. Finegan, "Areopagus," in *IDB* 1:217.
11. Bertil Gärtner, *The Areopagus Speech and Natural Revelation*, pp. 58-59.
12. For a brief account of current approaches to Paul's speech see the Introduction under "Theology."
13. F. Field, *Notes on the Translation of the New Testament*, p. 127.
14. Gärtner, p. 245.
15. H. P. Owen, "The Scope of Natural Revelation in Romans 1 and Acts 17," in *NTS* 5:138.
16. Gärtner, p. 188.
17. A. Harnack, *The Expansion of Christianity in the First Three Centuries* 1:333-34.
18. A. H. M. Jones, *The Greek City*, pp. 62-63.
19. Suetonius *Claudius* 25.4.
20. On the subject of Roman names, see H. J. Cadbury, *The Book of Acts in History*, pp. 69-71.
21. *IDB* 1:684a.

18:18—19:41

1. Josephus *Jewish War* 2.15.1.
2. D. T. Rowlingson, "The Geographical Orientation of Paul's Missionary Interests," *JBL* 69:341-44.
3. G. W. H. Lampe, *The Seal of the Spirit*, p. 66.
4. See George E. Wright and Floyd V. Filson, eds., *The Westminster Historical Atlas to the Bible*, rev. ed. (Philadelphia: Westminster, 1956), p. 91.
5. For a statement of the difficulties in the passage see Ernst Käsemann, *Essays on New Testament Themes* (Naperville, Ill.: Allenson, 1964), pp. 136-39.
6. Frederick Dale Bruner, *A Theology of the Holy Spirit*, p. 209.
7. H. A. W. Meyer, *A Critical and Exegetical Handbook to The Acts of the Apostles*.
8. A. Schlatter, *The Church in the New Testament Period*, p. 163.
9. E. Schürer, *The Jewish People in the Time of Jesus Christ* 2:3:152.

10. B. M. Metzger, "St. Paul and the Magicians," *Princeton Seminary Bulletin* (June 1944):27.
11. A. Deissmann, *Light from the Ancient East*, 4th ed., p. 260.
12. F. F. Bruce, *New Testament History*, p. 328.
13. James Hope Moulton and George Milligan, *The Vocabulary of the Greek Testament* (London: Hodder & Stoughton, 1930), s.v. *amphoteroi*.
14. W. L. Knox, *St. Paul and the Church of Jerusalem*, p. 345.
15. Oscar Broneer, "Corinth," *BA* 14:94.
16. William Ramsay, *St. Paul the Traveler and the Roman Citizen*, p. 277.
17. Ramsay, *The Church in the Roman Empire*, pp. 114ff.
18. Ibid., pp. 124-26.
19. Ibid., p. 134.
20. Ibid., pp. 135-39.
21. A. N. Sherwin-White, *Roman Society and Roman Law in the New Testament*, p. 90.
22. A. H. M. Jones, *The Greek City*, pp. 238-39.
23. F. D. Gealy, "Town Clerk," in *IDB* (Nashville: Abingdon, 1962), 4:676.
24. W. M. Ramsay, *The Letters to the Seven Churches of Asia* (Grand Rapids: Baker, 1963), p. 232.
25. Sherwin-White, p. 83.
26. Ibid., pp. 84-85.

20:1—21:16

1. F. F. Bruce, *New Testament History*, p. 354.
2. F. J. Foakes Jackson and Kirsopp Lake, *BC* 4:255, n.
3. F. F. Bruce, *Commentary on the Book of Acts*.
4. Johannes Munck, "Discours d'adieu dans le Nouveau Testament et dans la litterature biblique," in *Aux sources de la tradition chrétienne*; Jacques Dupont, *Le discours de Milet*. The latter volume is especially concerned with the pastoral values of the discourse.
5. Bo Reicke calls attention to the case of Ignatius. See "A Synopsis of Early Christian Preaching," in *The Root of the Vine: Essays in Biblical Theology*, p. 155.
6. Percy Gardner, "The Speeches of St. Paul in Acts," in *Cambridge Biblical Essays*, ed. H. B. Swete, pp. 401-3.
7. See Frederick Field, *Notes on the Translation of the New Testament*, p. 132; also Walter Bauer, *Greek-English Lexicon of the New Testament and Other Early Christian Literature*, trans. W. F. Arndt and F. Wilbur Gingrich (Chicago: U. of Chicago, 1957), s.v. *hypostellō*.
8. Dupont, p. 90.
9. B. F. Westcott, *St. Paul's Epistle to the Ephesians* (Grand Rapids: Eerdmans, 1950), p. 73.
10. For further discussion of this theme see the present writer's article, "The Tradition of the Sayings of Jesus," in *Toward a Theology for the Future*, ed. David F. Wells and Clark H. Pinnock, (Carol Stream, Ill.: Creation House, 1971), pp. 41-63.
11. William M. Ramsay, *St. Paul the Traveler and the Roman Citizen*, p. 293.
12. Field, pp. 134-35.
13. G. Campbell Morgan, *The Acts of the Apostles*, p. 481
14. Ramsay, pp. 301-2; *HDB*, 5:398.
15. Bruce, *The Book of Acts*, p. 429, n. 28.
16. Josephus *Antiquities* 19.6.1.
17. Ernst Haenchen, *The Acts of the Apostles*, p. 612.
18. F. J. A. Hort, *Judaistic Christianity*, p. 109.

21:27—23:35

1. Josephus *Jewish War* 6.2.4.
2. G. Dalman, *Sacred Sites and Ways* (London: Macmillan, 1935), p. 290.
3. Joachim Jeremias, *Jerusalem in the Time of Jesus*, p. 210.
4. T. Francis Glasson, *Moses in the Fourth Gospel* (Naperville, Ill.: Allenson, 1963), p. 21.
5. See William M. Ramsay, *The Cities of St. Paul*, pp. 85-244.

6. A. N. Sherwin-White, *Roman Society and Roman Law in the New Testament,* p. 179.
7. W. C. Van Unnik, *Tarsus or Jerusalem the City of Paul's Youth,* pp. 17-45.
8. Otto Michel, *Der Brief an die Römer* (Göttingen: Vandenhoeck &-Ruprecht, 1955); C. K. Barrett, *The Epistle to the Romans* (New York: Harper & Row, 1958).
9. Joseph Klausner, *From Jesus to Paul* (New York: Macmillan, 1943), pp. 309-11.
10. R. B. Rackham, *The Acts of the Apostles,* p. 423.
11. Francois Amiot, *The Key Concepts of St. Paul,* p. 22.
12. Sherwin-White, *The Roman Citizenship,* p. 189.
13. Sherwin-White, *Roman Society and Law,* pp. 154-155.
14. Ibid., p. 154.
15. Ibid., p. 148.
16. Ibid., p. 156.
17. J. M. Stifler, *An Introduction to a Study of the Acts of the Apostles* (New York: Revell, 1892), pp. 222-23.
18. R. P. C. Hanson, *The Acts,* p. 220.
19. Ernst Haenchen, *The Acts of the Apostles,* p. 643.
20. Claude A. Pierce, *Conscience in the New Testament* (Naperville, Ill.: Allenson, 1955), p. 96.
21. See F. F. Bruce, *The Book of Acts.* He points out that any contradiction with Romans 7:7ff. can thus be avoided.
22. *TDNT* 6:526, 534.
23. S. G. F. Brandon, *Jesus and the Zealots* (New York: Scribner, 1968), p. 111, n. 5.
24. A. Schlatter, *The Church in the New Testament Period,* p. 216.
25. Paton J. Gloag, *A Critical and Exegetical Commentary on the Acts of the Apostles* 2:324-25.
26. Josephus *Antiquities* 20.8.5.
27. Sherwin-White, *Roman Society and Law,* pp. 55-56.
28. Frederick Field, *Notes on the Translation of the New Testament,* p. 138.

24:1–26:32

1. A. T. Robertson, "Latin," in *ISBE* 3:1841a.
2. Josephus *Antiquities* 20.8.9.
3. A. N. Sherwin-White, *Roman Society and Roman Law in the New Testament,* p. 51.
4. Ibid., p. 50.
5. R. B. Rackham, *The Acts of the Apostles,* p. 443.
6. *BC* 4.
7. Johannes Munck, *The Acts of the Apostles,* p. 232.
8. T. W. Manson, *Studies in the Gospels and Epistles,* p. 61.
9. H. A. W. Meyer, *Critical and Exegetical Handbook to the Acts of the Apostles,* pp. 443-44.
10. J. E. H. Hull, *The Holy Spirit in the Acts of the Apostles,* p. 76.
11. Thomas Walker, *The Acts of the Apostles,* p. 509.
12. R. P. C. Hanson, *The Acts,* p. 228.
13. See A. T. Robertson, *Word Pictures in the New Testament* 3:421.
14. Josephus 20.7.1-2.
15. Ibid. 20.8.11.
16. C. F. D. Moule, *A Chosen Vessel,* pp. 69-70.
17. Sherwin-White, p. 67.
18. Ibid., p. 64.
19. Rackham, p. 461.
20. Sherwin-White, p. 51.
21. Adolf Deissmann, *Light from the Ancient East,* p. 354.
22. Josephus *Vita* 364.
23. Ibid. 359.
24. A. T. Robertson, *A Grammar of the Greek New Testament,* 4th ed. (New York: Hodder & Stoughton, 1923), p. 1179.
25. Josephus *Jewish War* 1.5.2.
26. Rackham.
27. Ernst Haenchen, *The Acts of the Apostles,* p. 684.

28. Pliny *Epistles* 10.96.
29. W. J. Sparrow-Simpson, *The Resurrection and Modern Thought* (London: Longmans, Green & Co. 1911), p. 145.
30. Munck, *Paul and the Salvation of Mankind*, pp. 20-22.
31. In his book *The Dynamic of Service* (Kansas City: Beacon Hill, 1924), Paget Wilkes develops the relevance of verse 18 for practical Christian work.
32. Rackham, p. 471, n. 2.
33. Nigel Turner, *Grammatical Insights into the New Testament*, p. 99.
34. Sherwin–White, p. 65.

27:1-44

1. James Smith, *The Voyage and Shipwreck of St. Paul*, p. xxxii.
2. Ibid., p. xlvi.
3. F. J. Foakes Jackson and Kirsopp Lake, *BC* 5:443.
4. Kirsopp Lake and Henry J. Cadbury, *BC* 4.
5. Smith, p. 76.
6. Ibid., pp. 76-77.
7. See the discussion by F. V. Filson, in *IDB*, s.v. "Phoenix."
8. Lake and Cadbury.
9. Smith, p. 102, n. 1.
10. Ibid., p. 108.
11. Ibid., p. 112.
12. Ibid., p. 102.
13. Ibid., pp. 124-28.
14. William M. Ramsay, *St. Paul the Traveler and the Roman Citizen*, p. 330.
15. Lake and Cadbury.
16. Adolf Deissmann, *Die Welt des Apostels Paulus* (Tübingen: J. C. B. Mohr, n.d.)
17. Josephus *Vita* 15.

28:1-31

1. William M. Ramsay, *St. Paul the Traveler and the Roman Citizen*, p. 343.
2. R. P. C. Hanson, *The Acts*, p. 253.
3. A. N. Sherwin-White, *Roman Society and Roman Law in the New Testament*, p. 110.
4. Ernst Haenchen, *The Acts of the Apostles*, p. 723.
5. Leonhard Goppelt, *Jesus, Paul and Judaism* (New York: Nelson, 1964), p. 131.
6. J. B. Lightfoot, *Saint Paul's Epistle to the Philippians* (London: Macmillan, 1913), p. 9, n. 3.
7. Sherwin-White, p. 114.

BIBLIOGRAPHY

General Works

Amiot, Francois. *The Key Concepts of St. Paul.* London: Nelson, 1962.

Barrett, C. K. *Luke the Historian in Recent Study.* London: Epworth, 1961.

Bruce, F. F. *New Testament History.* New York: Doubleday, 1971.

———. *The Speeches in Acts.* London: Tyndale, 1942.

Bruner, Frederick Dale. *A Theology of the Holy Spirit.* Grand Rapids: Eerdmans, 1970.

Burkitt, F. C. *Christian Beginnings.* London: U. of London, 1924.

Buttrick, George A. *Interpreter's Dictionary of the Bible.* 5 vols. Nashville: Abingdon, 1962.

Cadbury, H. J. *The Book of Acts in History.* New York: Harper, 1955.

———. *The Making of Luke-Acts.* New York: Macmillan, 1927.

———. *The Style and Literary Method of Luke.* Harvard Theological Studies, vol. 6. Cambridge, Mass.: Harvard U., 1919.

Caird, G. B. *The Apostolic Age.* London: Duckworth, 1955.

Conzelmann, Hans. *The Theology of St. Luke.* New York: Harper, 1960.

Craig, C. T. *The Beginning of Christianity.* New York: Abingdon-Cokesbury, 1943.

Deissmann, Adolf. *Light from the Ancient East.* 4th ed. New York: Doran, 1927.

Derwacter, F. M. *Preparing the Way for Paul.* New York: Macmillan, 1930.

Dibelius, Martin. *Studies in the Acts of the Apostles.* New York: Scribners, 1956.

Dix, Gregory. *Jew and Greek. A Study in the Primitive Church.* London: Dacre, 1953.

Dupont, Jacques. *Le discours de Milet.* Paris: Editions du Cerf, 1962.

———. *The Sources of the Acts.* New York: Herder & Herder, 1964.

Easton, B. S. *Early Christianity.* London: SPCK, 1955.

Ehrhardt, Arnold. *The Acts of the Apostles.* Manchester: U. Press, 1969.

Epp, Eldon Jay. *The Theological Tendency of Codex Bezae Cantabrigiensis in Acts.* Cambridge: U. Press, 1966.

Field, Frederick. *Notes on the Translation of the New Testament.* Cambridge: U. Press, 1899.

Filson, Floyd V. *A New Testament History.* Philadelphia: Westminster, 1964.

———. *Three Crucial Decades.* Richmond: Knox, 1963.

Foakes Jackson, F. J. *The Rise of Gentile Christianity.* London: Hodder & Stoughton, 1927.

Foakes Jackson, F. J., and Lake, K., eds. *The Beginnings of Christianity.* Vols. 1-3, 5. London: Macmillan, 1933.

414

Fuller, Daniel P. *Easter Faith and History*. Grand Rapids: Eerdmans, 1965.

Gärtner, Bertil. *The Areopagus Speech and Natural Revelation*. Acta Seminarii Neotestamentici Upsaliensis, vol. 21. Uppsala, 1955.

Gasque, W. Ward, "A Study of the History of the Criticism of the Acts of the Apostles." Doctoral dissertation, University of Manchester, 1969.

Gasque, W. Ward and Martin, Ralph P., eds. *Apostolic History and the Gospel*. Grand Rapids: Eerdmans, 1970

Goguel, Maurice. *The Birth of Christianity*. New York: Macmillan, 1954.

———. *The Primitive Church*. London: Allen & Unwin, 1964.

Goppelt, Leonhard. *Apostolic and Post-apostolic Times*. London: Adam & Charles Black, 1970.

Goulder, M. D. *Type and History in Acts*. London: SPCK, 1964.

Green, Michael. *Evangelism in the Early Church*. Grand Rapids: Eerdmans, 1970.

Halliday, W. R. *The Pagan Background of Early Christianity*. Liverpool: U. Press, 1925.

Harnack, Adolph. *The Expansion of Christianity in the First Three Centuries*. 2 vols. New York: Putnam, 1904.

Hastings, James, ed. *Dictionary of the Bible*. London: T. & T. Clark, 1909.

Hort, F. J. A. *Judaistic Christianity*. London: Macmillan, 1898.

Hull, J. H. E. *The Holy Spirit in the Acts of the Apostles*. London: Lutterworth, 1967.

Jaeger, Werner. *Early Christianity and Greek Paideia*. Cambridge, Mass.: Harvard, 1961.

Jeremias, Joachim. *Jerusalem in the Time of Jesus*. Philadelphia: Fortress, 1969.

Jones, A. H. M. *The Greek City*. Oxford: Clarendon, 1940.

Jones, Maurice. *St. Paul the Orator*. London: Hodder & Stoughton, 1910.

Keck, Leander E. *Mandate to Witness*. Valley Forge: Judson, 1964.

Kelso, James L. *An Archaeologist Follows the Apostle Paul*. Waco, Texas: Word, 1970.

Kittel, Gerhard, and Friedrich, Gerhard, eds. *Theological Dictionary of the New Testament*. Trans. Geoffrey W. Bromiley. 9 vols. Grand Rapids: Eerdmans, 1961-70.

Knox, W. L. *The Acts of the Apostles*. Cambridge: U. Press, 1948.

———. *St. Paul and the Church of Jerusalem*. Cambridge: U. Press, 1925.

Ladd, G. E. *The Young Church*. Bible Guides, ed. William Barclay and F. F. Bruce. Nashville: Abingdon, 1964.

Lampe, G. W. H. *The Seal of the Spirit*. London: Longmans, Green & Co., 1951.

Lietzmann, Hans. *The Beginnings of the Christian Church*. London: Nicholson & Watson, 1937.

Longenecker, Richard N. *The Christology of Early Jewish Christianity*. Studies in Biblical Theology, 2d series, vol. 17. London: SCM, 1970.

———. *The Ministry and Message of Paul*. Grand Rapids: Zondervan, 1971.

Macdonald, John. *The Theology of the Samaritans*. Philadelphia: Westminster, 1964.

Machen, J. Gresham. *The Origin of Paul's Religion.* New York: Macmillan, 1923.

Magie, David. *Roman Rule in Asia Minor.* 2 vols. Princeton: U. Press, 1950.

Marshall, I. Howard. *Luke: Historian and Theologian.* Grand Rapids: Zonder‹ van, 1971.

Metzger, Henri. *St. Paul's Journeys in the Greek Orient.* London: SCM, 1955.

Morton, H. V. *In the Steps of St. Paul.* New York: Dodd, Mead & Co., 1937.

Moule, C. F. D. *A Chosen Vessel.* London: Lutterworth, 1961.

———. *The Birth of the New Testament.* New York: Harper & Row, 1962.

Munck, Johannes. *Paul and the Salvation of Mankind.* Richmond: John Knox, 1959.

Ogg, George. *The Chronology of the Life of Paul.* London: Epworth, 1968.

O'Neill, J. C. *The Theology of Acts.* London: SPCK, 1961.

Orr, James, ed. *International Standard Bible Encyclopedia.* Grand Rapids: Eerdmans, 1930.

Purves, G. T. *Christianity in the Apostolic Age.* New York: Scribners, 1925.

Ramsay, W. M. *The Church in the Roman Empire.* New York: Putnam, 1893.

———. *The Cities of St. Paul.* New York: Armstrong, 1908.

———. *Pictures of the Apostolic Church.* Philadelphia: Sunday School Times, 1910.

———. *St. Paul the Traveler and the Roman Citizen.* New York: Putnam, 1904.

Reicke, Bo. *Glaube und Leben der Urgemeinde.* Zurich: Zwingli-Verlag, 1957.

———. *The New Testament Era.* Philadelphia: Fortress, 1968.

Ridderbos, H. N. *The Speeches of Peter in the Acts of the Apostles.* London: Tyndale, 1962.

Robertson, A. T. *Word Pictures in the New Testament.* Vol. 3. New York: Richard R. Smith, 1930.

Ropes, J. H. *The Apostolic Age.* New York: Scribners, 1906.

Scharlemann, M. H. *Stephen: A Singular Saint.* Rome: Pontificial-Biblical In- stitute, 1968.

Schlatter, A. *The Church in the New Testament Period.* London: SPCK, 1955.

Scott, E. F. *The Beginnings of the Church.* New York: Scribners, 1925.

Sherwin-White, A. N. *Roman Society and Roman Law in the New Testament.* Oxford: Clarendon, 1963.

Simon, Marcel. *St. Stephen and the Hellenists.* London: Longmans, Green, & Co., 1958.

Smith, James. *The Voyage and Shipwreck of St. Paul.* London: Longmans, Green, & Co., 1880.

Stanley, David M. *The Apostolic Church in the New Testament.* Westminster, Md.: Newman, 1967.

Stendahl, Krister, ed. *The Scrolls and the New Testament.* New York: Harper, 1957.

Stifler, J. M. *An Introduction to the Study of the Acts of the Apostles.* New York: Revell, 1892.

Stonehouse, N. B. *The Areopagus Address.* London: Tyndale, 1949.

Streeter, B. M. *The Primitive Church.* New York: Macmillan, 1929.

Talbert, C. H. *Luke and the Gnostics.* Nashville: Abingdon, 1966.

Telfer, W. *The Office of a Bishop.* London: Darton, Longman & Todd, 1962.

Tenney, Merrill C. *New Testament Times.* Grand Rapids: Eerdmans, 1965.

Thomas, W. H. Griffith. *The Acts of the Apostles.* Chicago: BICA, n.d..

Turner, Nigel. *Grammatical Insights into the New Testament.* Edinburgh: T. & T. Clark, 1965.

Van Unnik, W. C. *Tarsus or Jerusalem the City of Paul's Youth.* London: Epworth, 1962.

Weiss, Johannes. *Earliest Christianity.* 2 vols. New York: Harper, 1959.

Wilcox, Max. *The Semitisms of Acts.* Oxford: Clarendon, 1965.

Wright, W. B. *Cities of Paul.* London: Archibald Constable, 1906.

COMMENTARIES

Alford, Henry. *The Greek Testament.* Vol. 2. Chicago: Moody, 1958.

Bartlet, J. Vernon. *The Acts.* Century Bible. London: Caxton, n.d.

Bengel, J. A. *Gnomon of the New Testament.* Vol. 2. Edinburgh: T. & T. Clark, 1859.

Blaiklock, E. M. *The Acts of the Apostles.* Tyndale New Testament Commentaries. Grand Rapids: Eerdmans, 1959.

Bruce, F. F. *Commentary on the Book of the Acts.* Grand Rapids: Eerdmans, 1954.

———. *The Acts of the Apostles.* London: Tyndale, 1951.

Calvin, John. *Commentary on the Acts of the Apostles.* 2 vols. Grand Rapids: Eerdmans, 1949.

Foakes Jackson, F. J. *The Acts of the Apostles.* Moffatt Commentary. New York: Harper, n.d.

Gloag, Paton J. *A Critical and Exegetical Commentary on the Acts of the Apostles.* 2 vols. Edinburgh: T. & T. Clark, 1870.

Hackett, H. B. *A Commentary on the Original Text of the Acts of the Apostles.* London: Hamilton, Adams & Co., 1877.

Haenchen, Ernst. *The Acts of the Apostles.* Oxford: Blackwell, 1971.

Hanson, R. P. C. *The Acts.* The New Clarendon Bible. Oxford: Clarendon, 1967.

Knowling, R. J. *The Acts of the Apostles.* Expositor's Greek Testament, vol. 2. London: Hodder & Stoughton, 1917.

Lake, K., and Cadbury, H. J. *The Beginnings of Christianity.* Vol 4. London: Macmillan, 1933.

LaSor, W. S. *Church Alive.* Glendale, Cal.: Regal, 1972.

Lenski, R. C. H. *The Acts of the Apostles.* Columbus: Wartburg, 1944.

Macgregor, G. H. C. *The Acts of the Apostles.* Interpreter's Bible, vol. 9. Nashville: Abingdon, 1945.

Meyer, H. A. W. *Critical and Exegetical Handbook to the Acts of the Apostles.* New York: Funk & Wagnalls, 1883.

Morgan, G. Campbell. *The Acts of the Apostles.* New York: Revell, 1924.

Munck, Johannes. *The Acts of the Apostles.* The Anchor Bible. New York: Doubleday, 1967.

Page, T. E. *The Acts of the Apostles*. London: Macmillan, 1930.

Rackham, R. B. *The Acts of the Apostles*. Westminster Commentaries. London: Methuen, 1901.

Walker, Thomas. *The Acts of the Apostles*. Chicago: Moody, 1965.

Williams, C. S. C. *A Commentary on the Acts of the Apostles*. New York: Harper & Row, 1957.

Articles

Abrahams, Israel. "Rabbinic Aids to Exegesis." In *Cambridge Biblical Essays,* ed. H. B. Swete. New York: Macmillan, 1909.

Barrett, C. K. "Stephen and the Son of Man." In *Apophoreta,* ed. W. Eltester. Berlin: Töpelmann Verlag, 1964.

Best, Ernest. "Acts XIII. 1-3." *Journal of Theological Studies,* New Series 11 (Oct. 1960):344-48.

Broneer, Oscar. "Corinth. Center of St. Paul's Missionary Work in Greece." *Biblical Archaeologist* 14 (Dec. 1951):78-96.

Dupont, Jacques. "The Conversion of Paul, and Its Influence on the Understanding of Salvation by Faith." In *Apostolic History and the Gospel,* ed. W. Ward Gasque and Ralph P. Martin. Grand Rapids: Eerdmans, 1970.

Fitzmyer, Joseph A. "Jewish Christianity in Acts in Light of the Qumran Scrolls." In *Studies in Luke-Acts,* ed. Leander E. Keck and J. Louis Martyn. Nashville: Abingdon, 1966.

Gardner, Percy. "The Speeches of St. Paul in Acts." In *Cambridge Biblical Essays,* ed. H. B. Swete. New York: Macmillan, 1909.

Haenchen, Ernst. "The Book of Acts as Source Material for the History of Early Christianity." In *Studies in Luke-Acts,* ed. Leander E. Keck and J. Louis Martyn. Nashville: Abingdon, 1966.

Marshall, I. Howard. "The Resurrection in the Acts of the Apostles." In *Apostolic History and the Gospel,* ed. W. Ward Gasque and Ralph P. Martin. Grand Rapids: Eerdmans, 1970.

Mattingly, H. B. "The Origin of the Name *Christiani.*" *Journal of Theological Studies,* New Series 9 (Apr. 1958):26-37.

Metzger, B. M. "Ancient Astrological Geography and Acts 2:9-11." In *Apostolic History and the Gospel,* ed W. Ward Gasque and Ralph P. Martin. Grand Rapids: Eerdmans, 1970.

————. "St. Paul and the Magicians." *The Princeton Seminary Bulletin* 38 (June 1944):27-30.

Moehring, Horst R. "The Verb *akouein* in Acts 9:7 and 22:9." *Novum Testamentum* 3 (1959):80-99.

Morrice, W. G. "Mars' Hill or Court of Areopagus." *The Expository Times* 83 (Sept. 1972):377-78.

Mosley, A. W. "Historical Reporting in the Ancient World." *New Testament Studies* 12 (Oct. 1965):10-26.

Moule, C. F. D. "The Christology of Acts." In *Studies in Luke-Acts,* ed Leader E. Keck and J. Louis Martyn. Nashville: Abingdon, 1966.

————. "From Defendant to Judge—and Deliverer: An Enquiry into the Use and Limitations of the Theme of Vindication in the New Testament." In *Studiorum Novi Testamenti Societas*. Bulletin 3. Cambridge: U. Press, 1963.

Munck, Johannes. "Discours d'adieu dans le Nouveau Testament et dans la littérature biblique." In *Aux Sources de la Tradition Chrétienne*. Neuchâtel: Delachaux et Niestle, 1950.

Noack, Bent. "The Day of Pentecost in Jubilees, Qumran, and Acts." *Annual of the Swedish Theological Institute* 1 (1962): 73-95.

Owen, H. P. "The Scope of Natural Revelation in Romans 1 and Acts 17." *New Testament Studies* 5 (Jan. 1959):133-43.

Payne, D. F. "Semitisms in the Book of Acts." In *Apostolic History and the Gospel*, ed. W. Ward Gasque and Ralph P. Martin. Grand Rapids: Eerdmans, 1970.

Reicke, Bo. "A Synopsis of Early Christian Preaching." In *The Root of the Vine: Essays in Biblical Theology*, by Anton Fridrichsen et al. London: A. & C. Black, 1953.

Rowlingson, D. T. "The Geographical Orientation of Paul's Missionary Interests." *Journal of Biblical Literature* 69 (Dec. 1950):341-44.

Stanley, David M. "Paul's Conversion in Acts." *Catholic Biblical Quarterly* 15 (July 1953):315-38.

Van Elderen, Bastiaan. "Some Archaeological Observations on Paul's First Missionary Journey." In *Apostolic History and the Gospel*, ed. W. Ward Gasque and Ralph P. Martin. Grand Rapids: Eerdmans, 1970.

Moody Press, a ministry of the Moody Bible Institute, is designed for education, evangelization and edification. If we may assist you in knowing more about Christ and the Christian life, please write us without obligation to: Moody Press, c/o MLM, Chicago, Illinois 60610.